CW01035116

Medieval Domesticity

What did 'home' mean to men and women in the period 1200–1500? This volume explores the many cultural, material and ideological dimensions of the concept of domesticity. Leading scholars examine not only the material cultures of domesticity, gender, and power relations within the household, but also how they were envisioned in texts, images, objects and architecture. Many of the essays argue that England witnessed the emergence of a distinctive bourgeois ideology of domesticity during the late Middle Ages. But the volume also contends that, although the world of the great lord was far removed from that of the artisan or peasant, these social groups all occupied physical structures that constituted homes in which people were drawn together by ties of kinship, service or neighbourliness. This pioneering study will appeal to scholars of medieval English society, literature and culture.

MARYANNE KOWALESKI is Joseph Fitzpatrick S. J. Distinguished Professor of History and Director of the Center for Medieval Studies at Fordham University.

P. J. P. GOLDBERG is Reader in Medieval History in the Department of History, University of York.

Medieval Domesticity
Home, Housing and Household
in Medieval England

Edited by

Maryanne Kowaleski

Fordham University

and

P. J. P. Goldberg

University of York

CAMBRIDGE
UNIVERSITY PRESS

CAMBRIDGE UNIVERSITY PRESS
Cambridge, New York, Melbourne, Madrid, Cape Town, Singapore,
São Paulo, Delhi

Cambridge University Press
The Edinburgh Building, Cambridge CB2 8RU, UK

Published in the United States of America by
Cambridge University Press, New York

www.cambridge.org
Information on this title: www.cambridge.org/9780521899208

© Cambridge University Press 2008

This publication is in copyright. Subject to statutory exception
and to the provisions of relevant collective licensing agreements,
no reproduction of any part may take place without
the written permission of Cambridge University Press.

First published 2008

Printed in the United Kingdom at the University Press, Cambridge

A catalogue record for this publication is available from the British Library

ISBN 978-0-521-89920-8 hardback

Cambridge University Press has no responsibility for the persistence or
accuracy of URLs for external or third-party internet websites referred to
in this book, and does not guarantee that any content on such
websites is, or will remain, accurate or appropriate.

Contents

List of illustrations   *page* vii
List of tables   viii
List of contributors   ix
Acknowledgements   xiii
List of abbreviations   xiv

1. Introduction. Medieval domesticity: home, housing
    and household
    P. J. P. GOLDBERG AND MARYANNE KOWALESKI   1

2. 'Burgeis' domesticity in late-medieval England
    FELICITY RIDDY   14

3. Buttery and pantry and their antecedents: idea and
    architecture in the English medieval house
    MARK GARDINER   37

4. Building domesticity in the city: English urban housing
    before the Black Death
    SARAH REES JONES   66

5. Urban and rural houses and households in the late
    Middle Ages: a case study from Yorkshire
    JANE GRENVILLE   92

6. The fashioning of bourgeois domesticity in later medieval
    England: a material culture perspective
    P. J. P. GOLDBERG   124

7. Nuns at home: the domesticity of sacred space
    MARILYN OLIVA   145

8. 'Which may be said to be her own': widows and goods
    in late-medieval England
    JANET S. LOENGARD   162

9. Weeping for the virtuous wife: laymen, affective piety and Chaucer's 'Clerk's Tale'
   NICOLE NOLAN SIDHU   177

10. On the sadness of not being a bird: late-medieval marriage ideologies and the figure of Abraham in William Langland's *Piers Plowman*
   ISABEL DAVIS   209

11. Fragments of *(Have Your) Desire*: Brome women at play
   NICOLA McDONALD   232

12. Home visits: Mary, Elizabeth, Margery Kempe and the feast of the Visitation
   MARY C. ERLER   259

Consolidated bibliography   277
Index   310

Illustrations

3.1 Plan of the west hall at the Bishop's Palace, Lincoln *page* 38
3.2 Plan of Oakham Castle hall 50
3.3 Oakham Castle hall, looking towards the entrances to
the buttery and pantry 51
3.4 Doors in the north aisle to the ground-floor and
first-floor levels at Oakham Castle hall 52
3.5 View towards the service end of the west hall at the
Bishop's Palace, Lincoln 53
3.6 Axonometric projection of the plan of the hall at
Warnford (Hampshire) 55
4.1 An 'urban manor' and a burgage plot in early
medieval York 81
5.1 The standard layout of an open hall and two urban forms 94
5.2 The locations of York and Wharram Percy 99
5.3 Wharram Percy, showing the church, farm cottages and
earthworks of the deserted village 100
5.4 Wharram Percy: plan of the medieval village 101
5.5 Wharram Percy: plan to show successive peasant houses
in Area 10 106
5.6 Wharram Percy: plan to show phases of alteration to peasant
house in Area 6 108
5.7 Wharram Percy: schematic plan to show the two phases of
construction of the North Manor 110
5.8 Plans of three urban halls in York 116
5.9 Examples of the 'rent' at York, a distinctively urban type 120
11.1 The opening of 'The Book of Brome' 240
12.1 The Visitation in the Book of Hours of Catherine of Valois 263
12.2 The Visitation scene in the window of St Peter Mancroft,
Norwich 265

Tables

3.1 Inventory of goods in the St Paul's estate and their likely
    locations on the farmsteads   *page* 44
6.1 Analysis of a sample of urban and rural inventories   139

Contributors

ISABEL DAVIS, Lecturer in Medieval and Early Renaissance Literature, Birkbeck College, University of London. Author of: *Writing masculinity in the later Middle Ages* (Cambridge University Press, 2007); 'Men and Margery: negotiating medieval patriarchy,' in *A companion to 'The Book of Margery Kempe'* (D. S. Brewer, 2004); 'John Gower's fear of flying: transitional masculinities in the *Confessio Amantis*,' in *Rites of passage: cultures of transition in the fourteenth century* (York Medieval Press, 2004); 'Consuming the body of the working man,' in *Consuming narratives: gender and monstrous appetite in the Middle Ages and the Renaissance* (University of Wales Press, 2002); co-editor of: *Love, marriage and family ties in the later Middle Ages*, with M. Müller and S. Rees Jones (Brepols, 2003).

MARY C. ERLER, Professor of English, Fordham University, author of: *Women, reading and piety in late medieval England* (Cambridge University Press, 2002); 'Devotional literature,' in *The Cambridge history of the book in Britain*, vol. 3: *1400–1557* (Cambridge University Press, 1999); *Poems of Robert Copland* (University of Toronto Press, 1993). Co-editor of: *Poems of Cupid, God of Love* (Brill, 1990); *Gendering the master narrative: women and power in the Middle Ages* (Cornell University Press, 2003) and *Women and power in the Middle Ages* (University of Georgia Press, 1988).

MARK GARDINER, Senior Lecturer in Archaeology, Queen's University Belfast, formerly editor of *Archaeological Journal* (published by the Royal Archaeological Institute). Co-author of: *The south-east to 1000 AD* (London: Longmans, 1988); *Timber buildings in England and Wales, AD 900–1200* (forthcoming); author of 'Late Saxon settlement', in *A handbook of Anglo-Saxon archaeology* (Oxford University Press, forthcoming). Co-editor of *Romney Marsh: environmental change and human occupation in a coastal lowland* (Oxford University Committee for Archaeology, 1998); and *Medieval landscapes: landscape history after Hoskins* (Windgather Press, forthcoming).

P. J. P. GOLDBERG, Reader in Medieval History, University of York. Author of: *Women, work and life cycle in a medieval economy: women in York and Yorkshire c. 1300–1520* (Clarendon Press, 1992); *Medieval England: a social history 1250–1550* (Arnold, 2004); 'What was a servant?', in *Concepts and patterns of service in the later Middle Ages* (Boydell, 2000); 'Coventry's 'Lollard' programme of 1492 and the making of Utopia', in *Pragmatic utopias: ideals and communities 1200–1630* (Cambridge University Press, 2001). Editor and translator of: *Women in England c. 1275–1525: documentary sources* (Manchester University Press, 1995).

JANE GRENVILLE, Senior Lecturer in Archaeology and Pro-Vice-Chancellor for Students, University of York, and a Commissioner of English Heritage. Author of: *Medieval housing* (Leicester University Press, 1997); 'The archaeology of the late and post-medieval workshop', in *The vernacular workshop: from craft to industry, 1400–1900* (Council for British Archaeology, 2004); 'The material household' and (co-authored) 'Urban vernacular housing in medieval northern Portugal and the usefulness of typologies', in *The medieval household in Christian Europe, c. 850–c.1550* (Brepols, 2003); and 'The urban landscape', in *Gothic: art for England 1400–1547* (Victoria & Albert Museum, 2003).

MARYANNE KOWALESKI, Joseph Fitzpatrick S.J. Distinguished Professor of History and Director of the Center for Medieval Studies, Fordham University. Author of: *Local markets and regional trade in medieval Exeter* (Cambridge University Press, 1995); 'The demographic history of singlewomen in medieval and early modern Europe,' in *Singlewomen in the European past* (University of Pennsylvania Press, 1999), and other essays on medieval women, family, trade and towns. Editor and translator of: *Medieval towns: a reader* (Broadview, 2006) and two volumes of medieval accounts. Co-editor of: *Women and power in the Middle Ages* (University of Georgia Press, 1988) and *Gendering the master narrative: women and power in the Middle Ages* (Cornell University Press, 2003).

JANET S. LOENGARD, Professor Emerita, Moravian College. Author of: *London viewers and their certificates, 1508–1558* (London Record Society, 1989), and many articles, including 'Legal history and the medieval Englishwoman: a fragmented view', *Law and History Review* 4:1 (1986); '*Rationabilis Dos*: calculating the widow's "fair share" in the earlier thirteenth century', in *Wife and widow in medieval England* (University of Michigan Press, 1994); '"Of the gift of her husband": English dower and its consequences in the year 1200', in *Women of the medieval world* (Blackwell, 1985); and 'The action of nuisance' and 'Women and law', in *The Oxford encyclopedia of legal history*, volume on the English common law (forthcoming).

NICOLA MCDONALD, Senior Lecturer in English, University of York. Author of: 'Chaucer's *Legend of Good Women*, ladies at court and the female reader', *Chaucer Review* 35 (2000); 'Games medieval women play', in *The Legend of Good Women: reception and contexts* (Cambridge University Press, 2006). Editor of: *Pulp fictions of medieval England* (Manchester University Press, 2004), with essays on 'A polemical introduction' and 'Eating people and the alimentary logic of *Richard Coeur de Lion*' in the volume.

MARILYN OLIVA, Adjunct Associate Professor of History, Fordham University. Author of: *The convent and the community in late medieval England* (Boydell, 1998); 'All in the family? monastic and clerical careers among family members in the late Middle Ages', *Medieval Prosopography* 20 (1999); 'Unsafe passage: the state of the nuns at the Dissolution', in *Vocation of service to God and neighbour* (Brepols, 1998). Co-author of: *Religious women in medieval East Anglia* (University of East Anglia Press, 1993). Editor of: *Charters and household accounts of the female monasteries of Suffolk* (Boydell, forthcoming).

SARAH REES JONES, Senior Lecturer in History, University of York. Author of articles on the topography of medieval York, Thomas More's *Utopia*, Margery Kempe, the regulation of labour and the English urban household. Co-editor of six volumes of essays, including: *Pragmatic utopias: ideals and communities (1200–1630)* (Cambridge University Press, 2001); *Courts and regions in medieval Europe* (Boydell, 2000); and *The medieval household in Christian Europe* (Brepols, 2003). She is currently completing a major monograph on York between the Norman Conquest and the Black Death.

FELICITY RIDDY, Emerita Professor, University of York. Author of: *Sir Thomas Malory* (Brill, 1987); 'How the good wife taught her daughter', *Speculum* (1996); '"Women talking about the things of God:" a late medieval sub-culture', in *Women and literature in Britain, 1150–1500* (Cambridge University Press, 1993); 'Middle English romance: family, marriage, intimacy', in *The Cambridge companion to medieval romance* (Cambridge University Press, 2000). Editor of: *Prestige, authority, and power in late medieval manuscripts and texts* (York Medieval Press, 2000). Co-editor of: *Macmillan literary anthologies*, I, *Old and Middle English* (Macmillan, 1909); *Regionalism in late medieval manuscripts and texts* (D. S. Brewer, 1991) and *The uses of script and print, 1300–1700* (Cambridge University Press, 2004).

NICOLE NOLAN SIDHU, Assistant Professor of English, East Carolina University. Author of: 'Go-betweens: the old woman and the function of obscenity in the Old French fabliau', in *Comic provocations: exposing the corpus of Old French fabliaux* (Palgrave-Macmillan, 2006); 'Chaucer and the comic', in *The Palgrave advances in Chaucer studies* (Palgrave-Macmillan, forthcoming); 'All the king's married men: henpecked husbands, unruly wives, and royal authority in John Lydgate's *Mumming at Hertford*' (*Chaucer Review*, forthcoming). She is currently completing a book entitled *Strumpets, cuckolds and 'ryth wikked' women: the gender politics of obscene discourses in Middle English literature.*

Acknowledgements

The papers in this volume were among those given at the twenty-fifth annual conference of the Center for Medieval Studies at Fordham University in March 2005. The conference was co-sponsored with the Centre for Medieval Studies at the University of York, one of several co-operative ventures that our Centers in 'old' York and 'new' York have pursued in the last four years. We are especially grateful to Felicity Riddy for first proposing the idea of a programme of trans-Atlantic co-operation. The decision to focus the conference on the theme of 'medieval domesticity' was a natural one since it allowed us to capitalise on the expertise that the York Medieval Studies faculty has accrued through its Medieval Household Research Group.

The conference would not have been possible without the financial support of both Centers, as well as the generous funding provided by Nancy Busch, Dean of the Graduate School of Arts and Sciences, and John Hollwitz, then Academic Vice-President, both of Fordham University. Supplementary travel funds were supplied by the Centre for Medieval Studies, University of York. Kim Bowes, Dawn Ritchotte and Jocelyn Wogan-Browne helped Maryanne Kowaleski plan the conference programme, while Sarah Rees Jones, then the Director of the Centre for Medieval Studies at York, played a crucial role in facilitating the participation of both faculty and post-graduate students from the University of York. We also thank the speakers for giving a particularly stimulating set of papers. Finally, we are grateful for the help provided by Emily Hanson and Claire Serafin, graduate assistants at Fordham's Center of Medieval Studies, in assembling the final manuscript for publication.

When we wanted a speaker to open the conference with a keynote paper, Felicity Riddy seemed the obvious choice. Her stimulating discussion of issues around household and domesticity and her width of vision have been an inspiration for many scholars working in the field. It is for this reason that we dedicate this collection to Felicity with gratitude and admiration.

MARYANNE KOWALESKI
JEREMY GOLDBERG

Abbreviations

BL   London, British Library
EETS OS   Early English Text Society, original series
EETS ES   Early English Text Society, extra series
EETS SS   Early English Text society, supplementary series
HMSO   Her Majesty's Stationery Office
PL   Migne, J.-P. (ed.), *Patrologia cursus completus, series latina*,
            221 vols. Paris, 1861–5.
TNA   The National Archives, London

1 Introduction. Medieval domesticity: home, housing and household

P. J. P. Goldberg and Maryanne Kowaleski

'Home' was for women and men of the fourteenth and fifteenth centuries an evocative word that meant rather more than just a building or a place. As Chaucer's host noted, it was where a man might be master.[1] For others it was a place of refuge. In the ecstatic cry 'My delite and my hame, Ihesu, my blisful kynge', something of the deeper emotional resonances with which the word was freighted may be discerned.[2] For the author of *Cursor Mundi*, Heaven was 'þat rich ham' from which Adam was expelled at the Fall.[3] These meanings resonate in gentrywoman Jane Stonor's hope that 'Gode ȝeve yow goode nyghte and brynge yow welle home', expressed in a letter to her husband whose burden was all about his absence.[4] Home was associated with familiarity, friendship, nurturing and intimacy. These are the qualities implied by the epithet 'homli' so frequently found in religious discourses: for Margery Kempe, Christ was 'homly ... in hyr sowle'; the *Cloud of Unknowing* talks of 'þe Homliest freend'; the angel Gabriel at the Annunciation 'was homli and knowen wiþ þis ladi'.[5] 'Homli' was further used to denote sexual intimacy, but it also could imply meekness or simplicity, qualities that are again given religious significance by their literary use to describe Christ.[6]

---

[1] Geoffrey Chaucer, *The Canterbury Tales*, in *The Riverside Chaucer*, 3rd edn, ed. Larry Benson (Oxford University Press, 1987), line 1938: 'Thou art a maister whan thou art at hoom'.

[2] *Ihesu my lefe* in B. D. Brown, 'Religious lyrics in MS. Don.c.13', *Bodleian Quarterly Record* 7 (1932), 4–5.

[3] Richard Morris (ed.), *Cursor mundi (The cursur of the world): a Northumbrian poem of the XIVth century in four versions*, EETS OS vols. 57, 59, 99, 101 (Oxford, 1874–93), vol. I, p. 64, line 994.

[4] C. L. Kingsford (ed.), *The Stonor letters and papers, 1290–1483*, Camden Society 3rd series, vols. 29 and 30 (London, 1919), vol. I, p. 110.

[5] Sanford Brown Meech and Hope Emily Allen (eds.), *The book of Margery Kempe*, EETS OS vol. 212 (Oxford, 1940), p. 3, line 2; Phyllis Hodgson (ed.), *The Cloud of Unknowing and the Book of Privy Counselling*, EETS OS vol. 218 (Oxford, 1944; reprint 1981), p. 59, line 14.

[6] *Middle English dictionary* under *hōmlī*; accessed 12 October 2005 at http://quod.lib.umich.edu/m/med/.

The Middle English word *hous(e)hold* first appeared in the late four-teenth century, when, as today, it referred mainly to a group of people who lived and worked under the same roof.[7] The term thus alluded to a particular space (the house where they all lived) as well as to the relation-ships between the co-residents (relationships often overlaid with the ties of kinship), particularly such everyday, routine activities as eating and sleep-ing. And in later medieval usage, *household* need not mean just people; it could denote possessions. Thus Sir Roger Salwayn of York left his wife 'all my housholde holy' and Elizabeth Poynings likewise referred to 'all myne hole apparell and all my stuff of houshold being within my dwelling place' when she made her will.[8] The double meaning has particular pertinence to this present collection which locates people – householders and those who reside within the home – within the material fabric of the home. *Hous* or *house* itself is an ubiquitous term with meanings that overlap with modern meanings.[9]

The concept of 'domesticity', a much later usage, is historically con-tingent;[10] it means different things in respect of different kinds of people at different moments in time. Nineteenth- and early twentieth-century treat-ments of medieval domestic life usually linked it to 'home', and focused on everyday activities, the structure of houses and the objects found therein.[11] In addition to dwelling on the material culture of domestic life, these and other early works tended to adopt the mid-nineteenth-century Western

---

[7] For a useful discussion, see Felicity Riddy *et al.*, 'The concept of the household in later medieval England', in Sarah Rees Jones *et al.*, 'The later medieval English urban house-hold', *History Compass* 4 (2006), 5–10.

[8] E. J. Furnivall (ed.), *The fifty earliest English wills in the Court of Probate, London*, EETS OS vol. 78 (Oxford, 1882), p. 52; Norman Davis (ed.), *Paston letters and papers of the fifteenth century*, 2 vols. (Oxford: Clarendon Press, 1971–6), vol. i, p. 211. The object-centred approach to the household as the repository of possessions is also evident in recent archaeo-logical works; see, for example, Susan M. Margeson, *Norwich households: the medieval and post-medieval finds from Norwich survey excavations, 1971–1978*, East Anglian Archaeology Report no. 58 (Norwich, 1993); Geoff Egan, *The medieval household: daily living c. 1150–c.1450*, Medieval Finds from Excavations in London, vol. 6 (London, 1998).

[9] *Middle English dictionary* under *hous*.

[10] The earliest use of *domesticity* in our meaning would appear to date from 1726, while even the use of *domestic* dates no further back than 1521: *Oxford English dictionary* under *domesticity* and *domestic*; accessed 12 October 2005 at http://dictionary.oed.com.avoserv. library.fordham.edu/.

[11] For example, Thomas Wright, *The homes of other days: a history of domestic manners and sentiments in England* (London, 1871), a revised and expanded edition of his *A history of domestic manners and sentiments in England duing the Middle Ages* (London, 1862), which in turn was based on a series of papers he wrote for *Art Journal*; Marjorie Quennell, *A history of everyday things in England*, 2 vols. (London: Batsford, 1918). This was revised several times, with a separate volume for the Middle Ages: Marjorie Quennell and C. H. B. Quennell, *A history of everyday things in England*, vol. 1, *1066–1499*, 4th edn (London: Batsford, 1969). Both Wright and Quennell were copiously illustrated.

bourgeois ideal, found alike in Europe and North America, which designated separate spheres for men and women. Women were the home makers, the nurturers of children, the providers of domestic warmth and comfort, the guardians of purity and morality. Men, in contrast, were the bread winners, whose manly task it was to leave the safe haven of the house and venture into the polluting world of trade and manufacture. Such an ideology found cultural expression in art and literature, but also in contemporary architecture and furnishings.[12] This ideology of separate spheres, of woman's place within the home, of the domestic as antithetical to the world of work, colours our understanding of a comparatively recent past. What we all too easily lose sight of is the fact that ideologies represent ideals and that social practice may be more complex. The word *housewife*, for example, was being used by the early thirteenth century to denote a woman (usually the wife of the householder) who managed the everyday routine of her household, but it referred more to the work she did and was not freighted with all the meanings associated with its use in the nineteenth and twentieth centuries.[13] These meanings, moreover, reflected the same middle-class ideology evoked in the Western bourgeois ideal, which does not describe the experience of the labouring classes, although it was indeed the very irrelevance or inappropriateness of this ideology to the harsh realities of the socially less privileged that served to demarcate them from their middle-class neighbours.[14] As an ideology specific to an era of industrialisation, of factories and factory workers, and of growing population and urbanisation, it does not represent a model for other past societies, but it does offer a useful comparator against which we may set evidence for other and earlier eras where rather different socio-economic parameters applied.[15]

---

[12] For some American studies see: Elisabeth Donaghy Garrett, *At home: the American family 1750–1870* (New York: H. N. Abrams, 1990); Clifford E. Clark, 'Domestic architecture as an index to social history: the romantic revival and the cult of domesticity in America, 1840–1870', *Journal of Interdisciplinary History* 7 (1976), 33–56; Daphne Spain, *Gendered spaces* (Chapel Hill: University of North Carolina Press, 1992), ch. 5. The classic English study is Leonore Davidoff and Catherine Hall, *Family fortunes: men and women of the English middle class, 1780–1850* (Chicago: University of Chicago Press/London, Hutchison, 1987).

[13] *Oxford English dictionary* under *housewife*. For an example of the use of the term in an occupational sense, see Roger Virgoe, 'Some ancient indictments in the King's Bench referring to Kent, 1450–1452', in F. R. H. DuBoulay, (ed.)., *Documents illustrative of medieval Kentish society*, Kent Records vol. 18 (Ashford, 1964), p. 247.

[14] For a brilliant case study of rather different ideologies operating in rural peasant society see Martine Segalen, *Love and power in the peasant family: rural France in the nineteenth century*, trans. S. Matthews (Oxford: Blackwell, 1983).

[15] For a critique of how some scholars have applied the ideology of gendered separate spheres to the medieval peasantry, see P. J. P. Goldberg, 'The public and the private: women in the pre-plague economy', in P. R. Coss and S. D. Lloyd (eds.), *Thirteenth-century England III* (Woodbridge: Boydell, 1991), pp. 75–89.

In the context of the English later Middle Ages – loosely the era from the eve of the Black Death to the Henrician Reformation – the sense of familiarity, of intimacy, of emotional warmth and security that *home* and *homli* conveyed to contemporaries is perhaps a useful starting point for understanding 'medieval' domesticity. It is, however, necessary to address the diverse cultural, material and ideological paradigms in which people from varying levels of society lived their lives. The world of the great lord and his lady was far removed from that of the poor peasant, yet both occupied physical structures that constituted homes, which were built, organised and furnished in ways that are consciously or unconsciously reflective of their particular cultural values, and which brought together greater or lesser numbers of people tied by association of kinship, friendship, commerce, service or neighbourliness. This present collection places particular emphasis on the different values associated with townsfolk (especially the more well-to-do urban bourgeoisie) and peasants, who constituted the majority of the population throughout the medieval era. The rationale for this emphasis lies in the sense that emerges in a number of the chapters, and is prompted by Felicity Riddy's argument in the second chapter, that a distinctive bourgeois ideology of domesticity emerged in this period.

Riddy argues that 'domesticity' – even in its nineteenth-century form of a 'state of mind' defined by privacy and comfort within the physical structure of a house wherein the occupation of a domestic space by members of the family evolved into the concept of 'home' – was not a product of the modern period or even of seventeenth-century Holland, as other scholars have claimed, but of the fourteenth century.[16] Medieval domesticity was associated first with a specifically urban value system characteristic of the bourgeoisie, well-off artisans and merchants who lived in the multi-room timber-framed houses discussed in the chapters by Sarah Rees Jones and Jane Grenville, owned the variety of household goods analysed by Jeremy Goldberg and Janet Loengard and adhered to the marriage ethics identified by Nicole Sidhu Nolan and Isabel Davis. Often depicted in medieval discourses as worldly and successful, this social group developed a style of domestic living that, unlike that of their modern counterparts, combined working and trading with the everyday routines of domestic family life. In contrast to their poorer neighbours who lived in single rooms or simple cottages, the 'burgeis' had the rooms and space to separate these functions into what Riddy calls a 'domestic geography' that

---

[16] The definition is from John Tosh, *A man's place: masculinity and the middle-class home in Victorian England* (New Haven: Yale University Press, 1999), p. 4, as cited in Riddy's essay below, p. 16.

fostered hospitality, privacy, orderliness and the routine management of time within the stability and security of the home. These same domestic values can be seen, moreover, in the shops and work rooms attached to bourgeois houses, as evident in the mounting tide of urban and guild regulation that promoted industriousness in the (often live-in) apprentices and servants of the bourgeoisie and exercised quality control over the production and trading that occurred in these homes.

Several of the essays in this volume explore the influence of domestic ideologies on the development of the physical structure of the house. As Mark Gardiner points out, we can recognise ideas about domestic space – where certain rooms are located, what functions they serve – in the forms that houses took. He focuses in particular on two service rooms: the buttery (for storing drink and drink paraphernalia) and the spence or pantry (where food and tableware were stored), which occupied adjoining rooms off the screens passage or cross-entry of the main hall of the houses of the well-to-do. Why, he asks, were these two rooms distinguished from each other and not combined into one storage area? And why did the two rooms emerge in the plan of most hall houses in the late twelfth century, well before the late medieval domestic plan in which they so commonly figured? As Gardiner shows, the two rooms were not simply an architectural expression of the responsibilities of officials of the great household, but were related to the role that architecture played in the increasingly elaborate and hierarchical rituals associated with domestic dining in elite households. As behaviour surrounding dining rituals became more formalised and orderly, so too did the organisation of domestic space in the hall and its service rooms, which provided the food and drink that underlay the lord's generosity, and thus his honour. The architectural shift of the storage area for drink from a cellar or undercroft connected to the lord's chamber – and thus under his personal and direct control – to a room off the main hall, where the lord's generosity and hospitality were on display for all to see, also paralleled the growing hierarchical emphasis displayed in where one sat and what one was served in the lord's hall. The lord and his intimates sat on a central dais at one end of the hall, and directly opposite him were doors to the two service rooms, which allowed him to preside over the parade of food into the hall and up to the high table as it went by the other tables, all placed at right angles to the lord's raised table.

Sarah Rees Jones also tracks the social context of an architectural transformation: the emergence of a distinctive style of timber-framed housing in the late twelfth and early thirteenth century, the same period that Gardiner identifies as crucial for the development of the buttery and pantry in the houses of the wealthy. Compared to the flimsier housing that predominated in most tenth- and eleventh-century towns, timber-framed housing was sturdier and more durable, as well as larger and multi-storeyed, improvements that were made possible by new construction technologies. This type of housing, which provided both living spaces and working spaces and included an open hall on a smaller scale than the aristocratic hall studied by Gardiner, became the imagined site of the bourgeois domesticity so prevalent in late medieval texts, as discussed in Felicity Riddy's chapter. What is particularly significant about her analysis, however, is her argument that the spread of this new type of typically bourgeois housing went hand in hand with changes in legal practices that promoted security of tenure via written charters and the emergence of a burgage tenure free of seigneurial claims. Such security promoted investment in timber-framed housing by well-off artisans and merchants, who in turn used their houses to demonstrate their status to their poorer neighbours, who had to rent cheaper and smaller accommodation and never enjoyed the full rights of urban citizenship that owners of timber-framed houses possessed.

Gardiner's focus on the central hall as the heart of the high-status home of rural lords and Rees Jones's interest in tracing the origins and topographical location of the timber-framed urban hall house are echoed in Jane Grenville's chapter, which explores the relationship between rural and urban houses, questioning the degree to which town houses were distinctively different, as Sarah Pearson has recently argued, or, as W. A. Pantin claimed in 1962, simply adaptations of pre-existing rural forms.[17] In general Grenville sees town houses as in many ways quite distinctive structures meeting the very different demands of an urban economy based around trade and manufacture. By focusing, however, on the plebeian hall, apparently similar in form between peasant and bourgeois houses, she suggests that in this instance at least the urban model consciously borrows from its rural counterpart. Here she argues that familiarity of form would have helped to socialise the rural migrant, whether servant or apprentice, and helped him or her adapt to the power dynamics of the bourgeois household.

The hall may represent the setting in which the social dynamics of household life are played out and within which the different actors learn to play their parts, but the physical fabric is but part of a larger picture. We need also to explore the furnishings, the decoration, the things that we

---

[17] Sarah Pearson, 'Rural and urban houses: "urban adaptation" reconsidered', in Katharine Giles and Christopher Dyer, (eds.), *Town and country in the Middle Ages: contrasts, contacts and interconnections, 1100–1500* (Leeds: Maney, 2005), pp. 43–64; William Abel Pantin, 'Medieval English town-house plans', *Medieval Archaeology* 6–7 (1964 for 1962–3), 202–39.

would in our own age understand to transform the essentially impersonal 'house' into the individual 'home'. This is the theme of Jeremy Goldberg's chapter. The differences between peasant and bourgeois lifestyles appear sharply focused. Thus we may contrast the essentially pragmatic concerns with eating and sleeping suggested by peasants' parsimonious investment in furnishings with the comparative luxury and intimacy provided by the chamber within the bourgeois and mercantile house. The bourgeois hall may not have constituted intimate space, but with its benches, cushions and painted wall hangings it was visually unlike its country cousins. Here we find the mundane given devotional resonance. Cushions were fashionable must-have accessories in bourgeois halls and chambers from the earlier fourteenth century, but their use in chapels as kneelers or as rests for devotional books suggests that their function went beyond mere displays of wealth and comfort.

Attention to actual furnishings, this time of the domestic interior of the convent, is also central to Marilyn Oliva's chapter, which focuses on the essential domesticity of the lives of later medieval English nuns. Drawing on inventories, purchases recorded in household accounts and bequests in wills, Oliva shows the similar level of domestic comfort enjoyed by nuns and the gentry in the later Middle Ages: both scattered rushes or straw on their floors, draped their walls with (often decorated) hangings and slept on featherbeds with sheets, blankets, coverlets and pillows; both stored their bedding and valuables in chests and cupboards; had tables, chairs, benches, trestles and cushions in their halls; washed their hands in basins made of pewter or latten and dried their hands with linen towels; ate off earthenware plates laid on linen tablecloths; used utensils that included silver spoons; drank from bowls and cups that were often embellished with silver; and had a variety of other household fittings such as andirons and candlesticks. Most of these furnishings were also found in the homes of the wealthy merchant bourgeoisie. Oliva suggests that the nuns – most of whom came from the parish gentry, wealthy yeomen or urban bourgeoisie – were recreating the domestic environment with which they were most familiar.[18] The nuns' furnishings, however, were much more likely to be decorated with religious images than those owned by the gentry or bourgeoisie, and they also often put domestic items to devotional use, such as the linen housling towels which the nuns draped over the Eucharist chalice or around their missals and other service books when carrying them to chapel. This religious use of everyday domestic linens was

[18] For the social background of medieval English nuns, see Marilyn Oliva, *The convent and the community in late medieval England: female convents in the diocese of Norwich, 1350–1540* (Woodbridge: Boydell, 1998).

paralleled in the domestic furnishings of the specifically religious spaces of the convent. In decorating their chapels, vestries and churches with wall hangings, curtains, cushions and linens similar in material, form and adornment to those found in their cloistered dormitories, refectories, chapter rooms and inner halls and parlours, the nuns were domesticising their religious spaces in the same way that they sacralised their living quarters with religious imagery.

Several authors besides Oliva draw attention to the gendered dimension of household goods. Goldberg, for example, suggests that bourgeois wives – whose greater market involvement compared to peasant wives probably gave them more voice in household expenditure – may have focused their consumption choices on the bedchamber and its furnishings, the most intimate space in the house. This room was not only where such a wife and her husband slept, but also where she gave birth to her children, entertained female friends and kin, and said her prayers and other devotional practices.[19] In focusing on the legal boundaries of women's ownership of chattels, Janet Loengard points out how the gap between legal theory and practice illustrates medieval English society's understanding of the close association between women and certain types of household goods. Under common law, everything a woman owned became her husband's when she married; if he pre-deceased her, he was theoretically free to leave them to anyone he chose, or to his executor if he did not specify heirs. But husbands rarely did this. Many, indeed most, men made their wives their executors and/or explicitly bequeathed them properties and chattels. They chose in particular to exceed the common law definition of paraphernalia (most narrowly conceived of as the clothes on the wife's back) by bequeathing their widows virtually all their clothing and their bedroom furnishings, a finding that reinforces Goldberg's suggestion on women's close association with the bedchamber. Women's wills also considered these items theirs to give. And husbands sometimes gave back to their widows all the goods and property they had brought to the marriage (the cooking utensils, tableware and bedding so typical of later 'hope chests'), a 'gift' which, like the extended definition of paraphernalia, was supported by canon law. Borough customary law also was more liberal than common law; in many towns, a wife was automatically entitled to a percentage (usually one-third) of her husband's chattels for her lifetime, an arrangement that reinforces Riddy's arguments about the

---

[19] For the customisation of domestic spaces for devotional purposes by adding furnishings, particularly to the bedchamber, see Diana Webb, 'Domestic space and devotion in the Middle Ages', in Andrew Spicer and Sarah Hamilton (eds.), *Defining the holy: sacred space in medieval and early modern Europe* (Burlington, VT: Ashgate, 2005), pp. 27–47.

early emergence of a specifically 'bourgeois' domesticity. Both Loengard and Riddy, moreover, emphasise the impact that the intimacy of domestic living – of sharing a kitchen and bedroom and the routines of everyday life – must have had on the relationship between husband and wife and thus on the husband's decision to ignore common law restrictions.

Whereas 'house' could be understood as a primarily functional structure providing warmth, shelter and a place to sleep, but not necessarily the focus of significant social interaction, of intimacy, or of private devotion, 'home', the locus of domesticity, was an ideological construct that invested much greater cultural significance in the physical structure as a stage for playing out a range of social and gender relations.[20] The physical form of the house and the arrangement of rooms had meanings that were shaped by and shaped the lives of the people who used them. Thus the ubiquitous presence of buttery and pantry in well-to-do houses from the high medieval era can be tied *inter alia* to devotional constructions of sharing food, one of the primary functions of the household, a theme that forms part of Mark Gardiner's chapter tracing the evolution of these two rooms over several centuries. Here there are resonances with the Mass, that central institution of late medieval Catholicism. This we see, for example, with striking clarity in a visual parallel in the Luttrell Psalter: a depiction of the Last Supper, upon which the celebration of the Eucharist was based, is paired with Sir Geoffrey Luttrell, the Psalter's patron, seated at high table, drinking vessel in hand.[21] The Eucharistic resonances of dining at high table, reflected also in the symbolic parallel between hall and church in which high table and high altar occupy spatially congruent positions, immediately warn us that the sort of binary divide between the secular and the sacred that we take so much for granted worked differently in the later Middle Ages.[22] This is a theme that is central to Marilyn Oliva's and Mary Erler's studies and runs through a number of our other chapters; in a culture permeated by religion, people liked to make connections between this world and the next or to valorise their lives and their values by giving them devotional meaning.

---

[20] This observation is coloured by Judith Butler's understanding of gender as performative in her influential *Gender trouble: feminism and the subversion of identity* (New York: Routledge, 1990).

[21] Richard K. Emmerson and P.J. P. Goldberg, '"The Lord Geoffrey had me made": lordship and labour in the Luttrell Psalter', in James Bothwell, P.J.P. Goldberg and W.M. Ormrod (eds.), *The problem of labour in fourteenth-century England* (Woodbridge: York Medieval Press, 2000), pp. 45, 52–5.

[22] On the blurring of these boundaries, see also Jeanne Nuechterlein, 'The domesticity of sacred space in the fifteenth-century Netherlands', in Spicer and Hamilton (eds.), *Defining the holy*, pp. 49–79, and Webb, 'Domestic space and devotion'.

The complex intermeshing of the devotional and the mundane that seems so characteristic of bourgeois culture is again reflected in Nicole Nolan Sidhu's chapter on Chaucer's treatment of the Griselda legend in the 'Clerk's Tale'. Sidhu explores how Chaucer adapts a well-known story to provide a model of affective piety for the bourgeois home and for the bourgeois male in particular. In asking why late-fourteenth-century audiences found this tale of a husband's depravity towards his wife so compelling, her discussion takes us to the heart of gender and power relations within the later medieval household. Sidhu argues that women and male clerics were not especially drawn to the tale, but that laymen were, responding with anger and then empathy by imagining themselves as Griselda's protector. Chaucer, in fact, heightened aspects of Petrarch's version of the tale to augment the male emotional response, which was founded on notions of respectability that stressed the male householder's responsibility for the moral supervision not only of his own household, but of his local community. Bourgeois regulation of bad behaviour within the community, Sidhu argues, could thus take on the air of religious devotion. In the absence of an effective Church response to laymen's growing devotional demands for affective models of piety, laymen found their own outlets, such as the religious fraternities that proliferated during this period. These associations were most often associated with well-off artisans and the bourgeoisie, the same well-off burgess audience to whom Chaucer directed most of his writing. Griselda's own social position as a young peasant girl taken into the house of a wealthier man would also have resonated with married bourgeois householders' responsibility for the young female servants under their care. These same community expectations helped bourgeois laymen to imagine themselves intervening to safeguard Griselda. In doing so they were following medieval patriarchal dictates to nurture women: an ideal that suggests, according to Sidhu, a domestic model of female–male reciprocity, not an oppositional model in which men discipline women. Yet the reconciliation of Griselda and her cruel husband also justifies the husband's authority within marriage, albeit tempered by the bourgeois values of sobriety and seriousness.

Isabel Davis also discerns the emergence of a new bourgeois marriage ethic in the late fourteenth century, one that challenges the customary clerical privileging of virginity and chastity with an emphasis on the value of domestic conjugality. She traces this new ethic in William Langland's unusual deployment of the figure of Abraham in *Piers Plowman*, who in the B-text rendition displays a positive zeal for the married state. Langland draws upon the different iconographic and exegetical traditions surrounding the Old Testament figure to create a new Abraham in a way that emphasises his role as a *fleshly*, as well as a symbolic, husband and father. The moderation of Abraham's enthusiasm for marriage in the C-text revision, however, serves to emphasise the disruption that this new marriage ethic must have posed for Langland and his late medieval contemporaries. In locating and discussing a melancholy tone (the sadness of not being a bird, as the chapter title has it) that emerges in the discussion of marriage in *Piers Plowman* and other contemporary literature, Davis also highlights the themes of homelessness (for unmarried and unstable single people) and bereavement (for the paternal grief that Abraham and other fathers could experience) within late-medieval sexual ethics.

Conjugal sexual relations as a duty of the male householder also appear in the popular poem of advice, 'Arise Early', that accompanies the games copied into the Brome commonplace book considered by Nicola McDonald. But the promotion of sexual desire indicated by the last line of the poem acknowledges the desires of the householder's wife as well, a theme that McDonald pursues further in her discussion of the gentry household as a vehicle of domestic sociability that provides an erogenous space for the playing out of men and women's sexual yearnings. The various anti-feminist puzzle, cipher, fortune and dice games recorded in the commonplace book appear at first to reinforce the household as a locus of hierarchal domestic order and male authority because of their reliance on gendered stereotypes. Like Sidhu, however, McDonald finds more fluid and complex gender relations at work in these texts, arguing that the games were meant to provoke conversation and debate and hence gave women the opportunity to imagine and even articulate their own desires. The thrust of one dice game, called *Have Your Desire*, for example, was to dare its players to confess amorous or illicit thoughts. By naming desire, McDonald argues, women brought their desire into existence, and thus demarcated an erogenous space within the household where we can see female agency operating.

Female agency within the domestic space of the home is treated in Mary Erler's chapter as well, which also shows how late-medieval texts modelled explicitly or implicitly on the Visitation placed sanctity in a domestic setting, a theme pursued by several other contributions in this volume.[23] Erler argues that the new liturgies and devotional practices that sprang up around the occasion of the Visitation – by the pregnant Virgin Mary to her elderly but also pregnant cousin Elizabeth – celebrated the culture of

---

[23] For an extended analysis of domestic imagery in Middle English and Anglo-Norman texts, see Catherine Batt, Denis Renevey and Christiania Whitehead, 'Domesticity and medieval devotional literature', *Leeds Studies in English* new series 36 (2005), 195–250.

the home with its family visits, connections between kin, and female solidarities around pregnancy and birth. This culture, which placed family and home at the centre of spiritual life, is reflected in the mediations of Nicholas Love on the Visitation, which not only locate mothers and children at the heart of the house but also praise the spiritual edification that 'home visits' between devout men and women could promote. Margery Kempe's life illustrates this blending of spiritual visitation and conversation within a domestic setting that Love and visual images of the Visitation both highlight. Erler suggests that Margery's constant travels, whether on pilgrimage or more locally to speak with other devout women and men, were modelled on Mary's Visitation, but Margery reimagined her conversations during these visits as akin to preaching, thus capturing for women an apostolic vocation they were normally denied.

Although written by a range of scholars working on both sides of the Atlantic and rooted in a variety of different traditions and disciplines, this present collection offers a harmonious and complementary set of essays. What emerges is a culturally distinct understanding of bourgeois domesticity. This differs from peasant ideologies, but need not be unrelated to them. Implicitly it also differs and is distinguished from more plebeian urban values, since those renting modest premises and of necessity working for others were unlikely to have worked or even shared meals together. It also diverges from its nineteenth-century counterpart in that the home was not set apart from the world of work. Indeed work was integral to the bourgeois home. Nor was there a clear separation of gender roles into separate spheres (although several authors do see certain spaces and household goods as gendered female). Rather, there is emphasis on the partnership of husband and wife and a new sense that these two are bound, or ought to be bound, not as a consequence of dynastic ambition or patriarchal will, but by real affection rooted in shared ideals, shared tasks and shared ownership. We find again and again that the boundaries between the sacred and the profane, the spiritual and the secular, appear porous and even illusory. Indeed, it would seem a part of the construction of bourgeois domesticity continually to sacralise the home and its furnishings. At the same time, the home was taken into the church and domestic furnishings and clothing recycled for sacred use.[24] This is another reflection of the trend towards conspicuous piety that is the hallmark particularly of the more well-to-do at the end of the Middle Ages and is manifested in the proliferation

---

[24] Clothing and bed-hangings were sometimes bequeathed to make altar cloths and, to give a particularly striking if unusual example, a York woman left her bed to be used as an Easter Sepulchre: York, Borthwick Institute, Prob. Reg. 2 fol. 52v (Gateshed).

of guilds and chantry provision, and the material investment in church furnishings and fabric.[25] It was in the home, however, that children and servants were socialised in orderly and godly living, and husbands and wives led Christian lives manifested through the daily rituals of shared labour, shared meals and shared beds.

[25] See, for example, Katherine L. French, *The people of the parish: community life in a late medieval English parish* (Philadelphia: University of Pennsylvania Press, 2001); Eamon Duffy, *The stripping of the altars: traditional religion in England c. 1400–c. 1580*, 2nd edn (New Haven: Yale University Press, 2005).

2 'Burgeis' domesticity in late-medieval England

Felicity Riddy

There seems to be a consensus that domesticity is a product of the modern era, even though there is disagreement about how modern it is.[1] The central argument, for example, of Witold Rybczynski's engaging book, *Home, a short history of an idea*, which traces the concept of 'home' from the Middle Ages to the twentieth century, is that domesticity 'has to do with family, intimacy, and a devotion to the home, as well as with a sense of the house as embodying ... these sentiments'.[2] For Rybczynski, these are post-medieval developments. He suggests that there is a parallel between what he sees as the sparsely furnished medieval house, and the 'spare' self-consciousness of medieval people. Their lack of self-consciousness presumably had something to do with their lack of privacy: 'What is unexpected about medieval houses ... is not the lack of furniture ... but the crush and hubbub of people in them.'[3] He points out that the medieval urban house was a place of work as well as a place of residence, and this, he believes, contributed to its promiscuous publicness. This way of thinking seems to be indebted to Philippe Ariès's influential argument in *Centuries of childhood* that 'until the end of the seventeenth century, nobody was ever left alone. The density of social life made isolation virtually impossible ... everyday relations never left a man by himself.'[4]

For Rybczynski, domesticity first comes into being in seventeenth-century Holland. It is wonderfully and mysteriously depicted in Dutch genre paintings in which women are shown performing housewifely and

---

[1] During much of the period in which I have been thinking about medieval domesticity I have had the great privilege of working with colleagues at the Centre for Medieval Studies who have shared interests, especially Jeremy Goldberg and Sarah Rees Jones. What follows includes much that has been the subject of discussion, both at York and elsewhere, and I owe a great deal to the stimulus I have received from many other people. I have given earlier versions of this chapter at the universities of Auckland and Fordham, where I received some challenging questions for which I am grateful.

[2] Witold Rybczynski, *Home, a short history of an idea* (New York: Penguin Books, 1987), p. 75.

[3] Ibid., p. 28.

[4] Philippe Ariès, *Centuries of childhood: a social history of private life*, new edn, trans. Robert Baldick (London: Jonathan Cape, 1996), p. 385.

motherly roles in the plain interiors of bourgeois homes. Vermeer, Ter Borch, De Hooch and others irradiate everyday moments – a girl pouring milk, a woman caught in sunlight at a window, a woman peeling an apple for a child. They are moments of what Charles Taylor has called 'the affirmation of the ordinary,' which he sees as a hallmark of the modern mind.[5] Simon Schama in *The embarrassment of riches* has also used some of these paintings, though somewhat differently, to explore what he sees as the fundamental tensions in the *mentalité* of the period: '"Home" existed in the Dutch mentality,' he argues, 'in a kind of dialectical polarity with the world, and in particular the street, which brought the mire of the world, literally, to its doorstep. ... The struggle between worldliness and homeliness was but another variation on the classic Dutch counterpoint between materialism and morality.'[6] Wayne Franits's more recent study of women and domesticity in seventeenth-century Dutch art complicates but does not fundamentally query this model.[7] Domesticity, marked particularly by cleanliness, is represented as the sphere of moral virtue, in contrast to the street, which is associated with dirt and materialism. Domesticity is gendered, but it is not simply the case that women are associated with the domestic and men with the street; rather, domesticity is a means of identifying the good woman: she is the one who stays at home and manages her house, while the bad woman belongs on the streets. This way of thinking about women, virtue and the home is now familiar to medievalists and has been well explored.[8]

Another famous version of domesticity, of course, is the product of the nineteenth-century 'separate spheres' model of family and social life. This model has been related to the development of privacy, to the emergence of household management as a full-time occupation for middle-class women, and to the idea of the home as a source of moral and ethical value.[9] Here domesticity is again held to be the product of bourgeois social arrangements; now, however, the home is not contrasted with the

---

[5] Charles Taylor, *Sources of the self: the making of the modern identity* (Cambridge, MA: Harvard University Press, 1989), p. 13.

[6] Simon Schama, *The embarrassment of riches: an interpretation of Dutch culture in the golden age* (London: Collins, 1987), p. 389.

[7] Wayne E. Franits, *Paragons of virtue: women and domesticity in seventeenth-century Dutch art* (Cambridge University Press, 1993).

[8] See, for example, P. J. P. Goldberg, 'Pigs and prostitutes', in K. Lewis, N. J. Menuge and K. M. Phillips (eds.), *Young medieval women* (Stroud: Sutton, 1999), pp. 172–93.

[9] For a brief survey of the topic, see Michael Anderson, *Approaches to the history of the western family 1500–1914* (Cambridge University Press, 1995), pp. 31–3 and 71–2. A particularly influential study is Davidoff and Hall, *Family fortunes*, pp. 357ff.; for a critique of the model see Amanda Vickery, 'Golden age to separate spheres? A review of the categories and chronology of English women's history', *The Historical Journal*, 36 (1993), 383–414; for a

street but with work. The two spheres are thought of, again, as a polarity that is reinforced, though differently from before, by the gender divide: home is the proper sphere of women and work the proper sphere of men. The ideological separation of home from work marks the change from an older, pre-industrial set of social relations, nostalgically viewed as 'the world we have lost' (rather than escaped from).[10] With industrialisation, work moved out of the home which, now solely a residential space, was idealised as a source of different kinds of virtues from those of the workplace. Moreover 'work' came to mean exclusively 'work performed outside the home'; the female labour performed inside it was rendered invisible, and paid employment (of men) was privileged over unpaid employment (of women).

Many historians have been challenging the simplicities of this model, of course, although it still carries a residual power.[11] Feminist historians have shown, for example, that nineteenth-century British and American women were active outside the home in a variety of ways, while the British historian John Tosh has recently argued that home was as important as work for nineteenth-century middle-class masculinity – indeed, was one of its prime locations. Nevertheless he still thinks in terms of the separation of the spheres of work and home:

Domesticity ... denotes not just a pattern of residence or a web of obligations, but a profound attachment: a state of mind as well as a physical orientation. Its defining attributes are privacy and comfort, separation from the workplace, and the merging of domestic space and family members into a single commanding concept (in English, 'home'). Domesticity in this sense was essentially a nineteenth-century invention: socially it was inconceivable without large-scale urbanization; culturally it was one of the most important expressions of that awareness of individual interiority which had developed since the Enlightenment.[12]

So here domesticity rests on privacy and comfort and on an idea of home as separate from work; it is specifically urban and relates to individual interiority. Much of this is similar to the ideas of Rybczynski, who also sees domestic comfort as related to the interior life.[13]

If we accept these views, then it seems that there cannot have been a conception of domesticity in the late-medieval period, when the home was

---

reworking of the separate spheres model in relation to class as well as gender, see Elizabeth Langland, *Nobody's angels: middle-class women and domestic ideology in Victorian culture* (Ithaca: Cornell University Press, 1995).

[10] Peter Laslett, *The world we have lost: further explored*, 3rd edn (Cambridge University Press, 1983), p. 13.

[11] See, for example, Judy Giles, *The parlour and the suburb: domestic identities, class, femininity and modernity* (Oxford and New York: Berg, 2004).

[12] Tosh, *A man's place*, p. 4.

[13] See Rybczynski, *Home*, pp. 35–6.

also the place of work. Nevertheless, it is true that most of the character-istics that Tosh assumes for the nineteenth century can be shown to have been present in the late Middle Ages also. There was intense urbanisation in England from the thirteenth century on; rising standards of living at periods of economic prosperity, as in the later fourteenth century, were marked by increasingly comfortable housing;[14] Middle English had a subtle vocabulary relating to privacy and intimacy, and, *pace* Ariès, the privacy of individual households was in some towns protected by the law; the cultivation of individual interiority was encouraged through confes-sion and domestic prayer – one might think of the ubiquity of the book of hours in this period [15] – as well as by the propagation of secular modes of self-scrutiny (the lover's, for example); and powerful ideas of 'home' and 'homeliness' circulated in a world of migrants moving from smaller com-munities into towns.[16] The aim of this chapter is not simply to argue for a revised chronology of domesticity as a source of bourgeois identities, but also to show that domesticity as a 'state of mind' does not necessarily rest on a distinction between working and residing, or the home and the world, or on a separation of spheres along gender lines. For the pre-modern era, we need a different model.

I

Domesticity can be identified in fourteenth-century England as a specif-ically urban set of values associated with the particular mode of living of the 'burgeiserie' which might be translated into modern English as 'bur-gessry', if there were such a word. It was characteristic of the households of the 'burgesses', living and working together in multi-room houses which were increasingly built of timber-frame (a new technology in the thirteenth century) on several floors. These houses were not only residen-tial spaces but also sites of business and manufacture. They were family homes, not in the modern sense, but in the late-medieval sense of being places which accommodated *familiae*, or households: parents, children, apprentices and servants, and into which journeymen or day-labourers came to work.

---

[14] Christopher Dyer, *An age of transition? economy and society in the later Middle Ages* (Oxford: Clarendon Press, 2005), pp. 153–4.

[15] Eamon Duffy, *Marking the hours: English people and their prayers 1240–1570* (New Haven: Yale University Press, 2006).

[16] See Felicity Riddy, 'Looking closely: authority and intimacy in the late medieval urban home', in Mary C. Erler and Maryanne Kowaleski (eds.), *Gendering the master narrative: women and power in the Middle Ages* (Ithaca and London: Cornell University Press, 2003), pp. 212–28.

The major division in the social organisation of larger English towns in the later Middle Ages, when the processes of urbanisation were well established, was between those who were members of the franchise, or freemen, and thus were allowed to buy and sell retail, to train apprentices and to trade in other towns without paying tolls, and those who were not. Access to the freedom was generally by birth, by apprenticeship or by payment, and was not only for men: wives who traded *femme sole* and widows who took over their husbands' businesses were able to join the franchise, though they could not hold civic office. In some towns, such as York, the proportion of freemen was high, perhaps over 50 percent, while in Exeter it was much lower at just over 30 percent.[17] The members of the franchise were the privileged group from whom the towns' elites and officeholders were drawn. The rest – those who were not 'free' in this sense – would have included the practitioners of lesser-status crafts as well as journeymen and semi- and unskilled wage-labourers, and many women.[18]

In civic contexts by the fifteenth century the Middle English word 'burgeis' was applied to this group. It derives from the Latin *burgensis*, a coinage of the period of high-medieval urban expansion which first appears in England in Domesday Book to signify those resident in a borough who contributed to customary payments to the king, and it had the specialised meaning of freeman, citizen or master craftsman. Anglicised as 'burgeis', it long retained these technical senses. Thus a royal letter of 1422 begins: 'To oure right trusty and with al oure hert welbeloued, the Maire, Sherifs, Aldermen, bourgoys, and Communes of the Cite of London...',[19] while a petition from the citizens of Oxford to the king in 1455 asks that 'euery Burgeys of the said towne of Oxenford' should be allowed to take on apprentices who were not themselves the sons of freemen, as 'þe Citezens of the Citee of london doo.'[20] From earlier on, however, *burgeis* was used more loosely to mean simply a substantial townsman or townswoman: 'The burjays alle, curteys and

---

[17] See Maryanne Kowaleski, 'The commercial dominance of a medieval provincial oligarchy: Exeter in the late fourteenth century', in Richard Holt and Gervase Rosser (eds.), *The medieval town: a reader in English urban history 1300–1540* (London: Longman, 1990), p. 186.

[18] It seems clear that in towns such as York by the fifteenth century, for example, the attractions of the franchise were often outweighed by the burdens, mostly financial, so that men who were eligible by patrimony did not necessarily choose to become free.

[19] R. W. Chambers and Marjorie Daunt (eds.), *A book of London English, 1384–1425* (Oxford: Clarendon Press, 1931), p. 86.

[20] John H. Fisher, Malcolm Richardson and Jane L. Fisher (eds.), *An anthology of chancery English* (Knoxville: University of Tennessee Press, 1984), p. 290.

fre,/Welcomed him fair in to þat cite';[21] 'Burgeis and marchaundes and oþer riche comynes';[22] 'Thise burgeis wyves... riche ben and eke plesyng';[23] 'Leonele het his wiif / A fair buriays & joliif' (His wife was called Leonele, a pretty, good-humoured 'bourgeoise').[24]

There is a measure of approbation here, but at the same time clerical discourses used the term in ways that were explicitly critical of the affluence that is conventionally associated with the 'burgeis'. In *The book of vices and virtues* of around 1375 the active or worldly life of man on earth is compared to 'burgeiserie', which epitomises a dubious moral state: 'The burgeis hopeth to wynne and to gadre and chaffaren, and the ende of his entencion is al to be riche and noble in his lif holden and moche honoured.'[25] (The 'burgeis' wants to accumulate and amass and trade, and the goal of his desire is directed entirely to being rich and regarded as noble in his way of living and greatly honoured.) The lesson readers are supposed to learn is that they should be aristocratic, not bourgeois: like knights, they should aspire to an endless struggle up the high hill of perfection rather than amassing possessions and seeking status. *The book to a mother*, of around 1400, also uses the burgess as a metaphor for worldliness: 'Euerich man in dedly synne ys ... gon a pilgrimage fro Crist, his Fadur, to a fer contre of unliknesse, and haþ mad his couenaunt wiþ þe deuel, þat is a gret burgeis of þat contre.'[26] The country of unlikeness to which the sinner travels to make his pact with the devil is both exotic and familiar: it is the faraway place of pilgrimage and it is this world, near at hand, the world of dissimilitude in contrast with the changelessness of heaven. That is why the devil is one of its leading citizens and 'burgeiserie' is a state of moral alienation. Chaucer, who came from a 'burgeis' family himself, looks at the 'burgeiserie' more wryly, bringing together civic and moral senses when he says of the five guildsmen on the pilgrimage to Canterbury that

> Wel semed ech of hem a fair burgeys
> To sitten in a yeldehalle on a deys.   [guildhall [dais

[21] Ewald Zettl (ed.), *An anonymous short English metrical chronicle*, EETS OS vol. 196 (Oxford, 1935), lines 729–30.

[22] T. Arnold (ed.), 'A comment on the seven deadly sins', *Select English works of John Wyclif*, 3 vols. (Oxford: Clarendon Press, 1869–71), vol. III, p. 160.

[23] Geoffrey Chaucer, 'The Romance of the Rose', in *The Riverside Chaucer*, 3rd edn, ed. L. Benson (Oxford University Press, 1989), lines 6865–6.

[24] O. D. Macrae-Gibson (ed.), *Of Arthour and of Merlin*, EETS OS vol. 268 (Oxford, 1973), ll. 561–2.

[25] W. N. Francis (ed.), *The book of vices and virtues*, EETS OS vol. 217 (Oxford, 1942), p. 161.

[26] A. J. McCarthy (ed.), *A book to a mother* (Salzburg: Institut für Anglistik und Amerikanistik, Universität Salzburg, 1981), p. 100.

> Everich for the wisdom that he kan
> Was shaply for to been an alderman;   [suitable
> For catel hadde they ynogh, and rente,   [property
> And eek hir wyves wolde it wel assente.[27] [also

There is a very delicately observed conflation here of civic status ('fair burgeys'; 'alderman'), self-importance ('sitten in a yeldehall on a deys'), property ownership ('for catel hadde they ynogh, and rente') and the tyranny of the socially ambitious wife. So the 'burgeiserie' is that urban grouping which to outsiders was so closely associated with materiality – possessions, social difference, ambition – that they could stand metonymically for the world itself. They seem to be an affront on the one hand to the aristocrats because of their drive and upward mobility and on the other to the asceticism of the clergy in their pursuit of prosperity. There is something in all this of what Marx saw in the bourgeoisie: its rapacious energies and its unfettered creative drive. Domesticity may sound placid, but it is linked to the success in late-medieval England of this social group.

The 'burgeiserie', not surprisingly, saw themselves rather differently. That they were a grouping is clear: they use an egalitarian but exclusive language of fellowship, referring to one another as *concives*, or in English 'concitizeins' (fellow citizens) or 'comburgeis'; in some towns the term they use for themselves from the later fourteenth century is 'pers' or equals.[28] They intermarried and took one another's sons – and to a lesser extent daughters – as apprentices. They developed what Richard Britnell has described as a 'burgess-centred' commercial ethic which, although couched in the language of the common good (to which the 'burgeiserie' were particularly prone), in fact protected 'the rights of burgesses as consumers and manufacturers'.[29] And, as this chapter argues, they developed particular kinds of domestic living.

---

[27] Chaucer, 'General prologue', in *The Riverside Chaucer*, lines 369–74.

[28] See F. B. Bickley, *The little red book of Bristol*, 2 vols. (Bristol: W. C. Hemmons, 1900), vol. II, p. 152: 'Besecheth mekely your pouer Comburgeises, al the Maisters of the Craft of Barboures of the toune of Bristowe'; Travers Twiss (ed.), *Monumenta Juridica: the black book of the Admiralty*, vol. II, Rolls Series no. 55 (London, 1873), p. 171, from 'Le Domesday de Gipewyz': 'Such usages holdyn not but by twixe burgeys of the toun with inne, that men clepyth peeres and commouneres, and not betwixe burgeys foreyns'; W. Hudson and J. C. Tingey (eds.), *The records of the city of Norwich*, 2 vols. (London and Norwich: Jarrold, 1908–10), vol. I, p. 94: 'To wiche eleccion ye Meir & xxiiijti Concitezeyns of ye same Cite ... shal come.'

[29] R. H. Britnell, 'Urban economic regulation and economic morality in medieval England', paper delivered to the 75th Anniversary Conference of the Economic History Society (Glasgow, 2001), at www.dur.ac.uk/r.h.britnell/articles/Morality.htm; accessed 13 August 2006.

II

The demarcation within towns between those who were members of the franchise and those who were not, on which 'burgeis' status technically rested, was probably less visible on the street than another division, apparent from the early fourteenth century, between those who lived in one or two rooms and those who lived in a more spacious style in houses comprising anything between four or five rooms and more than twenty. This division is fundamental to the typologies which architectural historians have developed for discussing medieval English housing.[30] The significance of it, however, is not just a matter of size but of style: the multi-room house made possible a different way of living, a different mentality or, in Tosh's words, 'state of mind', which can be called 'burgeis' domesticity. This way of living assumes the possibility of the spatial and temporal differentiation of activities within the home. These activities include manufacture and trade, with all their routines, as well as feeding, sleeping, dressing and undressing, child-rearing, and the care of the sick and infirm, which are also routinised. Out of the management of these activities come particular notions of privacy, discretion and settledness, of industry and the pursuit of excellence, which may be at odds with actual social practice, but which nevertheless contribute to the making of bourgeois identities.

Chaucer's near contemporary, William Langland, author of *Piers Plowman*, uses the word 'burgeis' for a category of housing. He says of the nativity of Christ that: 'Ne in none beggers cote nas þat barne born / But in a burgeis place, of Bethlem þe beste' (Nor was that baby born in a beggar's hovel, but in a burgess's place, the best in Bethlehem).[31] The distinction Langland draws between the substantial 'burgeis place' and the beggar's 'cote' or hovel is one that is made in urban records. The medieval compilers of the Winchester tarrage survey of 1417 distinguish between the *tenementum*, denoting 'a built-up property of a certain minimum size' and the smaller *shopa* or *cotagium*, and this distinction is

[30] See Jane Grenville, *Medieval housing* (London: Leicester University Press, 1997), p. 171. Both the pioneering W. A. Pantin, 'The development of domestic architecture in Oxford', *Antiquaries Journal* 27 (1947), 120–50 and W. A. Pantin, 'Medieval English town-house plans', *Medieval Archaeology* 6–7 (1964), 202–39, and more recently John Schofield, *Medieval London houses* (New Haven: Yale University Press, 2003), pp. 27–60, identify a category of middling-sized houses.

[31] William Langland, *Will's visions of Piers Plowman, Do-Well, Do-Better and Do-Best*, ed. G. H. Russell and G. Kane (London: Athlone Press, 1997), Passus II, lines 146–7. This social inflation of Jesus' birthplace differs from the contemporary view in the Charter of the Abbey of the Holy Ghost: 'þanne was he born of his moder in an olde broken hous at Beedlem tounnys ende'. See C. Horstmann (ed.), *Yorkshire writers*, 2 vols. (London and New York: Sonnenschein, 1895–6), vol. I, p. 352.

standard elsewhere.[32] Many poor craftspeople, day-labourers and their families, as well as widows and other unmarried people, must have lived in one or two rooms only, or in a room over a shop, without cooking facilities or privies.[33] Not surprisingly, much less is known about these small houses than about bigger ones: the lives of the poor are scantily documented and the material evidence has mostly not survived, though there is some from Winchester,[34] Northampton,[35] Norwich, Hull, Hartlepool[36] and Perth.[37]

It seems that very large numbers of people lived in small homes: it has been calculated that in Winchester, for example, 22 percent of the residences were cottages and if shops are included, this figure rises to 31 percent. To these we can add an unknown number of single rooms within tenements let as independent or semi-independent accommodation. The kinds of people who lived in this way must have varied from students – like Nicholas in Chaucer's 'Miller's Tale', who has a 'chamber' in the lodging-house run by John, an Oxford carpenter – to poor widows, whose rights to live on in the family home were limited outside London and even there did not apply to rented accommodation. In York the Vicars Choral built cottages in the 1330s for the lower end of the market; these were rented by 'tenants employed in the building industry, in various types of service (as porters and cleaners), as well as in various aspects of the leather and clothing industries', while many of the cheapest houses were rented to women.[38] At the bottom were the people who had no

[32] See Derek J. Keene, *A survey of medieval Winchester*, 2 vols., Winchester Studies vol. 2 (Oxford: Clarendon Press, 1985), vol. I, p. 138.

[33] W. A. Pantin omitted single-room buildings in his influential typology of medieval urban housing; see Pantin, 'Medieval English town-house plans', 202–39. Keene, *Medieval Winchester*, argues that 22 percent of residences in Winchester were cottages, and that if shops are included this figure rises to 31 percent. In addition there was an unreckonable number of single rooms within tenements in which people lived independently. Keene provides evidence of poor tanners' widows in London in the first half of the fourteenth century living in single rooms: Derek Keene, 'Tanners' widows, 1300–1350', in Caroline Barron and Anne Sutton (eds.), *Medieval London widows, 1300–1500* (London: Hambledon, 1994), pp. 1–28.

[34] See Martin Biddle (ed.), *Winchester in the early Middle Ages* (Oxford: Clarendon Press, 1976), pp. 264–5.

[35] See John H. Williams, *St Peter's Street, Northampton: excavations, 1973–1976* (Northampton Development Corporation, 1979).

[36] See John Schofield and Alan Vince, *Medieval towns: the archaeology of British towns in their European setting* (London: Leicester University Press, 1994), pp. 76–85.

[37] See Philip Holdsworth, *Excavations in the medieval burgh of Perth, 1979–1981* (Edinburgh: Society of Antiquaries of Scotland, 1987).

[38] Sarah Rees Jones, 'Property, tenure and rents: some aspects of the topography and economy of medieval York', unpublished Ph.D. thesis, University of York (1987), p. 242; Sarah Rees Jones, 'Women's influence on the design of the urban home', in Erler and Kowaleski, *Gendering the master narrative*, pp. 190–211, especially pp. 204–9.

homes at all, who slept where they could, and seem to have been more or less permanently on the move.[39]

The ' burgeis place' is visible from the beginning of the fourteenth century at least, in surviving inventories of property, made when owners were distrained for debt, assessed for taxation or had died. The appraisers who compiled the inventories were fellow-citizens, usually engaged in the same or a related line of business. These men would have walked round the house in order to list and evaluate its contents, but they were not mapping it. For them the house was an accumulation of objects, some of which (the ones they were interested in) had a market value, while rooms – which they name – were a convenient means of categorising those objects under different headings. Among the earliest surviving inventories of urban housing are those made in Colchester in 1301 for the purposes of assessing citizens' tax liabilities. Most of those assessed lived in houses of only one or two rooms, the kind that later gets called a *cotagium* or *shopa*. Only a minority of Colchester tax-payers lived in larger houses: one of the biggest was Roger the Dyer's house which had four rooms – a *domus* or living room, a chamber, a kitchen and a brewhouse.[40] We can think of this as a small-scale 'burgeis place', in comparison with the houses of his contemporaries. It is very like the houses of Emma Hatfield, a London chandler's widow who died in 1373,[41] and Thomas Baker, a York stringer who died in 1436.[42] These both consisted of a hall, a shop, a chamber and a kitchen, and Emma Hatfield had a storehouse in addition.

The inventories show that there were conventions, shared by the inhabitants of geographically quite distant towns, about what kinds of objects went in which rooms: there was a shared understanding of the 'burgeis' organisation of space in these multi-room homes. It was because they knew the conventions that the appraisers were able to identify each room from its contents. There is always an *aula* or hall, that is, a room used for eating and other activities that earlier had the more generic name of *domus*. There is also always at least one room called a *camera*, in which people slept, though often not alone judging by the number of beds it contains. These rooms contained chests and cupboards for storage, but much more

[39] See, for example, Keene, *Medieval Winchester*, vol. I, pp. 235–6.
[40] J. Strachey (ed.), *Rotuli parliamentorum*, 6 vols. (London: s.n., 1767–77), vol. I, p. 243. See R. H. Britnell, *Growth and decline in Colchester, 1300–1525* (Cambridge University Press, 1986), p. 11. Britnell translates '*domus*' as 'living-room'. It is the room which is later more universally known as the '*aula*' or hall.
[41] A. H. Thomas (ed.), *Calendar of select plea and memoranda rolls of the City of London*, 3 vols. (Cambridge University Press, 1926–32), vol. II, pp. 150–62.
[42] Philip M. Stell (ed.), *Probate inventories of the York Diocese, 1350–1500* (York: York Archaeological Trust, 2006), pp. 552–4.

rarely benches or chairs. Frequently, but not always, there was a kitchen (*coquina*) that was sometimes part of the house and sometimes in a separate building at the back. There was, in addition, very often a *shopa* (and the English term can denote either a workshop or a retail space), a storeroom, a brewhouse and a boulting-house (where flour was sieved). Beyond these basic rooms, larger houses had other rooms such as a parlour, a wine-cellar, a grain-room, and occasionally a chapel and a counting-house or office, as well as additional chambers. A number of urban houses had gardens. Thomas Mocking, a London fishmonger who died in 1373, had eight rooms: two chambers, a hall with a 'fireplace' of iron, a storeroom, a parlour, a servants' room (which was evidently a workroom and not sleeping quarters since it contained only a chest and a table), a similar 'prentises chamber' with two tables and two forms, and a kitchen.[43] Robert Talkan, a York girdler who died in 1415, had a hall, a parlour, a chamber, a store-room, a kitchen, a brewhouse, a gyle-house (where beer was fermented) and a wine-cellar. In the 1430s John Cadeby, a Beverley mason, had a chamber, a hall, a parlour, a storeroom, a kitchen and several other rooms for brewing, a malthouse, an inner garden near the hall, an outer garden with outhouses and a larder. John Stubbes, a York barber who died in 1451, had a summer hall and several additional chambers as well as a range of service rooms. His house was a hostelry, like John the carpenter's in Chaucer's 'Miller's Tale', with around twenty rooms in all.

The ways in which rooms were used must have differed according to the time of day: the trestle table and the folding bed allowed for space to be used flexibly. The hall in the house of Hugh Grantham, a York mason who died in 1410, contained two spinning-wheels and a basket for wool as well as two trestle tables, so it must have been used by the women members of the household for spinning when it was not being used for meals.[44] Bristol regulations from 1438 specify that journeymen in that city belonging to certain 'craftes' who have not yet taken up the freedom of the city 'ne vse not no maner worke in here halles ne in here schoppes … til that they be burgeys'.[45] This suggests that in some 'burgeis' houses the hall was treated as a workroom. Chambers could likewise be both sleeping and working spaces; moreover, rooms which appraisers identify as parlours seem from their contents to have served quite different purposes in different houses, including relaxation, or storing goods, or working.[46] This

[43] Thomas (ed.), *Calendar of plea and memoranda rolls*, vol. II, pp. 50–62.
[44] Stell, *Probate inventories*, pp. 517–21, 523–5, 558–62, 579–83.
[45] Bickley (ed.), *Little red book of Bristol*, vol. II, p. 182.
[46] The parlour of John Carter, tailor, died 1485, contained 'A stone and a half of hemp 1s. 8d. A balloke, a form and all accessories for making bow strings 1s.': Stell, *Probate inventories*, p. 649.

suggests that it took some time for the parlour to acquire a settled meaning. A York barber-surgeon's house had a 'women's room', which was
evidently a work room of some kind.[47] The 1391 inventory of the goods of
Richard Toky, a London grocer, shows he had a hall, a chamber, a
kitchen, a pantry and buttery, a counting-house and a storehouse.[48]
Chaucer imagines a similar kind of domestic geography in the
'Shipman's Tale', where the merchant has an upstairs 'countour-hous'
in which he does his accounts.

The houses of these people were places of work, even when the head of
the household was employed outside the home. The house of the York
mason, Hugh Grantham, mentioned above, comprised a hall, a summer
hall, a chamber, a store-room, a kitchen and, like many merchants' and
artisans' homes, a brewhouse. Brewing in Grantham's establishment was
not just for domestic consumption, however, because he was owed money
for beer when he died. He also traded in grain and cloth.[49] Of his multiple
business interests, at least one – brewing – was clearly home-based and
may well have been managed by his wife, Agnes, who continued in the
trade after his death.[50] Among the possessions listed within the house of
Thomas Catton, a York weaver who died in 1413, are the two web looms
and their tackle which he used to practise his craft. The York houses of two
girdlers, a skinner, a stringer, a chapman, a barber, a pewterer, a tailor, a
shoemaker and a goldsmith all contain shops. 'Shop' is an ambiguous
term, as has already been suggested: it can imply 'workshop' as well as
'place of sale' because in some crafts – such as shoemaking and tailoring,
for example – goods for sale were made on the premises. On the other
hand, the shop of Thomas Gryssop, a chapman of York who died in 1446,
was wholly devoted to retail, not manufacture. It was stocked with a very
large number of small items, including cloth, paper, bonnets, gloves,
spectacles, spices and combs, that he presumably sold from home as
well as elsewhere. He had, unusually, a stable with two horses and owed
money to a London spicer and a London cap-maker, who must have been
among his suppliers. John Carter, a York tailor who died in 1485, had 'a
workshop for western cloth' and 'a workshop for southern cloth' in his
house, which seem to have been storerooms rather than workrooms.

---

[47] It contained a tub with lime, a steeping vat, a bucket and two tables or planks: Stell,
Probate inventories, p. 582.

[48] Thomas (ed.), *Calendar of plea and memoranda rolls*, vol. III, pp. 205–27.

[49] He was owed large sums at his death for cloth, barley and oats; see Jenny Kermode,
Medieval merchants: York, Beverley and Hull in the later Middle Ages (Cambridge University
Press, 1998).

[50] See P. J. P. Goldberg, *Women, work, and life cycle in a medieval economy: women in York and
Yorkshire c. 1300–1520* (Oxford: Clarendon Press, 1992), pp. 113–14.

Tailoring seems to have gone on in the 'shop'.[51] This was, by contrast with Gryssop's, clearly a place of manufacture as well as of sale, since it contained cloth, work tables, irons and shears.

III

These are homes, then, in which working, provisioning and living are not separate. Even members of the mercantile elite did not imagine a pattern of family life in which the husband went out to his business each day, leaving his wife at home with the servants to engage in solely domestic activities. In 1387, for example, during a period of crisis when Richard II moved from Windsor to the Tower of London, he proposed to commandeer lodgings for his followers in the city and suburbs in the way he usually did when the court moved round the country. According to the Westminster Chronicler, the mayor and aldermen of London told the king that

> the allotment of accommodation in this way was quite out of the question in London ... without their wares the merchants could not make their living there, and without their houses they had no means of showing them to purchasers, since they had no means of keeping them elsewhere.[52]

This confrontation is part of a larger narrative of struggles for authority between the king and the powerful men of the city; the arguments that the city fathers deploy are expediently mobilised for the purposes of political debate. Many of them would have sold from rented shops, but as Dyer has shown, there is plenty of evidence that buying and selling did in fact take place in people's homes.[53] The exchange seems to expose a gap between aristocratic and bourgeois conceptions of the home: the houses of members of the country gentry like the Pastons were places of production, where beer was made, bread was baked and wool was spun, but not of commerce or trade.[54] Sir Peter

---

[51] Stell, *Probate inventories*, pp. 649–50.

[52] Leonard C. Hector and Barbara F. Harvey (ed. and trans.), *The Westminster chronicle 1381–1394* (Oxford: Clarendon Press, 1982), p. 225.

[53] Christopher Dyer, 'The hidden trade of the Middle Ages: evidence from the West Midlands of England', in his *Everyday life in medieval England* (London: Hambledon, 1994), pp. 283–303.

[54] The inventory of goods listed as stolen when the Paston property at Heylesdon was broken into soon after 1465 includes equipment for brewing ale in the brewhouse: 'Brewerne Item in primis, a grett ledde to brewe v coumbe maltt wyth onys plawyng. Item, a macchefatt, ij geylyng fattys, vj kelers, a taptrowe, a temps to clense wyth, a sckeppe to bere maltt, a seve to syft malt, a bultyng pype, ij knedyng fattys, and a moldyng borde'. There was also a large amount of wool for spinning: 'Item, v ston of woulle. Item xxx woulle fellys', Norman Davis (ed.), *Paston letters and papers of the fifteenth century*, 2 vols. (Oxford: Clarendon Press, 1971–6), vol. I, p. 328.

Legh's grand house at Wollaton had a spinning-house and a bake-house;[55] Lady Margaret Pigott's house at Ripon had a brewhouse and a gyle-house.[56] The Paston family's anger about Margery Paston's clandestine marriage to their agent, Richard Calle, in 1465 must have had to do in part with ideas about the roles women played in the mercantile household where the home was also a shop: 'he shold neuer haue my good wyll for to make my sustyr to selle kandyll and mustard in Framlyngham',[57] sneers John Paston III to his older brother. His mother may brew or spin, or at any rate oversee these activities, but his sister may not sell.

The multi-room 'burgeis place' was also ideologically distinct from the one-room housing of the poor, in at least two important ways. The first is that in the former people were able, if they chose, to work, eat and sleep in different places, whereas in the latter they were not. Modern research into one-room family housing suggests that it is almost certainly a mistake to think of it (as at least one early modern archaeologist has done) as desirable open-plan living. Instead, it was no doubt endlessly frustrating and stressful, especially perhaps for women, as Langland suggests in his famous passage about the miserable lives of the urban poor:

And hemsulue also suffer much hungur	[themselves
And wo in winter tyme and wakynge on nyhtes	
To rise to þe reule to rokke þe cradle,	[regularly
Bothe to carde and to kembe, to cloute and to wasche,	[patch
To rybbe and to rele, rusches to pylie,	[clean flax [wind yarn [strip rushes
That reuthe is to rede or in ryme shewe	[pitiable
The wo of this women þat wonyeth in cotes.[58]	[live

('Cote', it should be noted, was the word Langland used in contrast to the 'burgeis place'.) The reference to 'reule' in the third line is revealing: it is less about imposing order than about being immersed in routine. Childcare and a range of work activities are grammatically and spatially undifferentiated, and the tyrannical succession of infinitives (to rise, to rock, to card, to comb, to clout, to wash, to rub, to reel, to strip) holds out no promise of completion. It seems to represent what de Beauvoir

---

[55] Stell, *Probate inventories*, p. 638.
[56] Ibid., p. 655.
[57] John Paston III to John Paston II, 1469; see Davis (ed.), *Paston letters*, vol. I, p. 541.
[58] Langland, *Piers Plowman: the C text*, Passus IX, lines 71–87.

has called 'the monotonous repetition of life in all its mindless factuality'.[59]

Langland's poor women in their 'cotes', cold, hungry, burdened with children, can be contrasted with the domestic regime that Chaucer imagines in his 'Shipman's Tale', written at much the same time. The merchant's wife and her husband, with their servants and an apprentice, live in a 'worthy hous', in which they entertain extensively. He works alone upstairs in his office all morning while she takes her maidservant into the garden. There she flirts with their visitor, a monk, until he looks at his portable time-piece and reminds her that it is time for dinner. She calls her husband down, they hear Mass (which suggests a private chapel) and then the tables are laid and they all eat a meal prepared by the cooks. Hospitality, orderliness, privacy, the imposition of routines and the management of time: these become more easily achievable domestic goals when a whole family does not occupy one room in which eating, sleeping, childcare and work endlessly overlap. The well-regulated household is one where these activities are all understood as separate but interrelated aspects of domestic life and ordered as such. The members of the well-regulated household were the nuclear family – parents and children – and apprentices and servants, engaged in diverse activities but contributing to a shared endeavour. There is a growing consensus among medieval demographic historians that in England the nuclear family goes back certainly to the late fourteenth century and probably to before the Black Death. Like the companionate marriage pattern, in which husband and wife are close in age and marry comparatively late, this may have developed earlier in towns than elsewhere. So a particular household formation, a way of living and the values underpinning these, all seem to go together.

Moreover, the 'burgeis place' allows activities to be located in the home which for the cottager have to take place outside it. The 'burgeiserie' could cook their food in their own kitchens instead of having to take their bread, pies and meat to the local baker's oven, or having to depend as the very poor must have done on the fast food industry which, as Martha Carlin has shown, was such a feature of the urban scene.[60] They could use their own

---

[59] Simone de Beauvoir, *The second sex*, trans. and ed. H. M. Parshley (London: Vintage, 1997), p. 616: 'It is natural for a woman to repeat, to begin again without even inventing, for time to seem to go round and round without ever leading anywhere ... Her life is not directed towards ends: she is absorbed in producing or caring for things that are never more than means, such as food, clothing and shelter.'

[60] See Martha Carlin, 'Fast food and urban living standards in medieval England', in Martha Carlin and Joel T. Rosenthal (eds.), *Food and eating in medieval Europe* (London: Hambledon Press, 1998), pp. 27–51.

privies instead of the common privy; their children could play indoors or in their gardens. At York in 1386 civic legislation was passed requiring people to lead and not drive their horses to the river for water because of the great danger they posed to children playing in the street.[61] 'Burgeis' domesticity locates these and similar kinds of activities – perhaps especially activities relating to regimes of the body – within the home and develops ideas of privacy to protect and sustain them.

During the course of the fourteenth and fifteenth centuries evidence from different parts of the country suggests that standards of 'burgeis' domestic comfort improved, at least as reckoned by the spaciousness and style of accommodation. The most obvious catalyst was of course the Black Death,[62] and the periodic recurrence of plague later in the century. One swift and brutal effect of this was to reduce housing densities in the towns. In London and Winchester, two places that have been closely studied, large numbers of very small shops disappeared; tenements that had been subdivided into numerous small units were restructured; in York by the fifteenth century, even in a period of economic decline, it was hard to find tenants for the very cheapest properties. Evidence of this kind suggests that, given the choice, people preferred larger houses to small ones. This is hardly a surprising conclusion to draw, and yet the picture may be more complicated and interesting than this, because the difference between the one or two-room cottage and the five or six-room house is not, as has already been suggested, merely a matter of size. What is at issue is also a mode of living, and what we may be seeing is the establishment of domesticity as a dominant urban value increasingly identified with 'burgeis' status and achievement. It is, moreover, no coincidence that the orderly and differentiated way of life – or rather the way of life that sets a value on orderliness and differentiation – should become visible during the period of the time revolution, with the invention of the fixed hour, in the fourteenth century.[63]

IV

The owners of the 'burgeis' houses I have described – many of whom, like Chaucer's family, must have been immigrants seeking better

---

[61] Maud Sellers (ed.), *York memorandum book, Part 1*, 2 vols., Surtees Society vols. 120, 125 (Durham, 1915), vol. I, p. 18. I owe this reference to Sarah Rees Jones.

[62] For urban mortality rates, see Jim Bolton, '"The world upside down": plague as an agent of economic and social change', in Mark Ormrod and Phillip Lindley (eds.), *The Black Death in England* (Stamford: Paul Watkins, 1996), p. 23.

[63] Gerhard Dohrn-van Rossum, *History of the hour: clocks and modern temporal orders*, trans. Thomas Dunlap (Chicago: University of Chicago Press, 1996).

opportunities – are in fact people on the move, on the make, reconstituting their households on the occasions of deaths and remarriages and constantly rebuilding their homes. We should see this group as always in process, restless, voracious and ambitious. Their flexible timber-frame homes acknowledge this: timber-frame construction was a new technology introduced at the turn of the thirteenth century, that made it possible to create buildings that were durable – hence the modern survivors – but easy to modify and adapt. Nevertheless, the 'burgeiserie' were differentiated from the mobile urban poor by a rhetoric of settledness; they were distinguished from itinerants in short-term lets. Sarah Rees Jones has argued that the householder emerges as a person with privileged status within urban administration in the fourteenth century, distinguished from the non-householder, the cottager or inmate, by virtue of his or her settled relationship with a house.[64] Nicholas Love's widely read, early-fifteenth-century account of the holy family in *The Mirrour of the Blessed Life of Jesus Christ*, manages to endow their lives of poverty after the escape into Egypt with a settled industriousness:

And þan wente þey to a Cite of þat londe that hiȝht Hermopolis or Lymopolis & þere þei hired hem sume symple house where þei dwelleden vij ȝere, as pilgrymes and straungeres, pore and nedy. Here mowe we deuoutly ymagyne and þenk of þe maner of lyuyng of hem in that vnkouh londe, & how oure lady wrouht for hir lyuelode, þat is to sey with nedil, sewyng and spinnyng, as it is writen of hir, & also Joseph, wirching in his craft of Carpentary, & how þe child blessed Jesus, aftur he came to þe age of v ȝere or þere aboute, ȝede on hir erndes & halpe in þat he miht, as a pore child to hem.[65]

There is a nice paradox here between the idea of home that this so palpably conveys, and the idea of outsiderliness. Mary and Joseph are represented as co-workers in an artisan household: Joseph as a carpenter (like John the Carpenter in Chaucer's 'Miller's Tale') and Mary as a sempstress, one of the traditional areas of paid female employment in early fifteenth-century England. They are 'straungeres' and thus not 'burgeis' in a technical sense – not members of the franchise and without the right to trade toll-free – yet they manage, working from home, to make a settled living in the city through their combined skills. There is a recognition here of the different male and female industrial roles within the home, which are unified by the activities of the five-year-old who is clearly a little trainee

---

[64] Sarah Rees Jones, 'Household and English urban government', in Myriam Carlier and Tim Soens (eds.), *The household in late medieval cities: Italy and northwestern Europe compared* (Leuven: Garant, 2001), pp. 684–98.

[65] Nicholas Love, *The mirror of the blessed life of Jesus Christ: a full critical edition*, ed. Michael G. Sargent (Exeter University Press, 2004), p. 53.

servant, running errands and helping them both. In this context, the industry, settledness and unity of the holy family in their 'simple hous' is clearly ideological: they are being dissociated from the shiftless, work-shy poor by a process of *embourgeoisement*. The holy family enables a rapprochement between the 'burgeis' and the cleric.

Other domestic values must have arisen from the fact that the 'burgeis' home is a place of work. To stability and industriousness can be added the values surrounding skill. From the fourteenth century, at least, the craft guilds strove to exercise rigorous quality control within the home. They checked on shoddy materials and poor workmanship; they regulated unsupervised working; they made sure apprentices were properly trained. The working household, like the modern university, was under a relentless external pressure to pursue excellence. Moreover, many craft and mercantile households supplied the late-medieval consumer boom which included luxury items – the leather goods, silkwork, many kinds of metalwork, fabrics, furs, food and wines – that shoppers sought in towns. We should not attribute the refinement of taste, aesthetic judgement and awareness of style required to produce these things only to the patron or consumer. In 1402 Elizabeth, Lady Zouche wrote from her home in Bedfordshire to her London friend John Bore, asking him to buy a gift for her mother on her behalf: 'I wolde a preyde ʒow þat ʒe wolde haue ordeyned me a peyre bedes of gold fore my lady my mother with þe queyntest pater noster þat ʒe can fynde wat so euer they coste.'[66] In this context 'queyntest' means a mixture of 'most elegant' and 'most skilfully wrought'. Lady Elizabeth assumes that John Bore will be able to buy beads of the quality she is after, ready-made, from a London goldsmith or jeweller. The skill required to make the 'queyntest pater noster' was what apprentices paid good money to acquire within their master's households, where they lived for many years. Since living and working took place in the same environment, workplace values relating to high-level craftsmanship and the quality of the product must have been domestic values as well.

V

All this suggests that the 'burgeis' home of late-medieval England was not, as Rybzcsinski, following Ariès, suggests, simply a public place. The records of the London assize of nuisance, which settled disputes between

---

[66] Rickert, 'Some personal letters of 1402', *Review of English Studies* 31 (1932), 257–63. 'I would like to ask you to choose a set of gold beads for my mother with the most elegant paternoster you can find, whatever the cost.'

neighbours arising from the regulations concerning buildings, seem to be evidence that the London 'burgeiserie' was engaged in the course of the fourteenth century in a process of defining where the public/private divide lay.[67] The records contain cases going back to before the Black Death in which people went to law to protect their *privata* or private business from intrusive neighbours. So in 1340 John de Hardyngham, clerk, complained that John de London, a tanner, and his wife had had three windows made 'in the wall of their solar, opposite his chamber and kitchen ... through which they and their household (*familiares*) can see his private business (*privata*)'.[68] In 1341 Isabel, widow of John Luter, complained that John Trappe, a skinner, had a tenement adjoining her property in which there were broken windows, enabling him and his servants to 'see into her garden'; she also complained of John de Thorp, another skinner, and Henry de Ware, while John le Leche, fishmonger, had a leaden tower on the wall of his property adjoining hers, 'upon which he and his household (*familiares*) stand daily, watching the private affairs of the plaintiff and her servants'; finally, she claimed that Joan, widow of Simon Corp, had twelve apertures overlooking Isabel's property through which she could see Isabel's 'private business'.[69] After an inspection, the court decided all these cases in Isabel Luter's favour, and her neighbours were required to repair the windows, take down the tower, and block the apertures. In 1356 John de Barton and his wife, who lived next door to the Prior of Holy Cross by the Tower of London, complained that the Prior's servants came through a door in the wall into the Bartons' garden, 'tread down the grass (*herbagia*) and other things growing there, and see and hear their private business'. Many of the assize of nuisance cases are between the kinds of people – a tanner, a skinner, a fishmonger – who lived in the multi-room homes that are the scene of 'burgeis' domesticity. In fact it looks as if what may be happening here is that the limits of the privacy of the home are being tested: the fact that the neighbours looked in the first place suggests that the home was not universally understood among that social group as a private sphere.

---

[67] See Diane Shaw, 'The construction of the private in medieval London', *Journal of Medieval and Early Modern Studies* 26 (1996), 447–77; Shannon McSheffrey, *Marriage, sex and civic culture in late medieval London* (Philadelphia: University of Pennsylvania Press, 2006), pp. 190–94.

[68] Helena M. Chew and William Kellaway (eds.), *London assize of nuisance 1301–1431. A calendar*, London Record Society vol. 10 (1973), 87. The assize of nuisance dealt with breaches of 'rules concerning walls, gutters, privies, windows, and pavements', p. x. It is particularly the rules about windows which raise privacy issues.

[69] Ibid, p. 88.

In these assize of nuisance cases, the private business that London citizens want to protect seems at first sight to have to do with modesty, with the boundary between the things that are done only in the presence of familiars and those that are the legitimate subject of outsiders' scrutiny. Among the kinds of activities deemed private might be those relating to bodily functions: getting washed and dressed, women dealing with their periods, both sexes defecating, as well as engaging in sexual activity, within marriage as well as outside it. Some of the fourteenth-century senses of the adjectives *derne* and *privé* (which both mean secret, secluded and private) support this: 'privé clothes' means underclothes; 'derne dede' and 'priué loue game' mean sexual intercourse; 'privé chose/lim/ membre' all mean sexual organs, as does 'derne lim'; 'privé womb' is the vulva; 'privé gagis' and 'privé harneis' are the male genitalia;[70] while the noun *privé* means a privy, and *commune privé* is, paradoxically, a public privy.[71] The privacy that is at issue here seems to be a matter of secrecy, of what should be hidden; not only a matter of modesty but also of its more extreme version, shame, whose converse is not publicness so much as boldness. This kind of privateness derives from the fact that the home is embodied: it is the place in which bodily functions are managed, the place of eating, sleeping, sex and sickness, as well as of hard work.

The converse of *privé* in Middle English is very often *apert*, meaning exposed to view. For example, in the late fourteenth-century version of 'Mandeville's' *Travels*, it is reported that 'Sum Sarzenes will drinke wyne gladly in priuetee, bot noȝt in apperte.'[72] Here, 'in priuetee' signifies the place where – or set of conditions under which – people do the things they want to do, while 'in apperte' is where they conform to what is expected of them. It may be that the London assize of nuisance was used by citizens to protect their 'privetee' in this sense, rather than their modesty or shame; that John le Leche standing on the top of his leaden tower was not a voyeur but a censor, and that he was made to take his tower down by a group of aldermen who perfectly understood the way 'Mandeville's' Saracens organised their lives. The luxury of being able to distinguish between private and public behaviours – between 'in privetee' and 'in aperte' – rests on the ability to withdraw from the eyes of the neighbours, of course, and particularly of being able to enforce this withdrawal in a court of law. The citizens who used the London assize of

[70] See *Middle English dictionary* under *privē* adj. 4 (a), (b), (c).
[71] *Ibid, privē* n. (2).
[72] G. F. Warner (ed.), *The buke of John Maundeuill*, Roxburgh Club vol. 119 (Westminster: Nichols and Sons, 1889), p. 17.

nuisance were all well-to-do;[73] the poor, as I have already suggested, must have lived exposed lives in which such possibilities for hypocrisy were not available.

Nevertheless privacy is not solitariness; in these assize of nuisance cases it is often the privacy of the *familia* or household which is at stake rather than that of the individual householder. *Privata* may not have related to particular actions at all. Instead, there may have been a sense that the home is, and ought to be, an unwatched place to which access is by invitation only, that is, that the intrusion relates not to specific conduct but to the meanings attached to certain kinds of intimate space, whatever people choose to do in it. The issue, then, is not modesty, shame or withdrawal, but power and possession. Its converse is free access: the publicness of the market or the street. As sites of manufacture and trade, urban households were increasingly subject from the late fourteenth century on to guild regulations forbidding householders and their apprentices to work beyond certain hours and giving guild officials rights of entry to examine the quality of the workmanship that went on in them. Nevertheless, an occasion such as that in 1378 when a York saddler, William Stillingfleet, refused the searchers of his craft access to his home on the grounds that they had been corruptly appointed, suggests that he at least had a strong sense of the limits of the publicness of the household.[74] And so we might want to link the sense of 'burgeis' domestic space as a place of *secreta* to the craft secrets that apprentices were not allowed to divulge.[75] We might also link it to the public-sphere virtue of discretion so sought after among urban elites. In some towns burgesses were required to swear an oath that they would 'conceal the counsels of the town'.[76] It seems that the formation of the 'wise and discreet' public man in fact took place within the home, understood as a place of *secreta* that were not to be seen or heard by outsiders.

Craft regulations also assume that it is possible to think of privacy within the working home. The York girdlers' ordinances of 1417, for example, forbid any apprentice or journeyman from doing any work pertaining to the girdler craft 'prevely in chaumbres, or oute of the house of ther maisters'.[77] Two or three decades earlier, Chaucer could imagine

---

[73] Chew and Kellaway (eds.), *London assize of nuisance*, p. xxxi.

[74] Sellers (ed.), *York memorandum book*, vol. I, p. 31.

[75] See, for example, the 1371 indentures of apprenticeship between Nicholas, son of John de Kyghlay, and John de Bradlay of York, bowyer, in which Nicholas is bound to carry out his master's orders, 'secreta sua celando' (concealing his secrets). See ibid., p. 54.

[76] For burgesses' oaths from Kings' Lynn, Ipswich and Maldon, see www.trytel.com/%7Etristan/towns/towns.html#menu; accessed 14 August 2006.

[77] Sellers (ed.), *York memorandum book*, vol. I, p. 182.

different kinds of solitariness within the urban household. In 'The Miller's Tale', Nicholas, who lodges in John the carpenter's house, has 'A chambre … in that hostelrye / Allone, withouten any compaignye'.[78] Parlours are mentioned in London inventories from the 1370s, and the collocation 'privé parlour' suggests they were withdrawal rooms, away from the business of the hall. In York, the earliest reference to a parlour in the surviving records is in the inventory of the house of Robert Talkan, a wealthy girdler and former mayor, who died in 1413.[79] His parlour seems to have been off the hall; it had a fireplace with a bench, a table and two chairs, and was presumably a place designed for comfortable and intimate conversation.

   Although there seems to have been a 'burgeis' domesticity in England from the fourteenth century, its realistic representation in art does not appear there until the sixteenth, with Holbein's portrait of the More family in their parlour, of which only a preliminary sketch survives. The reasons why England did not develop artistic styles in the fifteenth century that engaged with everyday domestic reality are no doubt complex. In the Netherlands, by contrast, we find from the 1420s on the detailed representation of bourgeois interiors in the works of Robert Campin, Petrus Christus, Rogier van der Weyden and others, as well as in manuscript illuminations such as those of the Master of the Hours of Catherine of Cleves. This new naturalism seems to emerge with the domestication and *embourgeoisement* of the life of Christ to which I have already referred, and to which the pseudo-Bonaventuran *Meditationes Vitae Christi* must have been a major contributor.[80] The graceful courtly realism of international gothic did not, it seems, value the ordinariness which is at the heart of 'burgeis' domesticity. For the Netherlandish school, the life of Christ provides a series of genre scenes – moments of stasis in the narrative – which can be appropriately rendered in a naturalistic mode. So initially the Annunciation, and then Mary nursing the Christ-child and other intimate scenes, come to be depicted within 'burgeis places', as everyday events in plain, conspicuously well-ordered chambers and kitchens, beside windows looking out on to contemporary towns. The ordinary is at first irradiated by religious significance, and then by its own. The same interiors are secularised, as in van Eyck's portrait of the merchant Arnolfini and his wife, and Holbein is an heir to this secular tradition. His 1527 sketch of the More *familia* in their parlour uses the tranquil setting of 'burgeis' domesticity to record the restless social processes that had always

[78] Chaucer, 'Miller's Tale', in *The Riverside Chaucer*, lines 3203–4.
[79] The contents are listed under 'Aula': Stell, *Probate inventories*, p. 524.
[80] See Nuechterlein, 'The domesticity of sacred space'.

been at its heart.[81] At the centre of the scene are three men: old judge John More, the London baker's son; his son, Thomas, the successful urban professional; and his son John, the husband-to-be of a landed Yorkshire heiress. Chaucer's family had shown the same pattern over three generations more than a hundred years before.

Specialised ways of domestic living were, I have argued, the source and location of a set of values that might be said to have created the 'burgeiserie' of the fourteenth and fifteenth centuries. These values had to do with imposing order and differentiation, both temporal and spatial, on the inescapable, everyday activities of the home: eating, sleeping, dressing, working, bringing up children and caring for the sick and the old. Domestic and personal privacy and the ethical norms of the working household – stability, industry, discretion, the pursuit of excellence, as well as the hypocrisy that privacy allows – seem to be aspects of this process. Its achievement, though, should be seen not simply as a process but also as a struggle, just as within the equilibrium of Vermeer's paintings there lie other, tenser feelings which suggest that the serenity of the domestic world is a matter of the play of light and belongs only to the moment at which the painter glimpsed and caught it.

---

[81] I have explored this idea more fully in Felicity Riddy, 'Fathers and daughters: Holbein's portrait of Thomas More's family', in Diane Wolfthal and Rosalynn Voaden (eds.), *Framing the family: narrative and representation in the medieval and early modern periods* (Tempe, AZ: Arizona Center for Medieval and Renaissance Studies, 2005), pp. 19–38.

3   Buttery and pantry and their antecedents:
     idea and architecture in the English
     medieval house

Mark Gardiner

The century between 1150 and 1250 was a crucial period in the emergence of the late-medieval domestic plan. By the middle of the thirteenth century, perhaps even by 1200, a consensus had largely emerged
about the organisation of domestic space. From then on, for the next
three hundred years almost every house in England was constructed
with three fundamental elements: the hall, chamber and services. Only
the smallest of houses, the urban and rural cottages, were too small to
accommodate these three rooms. The grandest buildings, of course,
had many other rooms, but these were subsidiary to the core elements
of the house. The late-medieval plan was flexible enough to reflect not
only the wealth of the owner, but also the constraints of particular sites.
The chamber block, for example, might be aligned with the hall or
turned sideways at right angles to form a cross-wing. But the hall,
chamber and services were always arranged in a recognisable manner,
so that a visitor entering any late medieval building could rapidly
comprehend the organisation of space.[1]

The late medieval domestic plan was not prescriptive, but was merely a
satisfactory way of arranging rooms which accorded with ideas of the
proper organisation of space. The hall was at the heart of the medieval
house, for this was the main ceremonial space in which guests were
received and meals consumed. It had a formal pattern with an entrance,
usually by means of a cross passage, at the 'low end' (Figure 3.1). The
householder and his or her family sat at a table at the 'high end', the
importance of which was sometimes emphasised by a raised dais and a
moulded beam or a hood to frame those seated there. A doorway commonly set at one side of the wall, either at the high end, or in the early
thirteenth century more commonly at the low end, provided access to the

---

[1] For a useful summary of the late medieval domestic plan, see Grenville, *Medieval housing*,
pp. 89–92.

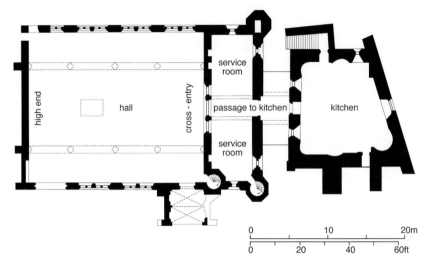

Figure 3.1 Plan of the west hall at the Bishop's Palace, Lincoln, showing thirteenth-century work only. Surviving masonry is shown in black and inferred walls in dashed outline. Adapted from P. A. Faulkner, 'Lincoln Old Bishop's Palace (SK 9777717)', *Archaeological Journal* 131 (1974), fig. 20.

owner's chamber or private room, often on the first floor. This was not only a bedroom, but also a place in which private matters might be discussed.[2] The service rooms where food and other domestic items might be stored, and food was prepared, were located on the ground floor at the low end of the hall. The hall was, therefore, not merely a room, but a hierarchical space with places for the owners of the house, and for their servants and guests according to their status. It provided a stage on which one of the central events of the day, the formal rituals of the serving and consumption of food, could take place.

Most recent work on the development of the late medieval domestic plan has viewed the problem from the perspective of the architectural historian.[3] The reasons why domestic space was organised in such a persistent and

---

[2] C. M. Woolgar, *The great household in medieval England* (New Haven: Yale University Press, 1999), p. 50; Felicity Heal, *Hospitality in early modern England* (Oxford University Press, 1990), pp. 40–4.

[3] John Blair, 'Hall and chamber: English domestic planning 1000–1250', in G. Meirion-Jones and M. Jones (eds.), *Manorial domestic buildings in England and northern France* (London: Society of Antiquaries, 1993), pp. 1–21; Mark Gardiner, 'Vernacular buildings and the development of the later medieval domestic plan in England', *Medieval Archaeology* 44 (2000), 159–79; Grenville, *Medieval housing*; Edward Impey and Roland Harris, 'Boothby Pagnell revisited', in G. Meirion-Jones, E. Impey and M. Jones (eds.), *The*

distinctive form remain almost entirely unexamined. A study of that prob-lem requires a rather different approach. Instead of taking a developmental view of architecture, seeking early prototypes and subsequent examples, buildings must be viewed as the realisation of ideas about domestic space. Concepts of domestic organisation must be regarded as primary: buildings must be interpreted as subsequent attempts to work out such ideas in physical space. The reasons underlying the organisation of domestic space can be more readily appreciated in the familiar context of the design of recent buildings. There is no plan which dictates the lay-out of rooms in modern houses and flats, but there are general precepts which architects recognise in designing domestic spaces and which the occupants expect. Bedrooms in English houses are normally set some distance away from the main entrance, but 'public' rooms for receiving guests are located near to the front door. The kitchen is situated away from the main entrance, but sufficiently close to the dining room. The toilet and bathroom must not be located anywhere near the kitchen. When these rules and other consider-ations were applied to the design of the inter-war semi-detached house in England, they tended to produce a standard plan in which the rooms had a 'natural' order. This applied equally to the exterior where one of the impor-tant considerations was to place the front doors of adjoining houses as far as possible from each other to give the illusion of separateness. The result was that builders tended to reproduce the same pattern in tens of thousands of houses constructed at this time, because there were few possible alternatives given the desires of purchasers and the constraints of space.[4]

My aim in this chapter is to examine the ideas underlying the service rooms in the late-medieval house, and how such concepts first developed and subsequently changed. Although the service rooms formed a small part of the late medieval house, they played an important role in the ceremony of serving food and dining. Unlike most rooms, which might have been used for a number of functions during the course of the day, the services had a limited purpose and in particular were associated with specific goods and utensils. We also need to understand the development of these rooms within the wider framework of the emergence of the late-medieval domestic plan, and examine how architecture was adapted to serve the growing formality of domestic life during the later twelfth and early thirteenth centuries. Thus, a study of the service rooms may be used to bring into relief the relationship between architecture, function and idea.

seigneurial residence in Western Europe AD c. 800–1600 (Oxford: Archaeopress, 2002), pp. 245–69; Anthony Quiney, 'Hall or chamber? That is the question. The use of rooms in post-Conquest houses', *Architectural History* 42 (1999), 24–46.

[4] F. E. Brown, 'Analysing small building plans: a morphological approach', in R. Samson (ed.), *The social archaeology of houses* (Edinburgh University Press, 1990), pp. 259–76.

The organisation of the services within the late-medieval house is so familiar that it barely occasions any comment from architectural historians. Two or three doorways led from the screens passage or cross-entry. If there were two doorways, they gave access to two equal-sized rooms, the buttery and pantry; if there were three doorways, the third led, either between the other rooms into a passage-way to the kitchen set beyond the main house or, if situated at one side, gave access to a chamber above the services (Figure 3.1). Our familiarity with this arrangement has tended to hide the fact that we understand very little about the way in which this pattern developed, particularly during the formative period in the later twelfth and first half of the thirteenth century when the domestic plan was still fluid. Indeed, there is very little real discussion about the reason for the distinction between the two rooms, and even exactly what functions were carried out in each. Margaret Wood, for example, in her detailed study of the medieval house which gives separate chapters to such minor features as porches and even garderobes (toilets), discusses the service doorways, but not the rooms themselves.[5] The subject is treated equally summarily in other more recent surveys.

The idea of two separate service rooms seems to have been well established in domestic planning by 1200 and it is found in most houses constructed in the following three hundred years. The longevity of these rooms suggests that they mattered to house-owners. It would have been possible for a single larger room to have accommodated the items stored in the two offices, but the construction of two equal and separate spaces suggests that the distinction between them may have been as much cultural as functional. In explaining the role of these rooms, we need to address three issues. The first is fundamental: what objects were associated with each of the two service rooms? If we can understand the reasons for grouping the contents of each and their associations, we may be able to ascertain the symbolism of the separate spaces. The second question is to consider how the rooms related to the organisation of the household. Large seigneurial households had separate officials responsible for the buttery and pantry, suggesting that these were not just rooms but were, in some respects, an embodiment of domestic order. Reversing this emphasis, the third issue is to examine the service rooms not merely as ideas, but as physical spaces within the architecture of the house. The buttery and pantry were located in relationship to other parts of the house and, in particular, had entrances which were visible from the public area of the hall. The evolution of these rooms in

---

[5] Margaret Wood, *The English mediaeval house* (London: Phoenix House, 1965), pp. 124–9.

the late-twelfth- and early-thirteenth-century house, when they first appear, is of especial interest.

The use of service rooms

De Nominibus Utensilium, written by Alexander Neckam, probably in the period 1177–90, provides a rare insight into the disposition of household items within an idealised lordly building. Neckam's main purpose in writing the work was, however, to introduce a wide range of Latin vocabulary and to provide a teaching aid for his students.[6] The immediate model for Neckam's work may have been the *Oratio de Utensilibus* by Adam of Balsham (alias Adam of Petit Pont), although, as Lendinara has pointed out, there are considerable differences in subject matter. Ultimately, the roots of *De Nominibus* lie in the tradition of didactic works of which the most relevant are the late-tenth-century *Colloquy* of Aelfric and, particularly, the colloquies of his pupil, Aelfric Bata. Neckam also drew upon classical authors and the seventh-century *Etymologie* of Isidore of Seville.[7] *De nominibus* describes the contents of each room in a large house, as well as the preparation of food and the character of castles. The author mentions more briefly the items used on a peasant farm. We must accept that the buildings and contents may not have been typical: the aim of the work was, after all, to use the widest possible vocabulary. However, the household must have been recognisable to his pupils in general terms if it was to act as a useful *aide-mémoire*. Neckam's method of teaching Latin vocabulary appears to have drawn upon a classic technique of memorisation described by Cicero.[8] The technique is summarised most clearly by Quintilian, who suggests that ideas may be remembered by associating

---

[6] The text of *De Nominibus* was printed in Thomas Wright (ed.), *A volume of vocabularies* (Liverpool: privately printed, 1857), pp. 96–119 from British Library, Cotton MS. Titus D. xx, and more recently by Tony Hunt, *Teaching and learning Latin in thirteenth-century England* (Cambridge: Brewer, 1991), pp. 181–90, plus further details in the erratum. On date, see R. W. Hunt, *The schools and the cloister: the life and writings of Alexander Nequam* (Oxford University Press, 1984), pp. 19–20, 125. Translations of passages from *De Nominibus* appear in Urban T. Holmes, *Daily living in the twelfth century* (Madison, WI: University of Wisconsin Press, 1953), *passim*.

[7] Patrizia Lendinara, *Anglo-Saxon glosses and glossaries* (Aldershot: Ashgate, 1999), pp. 357–78, reprinted from Patrizia Lendinara, 'The *Oratio de utensilibus ad domum regendum pertinentibus* by Adam of Balsham', *Anglo-Norman Studies* 15 (1993), 161–76; R. Ellis, 'A contribution to the history of the transmission of classical literature in the Middle Ages', *American Journal of Philology* 10 (1889), 159–62; Hunt, *Teaching and learning Latin*, p. 182 (fol. 105ra); Isidore of Seville, *Etymologie sive originum libri XX*, ed. W. M. Lindsay (Oxford University Press, 1910), xx, iii, translated in *The Etymologies of Isidore of Seville*, ed. S. A. Barney, W. J. Lewis, J. A. Beach and O. Berghof (Cambridge University Press, 2006).

[8] Cicero, *De oratore*, ed. E. W. Sutton (Heinemann: London, 1942), ii, lxxxvi. lines 350–3.

them with a series of places, particularly rooms within a building. The spaces are to be as varied as possible and he suggests using the forecourt, the living room, bedrooms and parlours.[9] Neckam is likely to have been aware of this technique and drew upon it in a very direct manner in using the spaces of a building to remind his students of their Latin vocabulary for household goods.

Neckam's description begins in the kitchen, where he lists the contents at length, and then continues in the pantry or spence where towels, tablecloths and knives were kept. A sauce dish, salt-cellar, cheese dish, candlesticks and baskets were also to be found there – all items for setting the table. The room called by Neckam the cellar or storeroom or foodstore (*promtuarium*), later known as the buttery from the *buttae* or barrels, contained cups, basins and spoons, in addition to the casks of wine, cider and beer.

It is interesting to contrast Neckam's *De Nominibus* with Adam of Balsham's earlier work, *Oratio de Utensilibus*. Adam taught in Paris from 1132, and although his work was not intended to be didactic, its value for teaching Latin was rapidly realised. The account begins with Adam's arrival in England on his return from France and continues with a description of the setting of the estate, before moving inside the castle. There, he walks around the buildings, providing an opportunity for a description of their contents.[10] Many of the items are again drawn from Isidore's *Etymologie*, particularly the contents of the storehouse which are taken directly from Book xx, iv–vii. It is true that Adam does not follow Isidore slavishly. He comments wryly, in an overt allusion to the *Etymologie*, that he saw no Arretine or Samian vessels. But the contents of Adam's storehouse do not resemble those of either a buttery or pantry, and instead include items associated with both. It seems that either Adam of Balsham's description leant so heavily on the *Etymologie* that it cannot be representative of practice in mid-twelfth-century England, or that there really were such storehouses at the time which combined the functions of buttery and pantry.

It is possible to pursue this further by comparing the descriptions of items in Neckam's and Balsham's fictional buildings with the goods listed in the twelfth-century stock-and-land leases of St Paul's, London. These provide an indication of the types of tools and utensils which might have been found on a manorial farm (*curia*). They can hardly be complete lists, even of the most important tools required for running a farm, but seem to

---

[9] Frances Yates, *The art of memory* (London: Pimlico, 1992), pp. 17–24; Quintilian, *Institutio oratoria*, 2 vols., ed. H. E. Butler (London: Heinemann, 1920–2), xi, p. ii, lines 17–22.

[10] The text is in Hunt, *Teaching and learning Latin*, pp. 172–6; discussed in Lendinara, *Anglo-Saxon glosses and glossaries*, pp. 357–75.

have been miscellaneous items, perhaps left by the previous tenants and found in the *curia* when the lease was drawn up. The goods on the manor farms of Walton-on-the-Naze and Thorpe (Essex) are particularly interesting. These were apparently listed by the canon who had been sent from London to execute the lease. The lease of Walton and Thorpe is not dated, but was drawn up sometime after the death of a former tenant, William of Ockendon, in 1150.[11]

The lists in the inventories appear to have both begun in the barns where carts were kept (Table 3.1). The appraiser at Walton evidently then moved to the granary, where there were *corbelli* – baskets often used specifically for carrying grain – and winnowing fans. After that he proceeded to the brewhouse, where he recorded a millstone for grinding malt, tubs and barrels, a lead boiler and casks. At Thorpe, the order seems to have been reversed with the brewhouse examined first, followed by the granary. The next items listed at Walton were three *tripodes*, though it is unclear whether these were three-legged stools, tables or even trivets. These are followed by a further distinctive group of goods – dishes, tablecloths, bowls and half a seam of salt. According to Neckam, these items for the table would typically have been stored in the pantry. Again, the Thorpe list is similar, but what is notable is the presence of two butts listed after the dishes and bowls of the pantry and presumably stored in a buttery. The trestle tables recorded in both lists suggest that recording continued in the hall where, at Thorpe, there was also a buffet with lathe-turned legs.[12] The recorder then returned to the farmyard or out-buildings where farm tools were noted, including iron teeth, presumably for a harrow.

It is clear from the order of the goods listed in both inventories that these were drawn up in a systematic way. Though the items on the two farmsteads differed, they were both inventoried by going around the farmstead, recording the goods found in each building or room. Two further inventories made around the same time for the demesne farm at Ardeley also order the items by room and building, though these are less comprehensive.[13] It appears that it was normal practice on the St Paul's manors to record the goods on demesne manors by progressing around

[11] William Hale Hale (ed.), *The Domesday of St Paul's of the year 1222*, Camden Society vol. 69 (London, 1858), pp. 129–32. For discussion of the leases, see Reginald Lennard, *Rural England 1086–1135: a study of social and agrarian conditions* (Oxford University Press, 1959), pp. 176–212. For the date of the death of William of Ockendon, see H. G. Richardson, Review of *Early charters of the cathedral church of St. Paul, London*, ed. M Gibbs, *English Historical Review* 57 (1942), 129.

[12] For an example of English lathe-turned furniture of about this date, see Penelope Eames, *Furniture in England, France and the Netherlands from the twelfth to the fifteenth century* (London: Furniture History Society, 1977), pp. 210–11, plates 54–5.

[13] *The Domesday of St Paul's*, pp. 136–7.

Table 3.1: *Inventory of goods in the St Paul's estate and their likely locations on the farmsteads*

I. Walton-on-the-Naze

barns?	iv carri	four carts
granary	iii corbelle	three baskets
	ii vanni	two winnowing fans
brewhouse	ii paria molarum	two pairs of millstones
	x cuve	ten tubs
	iv tunelle	four barrels
	ii plumbi super fornaces	two lead vessels on boilers
	ii tine	two casks
	iii tripod'	tripod, trivet or trestle
pantry	xx scutelle	twenty dishes
	ii nape quae sunt appreciate pro iv d.	two tablecloths worth 6*d*.
	vi ciphi	six bowls
	dimida summa de sale	half a seam of salt
?	ii secures	two ?hatchets
hall	una tabula cum trestlis	a table with trestles
farmyard	viiii esperdintes de ferr' et acerio	eight teeth of iron and steel
	v rusche	five bee hives

II. Thorpe

barns?	ii carri	two carts
brewhouse	vii cuvae	seven tubs
	i alge	one trough
	i plumbum super fornacem	one lead vessel on boiler
	una mola	one mill stone
	unum tunellum	one tun
granary	3 corbelle	three baskets
pantry	ii bacini	two basins
	ii ciphi	two bowls
	xii scutelle	twelve dishes
buttery	2 bucci	two butts
hall	una parva tabella cum trestlis	a small table with trestles
	unum branchum tornatile	a turned buffet
farmyard	una besca	a spade
	ii secures	two ?hatchets
	i uuogium	a pruning knife
	i tarambium	a gimlet
	vii esperdinte de ferro	seven iron teeth

Source: Hale, *The Domesday of St Paul's*, pp. 129–32.

the farmstead. We can pick out those items at Walton and Thorpe which were kept in the pantry for setting the table and, less confidently, identify the buttery from the mention of the butts for storing ale. The lists give weight to the veracity of Neckam's idealised text. The Walton list groups the salt and tablecloths with the dishes and bowls, implying that these were found together.

We can adopt a similar approach to an even earlier source. The Old English text called *Gerefa* purports to be advice to reeves on the management of a manorial farm. It survives in a single copy in handwriting of *c.* 1100, which must therefore be the latest date of composition. It is unlikely to pre-date the colloquies of Aelfric and Aelfric Bata, which appear to have been an influence. It can therefore be attributed to the eleventh century, though we cannot date it more precisely.[14] The most significant element of *Gerefa* for the present purpose is the lists of goods which the reeve should provide for work on the manor. There are two lists. The first (para. 15) begins with tools for building and proceeds to those items required for textile production. The author then states that 'nis ænig man þæt atellan mæge ða tol ealle ðe man habban sceal' ['there is no man that can enumerate all the tools which one must have'], but, contradicting that rhetorical statement, he immediately continues with a second list. This second list (para. 17) begins with farm equipment and a longer account of utensils which belong in domestic buildings. There is a strong argument, both grammatically and from the passage quoted above, that these two lists had separate origins and had been brought together in the surviving text.[15] The order of household utensils given in the second list (known as List B) is particularly significant. Christine Fell noted that these were organised by function, but this is only part of the explanation.[16]

A comparison of items in List B with those recorded in later sources suggests that the former were grouped by their location within the farmstead. The domestic utensils in List B were clearly associated with cooking, and we should expect to find them in the kitchen. They included not only large cooking vessels, but also a gridiron or trivet so they could be placed over the fire. The next section comprised items from the dairy, including buckets, churns and a cheese-vat. The third section is equally

---

[14] The text of *Gerefa* is printed in F. Liebermann, *Die Gesetze der Angelsachsen*, vol. I (Halle: Niemeyer, 1898), pp. 453–5. A translation is given in Michael Swanton, *Anglo-Saxon prose* (London: Dent, 1975), pp. 25–7. On the date, see P. D. A. Harvey, '*Rectitudines singularum personarum* and *Gerefa*', *English Historical Review* 108 (1993), 11–12, and C. P. Wormald, *The making of English law: King Alfred to the twelfth century* (Oxford University Press, 1999), p. 233.

[15] The lists are discussed further in Mark Gardiner, 'Implements and utensils in *Gerefa*, and the organization of seigneurial farmsteads in the High Middle Ages', *Medieval Archaeology* 50 (2006), 260–7 and in John Hines, '*Gerefa* §§ 15 and 17: a grammatical analysis of the lists of nouns', *Medieval Archaeology* 50 (2006), 268–70.

[16] Christine E. Fell, 'Some domestic problems', *Leeds Studies in English*, new series 16 (1985), 73–8.

clearly of items for cleaning the grain and included a range of sieves for removing straw, chaff and stones. The next group belonged to the buttery or the brewhouse, for here *Gerefa* lists items for making drinks (troughs and pails), and then items for storing it and consuming it (barrels for strong drink, dishes and cups). The inclusion here of beehives and honey bins is explained by Fell, no doubt correctly, by reference to the use of honey in sweetening drinks.[17] The strainer which concludes this group would have been used for removing any solid matter when the drink was decanted into jugs. The final group of utensils examined here can be recognised as belonging to the pantry – candlesticks, salt-cellar, spoon-case, pepper-horn – all items which would be set on the table, but also stools, seats and a yeast box.

The order of utensils recorded in List B, like those in the St Paul's inventories, was related to the places in which they were kept. It is possible again to distinguish groups of implements which were associated with the pantry and those associated with serving drink. This takes the distinction back into the eleventh century. The items listed by *Gerefa* and belonging in the buttery contained, inevitably, the barrels and other containers for drink and the cups from which it was consumed, but also troughs and containers for treading grapes. It suggests that the eleventh-century buttery was a place for making wine or ale, not merely for storing it, and this contrasts with the items in Neckam's list which include no items for producing alcoholic drink. The St Paul's evidence from the Thorpe inventory also tends to suggest a distinction between the places where drink was made and where it was stored. There are no such difficulties with those items which are connected with the pantry. The lists in *Gerefa*, in the St Paul's inventories and given by Neckam are similar and concern items associated with table-setting – tablecloths, napkins, salt dishes and lamps.

We have traced a long-standing distinction between the items associated with the buttery or the making of drink, and those connected with the spence or pantry. It has been followed backwards from Alexander Neckam's *De Nominibus* in the late twelfth century, by way of the St Paul's leases, as far as *Gerefa* which was written before *c.* 1100. The origin of the two service rooms lies, therefore, well before the late-medieval domestic plan became established and suggests that there was a basic, deep-rooted idea about separating items connected with drink from those associated with table-setting.

[17] Ibid., 73.

Household officials

It is quite possible that the root of the distinction between the buttery and pantry could lie even earlier and might be related to the organisation of great households. Typically, a seigneurial household had a steward responsible for ensuring the provision of food and a butler who had a similar duty for wine and ale. The two service rooms might relate to these two areas of responsibility. *Constitutio Domus Regis*, written in the period 1135×39, or perhaps originally compiled in 1108 and subsequently updated, provides the earliest full account of the organisation of the English royal household. There were five departments, each under a head or heads who were distinguished by payment at the substantial rate of 5*s*. a day. These were the chancellor, the steward, the butler (*dapifer*), the chamberlain and treasurer, and the constables.[18] It seems to be significant that the Pipe Roll of 1180–81, recording royal expenditure, mentions a payment for tablecloths (*napae*) and, separately, for barrels, casks and other items for the buttery. The wording suggests that accounts were rendered by separate officials with the tablecloths perhaps coming under the purview of the steward responsible for the pantry and the barrels under that of the butler.[19]

The Anglo-Saxon royal household of the mid-eleventh century had numerous officials, rather like its Anglo-Norman successor. However, the number of serving officials a century earlier was evidently much smaller.[20] King Eadred's will of 951×55 provides the clearest guide to the royal entourage. He bequeathed his most important officials one hundred gold coins each. These were the *discðegn* or steward, *byrele* or butler and *hrælglðegn* or chamberlain. There were no posts equivalent to the constables found in Henry I's household, and it is uncertain whether Eadred's *mæssepreost* or priest, who was given a bequest of fifty gold coins, performed any of the functions later exercised by the Norman chancellor. Certainly, the sum of money suggests he was of lesser importance than the

---

[18] C. Johnson (ed.), *Dialogus de scaccario and Constitutio domus regis*, revised edn by F. E. L. Carter and D. E. Greenway (Oxford University Press, 1983); Judith A. Green, *The government of England under Henry I* (Cambridge University Press, 1986), p. 27.

[19] *The Great Roll of the Pipe for the twenty-seventh year of the reign of King Henry the Second, A.D. 1180–1181*, Pipe Roll Society vol. 30 (London, 1909), p. 157.

[20] Simon Keynes, *The diplomas of King Æthelred the Unready, 978–1016* (Cambridge University Press, 1980), pp. 38–83, 134–53; Pierre Chaplais, 'The royal Anglo-Saxon "chancery" of the tenth century revisited', in H. Mayr-Harting and R. I. Moore (eds.), *Studies in medieval history presented to R. H. C. Davis* (London: Hambledon, 1985), pp. 41–51; cf. Simon Keynes, 'Regenbald the chancellor (*sic*)', *Anglo-Norman Studies* 10 (1988), 185–222.

other three posts.[21] Ninth- and tenth-century charters are attested by various *ministri* who are referred to in Latin or the vernacular as stewards, butlers or chamberlains, but these odd references do not allow a comprehensive picture of the royal household. Perhaps only the witness list of a charter bearing the date 892, and which includes Deormod *cellarius*, Ælfric *thesaurarius* and Sigewulf *pincerna*, gives us a more complete glimpse.[22] These offices of storekeeper, treasurer and butler seem to be comparable to those found later, particularly if the first was the equivalent of the steward.

The Carolingian court was broadly similar to the English royal household, although it had a more complex structure. Hincmar of Rheims noted in 882 that the chief officers of the palace were the chamberlain (*camerarius*), count of the palace (*comes palatii*), steward (*senescalcus*), butler (*buticularius*), constable (*comes stabuli*) and master of lodgings (*mansionarius*), as well as four chief hunters and one falconer. The description of the duties of these posts makes it clear that in the Carolingian court, as in the English royal household, there was division between those who oversaw the provision of food and of drink.[23]

The long-standing practice of appointing separate household officials to the posts of butler and steward seems to provide part of the explanation of the origin of the two service rooms, but that alone is not sufficient. The areas of responsibility of the butler and steward do not match very closely with the buttery and pantry. The butler was responsible not only for serving wine and ale, but also for procuring drink and storing it. Equally, the steward's field was much wider than suggested by the items in the pantry which, in the main, were for setting the table. It is, therefore, too simplistic to regard the two service rooms as an architectural expression of the roles of the household officials, although clearly there was a relationship. A deeper explanation is required to account for the symbolism of these rooms and the division of items

---

[21] L. M. Larson, *The king's household in England before the Norman Conquest* (Madison, WI: University of Wisconsin, 1904), p. 127; *Select English historical documents of the ninth and tenth centuries*, ed. F. E. Harmer (Cambridge University Press, 1914), no. 21.

[22] P. H. Sawyer, *Anglo-Saxon charters: an annotated list and bibliography* (London: Royal Historical Society, 1968), no. 348; discussed in Susan E. Kelly, *Charters of Abingdon Abbey, part 1* (Oxford University Press, 2000), p. 80. Keynes, *Diplomas of King Æthelred*, pp. 158–61.

[23] *Hincmarus de ordine palatii* (Monumenta Germaniae Historica, Fontes Iuris Germanici Antiqui, 3), lines 275–9, 323–94, translated in David Herlihy, *The history of feudalism* (Brighton: Harvester Press, 1970), pp. 216–20. I have, however, preferred my own translations of the posts.

between them, but it is necessary first to consider the architectural evidence.

Architectural evidence

Study of the architecture of standing buildings in conjunction with written evidence can allow us an insight into the way in which space was used during everyday life. Archaeological approaches to architecture have looked with increasing interest at the way in which light, embellishment and space were used to create an appropriate setting for formal events. This is most apparent in castles and larger houses, and it is in relationship with such buildings that it has been most commonly studied.[24] The owners of such buildings had the resources to spend on achieving the right effect and were particularly concerned with formal ceremony, the impact of which might be enhanced by its architectural setting. High-status buildings survive from an early date and it is through them that we can trace the emergence in the late twelfth century of the buttery and pantry as two separate service rooms at the end of the hall.

Margaret Wood considered the triple doorway found in the king's palace at Clarendon (Wiltshire) to be amongst the earliest examples. She dated these entrances to the buttery, pantry and to a passage-way through to the kitchen to 1176–7. Others have attributed the construction of the doorways to building work in the period 1181–3, when money was paid for 'the work of the hall'.[25] The archaeological evidence suggests a more complex story. The excavated stone service rooms are clearly later than the hall, but the presence of the doorways in the hall leading to rooms beyond seems to imply that there must have been an earlier buttery and pantry, perhaps built of timber.[26]

The evidence is much clearer in the hall at Oakham Castle (Rutland). The hall can be dated with some precision from the capitals of the pillars of the aisle arcade, which are very similar to work at Canterbury Cathedral and may even be the work of the same masons. These suggest that the Oakham hall was constructed in the 1180s.[27] At the east end of the hall

---

[24] For example, Philip Dixon and Pamela Marshall, 'The great tower at Hedingham Castle: a reassessment', *Fortress* 18 (1993), 16–23; Philip Dixon and Beryl Lott, 'The courtyard and the tower: contexts and symbols in the development of late medieval great houses', *Journal of the British Archaeological Association* 146 (1993), 93–101.

[25] Wood, *The English medieval house*, 124; R. Allen Brown, H. M. Colvin and A. J. Taylor, *The history of the king's works: II. The Middle Ages* (London: HMSO, 1963), pp. 911, 913.

[26] T. B. James and A. M. Robinson, *Clarendon Palace: the history and archaeology of a medieval palace* (London: Society of Antiquaries, 1988), p. 94.

[27] David Parsons, 'Transitional architecture in Rutland', *Rutland Record* 6 (1986), 195–201.

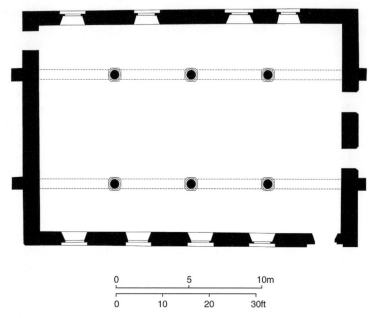

Figure 3.2 Plan of Oakham Castle hall (after C. H. Hartshorne, 'The hall at Oakham', *Archaeological Journal* 5 (1848), p. 141). The now-demolished chamber block with services to the left of the hall and the return aisle with chamber to the right are not shown.

were two centrally set doorways, each with two-centred heads (Figures 3.2 and 3.3). They led to part of the building to the east which no longer stands. A third doorway from within the aisle in the east wall had a round head and evidently gave access to another room on the ground floor, while a similar doorway above it, which must have been approached by stairs, led to rooms at first-floor level (Figure 3.4).[28] Much the same arrangement can be seen in the west hall at the Bishop's Palace, Lincoln, attributed to *c.* 1225. Two equal-sized doorways flanked a larger central entrance to a passageway to the kitchen (Figures 3.1 and 3.5). Above the two service rooms and passageway was the main chamber, which was thus located beyond the low end of the hall, rather than in the position which became common fifty years later, beyond the high end.[29] The

[28] P. A. Faulkner, 'Domestic planning from the twelfth to the fourteenth centuries', *Archaeological Journal* 115 (1958), 150–83.
[29] P. A. Faulkner, 'Lincoln Old Bishop's Palace (sk 9777717)', *Archaeological Journal* 131 (1974), 340–4.

Figure 3.3 Oakham Castle hall, looking towards the entrances to the buttery and pantry (now blocked). Reproduced with permission of Rutland County Council.

chamber at Oakham seems to have occupied exactly the same position. Although there was a room beyond the high end of the hall, it cannot have been the main chamber as it was accommodated in a single-storey return or end aisle.[30]

A further example of this arrangement can be identified from the excavations at the royal palace at Cheddar (Somerset), where the emergence of the buttery and pantry as separate rooms at the low end of the hall is particularly clear in the sequence of excavated buildings. East Hall I, built around 1100, had no attached services, nor apparently did its successor (II) which was constructed in *c.* 1150–70. East Hall III, which could not be closely dated but was attributed to the second decade of the thirteenth century, had a clear buttery and pantry with central passage

---

[30] One stone bracket for the low return aisle still remains *in situ* on the exterior of the west wall of the hall. The hole for a second bracket is visible.

Figure 3.4 Doors in the north aisle to the ground-floor and first-floor levels at Oakham Castle hall (now blocked). Reproduced with permission of Rutland County Council.

Figure 3.5 View towards the service end of the west hall at the Bishop's Palace, Lincoln (cf. Figure 3.1). The doorways to the service rooms and through to the kitchen lie to the left, the door to the bishop's chamber to the right and the entrance to the hall from the porch to the far right.

to the kitchen.[31] Again, accommodation, indicated by the presence of a garderobe and fireplace, was provided above the service rooms.

A clear pattern emerges from these high-status buildings and other contemporary halls.[32] It became common in the last two decades of the twelfth century and in the early thirteenth century, particularly in high-status halls, to construct service rooms at the low end of the hall and locate the main chamber above these. There were, of course, exceptions. The chamber at Farnham Castle, probably built during the episcopate of Henry Blois (1129–71), seems to have been situated well away from the kitchen

---

[31] P. A. Rahtz, *The Saxon and medieval palaces at Cheddar*, British Archaeological Reports, British Series vol. 65 (Oxford,1979), pp. 170–87. For revised dating, see Mark Gardiner, 'Timber buildings without earth-fast footings in Viking-Age Britain', in J. Hines, A. Lane and M. Redknap (eds.), *Land, sea, and home: proceedings of a conference on Viking Age settlement in the British Isles* (London: Society for Medieval Archaeology, 2004), p. 356, and John Blair, 'Palaces or minsters? Northampton and Cheddar reconsidered', *Anglo-Saxon England* 25 (1997), 116.

[32] For example, the hall at Bishops Auckland, County Durham, for which see J. Cunningham, 'Auckland Castle: some recent discoveries', in E. Fernie and P. Crossley (eds.), *Medieval architecture and its intellectual context: studies in honour of Peter Kidson* (London: Hambledon, 1990), pp. 81–90.

and services, and was placed at the opposite end of the hall.[33] Nevertheless, in many buildings the main chamber was situated at the low end of the hall. This is a surprising and unexpected observation, because the chamber in contemporary timber buildings of lesser status appears to have been situated beyond the high end of the hall, a position which became common in all buildings by the end of the thirteenth century.[34] However, the position of the chamber in late twelfth- and early thirteenth-century stone buildings may hold the key to understanding the development of the services.

John Blair has argued in a highly influential paper that the plan of the late medieval house developed by bringing together the hall and the free-standing chamber block. The detached chamber block is now acknowledged as a distinctive form of building and examples have been identified both in England and on the Continent.[35] A number of features are common to chamber blocks. Typically, they had living accommodation at first-floor level above an undercroft. The upper room was generally divided into two unequal parts, of which the larger was nearer the entrance and was sometimes provided with a fireplace, and the smaller one had access to a garderobe, if one was provided. There was an external entrance to the first floor and, less commonly, an internal vice (stair). The larger room on the first floor seems to have served as a withdrawing room, while the smaller was a bedroom. The floor of the undercroft was generally below the level of the exterior ground surface and it was sometimes divided into two parts, reflecting the division of the chamber above. If it was so divided, there were sometimes separate entrances to the two rooms, as at Boothby Pagnell (Lincolnshire).[36]

There is an obvious similarity of arrangement between these detached chamber blocks and the attached service rooms with chamber above in the late twelfth- and early thirteenth-century stone halls which have already been discussed. It is as if builders had simply brought together the two adjoining buildings – hall and chamber block – and placed the latter at the low end of the hall.[37] This is particularly clear in some buildings where the arrangement of services and chamber above still closely resembled the organisation of the chamber block. For example, the early-thirteenth-century building at Warnford (Hampshire), now ruined, comprised a three-bay aisled hall with services at the low end.

---

[33] H. E. Malden (ed.), *The Victoria history of the county of Surrey*, vol. 2 (London: Archibald Constable, 1905), pp. 599–603.

[34] Gardiner, 'Vernacular buildings and the later medieval domestic plan', 170–3.

[35] J. Blair, 'Hall and chamber', p. 1–21; Impey and Harris, 'Boothby Pagnell revisited', pp. 245–69.

[36] Cf. ibid., p. 251.

[37] Impey and Harris (ibid.) come to a similar conclusion about the incorporation of the chamber block into the hall.

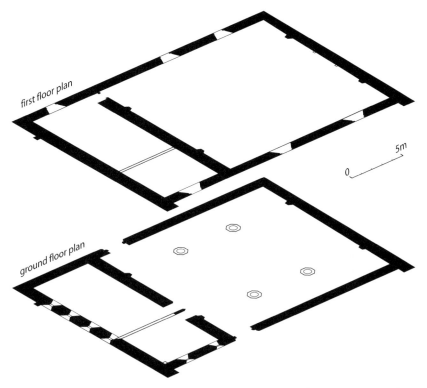

Figure 3.6 Axonometric projection of the plan of the hall at Warnford (Hampshire) as constructed.

The entrances to the services were, unusually, not set symmetrically along the axis of the hall, but to one side (Figure 3.6). The reason for this is only apparent from a close examination of the structure. The wall between the service rooms was dictated by the position of the wall within the chamber on the first floor. The floor was supported on timber joists, and therefore any first-floor stone wall had to be supported by a wall beneath, on the ground floor. Although neither wall survives, the position at first-floor level is apparent from the quoins which have been hacked back, and a wall is shown in that position at ground-floor level in a late eighteenth-century plan.[38] Thus the first-floor chamber had the

---

[38] H. P. Wyndham, 'Observations on an ancient building at Warnford, in the county of Southampton', *Archaeologia* 5 (1779), 357–66. See also Margaret Wood, *Thirteenth-century domestic architecture in England* (supplement to *Archaeological Journal* 105, 1950, London: Royal Archaeological Institute), pp. 27–9.

same plan found in chamber blocks, with one large room near the entrance and a smaller one beyond. There is one further point of similarity. The floor of at least one of the service rooms at Warnford, and possibly the other, was set down beneath the exterior ground level to create an undercroft or cellar.

The arrangement of the chamber end at Warnford helps to explain the arrangement at the Bishop's Palace at Hereford, where the services no longer survive. The hall itself has been dated by dendrochronology to 1179. The chamber and services were set in the now-demolished cross-wing at the end of the aisled hall. Our knowledge of the wing is dependent upon the interpretation of a plan of *c.* 1840. Two adjoining doorways led into two rooms, which were presumably the buttery and pantry. These were not set centrally on the axis of the hall, but rather awkwardly to one side of the nave of the hall, in much the same way as at Warnford.[39] The explanation there also seems to be that their position was dictated by the arrangements of rooms at first-floor level.

We have begun to see the way the late-medieval domestic plan crystallised around the turn of the thirteenth century and to discern the origins of the two service rooms. The services in stone buildings seem to have developed out of the rooms in the undercroft of detached chamber blocks. There is, however, one problem before we can accept this idea entirely. Few undercrofts within detached chamber blocks had two equal entrances, which is what we might have expected if they gave access to a pair of service rooms. However, we can be certain that the undercrofts were used for storage. The rooms were inadequately lit, generally by small windows, and they were set partially below ground, making them damp and quite unsuitable for accommodation. The one-room undercrofts could have served either as a buttery or a pantry, with a second service room in a separate building. In fact, it is more likely that the undercroft would have acted as the buttery, because barrels are best stored in damper conditions, while the items associated with the pantry were better kept in the dry. There is one further clue to the items stored in a chamber-block undercroft. A number of chamber blocks have an internal vice which provided access to the undercroft from the upper chamber. Examples include

[39] For the date, see D. Haddon-Reece, D. H. Miles and J. T. Munby, 'Tree-ring dates from the Ancient Monuments Laboratory, Historic Buildings and Monuments Commission for England', *Vernacular Architecture* 20 (1989), 46; John Blair, 'The 12th-century Bishop's Palace at Hereford', *Medieval Archaeology* 31 (1987), 59–72.

Christchurch Castle and Burton Agnes.[40] These internal stairs were not the main entrance to the upper floor, which was approached by an external flight of steps. An internal staircase is also likely in the undercroft at St Martin-at-Palace Plain, Norwich, discovered in archaeological excavation. The doorways to these undercrofts were shut and barred from the inside, suggesting that the only way out was by means of a ladder or stairs to the upper room and then down by the external stairs.[41] The occupant of the chamber therefore controlled access to the undercroft, and items stored in the undercroft needed to be accessible from the chamber above. The most likely conclusion is the one which has already been suggested using a different line of argument. The undercrofts of detached chamber blocks served for the storage of wine or ale. This was consumed privately in the chamber by the occupant after he or she withdrew from the hall.

It is useful at this point to summarise the argument so far. The literary and historical evidence has shown that from at least 1100 there were two separate rooms for the buttery and pantry, but the architectural evidence suggests that the formal pairing of buttery and pantry as two equal components within a single building did not occur before the late twelfth century. Before that time there may have been separate rooms in other buildings which served the same function. It is unclear whether these pantry and buttery buildings or rooms were treated as two equal, but separate, parts of a pair, though it seems unlikely. In some of the earliest stone houses with services, such as Oakham, the two offices were treated in architectural terms as equal. Conversely, at Hereford the two rooms were of different sizes, suggesting that in the late twelfth century it had not yet been accepted everywhere that the buttery and pantry were equal parts of a pair.

Transformations in ideas of domestic space

Houses are simultaneously metaphors for domesticity, the family and the proper order of society, and also physical structures in which people have their being and have to carry out daily tasks. In all houses there is a tension and an interplay between the ideal and imagined on the one hand, and the practical and experienced on the other. None of these elements stayed

---

[40] Margaret Wood, *Norman domestic architecture* (London: Royal Archaeological Institute, 1974), pp. 32–34, 54–56. Impey and Harris, 'Boothby Pagnell revisited', fig. 17, no. 8 suggest that the building at Eynsford is a chamber block; this does not seem likely. It is more probable that the large room at raised ground level was the hall.

[41] Brian Ayers, *Excavations at St. Martin-at-Palace Plain, Norwich, 1981*, East Anglian Archaeology vol. 37 (Dereham: Norwich Archaeological Unit, 1987), p. 157. The same pattern is found at Christchurch Castle.

fixed. The idealisation of space can change with new thoughts about domesticity, and this may in turn trigger the adaption of buildings to reflect novel concepts of the 'proper' design of a house.

One of the most obvious signs of the way in which domestic space was re-imagined is the change in the name of one of the service rooms. The terms used by Neckam were *disspensa* (spence) for the pantry and *promptuarium* or *celarium* (for the buttery). Boldon Book, written for the bishop of Durham at about the same time, refers to what seem to have been separate buildings, the *dispensa* and the *butilleria* (buttery).[42] Similarly, in 1234 timber was allowed by Henry III for the building of a *dispensa* and a *butilleria* at Winchester, and in 1252 the king sent instructions that the two services, similarly named, in his palace at Guildford should be roofed.[43] The word *panetaria*, 'pantry', is rarely used before the late thirteenth century to describe the room, although the post of pantler is mentioned. In the early-twelfth-century *Constitutio Domus Regis*, the office holder is called the *dispensator panis*, and he served within the steward's department.[44] However, by the end of the thirteenth and particularly during the course of the fourteenth century, the term *panetaria* replaced *dispensa* in Latin usage to describe one of the service rooms. For example, a lease of the manor of Belchamp St Paul (Essex) which can be attributed to the 1250s or 1260s mentions that beneath the chamber there was a *panetria* and a *botelaria*.[45] The will of Nicholas Longespee, bishop of Salisbury dated 1295 mentions the utensils of his pantry ('de panetrio meo'), and buttery. A century later it was common to refer, as John of Gaunt did *c.* 1383, to the officers of the *panetrye* and *butillerye*.[46] At the same time the word *spence* appears to lose its particular meaning in the vernacular and comes to refer to a room in which either food or drink or both were kept. Chaucer in the 'Summoner's Tale' could write 'al vinolent as botel in the

[42] David Austin (ed.), *Boldon Book* (Phillimore: Chichester, 1982), pp. 36–7. I have preferred *butilleria* (buttery), given in MS. B, to *bucheria* (butchery) in MS. A.

[43] *Calendar of close rolls preserved in the Public Record Office, 1234–37* (London: HMSO, 1909), pp. 36–7; W. W. Shirley (ed.), *Royal and other historical letters illustrative of the reign of Henry III*, 2 vols., Rolls Series no. 27 (London, 1866), vol. II, p. 66.

[44] For a discussion of the role of the pantler, see J. H. Round, *The king's serjeants and officers of state* (London: Nisbet, 1911), pp. 197–221.

[45] Guildhall Library (London), MS. 25,516, fol. 171. I am grateful to John Blair for notes on this document.

[46] A. R. Malden, 'The will of Nicholas Longespee, bishop of Salisbury', *English Historical Review* 15 (1900), 526; S. Armitage-Smith (ed.), *John of Gaunt's register*, Camden Society, 3rd series, vol. 21 (London, 1911), p. 342. For further examples, see F. J. Furnivall (ed.), *The fifty earliest English wills*, EETS OS vol. 78 (Oxford, 1882), p. 18; James Raine (ed.), *Testamenta eboracensia or, wills registered at York*, vol. 2, Surtees Society vol. 30 (Durham, 1855), p. 38; R. E. Latham *et al.* (eds.), *Dictionary of medieval Latin from British sources* (London: British Academy, 1975), *s.v.*

spence', although in earlier times bottles would have been kept in the buttery.[47]

The replacement of the term *spence* by *pantry* seems to reflect a wider shift in the associations of that room. It had earlier served for storing a number of items, of which bread was just one. A yeast box is included in *Gerefa* amongst the contents ascribed to the spence, suggesting an association with bread-making. This connection was certainly clear in the early thirteenth century when Henry III ordered the construction of a *granarium* or bin for grain or flour in the spence of his hall at Oxford.[48] The replacement of the word *spence* by *pantry*, a word derived from the Old French *paneterie*, 'bread store', argues that there was a shift in the perception of the function of this service room. It may have always had a connection with bread, but this was increasingly perceived as its primary function.

The pantry came to be closely connected with the pantler, just as the buttery was under the supervision of the butler. The rise of the pantler can be traced only in the barest outline, but seems to have been connected with the emergence of the formal ceremony of the service of meals. Bishop Robert Grosseteste's advice to the countess of Lincoln, written between 1245 and 1253, describes how the pantler with bread and the butler with cup should walk up in step to the high table before grace. They would have entered the hall, no doubt, from the service rooms and made their way between the expectant diners to the far end.[49] The two service rooms, and particularly their doorways which would have been seen from the hall, provided the setting for the formal ceremony marking the beginning of the meal. Those serving bread and serving wine were deemed equivalent, so that the mid-fifteenth-century *Boke of Curtasye* might refer to the pantler as the butler's fellow.[50] As a consequence, the service rooms took on the names of the officials with whom they were closely associated. The contents of the rooms do not seem to have changed, but greater importance was placed upon bread and its service.

[47] Robinson, *The complete works of Geoffrey Chaucer*, III (D), lines 1931–2. However, Chaucer's usage might also have been dictated by the need to rhyme 'spence' with 'reverence' in the subsequent line.

[48] W. H. Stevenson and C. T. Flower (eds.), *Calendar of the Liberate Rolls preserved in the Public Record Office*, vol. 1, *1226–40* (London: HMSO, 1917), p. 14; *Dictionary of medieval Latin from British sources*, *s.v.*, sense 2.

[49] Dorothea Oschinsky (ed.), *Walter of Henley and other treatises* (Oxford University Press, 1971), pp. 191–6, 402–5, cap. xxiv. On dating, see Louise J. Wilkinson, 'The *Rules* of Robert Grosseteste reconsidered', in Cordelia Beattie, Anna Maslakovic and Sarah Rees Jones (eds.), *The Medieval household in Christian Europe*, c. *850* – c. *1550* (Turnhout: Brepols, 2003), pp. 299–300.

[50] F. J. Furnivall (ed.), 'The Babees Book', in *Early English meals and manners*, EETS OS vol. 32 (Oxford, 1868), p. 312.

The role of architecture in the ceremony of the serving of food was clearly significant. The entrances at the low end of the hall provided the setting for the production of first the bread and drink, and then the food from the kitchen. The elaborate mouldings and columns around the service room doorways in the formal, western hall of the Bishop's Palace in Lincoln were clearly not intended to be hidden by screens, but to be seen as part of the spectacle of the formal ceremony of mealtimes (Figure 3.5). Bishop Grosseteste may have had this ceremony in his hall at Lincoln in mind when writing his *Rules*.

We might also wonder whether the performance of the production of wine and bread at domestic mealtimes may have evoked thoughts of the Eucharist in the bishop's mind, particularly as he had written on the subject of its proper performance.[51] Certainly the parallels between the two ceremonies must have presented themselves to many others, since, as the Fourth Lateran Council of 1215 instructed, all adult parishioners would have partaken of the Eucharist, usually once a year at Easter.[52] Similarities would also have been brought to mind by the organisation of space in the hall, which bore some resemblance to that in the church: both types of buildings had a clear hierarchy of space, with the more select places for the priest and the householder located towards the end most distant from the entrance.[53] The bread and wine in both ceremonies were brought from locked places – the pyx in the case of the church, as the Lateran Council required, and the buttery and pantry in the hall – up to the *mensa* (altar) or high table where the rituals were presided over by senior individuals present.[54] The parallels between the Eucharist, which re-enacted the Last Supper, and the domestic ceremony at the beginning of meals were appreciated sufficiently widely that the fourteenth-century Luttrell Psalter could allude to them. The illustration depicting the Luttrell family at table with two Dominican friars has a close resemblance to another in the same book showing the Last Supper. The association of the Luttrell meal and the Eucharist is made explicit by the depiction of Sir Geoffrey Luttrell, who is shown holding his cup about a plate decorated with the Greek cross.[55]

[51] Robert Grosseteste, *Templum Dei*, ed. J. Goering and F. A. C. Mantello, Toronto Medieval Latin Texts vol. 14 (Toronto: Pontifical Institute of Mediaeval Studies, 1984).

[52] Fourth Lateran Council, Canon 21.

[53] Kate Giles, *An archaeology of social identity: guildhalls in York, c. 1350–1630*, British Archaeological Reports, British Series vol. 315 (Oxford: Archaeopress, 2000), pp. 62–3.

[54] Fourth Lateran Council, Canon 20; Miri Rubin, *Corpus Christi: the Eucharist in late medieval culture* (Cambridge University Press, 1991), p. 45.

[55] R. K. Emmerson and P. J. P. Goldberg, '"The Lord Geoffrey had me made": lordship and labour in the Luttrell Psalter', in James Bothwell, P. J. P. Goldberg and W. M. Ormrod (eds.), *The problem of labour in fourteenth-century England* (York Medieval Press, 2000),

The increasing emphasis given to the Eucharist in the early thirteenth century drew attention to the particular ritual significance of wine and bread.[56] These began to be regarded as natural counterparts, and this was, no doubt, aided by the growing availability of wine. The volume imported from France increased considerably after 1199 when King John attempted, though not entirely successfully, to regulate its price. However, one consequence of his measures, according to Roger of Hoveden, was a great rise in wine consumption.[57] It was in this context that the spence was gradually replaced in name by the pantry.

There was no sense that the domestic ceremony of the production of wine and bread was mocking religious practice; rather the daily act of dining borrowed from church services some of the solemnity of ritual. The growing number of courtesy books which appeared in the late twelfth and early thirteenth century suggest that the rituals surrounding eating and the behaviour required from those at dinner were becoming more formal.[58] Mealtimes tend to be one of the most rule-bound and difficult of social situations, and naturally enough courtesy books devoted considerable space to the subject of behaviour at table. The importance of the meal can be gauged from the longest of the courtesy books of this period, *Urbanus Magnus* by Daniel of Beccles, written in the late twelfth century. More than a tenth of the text is devoted to the subject of table manners. The question of table service and foods to be eaten are no less important in this work and form a similar proportion.[59] Running through courtesy books of this period is an expectation that diners ought to behave in a respectable manner, as well as respectfully to their host.

The growing interest in formal behaviour and the developing ritual of domestic dining in the late twelfth and thirteenth century are likely to have had a broader impact in the architectural plan. The emergence of the late medieval domestic plan is likely to be connected with a stricter code of behaviour and developing domestic ceremony. The plan formalised the organisation of space in exactly the same way as the courtesy books formalised acceptable behaviour. It was only possible to partake of strict ceremony in an unfamiliar building if it was structured in a recognisable

---

pp. 52–3. For further comments on this scene and the parallels with the illustrations of the Last Supper, see Michael Camille, *Mirror in parchment: the Luttrell Psalter and the making of medieval England* (London: Reaktion Books, 1998), pp. 84–90.

[56] Rubin, *Corpus Christi*, pp. 54–62.

[57] W. Stubbs (ed.), *Chronica Rogeri de Houedene*, 4 vols., Rolls Series no. 51 (London, 1868–71), vol. 4, pp. 99–100.

[58] The dating, manuscripts and editions of courtesy books of this period are discussed in J. Nicholls, *The matter of courtesy: medieval courtesy books and the Gawain-Poet* (Woodbridge: Brewer, 1985), pp. 145–52, 179–85.

[59] J. G. Smyly (ed.), *Urbanus Magnus Danielis Becclesiensis* (Dublin: Hodges, Figgis, 1939).

manner. The late-medieval plan established rules about the arrangement of space which made any building readily comprehensible, even to a stranger. The plan also allowed diners to be placed within the hall according to their status, the most important sitting at the high end and the least closest to the door at the low end. Early courtesy books are also much concerned with the proper display of social hierarchy. The position of the service rooms was no less important. Food was stored there, and bread and wine were brought forth from beneath the householder's chamber. The food which was served was thus both symbolically and physically under his or her control. The production of food was demonstrably an expression of the householder's hospitality and generosity, and an action which reflected upon his or her honour.[60]

The late twelfth century has emerged as a significant moment in the development of the two-service arrangement, but, as has already been shown, the idea of the separation of the buttery and spence (later the pantry) dates back to before the beginning of the twelfth century. It is the nature of the distinction between these two which must now be considered. The obvious contrast between the items stored in the buttery and those in the spence was between those which were wet and those which were dry. The buttery was self-evidently the place in which wet materials – drink of various sorts – and items for serving liquids were stored. Conversely, the pantry was linked with dry items. The order of items in *Gerefa* suggests that those utensils connected with the building which served as the spence included candlesticks, a salt-cellar and a yeast box. The first of these has clear associations with fire, the obvious opposite of water, and the last two require dry conditions for storage. Napery – cloths and towels – was stored in the pantry, as Neckam says, and presumably also bread. Again, towels have obvious connections with drying, while bread is preferably stored in such conditions to prevent it becoming mouldy.

The division between wet and dry items might suggest a connection with the classical theory of the four humours. Humoral theory is widely associated with the writings of Galen, but he lent his authority to ideas already established in Greek medical practice. Galen suggested that good health resulted from a proper balance of hot and cold, moist and dry, components in the body. A balance might be maintained by eating appropriate foods to ensure none of the four humours was in excess. Knowledge of the humours persisted into the early medieval period, and the importance of a balance of appropriate foods is mentioned in Bald's *Læceboc*, composed in the

[60] Julie Kerr, 'The open door: hospitality and honour in twelfth/early thirteenth-century England', *History* 87 (2002), 322–35.

early tenth century. Byrhtferth's *Enchiridion*, written *c.* 1011, makes an association between the four humours, the elements, the seasons and the ages of man. Yet in spite of these references, the literary and linguistic evidence suggests that humoral theory was not common knowledge in pre-Conquest England and played little part in medical practice.[61]

Wider dissemination of the concept of the four humours had to await the translation from Arabic into Latin of a number of texts in the middle of the twelfth century, including *Kitāb sirr al-asrār*, translated first by John Hispaniensis and later by Phillip Triplitanus in the first half of the thirteenth as the *Secretum secretorum*.[62] Chaucer makes a number of references to the relationship between food and the balance of humours in the *Canterbury Tales*, beginning with his description of the Doctor of Physic in the General Prologue. He 'knew the cause of everick maladye, were it of hoot, or coold, or moyste, or drye'.[63] The Franklin's character is carefully sketched by Chaucer to reflect the humoral character of the foods he is described as eating.[64] Late-medieval recipes carefully describe the procedures for 'tempering' food so that the humoral balance of any dish tended towards the warm and moist, which was the natural condition of the average healthy person. To achieve this, it was necessary to offset any imbalance in the dish resulting from the humours of the constituents. Liquids were self-evidently moist, but while water was cool, wine was warm, with red more so than white. Bread as a dry food might be used to temper or counteract the moist, warm qualities of wine or ale.[65]

The timing of the spread of humoral theory suggests that it does not provide an explanation for the origin of the buttery and pantry or spence. The theory was not widely known until the middle of the twelfth century at the earliest, when the separation of items associated with the spence and buttery was long established. It seems probable that, as the idea of the humoral qualities of food became more widely disseminated, it was associated with the existing dry/moist division between items in the two rooms.

---

[61] M. L. Cameron, 'Bald's Leechbook and cultural interactions in Anglo-Saxon England', *Anglo-Saxon England* 19 (1990), 11–12; P. S. Baker and Michael Lapidge (eds.), *Byrhtferth's Enchiridion*, EETS SS vol. 15 (Oxford, 1995), pp. 10–15; L. Ayoub, 'OE *wæta* and the medical theory of the humours', *Journal of English and Germanic Philology* 94 (1995), 332–46.
[62] M. A. Manzalaoui (ed.), *Secretum secretorum: nine English versions*, vol. 1, EETS OS vol. 276 (Oxford, 1977), pp. xiv–xv.
[63] Robinson, *Complete works of Geoffrey Chaucer*, I (A), 419–20.
[64] J. A. Bryant, 'The diet of Chaucer's Franklin', *Modern Language Notes* 63 (1948), 318–25.
[65] Terence Scully, 'Tempering medieval food', in M. W. Adamson (ed.), *Food in the Middle Ages: a book of essays* (New York: Garland, 1995), pp. 3–23.

Conclusion

The buttery and pantry, like many enduring symbols, were endowed with new meanings and significance as ideas about the house evolved during the course of the twelfth and early thirteenth centuries. This appears to have been a particularly important period in the development of the domestic plan as ideas of social order and appropriate behaviour were established. It was a period of change and experimentation in concepts of domestic space. Once the domestic plan was established, it remained almost exactly the same until the sixteenth century. Similarly, courtesy texts written during the later twelfth and early thirteenth century continued to appear in books of the fourteenth and fifteenth centuries, suggesting that once the rules of behaviour had been established, they too persisted, little altered, throughout the later Middle Ages.[66] Social behaviour and architecture therefore marched together: both saw a period of change followed by centuries when ideas remained largely the same.

It has been suggested that there were separate rooms or buildings for the storage of table items, and for drink and the vessels for serving drink, before the late twelfth century. The services were accommodated in buildings separate not only from the hall, but possibly from each other. That seems to be the implication of the entry in *Boldon Book*. In the largest households there was an official who had responsibility for the supply and the service of food and another for drink. During the twelfth century these elements were configured in a new and more systematic manner. The services appeared below the chamber at the end of the halls of the nobility. This was achieved by integrating the once separate chamber block and hall.

The pattern of two equal service rooms appeared in the second half of the twelfth century, although it was not immediately and universally accepted. It was perfectly possible to construct an asymmetrical arrangement at the Bishop's Palace, Hereford and later at Warnford. However, the growing importance of the Eucharist helped to establish as a common the duality of bread and wine, not only in a sacred context, but also in a secular one. This, translated into architecture, took the form of the symmetry of the two doorways to the service rooms, sometimes flanking a central door to the kitchen. The internal symmetry of the hall along its long axis is a principle of the late-medieval plan. The typical large hall had tables set parallel to the long walls and a single high table on the dais at the high end set at right angles. Consequently, the only individual who sat on

---

[66] See the lists of manuscripts of, for example, *Stans puer ad mensam* and *Facetus: 'cum nihil utilius'* in Nicholls, *The matter of courtesy*, pp. 181, 184 and more generally, pp. 161–71.

the line of symmetry when dining was the head of the house. His or her axial position emphasised the centrality of his or her role in the household. The ordered domestic world described in courtesy books was reflected in the architecture of the house. The service rooms acquired new associations: the spence became the pantry to reflect its connection with bread. Under the new domestic order officials – the butler and pantler – were placed in charge of their offices and answerable for the food and drink which passed through their services. The architecture was not only an expression of the status of the householder, but a statement of the good order which prevailed within the household.

The task of tracing the development of the buttery and pantry is not a simple one. There was no straight line of development of either concept or architecture which by the middle of the thirteenth century had led to the widely accepted plan with two service rooms located beyond the low end of the hall. Instead, builders and the owners of houses grappled with developing ideas about the organisation of domestic space which seem to have been particularly fluid in the century between 1150 to 1250. Running alongside the questions of architectural organisation was the changing conceptualisation of what houses meant. Late-medieval houses were very carefully structured spaces with public and private areas, high and low ends for those with power and those without. The opposition of wet and dry, which is a recurrent feature of the contents of the two service rooms, was a not insignificant aspect of the division of the space, but one of the many ideas about objects, food, society and space which came together in the physical organisation of the medieval house.

Acknowledgements

I am indebted to the British Academy for a travel grant to visit the standing buildings discussed here, to Christopher Whittick who accompanied me on a number of occasions and discussed the structures, to Libby Mulqueeny who prepared the line drawings and to the editors who suggested various lines of argument. The photographs of Oakham Castle hall are reproduced with permission of Rutland County Council.

4   Building domesticity in the city: English urban housing before the Black Death

Sarah Rees Jones

The urban housing of later medieval England, particularly in the two centuries after the Black Death, is the subject of a growing literature by scholars working in a variety of disciplines. The rich evidence of both surviving and excavated buildings is steadily being recorded and published, and scholars are moving far beyond description to consider the cultural and social values attributed to domestic spaces.[1] Their considerations include the extent to which domestic spaces reflected or aided in the construction of social hierarchies of gender and labour, and how they were used in the negotiation of domestic roles and relationships such as courtship, marriage and working life.[2] Questions about the nature and use of urban domestic space have thus been integrated into studies focusing on the emergence and development of bourgeois family values in the generations traumatised and transformed by the impact of the Black Death and its aftermath. Our knowledge and understanding of urban domestic building between the Norman Conquest and the Black Death, however, is much slighter. Yet this was the very period in which urban houses were transformed through the introduction of new building materials and technologies, including greater use of stone and the development of timber framing, and in which the hall houses and cottages that are the imagined sites of later-medieval bourgeois domesticity first emerged.

---

[1] Schofield, *Medieval London houses*; Grenville, *Medieval housing*; Anthony Quiney, *Town houses of medieval Britain* (New Haven: Yale University Press, 2003).

[2] P. J. P. Goldberg, 'The public and the private: women in the pre-plague economy,' *Thirteenth-century England* vol. III, pp. 75–89; Barbara Hanawalt, 'At the margins of women's space in medieval Europe', in Barbara Hanawalt, *'Of good and ill repute'. Gender and social control in medieval England* (Oxford University Press, 1998), pp. 70–87; Jane Grenville, 'Houses and households in late medieval England: an archaeological perspective', in Jocelyn Wogan-Browne *et al.* (eds.), *Medieval women: texts and contexts in late medieval Britain. Essays for Felicity Riddy* (Turnhout: Brepols, 2000), pp. 309–28; Peter Arnade and Martha C. Howell, 'Fertile spaces: the productivity of urban space in northern Europe', *Journal of Interdisciplinary History* 32 (2002), 515–48; Felicity Riddy, '"Burgeis" domesticity in late medieval England', this volume; Rees Jones, 'Women's influence on the design of the urban home'; Shannon McSheffrey, 'Place, space, and situation: public and private in the making of marriage in late medieval London', *Speculum* 79 (2004), 960–90.

If we are to understand more fully the better-recorded domestic cultures of the later Middle Ages we must seek some understanding of the pre-plague contexts out of which they developed.

The great transformation of urban building, 1100–1300

Domestic architecture in England was revolutionised between 1100 and 1300 as a distinctively urban style of housing emerged.[3] The revolution can be traced both in the technology of building construction and in the form of the urban house. In the eleventh century most houses built out of timber were comparatively small and insubstantial and were of single storey construction, although some contained raised floors over sunken storage areas.[4] The stability of these buildings was provided by posts sunk into the earth, or slotted into wooden sill beams resting directly on the ground, and their roofs were usually thatched. As a consequence they were prone to rot and fire and needed rebuilding relatively frequently.[5] The assumption that houses would be regularly consumed by fire is indicated in an agreement of 1212–25 between two neighbours in York who agreed to maintain the fence and gutter between their two properties until the first fire ('ad primam combustionem'), after which the boundary would be adjusted.[6] By 1200 the threat from fire was central to the creation of London's by-laws regulating domestic building, and indeed the construction of whole houses in stone was in part a response to the problem of fire in the twelfth and thirteenth centuries before timber-framing techniques had reached maturity.[7]

In timber buildings the threat from fire was also gradually countered by the use of more fire-resistant materials, especially tile, in the floors,

---

[3] David M. Palliser, T. R. Slater and Elizabeth P. Dennison, 'The topography of towns 600–1300', in David M. Palliser (ed.), *The Cambridge urban history of Britain*, vol. 1, *600–1540* (Cambridge University Press, 2000), pp. 181–5; Quiney, *Town houses of medieval Britain*, pp. 133–42, 173–186, 235–268; Pearson, 'Rural and urban houses 1100–1500', pp. 43–63.

[4] Valerie Horsman, Christine Milne and Gustav Milne, *Building and street development near Billingsgate and Cheapside: aspects of Saxo-Norman London I*, London and Middlesex Archaeological Society Special Paper no. 11 (London: London and Middlesex Archaeological Society, 1988), p. 108; R. A. Hall and K. Hunter-Mann, *Medieval urbanism in Coppergate: refining a townscape. The archaeology of York* 10/6 (London: Council for British Archaeology, 2002), p. 818.

[5] Horsman *et al.*, *Aspects of Saxo-Norman London*, p. 109; Grenville, *Medieval housing*, pp. 30–4.

[6] William Farrer and C. T. Clay (eds.), *Early Yorkshire charters*, vol. 1 (Edinburgh: Ballantyne, Hanson and Co., 1914), p. 178, no. 213.

[7] H. T. Riley (ed.), *Liber Albus: the white book of the city of London, compiled A.D. 1419 by John Carpenter, common clerk. Richard Whittington, mayor* (London: R. Griffin, 1961), pp. 284–5.

roofs and walls. The threat from rot was much reduced by devising ways of raising the timber parts of the structure off the ground, until eventually they were placed on foundation walls of stone. Such buildings lacked the lateral stability that had previously been achieved by sinking the upright structural posts into pits in the ground. Instead carpenters developed systems of joints and trusses in order to stabilise their structures, and by the fourteenth and fifteenth centuries builders were constructing fully timber-framed houses that were capable of surviving hundreds of years.[8] There are thousands of surviving examples in English towns, where their elaborate and sometimes decorative timber frames became a characteristic feature of later medieval and early modern domestic architecture, outnumbering and sometimes even replacing stone houses.

The new building technologies of timber framing emerged in London between 1180 and 1220 and developed slowly throughout the country over the course of the thirteenth century.[9] Timber framing permitted the construction not just of more durable homes, but also of larger buildings. In Coppergate, York, the first properly timber-framed buildings dated from the mid to late thirteenth century and were considerably larger than their predecessors. On one plot an eleventh-century building which occupied a footprint of 3 m by 10.2 m was eventually replaced in *c.* 1280 by a timber-framed building of 4 m by 26 m.[10] Timber framing also allowed builders to construct taller houses incorporating two or more storeys.[11]

Hall houses and small houses

The larger timber-framed houses of the fourteenth and fifteenth centuries were more complex in design than earlier timbered structures and usually filled the building plot on which they were constructed. Although many occupied narrow plots that were no more than twenty feet wide facing the street, their accommodation extended both upwards over upper stories and backwards around yards and even gardens set well back from the street frontage. They typically contained a hall with several smaller rooms such as parlours, chambers and shops within a single structure, plus a

---

[8] Grenville, *Medieval housing*, pp. 34–52; Richard Harris, *Discovering timber-framed buildings* (Haverfordwest, Pembrokeshire: Shire Publications, 1993).
[9] Gustav Milne, *Timber building techniques in London c. 900–1400*, London and Middlesex Archaeological Society Special Paper no. 15 (London, 1992).
[10] Hall and Hunter-Mann, *Medieval urbanism in Coppergate*, Buildings c6b and c6f, pp. 795–9, 818–22.
[11] Pearson, 'Rural and urban houses', pp. 47–50.

kitchen or other outbuilding and a garden or yard.[12] Since most work was done in workshops within households, their design therefore provided both working spaces and living spaces, productive spaces and ceremonial spaces, spaces which could be either intimate or very public, depending on the ways in which access was controlled, the ways in which they were furnished or simply the ways in which they were used.

The inclusion of open halls in these urban domestic buildings has been a particular subject of debate because of what it might reveal about social hierarchies in towns and about the evolutionary relationship between rural and urban forms of house and household.[13] Halls were constructed both parallel to the street and at right angles to it, but were nearly always located away from the street frontage either on the ground floor accessed by a narrow lane off the street, or on the first floor of a house above storage and retail spaces. They were large rooms, usually open to the rafters, often of two stories in height, and most were heated by an open hearth at the centre. By the fourteenth and fifteenth centuries the inclusion of an open hall with an open hearth was an 'ubiquitous' and distinctive feature of middling and larger town houses in England and Wales, but was not found in houses of equivalent status on the continent.[14] Why was the inclusion of a hall so desirable in an English urban context? William Pantin argued that the prevalence of the open hall in English town houses was a result of 'urban adaptation' as townspeople emulated the architectural features of the rural houses of the nobility and gentry, but this has been refuted in more recent literature.[15] Although Mark Gardiner agrees that the basic elements of the tripartite plan of domestic architecture, including a large open hall-like space with service rooms at one end and smaller living spaces at the other, originated in the countryside, he places

[12] Keene, *Survey of medieval Winchester*, vol. 1, pp. 156–9; Schofield, *Medieval London houses*, pp. 61–93; Schofield, 'Urban housing in England, 1400–1600', in David Gaimster and Paul Stamper (eds.), *The age of transition. The archaeology of English culture 1400–1600* (Oxford: Oxford University Press, 1997), pp. 127–44; Schofield and Vince, *Medieval towns*, pp. 63–98; Grenville, *Medieval housing*, pp. 157–93.

[13] Pantin, 'Medieval English town-house plans'; Pantin 'Chantry priests' houses and other medieval lodgings', *Medieval Archaeology* 3 (1959), 216–58; Pantin, 'The merchants' houses and warehouses of King's Lynn', *Medieval Archaeology* 6–7 (1964 for 1962–3), 173–81; Faulkner, 'Domestic planning from the twelfth to the fourteenth centuries'; Faulkner, 'Medieval undercrofts and town houses', *Archaeological Journal* 123 (1966), 120–35; Schofield, *Medieval London houses*, pp. 61–93; Pearson, 'Rural and urban houses', pp. 43–63; Jane Grenville, 'Urban and rural houses and households in the late Middle Ages: a case study from Yorkshire', this volume.

[14] Pearson, 'Rural and urban houses', pp. 50–52.

[15] William A. Pantin, 'Some medieval townhouses: a study in adaptation', in I. Ll. Foster and L. Alcock (eds.), *Culture and environment. Essays in honour of Cyril Fox* (London: Routledge and Kegan Paul, 1963), pp. 445–78.

their origin much earlier, in the tenth to twelfth centuries, demonstrating that the essential tripartite form developed independently of the new building technologies of either stone-built housing or timber framing.[16] He also refutes Pantin's theory of social emulation, arguing that the essential principles of the tripartite plan could be found in peasant timber structures, such as the longhouse, as well as in gentry housing, while Sarah Pearson has reversed Pantin's argument altogether, suggesting that the commonest version of the urban tripartite hall, with two-storied solar and service blocks at either end of the central hall, originated in towns and only later moved from the town to the country.[17]

Simpler urban homes, with just one or two rooms and without halls and kitchens, have received less attention in the literature.[18] Fewer examples survive, and they are less prominent in the narratives found in both court records and fictional works of the period. Nevertheless, they were an important part of the domestic landscape of towns. Cottages and even smaller accommodations probably outnumbered the larger hall houses in towns. Even in a middling-sized town such as Winchester, by 1417 cottages and shops accounted for a third of all residences in the city, with an unknown number of other households living in sublet rooms or as vagrants, while Rutledge has estimated that as much as 75 per cent of the population of one central ward in Norwich in the early fourteenth century lived in rented accommodation including smaller houses.[19]

Smaller houses in later medieval towns took a variety of forms. The 'tripartite' design of many urban hall houses, including private rooms in a solar block of two or more storeys, and service rooms in a second two-storey block, at opposite ends of an open central hall might be adapted to a number of different uses. A common adaptation in towns was the construction along the street frontage of additional two-storied single-bay blocks.[20] These smaller units attached to larger houses might be let as one-up, one-down cottages, or the groundfloor shops and upper rooms might be sublet independently. Other small houses were constructed either as stand-alone structures or in freestanding rows of

---

[16] Gardiner, 'Vernacular buildings and the development of the later medieval domestic plan in England'; Gardiner, 'Buttery and pantry and their antecedents: idea and architecture in the English medieval house', this volume.

[17] Pearson, 'Rural and urban houses', pp. 50–2.

[18] Keene, *Survey of medieval Winchester*, vol. 1, pp. 162–5.

[19] Ibid., pp. 235–6; Elizabeth Rutledge, 'Landlords and tenants: housing and the rented property market in early fourteenth century Norwich', *Urban History* 22 (1995), 10.

[20] Pantin, 'Some medieval townhouses', pp. 445–78; Pantin, 'The halls and schools of medieval Oxford: an attempt at reconstruction', in *Oxford studies presented to Daniel Callus*, Oxford Historical Society n.s. vol. 16 (Oxford, 1964), pp. 31–100; Keene, *Survey of medieval Winchester*, vol. 1, pp. 162–5.

cottages.[21] Most surviving examples of such smaller houses occupy street frontage sites.[22] This pattern of survival obscures the wider variety of contexts in which such houses were erected.[23] Whole house plots might be developed with rows or courtyards of small single-bay houses of either one or two stories, constructed as timber-framed terraces. Similar rows of small houses might also be built on other sites, such as in the cemeteries of churches, around the perimeter of the precincts of religious houses, or on sites encroaching on market places or city defences.[24] There has been little discussion of these smaller homes beyond the observation that such rows were often constructed by landlords in order to raise an income from rents (indeed such small houses were often called 'rents').[25]

This binary of hall and small houses may oversimplify the range of later medieval housing, but by the fifteenth century the implied social hierarchy of these two styles of house was explicit in civic discourse. In Coventry and Bristol the terminology of 'hallholder' and 'cottager' was used in civic records to distinguish different classes of urban resident, while elsewhere a similar distinction between tenement and cottage was used.[26] This use of the language of housing in civic discourse reflected a social hierarchy related to the organisation of work in towns, and

[21] Quiney, *Town houses*, pp. 255–68.

[22] In York many smaller houses in courtyards behind streets were cleared away in the nineteenth century: York City Archives, York Board of Health.

[23] Because so many surviving examples of rows of small houses occupy positions on street frontages other examples have been overlooked.Two cases in York illustrate this point. The first is a surviving range at 87 Low Petergate which has been misinterpreted as a single building of five equal bays, but which documentary evidence confirms was originally a row of houses fronting on a lost side lane (Royal Commission of Historical Monuments of England, *An inventory of the historical monuments of the city of York*, volume v, *The central area*, London: HMSO, 1981, p. 196 no. 367; York Minster Library vc 6/2/44 [1409] *et seq.*, Rents of St Edward's Chantry in Petergate). The second is an excavated building of *c.* 1280 in Coppergate which has been interpreted as a long tripartite timber-framed hall house set behind buildings on the street frontage. The supposed 'hall' here is identified as a single bay of less than 8′ flanked by supposed solar and service blocks of two bays each with an access path running the full length of the building (Hall and Hunter-Mann, *Medieval urbanism in Coppergate*, pp. 724, 820). An alternative interpretation of this structure as a row of small houses built along the length of the plot seems plausible.

[24] P. Short, 'The fourteenth century rows of York', *Archaeological Journal* 137 (1980), 86–136; S. Rees Jones, 'Historical background', in R. A. Hall *et al.*, *Medieval Tenements in Aldwark*, The Archaeology of York 10/2 (London: Council for British Archaeology, 1988), pp. 1–8.

[25] Derek Keene, 'Landlords, the property market and urban development in medieval England', in F. Eliassen and G. A. Ersland (eds.), *Power, profit and urban land: landownership in medieval and early modern European towns* (Aldershot: Scolar Press, 1996), pp. 108–9.

[26] M. D. Harris (ed.), *The Coventry Leet book, or mayor's register, containing the records of the city court leet or view of frankpledge, A.D. 1420–1555, with divers other matters*, vol. 1, EETS OS vol. 134 (London, 1907), pp. 59, 234; Keene, *Survey of medieval Winchester*, vol. 1, p. 138.

emerging ideas of citizenship in which master craftsmen were privileged over waged labourers.[27] In London, for example, journeymen and other hired labourers were discouraged from setting up large households which might lead them into competition with their employers, and the marriages of servants were closely regulated by masters for similar reasons. Social hierarchies constructed in the households and workshops of master crafts-men influenced both the language and the concrete form of domestic housing, in which non-masters were relegated to subtenancies in tiny properties which restricted their opportunities for social advancement through either work or marriage.[28] In both rhetoric and practice the command of a substantial household was regarded as necessary for suc-cess as a master within post-plague civic society.

It is now time to extend our understanding of the social context within which housing developed in English towns back into the three centuries preceding the Black Death. While much interpretative work has focused on the better surviving structures and records of the later Middle Ages, little work has addressed the issue of how and why this architectural binary of hall houses and small houses developed in towns during the pre-plague centuries. The new technology of timber framing permitted the construction of larger timber houses, but why did they take on the part-icular forms that they did? How distinctive were urban and rural forms of property and what were the social and cultural contexts in which different kinds of town house were constructed?

The place of property in the town plan

How were domestic buildings located in the town plan and related to units of property ownership? We now have a good general understanding of the morphology of towns and the evolution of street plans and property boundaries between the ninth and the thirteenth centuries, and there is a great deal of evidence to suggest considerable continuity in the re-use and survival of property boundaries down to modern times.[29]

Detailed research into towns planned before the twelfth century has also revealed a hierarchy of units of property ownership represented in the

---

[27] Sarah Rees Jones, 'Household, work and the problem of mobile labour: the regulation of labour in medieval English towns', in Bothwell, Goldberg and Ormrod (eds.), *The problem of labour in fourteenth-century England*, pp. 133–53; Rees Jones, 'The household and English urban government', in Myriam Carlier and Tim Soens (eds.), *The household in late medieval cities: Italy and north-western Europe compared* (Leuven: Garant, 2001), pp. 71–88.

[28] Rees Jones, 'Women's influence on the design of the urban home', pp. 194–5.

[29] Palliser, Slater and Dennison, 'The topography of towns 600–1300', pp. 161–7, and see references cited there.

original settlement of towns. At the top of this hierarchy were quite large units in the town plan which formed the primary units of landownership. In the commercial northern *burh* at Worcester, which was laid out in the 890s, primary units consisted of blocks of land approximately ten perches (165 feet or 50.29 metres) in width along the High Street, and which extended the full width of an *insula* (or block) in the street plan from one street frontage to another.[30] In older towns of Roman origin which were refashioned in the ninth to eleventh centuries, such as Winchester, Oxford, London and York, the large primary units took a less regular form and the primary units which can be most easily detected in later records are those associated with the ownership of neighbourhood churches established during the period of refashioning. In these cases the church was owned in association with a number of adjacent properties and the extent of this urban estate came to define the extent of the parish as the parochial system developed. These primary units associated with churches have sometimes been described as 'urban manors' with the church providing their administrative heart.[31]

Such primary units were often subdivided, right from their inception, into smaller plots of between one and three and a half perches (approximately 16–60 feet or 4.87–18.28 metres) in width along the street frontage; such smaller plots were also characteristic of newer towns planned after the Conquest.[32] These narrower plots were particularly influential in the developing vernaculars of urban domestic and commercial architecture. Indeed Pantin's typology of 'right angle' and 'parallel'

---

[30] Nigel Baker and Richard Holt, *Urban growth and the medieval church: Gloucester and Worcester* (Aldershot: Ashgate, 2004), pp. 171–2.

[31] Biddle, *Winchester in the early Middle Ages*, pp. 452–4; John Blair, *Anglo-Saxon Oxfordshire* (Stroud: Sutton, 1994), p. 151; Anne Dodd, 'Synthesis and discussion', in Anne Dodd (ed.), *Oxford before the university: the late Saxon and Norman archaeology of the Thames crossing, the defences and the town*, Thames Valley Monographs no. 17 (Oxford University Press, 2003), p. 30; Derek Keene, 'London from the post-Roman period to 1300', in David M. Palliser (ed.), *The Cambridge urban history of Britain*, vol. 1: *600–1540* (Cambridge University Press, 2000), pp. 206–7; John Blair, *The church in Anglo-Saxon society* (Oxford University Press, 2005), pp. 337–40, 402–7. Some scholars use the Old English *haw* or *haga* to describe primary property holdings in towns. *Haga* however is a regional term which is not found outside Wessex and Mercia. Some similar primary units in York are discussed in more detail below.

[32] The perch varied between 16.5 feet and 20 feet in length in different parts of the country and there was also some variation in the length of the foot: P. Crummy, 'The system of measurement used in town planning from the ninth to the thirteenth centuries', in S. C. Hawkes, D. Brown and J. Campbell (eds.), *Anglo-Saxon studies in archaeology and history*, British Archaeological Reports, British Series vol. 72 (Oxford, 1979), pp. 149–63; T. R. Slater, 'Domesday village to medieval town: the topography of medieval Stratford-upon-Avon', in Robert Bearman (ed.), *The history of an English borough: Stratford-Upon-Avon 1196–1996* (Stroud: Sutton Publishing, 1997), pp. 34, 37–9.

later-medieval urban hall houses was based on the relationship between the house and its plot. The common right-angular hall houses are so called because their roof ridges ran at right angles to the street and they were frequently built on plots that were one perch wide.

The prominence of the perch-wide building plot in medieval townscapes has led some authors to describe them as burgage plots and thus to associate these houseplots with the legal units of freehold burgage tenure in towns. This is an oversimplification of a more complicated pattern of landownership and planning in towns. In twelfth-century Stratford-upon-Avon units held in burgage were three and a half perches wide, as were the new burgages laid out in the new 'French' quarter of Norwich immediately after the Conquest.[33] In York the size of burgage plots is indicated by the payment of husgabel, or burgage, rents which are first recorded in *c.* 1284 and in which the commonest payment was 2d, equivalent to two house gable's worth of land.[34] The dimensions of one such burgage were revealed for a site in Skeldergate, York, where excavation revealed two house plots whose boundaries were established in the late ninth century, and which together occupied a street frontage of about 50 feet (or three perches).[35] Yet in the late thirteenth century the two plots were owned as a single burgage unit by the Stavely family, who paid 2d husgabel rent to the crown in 1284.[36] Thus evidence from Norwich, Stratford, York and other towns suggests that plots owned in burgage were normally two to three perches wide, but from their inception might be subdivided longitudinally by their tenants into house plots of one perch in width.

The evidence of property boundaries thus indicates a complex hierarchy of settlement. Primary units, or urban manors, might be divided into substantial burgage plots which were in turn often divided into individual house plots of one perch in width. As we shall see, even these individual house plots might be further subdivided horizontally to provide more than one dwelling space.

[33] Slater, 'Domesday village to medieval town', pp. 37–9; Brian Ayers, 'The urban landscape', in Carole Rawcliffe and Richard Wilson (eds.), *Medieval Norwich* (London: Hambledon, 2004), p. 17.

[34] David M. Palliser, 'York's earliest administrative record, the Husgabel roll of c. 1284', *Yorkshire Archaeological Journal* 50 (1978), 81–91.

[35] Gillian Andrews, 'Archaeology in York: an assessment', in P. V. Addyman and V. E. Black (eds.), *Archaeological papers from York presented to M. W. Barley* (York Archaeological Trust, 1984), p. 201, no. 56.

[36] W. Brown and C. S. Clay (ed.), *Yorkshire deeds 1*, Yorkshire Archaeological Society Record Series vol. 39 (Leeds: Knight and Forster, 1909), p. 216; TNA, Enrolled Deed, De Banco Roll, 142/211; 'Husgabel Roll', p. 90, no 315. Husgabel rents were assessed at 1d per house gable along the street frontage.

Archaeology provides evidence of the houses constructed on these primary, secondary and tertiary units. Excavations on a number of sites in the City of London have established a sequence for the establishment of streets and side streets between the tenth and twelfth centuries, and recorded the progressive subdivision of units of occupation. On sites near the river frontage early building development occurred on the street frontage of plots as well as to their rear, but on sites further away from the river (for example to the north of Cheapside) the earliest buildings were located away from the street frontage.[37] Buildings on the street frontage were smaller and laid on the surface, while larger buildings with open structures, similar to halls, over shallow cellars were found towards the rear of plots. Similarly, excavations on several sites in central Oxford, but not in waterfront locations, suggest that initial development of the primary unit in the ninth to tenth centuries consisted of a substantial house set well back from the street within an enclosed precinct containing service buildings and yards or gardens within a relatively spacious site.[38] Intensive development of the street frontage with commercial buildings often occurred somewhat later, for example in the eleventh century, in response to the further commercial development of the local economy and the town. On secondary plots of approximately 2 perches (32 feet 10 inches or 10 metres) in width a similar pattern of occupation was observed with larger buildings, some in the form of hall-like structures over sunken cellars, toward the rear of the plot, and smaller surface-laid buildings some of no more than half a perch (5 feet 2 inches or 2.50 metres) in width along the street frontage. Over the centuries that followed commercial development along street frontages was not simply incremental; there were phases of retrenchment as well as growth – yet the overall integrity of the unit of property ownership was not much compromised.

The first of the two London models of development can also be seen in the excavations at Coppergate in York, which also occupies a waterfront site. Relatively narrow perch-wide building units were a feature of the site from the later tenth century and persisted down to the post-medieval period. As we have seen, the large timber-framed house of the later thirteenth century occupied the same narrow plot, towards the middle of the site, as did its much smaller eleventh-century predecessor. In their interpretation of the site, however, Richard Hall and Kurt Hunter-Mann suggest that stability in the existence of plot boundaries was compatible

---

[37] Horsmann et al., *Building and street development*, pp. 112–16.
[38] Dodd (ed.), *Oxford before the university*, pp. 30, 35–41.

with the changing use and significance of those boundaries.[39] In the eleventh and twelfth centuries the boundaries between building plots were not always marked by physical barriers. A strip of unbuilt land down either side of the house separated each plot from its neighbours (indeed a minimum gap of two feet was required in Canterbury in the ninth century).[40] Where boundaries between plots were marked by fences, and more rarely ditches, these were often relatively slight and permeable. Fences were perhaps no more than 1 foot 8 inches (0.5 metres) high and they did not necessarily run the full length of the boundary. The lack of significant fencing suggests frequent and easy communication between houses on neighbouring plots and possibly some kind of shared or common use of yards, all of which would support the idea that perch-wide building plots were not treated as independent units of ownership but were occupied in co-dependence with immediate neighbours within larger units of landholding.

At a later date, after *c.* 1250, when larger timber-framed buildings were built right up to the boundaries of the plots, physical barriers between adjacent plots were considerably more obvious. At this later date new paths were created to mark the boundaries between plots and such access routes from the street separating neighbouring houses were often the subject of legal agreements (and disputes) in the later Middle Ages.[41] 'Vertical' access routes along the length of plots thus came to predominate over 'horizontal' access routes between plots. We may use this evidence to suggest that occupation and possibly ownership of houses on separate plots became more distinct after *c.* 1250, and that as a consequence notions of maintaining privacy between plots became greater than they had been before, when visible access and movement across and between neighbouring plots would have been physically easier. It is interesting to note that it is also in the middle of the thirteenth century that we begin to have documentary evidence of concerns about privacy between adjacent houses in the London assizes of building and nuisance which regulated against buildings having windows overlooking their neighbours' gardens at a height of less than 16 feet from the ground.[42]

---

[39] For the following discussion of Coppergate boundaries see Hall and Hunter-Mann, *Medieval urbanism in Coppergate*, pp. 807–10.
[40] Nicholas Brooks, *The early history of the church in Canterbury* (Leicester University Press, 1984), p. 27.
[41] Rees Jones, 'Historical introduction', pp. 695–6.
[42] Chew and Kellaway (eds.), *London assize of nuisance*, pp. 103–4; Vanessa Harding, 'Space, property and propriety in urban England', *Journal of Interdisciplinary History* 32 (2002), 560.

Thus, however visible and durable single perch-wide building plots may have been in the evolving domestic built environment of the town, they obscured an underlining hierarchy of landownership and land use in which clusters of adjacent plots were often owned and managed together as larger social units. By the eleventh century a common pattern had emerged of larger houses set back behind the street frontage, often constructed with large open hall-like structures above sunken cellars, while the street frontage itself was likely to be developed with smaller and less substantial structures which might be no more than half a perch wide. The comparatively rare written evidence of such small housing provided by the reference in Domesday's account of York in 1086 to William de Percy owning the church of St Cuthbert together with seven small houses occupying a site 50 feet wide can now be set in the context of an increasingly large body of archaeological evidence for similar structures in other towns.[43] This model of large and small domestic buildings has been found both on the larger primary units, and on their subdivisions of just one or two perches in width, suggesting a common and shared perception of the ideal arrangement of domestic space by 1100. The larger and technically more sophisticated timber-framed hall houses of the later thirteenth, fourteenth and fifteenth centuries reproduced an essentially similar hierarchy of domestic spaces, but within a single architectural structure.

The place of urban property in society

What do we know about the owners and occupants of these different units of urban property? The increase in the use of written deeds of title to urban property in the twelfth and thirteenth centuries allows us to see more clearly the relationship between this hierarchy of property types in the town plan and the social structure of the town and its rural hinterland.

The physical hierarchy of urban property units reflected a social hierarchy of land ownership. In Worcester, for example, the primary units in the new *burh* of the 890s were given to privileged tenants, including lay servants of the cathedral community, who were responsible for attracting settlers to the town by subletting the smaller building plots within their new urban estates or 'manors'.[44] Here, as also in other cities such as

---

[43] Margaret L. Faull and Marie Stinson (eds.), *Domesday Book*, vol. 30, *Yorkshire* (Chichester: Phillimore, 1986), fol. 298a; David Palliser, *Domesday York*, Borthwick Papers no. 78 (York: Borthwick Institute, 1990), p. 16.

[44] Baker and Holt, *Urban growth and the medieval church*, pp. 263–7.

London, the landlords of primary units in the town also owned significant rural estates.[45] Their urban properties thus provided a bridge between the society of town and country and were one of the means by which towns were populated and developed a commercial hinterland.[46] For example, the urban manor might be used as a principal residence by its owner, supplied from his or her rural estates. In Coventry in the twelfth and thirteenth centuries, surplus produce from the countryside was marketed through such urban and suburban estates, facilitating the commercial development of both town and countryside.[47] Urban manors also provided the tenants of rural estates with a safe refuge in the defended town in times of war. In 1175 × 89 Richard de Hudleston granted to Avenel his chief residence in Clementhorpe by the river Ouse in York for 2s a year, on condition that he (Hudleston) might continue to lodge there on his visits to the city and that in time of war the main house would revert to Richard while Avenel stayed in other houses in the court (*curia*).[48] Thus, in the main period of both town and village formation between the ninth and early thirteenth century, rural landowners often lived in towns and engaged in trade.[49] The commercial development of town and country was interlinked and supported through an extensive network of property ownership and, indeed, both urban and rural village settlements planned during this period developed very similar plan forms.[50]

The integration of the urban and rural property markets was reflected in other aspects of the early management of urban estates. Urban landlords of primary units sometimes exerted an influence over their urban tenants similar to those exercised by a manorial lord of rural estates. The monastic landlords of the 'urban manor' of Godbegot in Winchester maintained a seigneurial jurisdiction over their tenants into the sixteenth century.[51] In twelfth-century York and thirteenth-century Coventry several landowners, including even burgesses, held courts for their

---

[45] Keene, 'London from the post Roman period to 1300', pp. 204–7.

[46] Blair, *Anglo-Saxon Oxfordshire*; Dodd, *Oxford before the university*, p. 30.

[47] Peter Coss, *Lordship, knighthood and locality, a study in English society c. 1180–c. 1280* (Cambridge University Press, 1991), pp. 61–92; Richard Goddard, *Lordship and medieval urbanisation: Coventry, 1043–1355* (Woodbridge: Boydell and Brewer, 2004), pp. 200–10.

[48] *Early Yorkshire charters*, vol. 1, p. 180 no. 216. Huddleston is about eighteen miles south west of York, and the site of important quarries of magnesian limestone which was transported up the Ouse and used in the construction of York Minster. By the thirteenth century the Huddleston family occupied a substantial manor house there.

[49] Robin Fleming, 'Rural elites and urban communities in late-Saxon England', *Past and Present* 141 (1993), 3–37.

[50] For a review of the literature on the similarities in town and village planning see David M. Palliser, 'Town and village formation in medieval England', in Palliser, *Towns and local communities in medieval and early modern England* (Aldershot: Ashgate, 2006), pp. 1–24.

[51] Keene, *Survey of medieval Winchester*, vol. 2, pp. 486–7.

tenants.[52] One powerful landlord, the abbey of St Mary's, still required its burgage tenants in the suburb of Bootham in York to provide labour services in harvesting hay from its extensive meadows nearby in the 1260s.[53] Primary units of landholding in towns were also associated, as we have seen, with the ownership of churches, and might also control other essential common facilities, such as ovens, semi-public meeting spaces (such as halls used by craft associations) and charitable works such as hospitals. In Coppergate in York two such primary units near the city's main grain market included ovens by the twelfth century, while an estate between St Sampson's church and the new civic market in Thursday Market (now St Sampson's Square) included a horse mill.[54] Similarly in Coventry in 1280, a single burgage belonging to Richard de Burton and Petronilla his wife contained seven subtenancies for cottars together with a common oven within their lordship (*dominico*) which the cottagers were obliged to use by custom.[55] Landownership in towns therefore carried with it some attributes of the patronal lordship exercised over rural manors and submanors, in which subtenants were treated as dependents of their landlords. The integration of urban and rural estates and the seigniorial dependence of some urban tenants in the period of urban development between the tenth and thirteenth centuries provide one important context for evaluating the relationship between urban and rural house forms. First it suggests that a simple model of emulation of rural building by townsmen or vice versa is unsupportable because it misses the integrated nature of the two societies in this early and influential period of settlement. Secondly it suggests that the hierarchies of larger and smaller buildings found within both primary units and smaller house plots reflected hierarchies of legal and social dependence between landowners and their subtenants.

Once we move inside the town, we can see further correlations between the status of different social groups and the types of domestic property they owned. In York between the twelfth and the fourteenth centuries, the families which owned the larger primary units might be drawn from the greater barons such as Roger Mowbray who owned *Mulbraihalle* (near modern Mulberry Hall) in Stonegate in the twelfth century, or the Scropes of Masham who acquired the primary unit, including the church of

[52] BL, Cotton MS. Claudius D. xi, fol. 201v; P. R. Coss (ed.), *The early records of medieval Coventry*, British Academy Records of Social and Economic History n.s. vol. 11 (London: Oxford University Press, 1986), p. xxii.

[53] John Rylands Library (Manchester) MSS. 220–1, fols. 20, 24, 26.

[54] The Coppergate oven was described as a *sequela* for the larger holding, which consisted of seven gable fronts (or house plots) and was held exempt from the payment of husgabel: BL, Cotton MS Nero D iii, fols. 168–72; *Early Yorkshire Charters*, vol. 1, pp. 181–3.

[55] Coss (ed.), *The early records of medieval Coventry*, p. 372. Richard de Burton, *alias* Richard de Aula, was an official of the Earl of Chester, lord of Coventry.

St Martin in Micklegate, for their town house in the early fourteenth century.[56] More commonly the owners of primary units belonged to the families which provided the leaders of the civic community. The form of this leadership changed over time: from hereditary judges at the time of the Conquest, whose descendants in the twelfth century owned four major primary units and their churches in the Walmgate area,[57] to the families of the royally appointed reeves who accounted for the city to the county sheriffs in the later twelfth century, including William Fairfax who held the primary unit of seven house plots with an oven between Ousegate and Coppergate as well as other York properties,[58] to the elected leaders (a mayor and three bailiffs) who presided over the civic government of York from the reign of King John onwards.

Although these city offices were not hereditary they were commonly dominated by a small group of interrelated families over several generations. For these families the ownership and occupation of primary units, particularly those associated with parish churches, provided an important base for their power both in their neighbourhood and in the city as a whole. In several cases it can be demonstrated that the ownership of these prominent domestic sites passed between successive leaders of the civic community, from one generation to the next, from the later eleventh into the fifteenth century. One example in Castlegate is enough to illustrate the pattern (Figure 4.1). This 'urban manor' lay outside the entrance to York Castle and coincided in extent with the parish of St Mary Castlegate. It was first mentioned in 1086 as a possession of the French knight William de Percy, one of the first custodians of the castle, patron of the church and owner of an estate of fourteen house plots in Castlegate.[59] By the fourteenth century the same property was in the hands of the Gra family and later passed to Thomas Holme, leading members of two of the greatest mercantile and mayoral dynasties of York in the later Middle Ages.[60]

---

[56] Rees Jones, 'Property, tenure and rents', vol. 1, pp. 112–3; S. Rees Jones and F. Riddy, 'The Bolton Hours of York: female domestic piety and the public sphere', in Anneke B. Mulder-Bakker and Jocelyn Wogan Browne (eds.), *Household, women and Christianities in late Antiquity and the Middle Ages* (Turnhout: Brepols, 2005), pp. 241–2.

[57] *Early Yorkshire charters*, vol. 1, pp. 240–50.

[58] BL, Cotton MS Nero D iii, fols. 169–72.

[59] *Domesday*, f. 298a; P. M. Tillot (ed.), *Victoria county history of Yorkshire: The city of York* (London: Oxford University Press, 1961), p. 392.

[60] York City Archives G70.16; TNA, C143 243/15, 394/24; Borthwick Institute Probate Registers 1, fol. 42v, 3 fol. 236v; Rees Jones, 'Historical introduction', pp. 693–4. For the Gra and Holme families see J. S. Roskell, L. S. Clark and C. Rawcliffe, *The House of Commons, 1386–1421* (Stroud: Sutton, 1993); Kermode, *Medieval merchants*, pp. 338–9; Christian D. Liddy, *War, politics and finance in late medieval English towns: Bristol, York and the Crown, 1350–1400* (Woodbridge: Boydell and Brewer, 2005), pp. 131–9, 172–3, 203–10, 231–2.

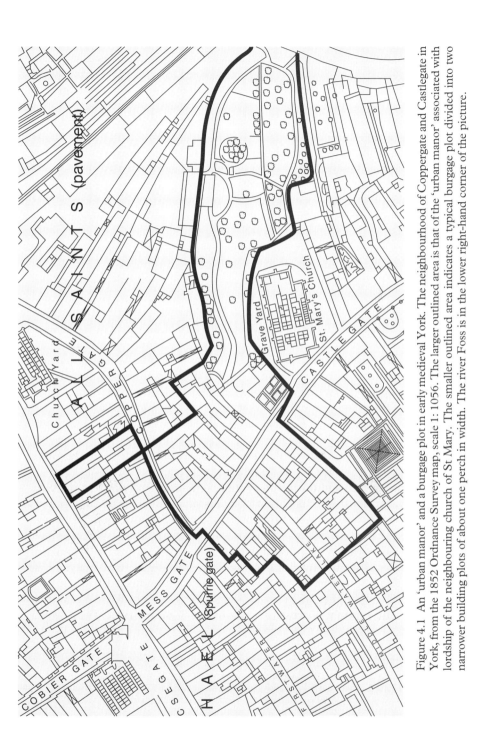

Figure 4.1 An 'urban manor' and a burgage plot in early medieval York. The neighbourhood of Coppergate and Castlegate in York, from the 1852 Ordnance Survey map, scale 1: 1056. The larger outlined area is that of the 'urban manor' associated with lordship of the neighbouring church of St Mary. The smaller outlined area indicates a typical burgage plot divided into two narrower building plots of about one perch in width. The river Foss is in the lower right-hand corner of the picture.

Several other primary units in other city parishes enjoyed a similarly long life as the focus of dominant households within the city. A few developed more formal public functions. The stone hall in Coney Street belonging to Hugh son of Lefwin son of Thurwif, one of the most powerful of York's burgesses at the end of the twelfth century, was transformed during the thirteenth century into the civic Guildhall (or town hall),[61] while the Mercers Hall, constructed in Fossgate in 1357, also seems to have been built on the site of an older stone house.[62]

The continuing prominence of such domestic sites in the civic landscape over so many centuries, and the conversion of others into civic buildings, suggests a considerable continuity in the manifestation of authority in the city between the tenth and the fifteenth centuries, and of the familial and parochial foundations upon which a civic power base was built. Such households were necessarily complex. In Castlegate, by 1400, much of the parish was still encompassed within the dominant household of the Gra family.[63] The main house was built on the south side of the road approaching the castle entrance while large gardens, described as the 'fief' of the main house, occupied the opposite side of the street and extended around the parish church and down to the river Foss. The owners of the house were also the constables of Castlegate Ward and dominant patrons of the parish church. They housed some of the parochial clergy in their own property and were patrons of a small hospital next to the church. The parts of the estate nearer the market street of Coppergate were subdivided into tenancies for sublets, including a bakehouse. The influential position of such domestic establishments in the community, and their longevity as sites of power, suggests that their owners would have been likely role models for those aspiring to join their ranks.

In the twelfth and thirteenth centuries the next level down in the civic hierarchy consisted of those householders who were of sufficient standing to act regularly as witnesses and jurors in their neighbourhoods and in the borough court, including several who were successful artisans. Such men were leaders within their neighbourhoods and played a part in city politics without necessarily ever rising to become leaders of the entire city. Their local standing within the city is even sometimes indicated by their very names: for example, Nicholas of Bretgate and Henry of Fishergate took their names from the streets in York in which they lived.[64] They owned

---

[61] *Early Yorkshire charters*, vol. 1, pp. 198–200; York City Archives, G16; TNA, PRO, SC6/708 m.10; Rees Jones, 'Property, tenure and rents', vol. 1, p. 72.

[62] Giles, *An archaeology of social identity*.

[63] Rees Jones, 'Historical introduction', pp. 693–4.

[64] Brown and Clay, *Yorkshire deeds*, vol. 2, Yorkshire Archaeological Society Record Series vol. 50 (1914), p. 203; Bodleian Top. Yorks. C72 fol. 48.

stone houses, on burgage plots of two to three perches in width. Some of these stone houses were complex structures built on to the street front with spaces for shops in undercrofts or cellars opening on to the street, and with halls or private chambers either behind or above these cellars. In 1326, for example, John de Selby, an apothecary, owned a hall over three stone cellars in Fossgate.[65] In other cases stone houses or halls were set back from the street frontage, with separate shops built out of timber on the street frontage. By 1276 Richard le Spicer, an apothecary, occupied one such stone hall in Petergate which is first recorded in *c*. 1201.[66] The hall occupied the rear of the site while the street frontage was developed with *bothis* (booths or stalls) constructed out of timber.

The large number of stone houses mentioned in the records suggests that they were popular with prominent artisans and traders. Stone houses were a significant investment for such men of middling status.[67] They were more durable than earth-fast timber structures and they allowed much greater versatility in the development of buildings of more than one storey. The complexity of the structures suggests, however, that they were also designed to accommodate a similar hierarchy of dependencies and sublets to that found on the larger estates of the civic leaders. A hierarchy of larger and smaller domestic spaces was built into their design, reproducing in a single complex the familiar hierarchy of domestic spaces found on larger sites and in earlier phases of exclusively timber development. Stone houses were common but not ubiquitous in the city. They surely represented not just a functional development, but also their own-ers' desire to emulate the architecture of the even larger homes of more prominent civic leaders, to demonstrate their position within their local neighbourhood, to convey their social aspiration in the wider city, and to provide a stable basis for the perpetuation of their family's local power.

While the use of stone permitted much more elaborate domestic structures, it seems that upper and middling elites in the town were

---

[65] Nigel Tringham (ed.), *Charters of the vicars choral of York Minster, city of York and its suburbs to 1546*, Yorkshire Archaeological Society Record Series vol. 148 (Leeds: Knight and Forster, 1993), pp. 60–3; York Minster Library, Vicars Choral, 4/1/1, 6/2/3. Stone cellars are recorded in a number of York streets. They are described as lying beneath a hall, or below solars or chambers (*camerae*) some of which probably served a function similar to a first-floor hall. They are particularly frequently mentioned in market streets close to the two bridges, over the rivers Foss and Ouse, and in the streets near the Minster. They may have been similar to the surviving stone houses in Lincoln: Quiney, 'Hall or chamber?', 38–40.

[66] BL, Cotton MS Claudius B iii, fol. 67; York Minster Library, L2/1 pt iv, fol. 44; L2/2a, fol. 21v; Rees Jones, 'Property, tenure and rents', vol. 2, pp. 78–82.

[67] While title deeds are usually uninformative about the buildings on properties, they were more likely to mention houses of stone than any other kind, thus indicating their special value.

conservative in their conceptualisation of domestic space, and used the new technology primarily to reproduce the familiar hierarchy of domestic spaces which was well established before 1100. As even newer technologies of timber framing became available by the end of the thirteenth century, they in turn reproduced the same familiar hierarchy of larger houses with halls in the centre of plots and smaller units around the periphery. So burgage plots supported small communities, under the authority of the head of household, which mirrored in microcosm the wider collectivities of parish and even town.

The construction of larger houses with halls or grand upper chambers, combined with the construction of much smaller units along the street frontage, was thus not a feature of new forms of domesticity in the fourteenth century or the post-plague decades, but reflected arrangements that had emerged over centuries of urban development. These arrangements were predicated on a form of social organisation in which households were grouped together in collective dependencies having in common certain quotidian facilities such as yards, ovens and even halls. Even single house plots could be developed to support small communities of this nature. The final question which remains, therefore, is what kinds of relationships existed between the occupants of the larger and smaller domestic buildings in individual house plots. It is only when we turn to think about the processes of law through which entitlement to property in housing was created that we gain glimpses of these social relationships and begin to see real and significant changes in the ownership and occupation of housing in the city.

Property and writing

The transformation in the technology of building in England between 1100 and 1300 coincided with a transformation in the processes and practices of conferring legal title to property, and particularly in the rapid rise and diffusion of the use of writing. The use of written charters conferring title to property increased in the twelfth century, but it was only in the thirteenth century that town courts began to keep written registers of transactions of burgess property made before the borough court.[68] Such witnessed transactions need not involve a written charter, but there was a growing emphasis on the use of written charters and by the early fourteenth century urban land registries were increasingly used for

---

[68] Geoffrey Martin, 'The registration of deeds of title in the medieval borough' in D. A. Bullough and R. L. Storey (eds.), *The study of medieval records: essays in honour of Kathleen Major* (Oxford University Press, 1971), pp. 151–73.

registering charters of title to land. Over the course of the thirteenth century possession of title to land thus came to depend less on the owner-ship of land being known, remembered and witnessed by the local com-munity and more on the ownership and recognition of a correct form of written title. Property ownership by charter therefore supported an increased fluidity in the property market, and the use of written titles spread down the social hierarchy to the owners of individual perch-wide building plots at just the same time as we find increasing concern about the privacy of those plots in contemporary nuisance law and in contemporary building practice.[69]

The rise of the urban land registry and the use of publicly recognised written titles to urban land can also be understood as part of the context in which landlords were progressively deprived of their private jurisdictions over free tenants as the English crown developed and extended the authority of royal courts. English common law did not provide a concept of ownership equivalent to that in current modern usage, but it did provide a simplification of complicated tenurial hierarchies of interrelated rights to land, and certainly after 1290 reduced the numbers of different parties who might claim title to a piece of land.[70] These developing notions of property under the common law brought clearer definitions of burgage tenure in the boroughs in contrast to servile tenure on rural manors, freeing the former and stimulating a dramatically increased use of written charters of titles among such free burgage tenants. By the middle of the thirteenth century the possession of urban land by charter was probably the most effective means of proving burgess status, and indeed this was one reason why urban courts developed registries of titles for burgage owners to ensure that they were publicly recorded.[71] It is a popular misconception that anybody could earn their freedom by moving to a town and living and working there for a year and a day. Rather, such new burgesses had to prove that the burgess community had accepted them, and the commonest form of proof was the possession of property in burgage tenure and its recognition before the borough court.[72]

Both the registration of titles and the use of charters in borough courts increased over the course of the thirteenth century, and after 1272 were given added impetus by the legal reforms of Edward I's reign, which emphasised the importance of written titles to any legal privilege.[73] When

---

[69] See above, notes 38–41.
[70] Harding, 'Space, property and propriety in urban England', 549–69.
[71] Adolphus Ballard (ed.), *British borough charters, 1042–1216* (Cambridge University Press, 1913), pp. xliv–xlv.
[72] Ibid., p. li.   [73] Martin, 'Registration of deeds of title', pp. 166–7.

royal officials launched a national series of inquisitions, the *Quo Warranto* proceedings, demanding to know the written titles by which local communities enjoyed various privileges, boroughs responded in a variety of ways, but in Coventry in 1280 a long and detailed list was produced of those who claimed to be burgesses by listing their burgages and the charters by which they held them.[74] By contrast, servile tenants of rural estates were not supposed to possess written charters.[75] Tenants in villeinage may have had the compensation of securities provided by the use of the manor court, but the prohibition on selling land by charter remained a major grievance.[76] Villeins' subtenants did not even have the protection of the manor court.[77]

The possession of written charters of title to land, and the use of a borough land registry, thus became the first symbols of urban freedom and bourgeois identity which distinguished burgesses from both servile tenants on rural manors and, importantly, from their uncharted neighbours in towns. For just as in the countryside, so in the town: subtenants of burgesses could not claim the protection of written charters. Thus, in 1271 William son of Thomas the goldsmith was unable to inherit his father's property in York since his father had never had a charter of enfeoffment because he held the messuage as a tenant at will without any writing.[78]

William son of Thomas's case suggests that the new legal practices were hardening distinctions in the ownership of urban property, defining more strictly the distinction between those who would in future be regarded as owners and those who would be regarded as tenants together with their respective and very different, rights over property. In this developing distinction traditional practices in building were influential in determining how the two groups were defined. William son of Thomas's property was a shop, occupying a small subdivision of a larger burgage plot. Although shops and cottages were sometimes valuable and highly sought after, there is little evidence in this period of them developing into permanent autonomous units of ownership. Prior to 1300 shops and cottages might be bought and sold, but more often they were leased, or the rental

---

[74] Coss (ed.), *Early records of medieval Coventry*, pp. 370–94.

[75] Paul Hyams, *Kings, lords and peasants in medieval England* (Oxford: Clarendon Press, 1980), pp. 43–65.

[76] Leon A. Slota, 'Law, land transfer and lordship on the estates of St Alban's abbey in the 13th and 14th centuries', *Law and History Review* 6 (1988), 119–38; Paul Hyams, 'What did Edwardian villagers understand by law?', in Zvi Razi and Richard M. Smith (eds.), *Medieval society and the manor court* (Oxford: Clarendon Press, 1996), pp. 82–3.

[77] H. S. A. Fox, 'Exploitation of the landless by lords and tenants in early medieval England', in Razi and Smith (eds.), *Medieval society and the manor court*, pp. 518–68.

[78] BL, Cotton MS Claudius B iii, fol. 42.

income from them was bought and sold. In the majority of cases they were let without written title, and they and their occupants remained dependent on the ownership and investment of the owner of the larger burgage unit on which they were built. In Norwich this dependency was formally recognised in *c.* 1300 in the expectation that the owner would take legal responsibility for the tenants of his 'rents' in the city courts.[79] Similarly the evidence of rent accounts from York before 1310 suggests that the subtenants of shops were treated as the dependents of free tenants and were seldom entered in written records. For example, Richard le Spicer was named as the single occupant of his dwelling in Low Petergate in 1276.[80] Even though there is other evidence that by 1201 there were already several shops on the plot he occupied, the subsidiary rents from these were not individually assessed and accounted for separately in the written record until 1364, when twelve shops were listed.[81] Around 1300 the vast majority of subtenancies of shops, cottages and single rooms were held by tenants at will without any security of tenure, rights to inheritance or written record to bring them to the historian's attention, and the occupation of a shop or cottage rarely secured independent rights of burgage tenure.

The impact of the use of written titles in distinguishing between owners of full burgages and tenants of their subdivisions is made clear when we consider the different types of property that began to be conveyed by charter. In the twelfth century use of charters remained relatively unusual in the conveyance of urban property. When charters were used they often described quite large properties some two perches or more in width. As the use of charters became more common during the thirteenth century, smaller units became the subject of written transactions. Detailed studies of sales of property around 1300 in several towns, including Oxford and York, suggest that original burgage plots were often divided into single perch-wide units for the purposes of newly chartered ownership. Sometimes, as in the examples in Coppergate or Skeldergate in York which have already been discussed above, this new division of ownership reflected an already existing physical division into perch-wide units of occupation, in other cases the physical division was new.[82] It was the owners of these properties who embraced the new technology of timber framing, adapting it to the construction of the multi-storied perch-wide timber-framed hall houses studied by Pantin and others. The increased

[79] Rees Jones, 'The household and English urban government', pp. 73–83.
[80] See note 65 above.   [81] York Minster Library, M2/4g, fol. 40v.
[82] Julian Munby, 'Zacharias's: a 14th-century Oxford New Inn and the origins of the medieval urban inn', *Oxoniensia* 57 (1992), 258–61.

use of written charters extended the privileges of chartered burgage status to the freeholders of single perch-wide building plots, providing them with the security and autonomy necessary to invest in buildings of substance, even if they lacked the wealth or the land to invest in constructions of stone. At the same time the use of charters enhanced the legal and civic distinctions between them and their subtenants. It is perhaps not surprising that their timber-framed houses emulated the architectural form of those older houses of the civic hierarchy they aspired to join, including the incorporation of a hall in the more secluded parts of the house and the reservation of the street frontage for smaller rooms and shops for subletting.

The incorporation of such subtenancies into the very fabric of urban houses thus raises the final question of the social relationships between the chartered owners of building plots and their unchartered subtenants. Scholars have tended to assume that the major reason for the multiplication of shops and cottages on such plots was commercial, as property owners responded to the demand for such accommodation as urban economies grew. Thus, as we have seen, the first intensive developments of street frontages with small buildings identified in archaeological excavations of tenth and eleventh century towns were on streets close to wharves, bridges and market places. It is only rarely that we gain a glimpse of the creation of such subtenancies in the documentary record before 1300. One lease of the mid-thirteenth century described a plot of land with buildings in Castlegate, York, which the tenant was to divide into four small houses to yield an annual rent of 18s.[83] This confirms our expectation that one function of subtenancies was to produce a rental income for their owners and that there were tenants ready to pay high rents for small properties in the right location. This impression is readily reinforced by the later medieval description of this kind of small-house accommodation in so many towns as 'rents' and by the substantial evidence for the construction of rows of both houses and shops to produce a rent by many urban landlords, both lay and ecclesiastical, in the later thirteenth and early fourteenth centuries. As the first urban rent accounts begin to survive these speculative developments become easier to detect. Between 1304 and 1347 the vicars choral in York added nearly fifty new houses to their rental by constructing nine new rows of small houses in five streets near the Minster and their college.[84] The tenants in these

[83] Judith A. Frost, 'An edition of the Nostell Priory cartulary: London, BL, Cotton Vespasian E XIX', unpublished PhD thesis, University of York (2005), p. 632 no. 693.
[84] York Minster Library, Vicars Choral 4/1/3, 7, 6/2/3, 12; Rees Jones, 'Property, tenure and rents', vol. 1, pp. 207–210.

properties included a number of men and women, clerical and lay, several of whom were members, servants or employees of the college community.[85] At least five York parish churches are also recorded as constructing rows of small single-bay houses between 1316 and 1340 in order to raise rents to support chantries.[86] Similar developments have been recorded in pre-plague Oxford, Winchester, Canterbury and London.[87]

It is worth noting, however, that although the development of street frontages with tiny units was a well-established practice by the eleventh century, the introduction of the term 'rent' as a generic term for such subtenancies seems to have been a novelty in the years around 1300.[88] We should therefore be alert to other ways in which subtenants were once regarded as the dependents of their landlords in non-commercial relationships. We have already seen that the freeholders of burgage tenants might be expected to exercise patronal rights and responsibilities over their subtenants, providing them with shared facilities in common ovens and yards and representing them in the courts. These practices may already have been waning and somewhat archaic by the time they are recorded in the later thirteenth century, but they hint at a time when subtenants were indeed the co-dependents of the major householder and burgages may have housed little collectivities of small communities or perhaps extended family networks. In York around 1300 there were stem family households, such as the household of Thomas le Horner on the corner of Loplane and Petergate, where adult sons and daughters, both married and unmarried, occupied shops, cottages and single rooms around the perimeter of the main family hall.[89] There were also units which look rather like *frèrèches*, such as that of the two Santon brothers who occupied neighbouring

[85] Rees Jones, 'Women's influence', pp. 208–210; S. Rees Jones, 'God and mammon: the York estate of the vicars choral of York', in David Stocker and Richard Hall (eds.), *Cantate Domino: colleges of vicars choral* (Oxford: Oxbow, 2005), pp. 197–9.

[86] These were Lady Row by Holy Trinity, Goodramgate (*Calendar of patent rolls preserved in the Public Record Office, 1313–17*, London: HMSO, 1898, pp. 476–7), and rows in the churchyards of St Martin Coneystreet, All Saints Pavement, St Sampson in Newgate and St Michael Spurriergate (*Calendar of patent rolls, 1334–38* (London, HMSO, 1895), pp. 121, 385, 399, 458).

[87] A. F. Butcher, 'Rent and the urban economy: Oxford and Canterbury in the later Middle Ages', *Southern History* 1 (1979), 11–43; Mavis Mate, 'Property investment by Canterbury cathedral priory', *Journal of British Studies* 23 (1984), 1–21; Keene, *Survey of medieval Winchester*, vol. 1, pp. 237–43.

[88] Geoffrey Martin, 'The governance of Ipswich from its origins to 1550', in David Allen (comp.), *Ipswich borough archives 1255–1835*, Suffolk Records Society vol. 43 (Woodbridge: Boydell, 2000), p. xxii.

[89] York Minster Library, M2/2a fos 32v–39; Rees Jones, 'The household and English urban government', pp. 81, 87.

houses, probably on the same two-perch burgage plot in Ousegate.[90] Another example is Robert son of John de Hull, who assigned a corner plot within his property, between his own house and the church of St Martin in Coneystreet, to his sister Eve on her marriage to John de Brayton in 1271.[91] The plot measured 10 feet by 19 feet, enough for a small house, which later passed to Eve's son Hugh, who became a deacon of the church. In all these cases the different houses on the burgage plot did not form separate 'nuclear' households but sustained a variety of interlocking relationships with the principal householder. It would make perfect sense that these extended groups should use some expensive facilities, even including the hall in the principal house, in common. It was only when such small houses became detached from the patronage of the main householder that their lack of such facilities or protection became problematic. Thus by the 1420s it was a recognised problem that the inhabitants of 'rents' in London, lacking privies of their own, threw their urine and faeces into the streets.[92] What had once been a private concern, as landowners provided privies for their subtenants in their shared yards, became a public matter for civic government. The ownership of a burgage plot, with its variety of domestic spaces, offered many opportunities for communal as well as nuclear living, and it would be wrong to imagine that all subtenancies were commercial ones. Even tenants who paid rent might belong to the extended familial network of their landlord.

Conclusion

The gradual development of the common-law concept of burgage tenure between *c.* 1150 and 1300, and the extension of chartered rights of burgage tenure to the occupants of the perch-wide building plots in towns, liberated the already swelling ranks of the house-plot owners from any lingering sense of subservience to seigniorial lords. Indeed, these owners were the successful artisans and petty merchants who were to lead the radical movements for more open government in England's towns during the long fourteenth century. It cannot be just a coincidence that it was over the same period that the evolution of timber framing also finally permitted

---

[90] Carol Fenwick (ed.), *The poll taxes of 1377, 1379 and 1381*, vol. 3, *Wiltshire – Yorkshire*, British Academy Records of Social and Economic History n.s. vol. 37 (Oxford University Press, 2005), p. 142.

[91] C. S. Clay (ed.), *Yorkshire deeds*, vol. 6, Yorkshire Archaeological Society Record Series vol. 76 (Leeds: Knight and Forster, 1930), pp. 168–73.

[92] A. H. Thomas (ed.), *Calendar of select plea and memoranda rolls of the city of London, 1413–37* (Cambridge: Cambridge University Press, 1943), p. 23.

English burgesses to demonstrate their status in well-appointed and durable homes on narrow perch-wide building plots.

Along with the charter, the timber-framed right-angle urban hall house was the most obvious visible symptom of the first rise of the bourgeoisie. They were a product of urban civic literacy and an expression of the new freedoms brought about by writing. Timber framing was to persist into the eighteenth century and in contexts and cultures, even in the later Middle Ages, which had very different notions of urban citizenship. But in looking back at the historical context out of which the very first timber-framed hall houses developed, we can see that they brought with them a number of cultural associations inherited from the much more ancient ideal of the 'urban manor'. They represented collective hierarchies of dependency which operated at a domestic as well as a parochial level, were fundamental to civic society, and conferred an ingrained sense of privilege among the burgesses over their un-chartered and un-halled urban neighbours.

5   Urban and rural houses and households in the late Middle Ages: a case study from Yorkshire

Jane Grenville

This chapter addresses the similarities and differences in rural and urban houses and in particular considers how these related to the broader issues of household and domestic identity. At its core lies a hypothesis very familiar to all medieval archaeologists, proposed by William Pantin more than forty years ago, that urban houses in late-medieval England represent an adaptation of rural plans to suit the new economic and social conditions of the town.[1] This view, which has provided a platform for debate among scholars of medieval urbanism ever since it was proposed, has most recently been challenged by Sarah Pearson, who notes that 'it assumes that urban and rural populations shared enough of the same needs to aspire to the same type of house'.[2] My purpose here is to explicate the two views and to use evidence from Yorkshire to examine the assumption that populations in towns and their hinterlands shared common aspirations. In so doing, I am much indebted to my York colleagues, Sarah Rees Jones, Jeremy Goldberg and Felicity Riddy, with whom I have spent many happy hours in debate and who have generously shared their ideas derived from the rich documentary and literary sources for York, London and other English towns.[3] Their thinking provides arguments related to my own and by different routes, we sometimes arrive at strikingly similar conclusions, as I shall demonstrate here. I also hope to contribute to the debate about whether there was, as Gervase Rosser has suggested, a distinctive urban culture in the later Middle Ages, such that 'the old assumption ... that the contemporary cultural environment was overwhelmingly rural needs to

---

[1] Pantin, 'Medieval English town-house plans'.
[2] Pearson, 'Rural and urban houses 1100–1500', p. 43.
[3] P. J. P. Goldberg, 'Household and the organisation of labour in late medieval towns: some English evidence', in Carlier and Soens, *The household in late medieval cities*, pp. 59–70; Rees Jones, 'Women's influence on the design of urban homes' and 'The household and English urban government'; Riddy, 'Looking closely'. These articles all owe much to the shared research agenda of the York Households Group, as does this chapter.

be set aside'.[4] I shall argue that the archaeological evidence suggests that although there was a new urban consciousness, the ties to the countryside remained real and active and that these tensions resulted in two distinct traditions of urban building, one truly innovative and the other interestingly conservative.

Pantin was completely explicit about his assumption that the town house represents a rural model adapted to urban conditions: 'this *rus in urbe* tradition, like the townsman's cattle in the common fields and the "broad gates" and miniature farmyard that sometimes occupied part of his tenement, reminds us how much the medieval town remained part of the countryside'. The widely accepted 'standard' plan type for the medieval manor house is that of the tripartite subdivision of central hall open to the rafters, flanked by wings usually divided into two storeys and containing service rooms at one end and a solar or private apartment for the lord at the other.[5] Using forty examples from various towns around England, Pantin looked at the relative positions of the open hall, the service rooms and the solar or principal chamber, and developed a typology whose principal attribute was the orientation of the central hall to the street – hence parallel and right-angled hall types form the basis of his classification (Figure 5.1). Crucially, he restricted his investigations to buildings with open halls at their core, excluding both smaller houses 'where the hall plan, if it can be said to be applied at all, is applied vertically' and very large houses such as Arundel House in the Strand in London 'where there was so much space that the introduction of a complete manor-house plan presented no problem of adaptation at all'. His sample, then, has an inbuilt bias and this perhaps underlies the fact that he does not seem to question the desirability to the medieval urban population of importing a rural plan type to the town, having simply omitted those structures that do not conform to his preconception.[6]

Sarah Pearson, in a recent paper reconsidering the evidence for urban building from the twelfth to the fifteenth centuries challenges this assumption that the urban type simply represents the countryside brought to the town. She goes on to suggest that, far from conforming to the tripartite type, early (that is late twelfth and early thirteenth century) urban house forms demonstrate considerable variety and flexibility in their design and layout. Looking at later buildings she argues that storied construction may be initially an urban innovation, since 'in the countryside, space was not

---

[4] Gervase Rosser with Patricia E. Dennison, 'Urban culture and the church', in David M. Palliser (ed.), *The Cambridge urban history of Britain*, volume 1: *600–1540* (Cambridge University Press, 2000), p. 337.
[5] Grenville, *Medieval housing*, pp. 89–92.   [6] Pantin, 'Town-house plans', 202.

a) Schematic open hall plan

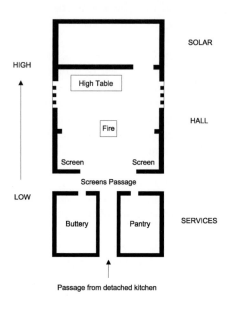

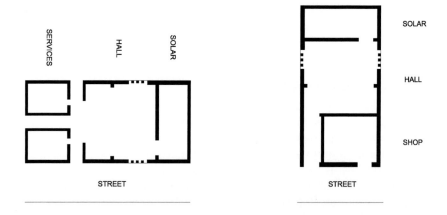

b) Schematic parallel hall

c) Schematic right-angled hall

Figure 5.1 Above: the standard layout of an open hall. Below: two urban forms, showing different orientations of hall to street frontage (author/Alex Holton).

such an important issue and first floor accommodation was unnecessary'.[7]
She discusses the plan forms of later urban houses with open halls and
concludes that tripartite forms are relatively unusual in urban contexts
and that 'the evidence leads to the suspicion that, except at the very
highest social levels, urban dwellers had no need for the hierarchic
arrangement of rural houses, nor for rooms in which to perform essentially
rural functions. Instead, emphasis was on commerce, workshop space,
and storage'.[8] These are conclusions that demand closer investigation.
As Pearson notes, 'a great deal of work has been done on rural houses.
We know far less about urban ones ... Much more work is still required to
tease out the complex relationship between the two.'[9]

In explaining the differences between town and country, Pearson
repeatedly returns to the social and economic issues of space – the need
for hierarchical space, the need for commercial space and so forth – and
suggests that these vary between urban and rural contexts. Where similarities are found, as in the introduction of storied construction, an
explanation is sought in terms of emulation, whatever the disagreements
about the direction in which the influences moved. In broadly agreeing
with this analytical approach, I will argue first that the social use of space is
perhaps even more central to understanding these buildings than Pearson
suggests and then provide an empirical example by considering the complex relations between town houses and their rural counterparts in late-
medieval Yorkshire. This leads me to disagree with her conclusion in part:
I shall show that some buildings seem to depend on the direct and explicit
relationship between town and country while others emphatically do not,
but rather represent a distinctively urban type.

Space as an agent of social and economic relations

Archaeologists have been much influenced over the last quarter century
by general theories of how people relate to space in terms of both buildings
and landscapes. The work of the space syntax research group at University
College London, led by Bill Hillier and Julienne Hanson, has been
hugely influential, as has related research by Thomas Markus and a
different, more anthropological, approach to non-verbal communication
by Amos Rapaport.[10] Pierre Bourdieu's concept of *habitus*, that sense of
understanding one's place and role within one's physical lived environment
and the practical logic and sense of order that is culturally transmitted and

---

[7] Pearson, 'Urban and rural', p. 49.   [8] Ibid., p. 59.   [9] Ibid.
[10] Bill Hillier and Julienne Hanson, *The social logic of space* (Cambridge University Press,
1984); Julienne Hanson, *Decoding homes and houses* (Cambridge University Press, 1998);

varies from culture to culture, has been influential along with that of his fellow French post-modern theorist, Henri Lefebvre, who argues that it is the social *production* of space rather than the description of its configurations that must be the subject of study.[11] Finally, the work of British sociologist Anthony Giddens has given prominence to the active agency of space, which he terms 'locale', in determining social practice.[12]

The impact of such theorising on archaeology may be seen in a disparate group of edited volumes of the early 1990s.[13] Two major monographs of particular interest to medievalists were Roberta Gilchrist's 1994 study of medieval nunneries and Matthew Johnson's 1993 consideration of Suffolk vernacular housing of the sixteenth and seventeenth centuries.[14] Gilchrist looked at gender relations and Johnson at household dynamics (between servants and masters as well as parents and children), and both used their subjects to provide an exegesis of the broader thesis, that 'material culture is *active* in social relations. Far from merely *reflecting* society, material culture can be seen to construct, maintain, control and transform social identities and relations.'[15] For Gilchrist, the methodology for articulating this understanding came from the notion of *habitus* as defined by Pierre Bourdieu, while Johnson took a more rigorously structuralist view. Kate Giles's work on York guildhalls explores these theoretical approaches in greater detail in a study that is directly relevant to the argument presented here.[16]

The arguments presented in these works are complicated and sometimes expressed in abstruse language. Nevertheless, it is important at the outset to elucidate some of these ideas in non-theoretical vocabulary, as they are critical to the thinking behind this chapter. A pair of simple modern examples will suffice to make the point. We can all remember our

---

Bill Hillier, *Space is the machine: a configurational theory of architecture* (Cambridge University Press, 1996); Thomas Markus, *Buildings and power: freedom and control in the origin of modern building types* (London: Routledge, 1993); Amos Rapaport, *The meaning of the built environment*, 2nd edition (Tucson: University of Arizona Press, 1990).

[11] Pierre Bourdieu, *Outline of a theory of practice* (Cambridge University Press, 1977); Henri Lefebvre, *The production of space*, trans. Donald Nicholson-Smith (Oxford: Blackwell, 1991).

[12] Anthony Giddens, *The constitution of society: outline of the theory of structuration* (Cambridge: Polity Press, 1984).

[13] Susan Kent (ed.), *Domestic architecture and the use of space* (Cambridge University Press, 1990); Ross Samson (ed.), *The social archaeology of houses* (Edinburgh University Press, 1990); Martin Locock (ed.), *Meaningful architecture: social interpretations of buildings* (Aldershot: Avebury, 1994); Michael Parker Pearson and Colin Richards (eds.), *Architecture and order* (London: Routledge, 1994).

[14] Roberta Gilchrist, *Gender and material culture: the archaeology of religious women* (London: Routledge, 1994); Matthew Johnson, *Housing culture: traditional architecture in an English landscape* (London: UCL Press, 1993).

[15] Gilchrist, *Gender and material culture*, p. 15.   [16] Giles, *An archaeology of social identity*.

first day at school. The change in scale from the domestic to the institutional building and from the family to the large group of kids supervised by unknown adults was novel. For some of us it engendered terror, for others an excited 'butterflies in the tummy' sensation. We were lost, physically and metaphysically. As we moved on through the educational system, changing schools, similar feelings were induced, but the codes of the institutional building and of institutional behaviour were by now better understood and the foreignness of the situation was less acute. By the time we arrived at university, the vocabulary of educational architecture was thoroughly embedded and it was the specifics of the new place rather than its underlying social structure that needed to be learned. Space directs us and different social structures inhabit, manipulate and are manipulated by different spatial configurations, and in this respect the production of social space is an intrinsic aspect of *habitus*. My second example concerns the way in which material culture may be used explicitly to differentiate between social groupings in different contexts – as, for instance, the way in which modern urban and rural communities differentiate themselves and the way in which individuals move between the two and vary not only their behaviour but also their lifestyle choices depending on location, both physical and social. 'Country clothes' and pick-up trucks may have a functional purpose which would serve equally well in the city, but most rural dwellers will modify their dress code for a trip to London. Yet I was struck by the television footage of protesters against the banning of hunting with dogs, whose demonstrations were a feature of the British political scene in the opening years of the twenty-first century: in this situation the distinction was clearly and aggressively drawn, not only verbally in the slogans and chants, but also in terms of appearance, for they came in their country clothes, Barbour jackets and green Wellington boots. A distinction between two cultures that is normally less sharply drawn was deliberately intensified through the use of material culture, and there was sufficient common ground for the vocabulary to be clearly understood by the urbanites, whatever their views on the political issue at hand.

With these modern examples in mind, I wish now to return to the medieval period and to Rosser's contention that in the later Middle Ages there 'was a prevalent perception in the medieval town that urbanity was distinguished from an alien countryside'.[17] Pursuing the arguments outlined above that material culture is an engine of social practice, rather than a mere reflection of it, I shall argue that deliberate choices were made about how to signal a specifically urban identity in such a way that

---

[17] Rosser and Dennison, 'Urban culture', p. 338.

country cousins would recognise it and understand the implications. Although there are many categories of material culture that could be considered in this way (pottery and personal belongings spring immediately to mind), I shall concentrate here on the house as the locale of the household.[18] I shall address the question through the lens of two of the most famous projects in English medieval studies: the archaeological investigation of the deserted village site of Wharram Percy in North Yorkshire and the extensive studies made of medieval York, through the recording and analysis of its surviving buildings, the excavation of its subsurface remains and the work of historians on its extensive archival records. My period is *c.* 1300 to *c.* 1520, when the rural population was under considerable economic stress, the nature of which varied across this long time span, and when migration into the towns was common amongst young adults.[19] How would a teenager from Wharram relocating to the city have perceived and understood the physical appearance of York's buildings? How was material culture in its architectural manifestation used passively to signal and actively to structure the contrasts and familiarities between rural and urban society? Sarah Pearson suggests that we are still relatively ignorant about what the people who lived in these urban houses expected of their homes and whether they had any use for the sort of accommodation found in rural areas.[20] By looking in some detail at those buildings and at the historical evidence for the people who occupied them, I shall argue that there are social and economic imperatives that demand both difference and familiarity in the same locale. I begin by introducing my two sites.

Wharram Percy and York

Wharram Percy lies eighteen miles to the north-east of the city of York near the north-western edge of the chalk uplands known as the Yorkshire Wolds, in an area now given over to cereals and grazing (Figure 5.2). The only standing buildings on the site are a ruined medieval church and a pair of deserted brick-built farm cottages which date from the middle of the nineteenth century but sit on the foundations of an eighteenth-century

---

[18] C. G. Cumberpatch, 'Towards a phenomenological approach to the study of medieval pottery', in C. G. Cumberpatch and P. W. Blinkhorn (eds.), *Not so much a pot, more a way of life* (Oxford: Oxbow, 1997), pp. 125–51; P. J. P. Goldberg, 'The fashioning of bourgeois domesticity in later medieval England: a material cultural perspective', this volume; Geoff Egan, 'Urban and rural finds: material culture of country and town', in Katherine Giles and Christopher Dyer (eds.), *Town and country in the Middle Ages, contrasts, contacts and interconnections, 1100–1500* (Leeds: Maney, 2005), pp. 197–210.
[19] Goldberg, *Women, work, and life cycle.*   [20] Pearson, 'Urban and rural', p. 55.

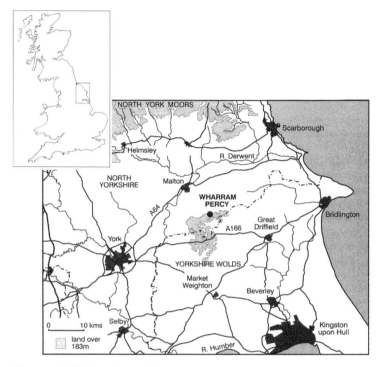

Figure 5.2 The locations of York and Wharram Percy (reproduced with permission of English Heritage–NMR).

range of farm buildings (Figure 5.3). It is part of the folklore of English medieval studies that it was to this site that a young economic historian from the University of Leeds, Maurice Beresford, came on a hot June day in 1948 to seek out empirical proof for his contention, offered at a seminar in Cambridge a few weeks earlier, that deserted villages were not a feature peculiar to the Midland plain but could be found elsewhere and more plentifully than had been supposed.[21] At Wharram he saw, clearly delineated as earthworks, the remains of about thirty houses laid out in two facing rows. The longer one to the west sits at the top of an escarpment, while at the foot of the hill is the shorter eastern row – and all of this could be observed in the humps and bumps in the ground. To the north a distinctly separate unit was observable, subsequently, and correctly, identified as the site of a manor house complex (Figure 5.4). The site

[21] M. W. Beresford and J. G. Hurst, *Wharram Percy: deserted medieval village* (New Haven: Yale University Press, 1990), 20.

Figure 5.3   Wharram Percy, showing the church and the farm cottages with the earthworks of the deserted village on the hillside beyond (photo: author).

became the subject of intensive study over the next forty years. Though the main series of excavations ended in 1990, study continues, with a detailed re-survey of the earthworks by English Heritage in 2002 and continuing survey and small-scale excavation in the vicinity by the Department of Archaeology of the University of York up to and including the summer of 2005.[22]

Documentary evidence for Wharram is scant. Domesday Book recorded two manors, which seem to have amalgamated by 1254. Valuations suggest a sharp decline in the overall value of the holding in the early fourteenth century.[23] Following the ravages of the Black Death, a tax return of 1352

[22] A. Oswald, *Wharram Percy deserted medieval village, North Yorkshire: archaeological investigation and survey*, Archaeological Investigation Report Series AI/19/2004 (Swindon: English Heritage 2004); University of York Department of Archaeology, *The Wolds research project* (at http://www.york.ac.uk/depts/arch/Wolds/index.html).

[23] M. W. Beresford, 'Documentary evidence for the history of Wharram Percy', in D. D. Andrews and G. Milne (eds.), *Wharram, a study of settlement on the Yorkshire Wolds I: domestic settlement I: Areas 10 and 6* (London: Society for Medieval Archaeology, 1979), pp. 5–25; Philip Rahtz and Lorna Watts, *Wharram, a study of settlement on the Yorkshire Wolds IX: the north manor area and north-west enclosure*, York University Archaeological Publications no. 11 (York, 2004), pp. 2–5.

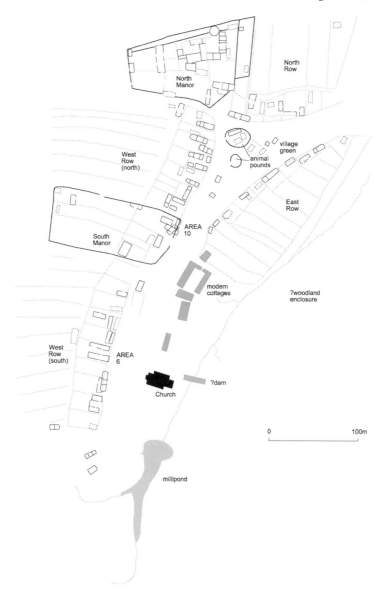

Figure 5.4 Wharram Percy: plan of the medieval village (reproduced with permission of English Heritage–NMR).

and an inquisition *post mortem* of 1368 suggest a measure of recovery, with all the uncultivated land of 1323 back in production and thirty houses occupied. After the middle of the fifteenth century, however, the population declined significantly, presumably as a result of putting the land down to pasture (see below), and a 1517 Commission of Enquiry provides evidence for the eviction of the last four families and the destruction of their houses at some stage between 1488 and 1506. Archaeological work has demonstrated the location of the two manors, one of which lay hidden beneath the later peasant houses, the other being visible as a series of earthworks on the northern edge of the village as mentioned above. The subsurface remains of peasant houses have been examined in two locations, generally referred to by the site codes they were given by the excavators, Areas 6 and 10. Publication of the project continues, but much is already in the public domain.[24]

Throughout the later Middle Ages York, along with Bristol and Norwich, was one of the most important provincial towns of later medieval England.[25] Its strong position might be ascribed to a mixed economic base: as a trading centre on both a national and an international stage; as an ecclesiastical centre, housing both the archbishopric and the richest Benedictine house in northern England, let alone all four orders of mendicant friars; and last, though by no means least, its political importance as a strategic location ensured frequent royal attentions. Described by William of Malmesbury in the late twelfth century as 'urbs amplissima et metropolis',[26] it retained its importance until the later fifteenth century, underpinned by its service function to what has been described as 'one of the largest and, perhaps, most self-indulgent consumer populations in the North', resulting in 'a rich mix of skills, commerce and cultures,

[24] Beresford and Hurst, *Wharram Percy*; and Susan Wrathmell, *Wharram Percy deserted medieval village* (London: English Heritage, 1996) remain the most accessible introductions. For more detailed reports on the later medieval phases, readers are directed to R. D. Bell and M. W. Beresford, *Wharram, a study of settlement on the Yorkshire Wolds I* (London: Society for Medieval Archaeology, 1987); J. G. Hurst, 'The Wharram research project: results to 1983', *Medieval Archaeology* 28 (1984), 77–111; J. G. Hurst, 'The Wharram research project: problem orientation and strategy 1950–90', in Della Hooke (ed.), *Medieval villages: a review of current work* (Oxford University Committee for Archaeology, 1985), pp. 200–4; P. Stamper and R. Croft, *Wharram, a study of settlement on the Yorkshire Wolds VIII: The south manor area*, York University Archaeological Publications no. 10 (York, 2000); Stuart Wrathmell, *Wharram, a study of settlement on the Yorkshire Wolds VI: domestic settlement 2: medieval peasant farmsteads*, York University Archaeological Publications no. 8 (York, 1989).
[25] Alan Dyer, 'Ranking lists of English medieval towns', in David M. Palliser (ed.), *The Cambridge urban history of Britain*, vol. 1: *600–1540* (Cambridge University Press, 2000), pp. 747–70.
[26] William of Malmesbury, *Willelmi Malmesbiriensis monachi De gestis pontificum Anglorum libri quinque*, ed. N. E. S. A. Hamilton, Rolls Series no. 52 (London: Longman, 1870).

unrivalled outside London'.[27] It is now generally accepted that the thriving population of York, and of other towns, was the result of inward migration from the countryside.[28]

Like other urban centres, York was badly affected by the Black Death and subsequent epidemics. It is estimated that 40 to 45 per cent of the rural Yorkshire population was lost and that the proportion may have been higher in the towns; yet it has been argued that paradoxically, this disaster may be measured by the buoyancy of urban populations rather than their collapse, for the later Middle Ages show a spectacular increase in admissions to the freedom of the city.[29] In the Yorkshire Wolds, arable husbandry declined as the cost of labour rose very swiftly after the Black Death and when grain prices started to fall significantly from the 1370s. Jeremy Goldberg has argued that a principal demographic impact of disease was the accelerated migration of peasants from the countryside, where land was being turned over from labour-intensive arable farming to pastoral production and smallholdings were being rolled up into the larger land parcels of richer peasants, at the expense of their poorer neighbours. In particular, women seem to have been more mobile.[30] Goldberg has suggested that in the later fourteenth and early fifteenth centuries in Yorkshire, women achieved a measure of independence, both economic and marital (in terms of entering marriages late or not at all, and playing a more proactive role in choosing marriage partners). Young men, too, were entering service in the city, and a new class of young, single, relatively unsupervised and independent town-dwellers seems to be emerging. Some of them returned to the countryside after a period of service; others remained in town, married or not. My chief concern in the rest of this chapter is to explore the houses with which they would have been familiar, both in the city and in the village, and to explore further Sarah Pearson's suggestions about the direction of influence.

Houses and households in medieval Yorkshire

How did household structure relate to the plan of the later medieval house, in town and country? To answer this question we need to look in some detail at the configuration of rural and urban buildings and consider the social groups that occupied them, in the context of the likely links

---

[27] Jennifer Kermode, 'Northern towns', in Palliser (ed.), *The Cambridge urban history of Britain*, volume 1: *600–1540*, p. 678.

[28] Ibid., p. 676.

[29] Ibid.; R. B. Dobson, 'Admissions to the freedom of the city of York in the later Middle Ages', *Economic History Review* 2nd series, 26 (1973), 16–22.

[30] Goldberg, *Women, Work and life cycle*, passim.

between them provided by the migrant workers discussed above. The construction of a familiar *habitus* is an important part of this argument. If the migrants were drawn from the peasant classes, what sort of buildings would they have been familiar with in their natal villages? A recent review of the late-medieval plan form reinforces earlier observations on the ubiquity from about 1250 onwards of the three-or four-unit house: a cross passage with service rooms to one side, a hall on the other side and a chamber, or inner room, beyond.[31] In its disposition of space, if not the fixtures and fittings, this is reminiscent of the linear tripartite plan of the later medieval manor house, where the solar lay beyond an open hall with a dais at the high end for the lord's table, accentuated by a coved canopy looking down towards a screens passage which separated off the service rooms, the buttery and pantry. The linear configuration materialised and embodied social hierarchies in a formal setting, with clear visual cues in the fixtures and fittings to signal the social status of the high end.

The peasant house had a similar linear arrangement, with an open central room entered via a cross passage at one end, dividing off service rooms, or in some cases, animal accommodation. At the other end, a separate room provided private space for the head of the household and the immediate family. This arrangement lacked the dais, the canopy and screens, but it has been argued by David Austen and Julian Thomas that the repetition of these features encapsulated 'a mental template of the habitual space espoused by an extensive group ... it had ... three-dimensional reality ... functional purpose and symbolic meaning, all of which might shift through time'.[32] Crucial to their argument is a combination of ethnoarchaeological evidence from western Ireland and the interpretation of the functional logic of the disposition of space between humans and animals and between open and enclosed spaces, to suggest a hierarchical arrangement of symbolic space, similar to that of the manorial hall, but not signalled by the fixtures and fittings associated with the higher-status buildings. It is argued that the space alone, combined with the positioning of human actors within it at different times of the day and year, is enough in itself to indicate the hierarchical nature of the group that lives there. 'The interiors of English medieval houses are, then, repeated and familiar spatial maps of late feudal social relations, with emphasis on the core family but with material differences from rank to

---

[31] Gardiner, 'Vernacular buildings'; Gardiner, 'Buttery and pantry, and their antecedents'.
[32] David Austin and Julian Thomas, 'The "proper study" of medieval archaeology: a case study' in D. Austin and L. Alcock (eds.), *From the Baltic to the Black Sea: studies in medieval archaeology* (London: Unwin Hyman, 1990), pp. 43–78.

rank and from region to region.'[33] Such a conclusion is necessarily speculative, but I propose to investigate its load-bearing capacity by applying the theoretical argument about mental templates and *habitus* to the evidence for rural and urban housing in Yorkshire set in its socio-economic context.

Taking the rural evidence first, the substantial remains of three medieval domestic and agricultural complexes have been excavated at Wharram Percy. The general layout of Wharram is one of long narrow crofts (paddocks) with tofts (farmhouse and outbuildings) at their street frontages comprising a house and ancillary buildings within a garden enclosure.[34] The regularity of the layout suggests a degree of planning (see Figure 5.4).[35] Croft sizes vary in area, the largest being *c.* 0.82 acre and the smallest at *c.* 0.15 acre. Two peasant holdings (Area 10 and Area 6) were excavated in detail over the long period of investigation, and others were looked at partially. Excavation of Area 10 revealed that the toft and croft occupy the former site of the south manor house. The form and finds from the later peasant house seem to indicate a property of some status (Figure 5.5). It is unusually large and although the evidence is ephemeral, it seems to have a heated and an unheated end.[36] Indeed, it has been suggested by the Wharram team, on the evidence of a 1323 inquisition *post mortem*, that this farmstead, together with the more fragmentary remains found on the next plot to the south, was of higher social status than its neighbours.[37] The 1323 document also provides an important piece of evidence for our understanding of town/country relations in that it highlights the declining fortunes of Wharram at this date, with the total valuation of the manor down from £21 12s 2d in 1266–7 to £12 6s 4d, and two-thirds of the demesne bovates lying fallow.[38] These signs of rural recession before the Black Death are important and I will return to them in

---

[33] Ibid., p. 59.

[34] Grenville Astill, 'Rural settlement: the toft and croft', in Grenville Astill and Annie Grant (eds.), *The countryside of medieval England* (Oxford: Blackwell, 1988), pp. 36–61, provides a general introduction for the uninitiated.

[35] Wrathmell, *Medieval peasant farmsteads*, pp. 41–5; Oswald, *Wharram Percy*, figure 27.

[36] The first phase (Building 4), which Wrathmell has convincingly shown to have consisted of a well-built cruck structure, was a long narrow building of the common tripartite plan type, aligned north–south along the frontage of the plot, dated on pottery evidence to *c.* 1300, modified at a later by the addition of Building 2 to the south. The buildings are about 4 m or 13 ft wide internally and at least 21.75 m (84 ft 6 ins) long (the southern extent of Building 4 was not identified so this represents a minimum length). This would give a minimum internal area of 87 m^2 or 936½ sq ft. This is a generous size: even if we assume that part of this structure was used to house animals, the domestic accommodation is considerable.

[37] Wrathmell, *Medieval peasant farmsteads*, p. 23.

[38] Beresford, 'Documentary evidence', p. 11.

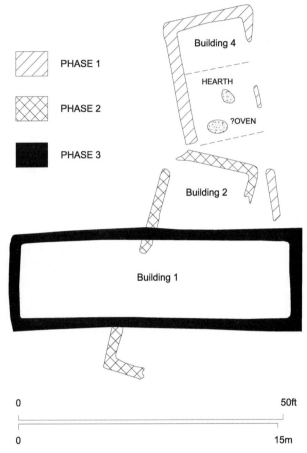

Figure 5.5 Wharram Percy: plan to show successive peasant houses in Area 10 (after Wrathmell, *Wharram, a study of settlement on the Yorkshire Wolds VI*).

my discussion of urban building. A later building on the site, Building 1, lies at right angles to the earlier structures and seems to be an agricultural building, which, together with other structures from this toft and its two southern neighbours, belongs to one of the larger amalgamated farmsteads that characterise the final phase of occupancy of the village in the late fifteenth century.[39]

---

[39] Wrathmell, *Medieval peasant farmsteads*, p. 21; Oswald, *Wharram Percy*, p. 58.

The second main area of peasant house excavation took place to the south, in what was known to the excavators as Area 6. Here two buildings, Building 1 and Building 4, lie on an east–west alignment at right angles to the street frontage, with Building 1 to the south. Building 1, dated by pottery finds to the first half of the fourteenth century, follows the familiar tripartite plan, with a cross passage separating a heated from an unheated end (Figure 5.6).[40] It had low stone side walls whose separate stretches allowed the excavators to identify bay lengths of between twelve and sixteen feet, entirely consonant with evidence from both excavated and standing buildings. On top of these low walls, seated on wide flat stones known as padstones, would have been curved cruck timbers, carrying the weight of the roof and walls. This would have provided a well-built and repairable structure, which would have represented an item of significant value within the estate of its holder. Like the structure in Area 10, the building was large.[41] It was also sturdily built and thus presumably inheritable: we are looking at the houses of fairly wealthy peasants who were able to support relatively large families. The interpretation of the similarly sized Building 4 to the north has changed over the long period of study at Wharram. The original interpretation was as an earlier longhouse, but it has subsequently been reinterpreted as a barn contemporary with the house to the south, although firm information on its function is scarce. Analogies suggest a farmyard disposition here, and the excavated evidence provides us with a plan of two structures divided by a yard which could be closed off by gates.

Areas 10 and 6, then, show us something of the domestic and agricultural buildings of two of the better-off peasant families at Wharram. It would be interesting indeed, in future excavation campaigns, to return to some of the smaller holdings to investigate the nature of those houses. Would they differ significantly from the tripartite plan we see here? This consists of a communal central area, perhaps better referred to by the post-medieval term 'houseplace' than 'hall', which conjures up visions of the screens passage, service end and solar of the manorial hall. This houseplace is a multi-purpose functional area, without the trappings of the higher-status hall, but, as I have suggested above, its basic spatial layout is enough to ensure that the social syntax of authority is embedded within

---

[40] Andrews and Milne (eds.), *Wharram Percy I*, p. 105.
[41] The internal proportions of the first phase of the building are 27.5 m (90 ft) by *c.* 5 m (*c.* 16 ft 6 ins), giving an internal area of 1,485 sq ft, even larger than the Area 10 building discussed above. If we assume that the lower end was used as an animal byre and measure the internal area from the cross passage westwards, the area of putative domestic occupation is 726 sq ft.

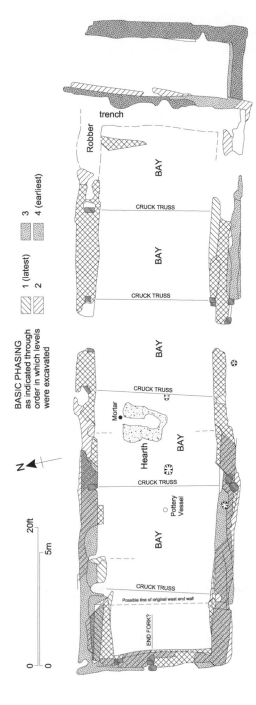

Figure 5.6 Wharram Percy: plan to show phases of alteration to peasant house in Area 6 (after Wrathmell, *Wharram, a study of settlement on the Yorkshire Wolds VI*).

the plan. The idea of graduated space, with higher status furthest away from the entrance passage (here a simple cross passage rather than articulated by a screen) is strong. Both Mark Girouard and Matthew Johnson have argued for the importance of the open hall as a means of exercising social control over subordinates in aristocratic houses: lack of physical segregation ensured a high degree of surveillance, while embedded cues of social difference, such as the raising of the dais at the high end of the noble hall and its location beneath a canopy, acted to reinforce a patriarchal, hierarchical system.[42] Although the dais and canopy are not observable in the peasant house (although the archaeological adage that absence of evidence is not evidence of absence should perhaps be noted here and it could be that visual cues such as these simply have not survived the taphonomic process), the persistence of the tripartite plan, coupled with the interpretation of the disposition of heated and unheated areas, suggests a plan type which, in Gardiner's words, 'was sufficiently flexible to be adapted to serve the purposes of both peasants and their lords' and which 'reflects a remarkable consensus about the organization of social space'.[43]

Turning, then, to the manorial hall at Wharram, the site of the North Manor has had but few trenches dug across it, and none in the area that has been identified as the hall (Fig 5.7).[44] Such an undertaking would doubtless yield fascinating results, but in the meantime it is possible to say a little about the lordly domestic accommodation from the work done by the original surveyors, supplemented by the more recent topographical survey undertaken by English Heritage.[45] Here the main hall range is identifiable from surface earthworks and is clearly subdivided into three elements, as we might expect for a typical high-status hall, split into hall, service rooms and solar. The English Heritage team argues that a second phase of expansion saw the construction of a new hall range to the east.[46] Within the extent of the whole *curia* (approximately 2.5 acres) are a barn, various stockyards and, in the second phase, a circular dovecote, a clear expression of lordly status.[47]

[42] Mark Girouard, *Life in the English country house: a social and economic history* (New Haven and London: Yale University Press, 1978), p. 30; Johnson, *Housing culture*, pp. 52–9.

[43] Gardiner, 'Vernacular buildings', 178–9. Taphonomy is the process by which archaeological material decays and decomposes in the ground.

[44] Rahtz and Watts, *North manor*, pp. 6–8.   [45] Oswald, *Wharram Percy*, pp. 41–8.

[46] The hall element of the first phase is approximately 11 m × 6 m (36 ft × 19 ft 8 ins), giving a floor area of 709 sq ft as the public space with the lord's household, where the manor court was invariably held. To this one could add the 1163 sq ft of domestic accommodation represented by the solar block and 430½ sq ft of service rooms (with a possible detached kitchen to the north-west joined to the rest of the complex by a corridor).

[47] John McCann, 'An historical enquiry into the design and use of dovecotes', *Transactions of the Ancient Monuments Society* 35 (1991), 89–160.

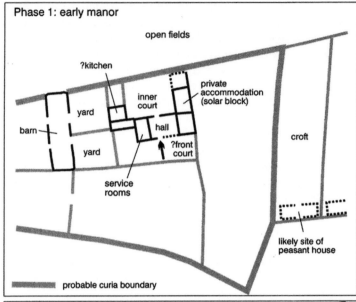

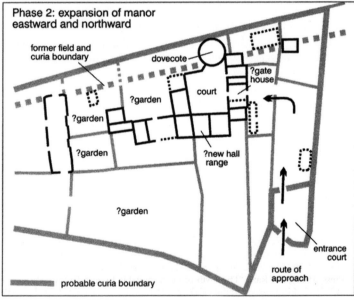

Figure 5.7 Wharram Percy: schematic plan to show the two phases of construction of the North Manor (reproduced with permission of English Heritage–NMR).

To sum up the archaeological evidence for domestic accommodation from Wharram, both lordly and peasant dwellings seem to have conformed to the tripartite layout that seems so ubiquitous in the English medieval countryside. A central open area is a main occupation space in the peasant house and has an open fire, but the manorial hall demonstrates a greater complexity, with separate areas for services and private accommodation. Plentiful evidence from surviving manorial halls of the later Middle Ages suggest additional features such as screens passages at the low end, and a dais and canopy at the high end.[48] In the case of the peasant buildings, the assumption has been made, based on the evidence of later vernacular buildings, that the space on the other side of the cross passage is taken up with animal accommodation.[49] If the peasant buildings were *not* subdivided between domestic and agricultural purposes, then the available floor space would indicate either very generous allowances or very large families. It is to the historical evidence for that rural household structure that we now turn.

The historiography for the study of the domestic arrangements of the medieval peasantry is very substantial and it would be futile for an archaeologist to attempt to summarise it in any detail. Peasant household size and structure has most commonly been analysed through the use of poll tax returns and manorial court rolls; it is a field in which there remains considerable debate over both the general trends and the detail of family structure and over the causes and rate of change.[50] Historians share with archaeologists the problems of partial survival of evidence and difficulties in interpreting what there is, given that the records were never written down with the historians' purposes in mind; the literature reflects this, but a measure of consensus is emerging.[51] It is suggested that there is a tendency over the period from the early fourteenth century for households to manifest themselves as nuclear rather than extended families.[52] Bearing in mind that there were households that consisted of solitaries (either unmarried or widowed) or childless couples, and given exceptionally high rates of childhood death, raw figures for family size are not particularly

---

[48] Grenville, *Medieval housing*, pp. 89–120.
[49] Wrathmell, *Medieval peasant farmsteads*, p. 28.
[50] See Richard M. Smith (ed.), *Land, kinship and life-cycle* (Cambridge University Press, 1984); R. H. Hilton, *The English peasantry in the later Middle Ages* (Oxford: Oxford University Press, 1975); Zvi Razi, 'The myth of the immutable English family', *Past and Present* 140 (1993), 3–44; Peter Fleming, *Family and household in medieval England* (Basingstoke: Palgrave, 2001).
[51] Zvi Razi, *Life, marriage and death in a medieval parish: economy, society and demography in Halesowen, 1270–1400* (Cambridge University Press, 1980); Richard M. Smith, 'Families and their land in an area of partible inheritance: Redgrave, Suffolk, 1260–1320', in Smith, *Land, kinship and life-cycle*, pp. 135–95. In particular see Razi, 'The myth', *passim* for sources.
[52] Fleming, *Family and household*, pp. 66–7.

helpful. Zvi Razi has shown that while single conjugal units tended to occupy individual houses (that is, in nuclear families), networks of extended kin remained centrally important, in the West Midlands at least, until well after the worst years of plague epidemics in the mid to late fourteenth century, while in East Anglia, Smith and others have been able to demonstrate how these networks broke down more quickly in an area where manorial control was weaker, population denser, the land market more active and economic systems more diversified. Thus the nuclear family appears earlier in East Anglia than elsewhere. The important point, for the purposes of this argument, is that peasant households were living and working together, not only in the fields but also in the house, where the configuration of space suggests that a high degree of intervisibility allowed the parents to observe and supervise the play, table manners and work of their children. Peasant families were used to operating, both indoors and outside, in conditions where the junior members could be seen and controlled by the senior members.[53] In the manor house complex, more segregation of tasks is implied by the greater number of subsidiary buildings, but here the hierarchical nature of the domestic unit (including the family and its servants and labourers, both high and low status, comprising the *familia*) is reinforced by the open hall with its explicit emphasis of social status through the visual cues of graduated space, dais and canopy. The importance of oversight is central.

A second area of research by historians has focused on migration from the countryside to the towns. Again the literature is substantial, but there is a clear consensus that inward migration occurred both in periods of relative prosperity in the countryside and, conversely, when there was simply not enough land to go round. There is evidence to suggest that in the thirteenth and early fourteenth centuries, the children of families with insufficient land left for work in the towns. Jeremy Goldberg argues that before the Black Death 'underemployment and unemployment must have been features of rural life ... for the poor and the destitute towns offered the chimera of work and opportunity'.[54] His work, based largely on the evidence of depositions in the ecclesiastical courts, and that of Peter McClure on surname evidence, bring the city of York into sharp focus and we find large-scale immigration throughout the later Middle Ages, notably from a wider catchment area after the Black Death than

---

[53] Ibid., pp. 63–4; Barbara Hanawalt, *The ties that bound: peasant families in medieval England* (Oxford University Press, 1988), pp. 156–68.

[54] Goldberg, *Women, work and life cycle*, p. 283. It is fair, however, to say that the social status of those going into service in towns has yet to be adequately addressed by historians (Goldberg, pers. comm.). Perhaps the suggestions made in this chapter on the strength of the archaeological evidence will spur them into action.

before.[55] Changes in economic circumstances in the later fourteenth century did nothing to stem the tide of migration, although the reasons now were different, with the loosening of manorial control and changes from arable to pastoral farming as the former became unsustainable with the drop in the labour force.[56] It is widely agreed that migration from the countryside buoyed up the population levels of plague-hit cities, for 'no late medieval urban community seems to have been capable of replenishing its population by means of natural regeneration'.[57] There is evidence to suggest that women were more mobile than historians had previously noted, and Goldberg has considered this phenomenon in detail. He makes the interesting suggestion that 'the factors that may have motivated the young, and young women in particular, to migrate from the countryside into the town must be understood in terms both of the particular attractions of urban society, be they economic or social, and the restrictions of rural life. Migration in search of employment, particularly by the young and unmarried, seems to have been a characteristic feature of pre-industrial society.'[58]

To summarise: the households that occupied the larger peasant tofts were hierarchical, with parents exercising considerable surveillance over their children. These children, as they approached adulthood, might well make their way to the towns, to serve in artisanal or merchant households. Furthermore, others have argued that the medieval peasant was inherently conservative.[59] The Wharram evidence reviewed above indicates that this hierarchical household was accommodated in a building where the principal room was an open hall. While there are indications of a hierarchical subdivision of space, its subtler material manifestations are less easy to detect than in buildings of manorial status; however, the documentary evidence suggests that social order was maintained by the watchful parental eye in a locus where intervisibility was all-important. I am arguing that the interdisciplinary evidence combines to suggest that shape, size and social differentiation are critical to our understanding of the function of the peasant open hall. In the discussion of the urban hall that follows, I will argue that these rural notions of household hierarchy, obedience and

---

[55] Goldberg, *Women, work and life cycle*, pp. 280–304; Peter McClure, 'Patterns of migration in the late Middle Ages: the evidence of English place-name surnames', *Economic History Review* 2nd series, 32 (1979), 167–82.
[56] P. J. P. Goldberg, *Medieval England: a social history 1250–1550* (London: Arnold, 2004), p. 168.
[57] R. B. Dobson, 'General survey 1300–1540', in Palliser, *The Cambridge urban history of Britain*, vol. 1, p. 277; see also Jennifer Kermode, 'The greater towns 1300–1540', *ibid.*, p. 444; Heather Swanson, *Medieval British towns* (Basingstoke: Palgrave, 1999), p. 113; Goldberg *Women, work and life cycle*, p. 77.
[58] Ibid., p. 294.   [59] Discussed by Goldberg, *Medieval England*, pp. 11–12.

discipline on the part of the younger members of the household combined with innate conservatism and found one element of expression in the persistence of the open hall in an urban context in which it could well have seemed, in functional economic terms, a waste of space. The powerful desire for ontological security translated in material terms into the disposition of the urban house: the urban open hall of the merchant or wealthy artisan is, within Pantin's paradigm, an expression of *rus in urbe*.

To explore this suggestion in more detail, we must address briefly the issues of servanthood that have been so thoroughly considered by medieval historians. In particular, arguments have been advanced for 'life-cycle service', that is, a period of service undertaken in late teens and early twenties that was a common feature of adolescence and early adulthood among the lower and middling orders (and, on a different status level, among the aristocracy too).[60] For the young immigrants into towns identified above, the advantages were legion, with access to training and opportunities to develop social skills and more extended networks and, perhaps most importantly, to seek out marriage partners. For those who had lost their parents, the chance to achieve a degree of security in another household may well have been a principal attraction.[61] It also represented an opportunity to escape the conservative patriarchy of the rural household, and that opportunity to undermine the *status quo* may well have held attractions. For parents, this possibility of subversion must have been seen as a threat among the other palpable benefits of service for older children: that it provided a comparatively secure environment away from the village where economic opportunities were limited, and enhanced future prospects. Parents would also wish to be assured that a move to town would guarantee appropriate socialisation and discipline, and to that end, a reassurance that the same values obtained in the employer's home as in the natal family would have been important. Employers, for their part, found life-cycle servants comparatively inexpensive and a flexible workforce. Thus servants and apprentices became an integral part of many merchant and artisanal households in towns, and, to a lesser degree, in the households of richer peasants in the countryside. Hence we should, perhaps, not be surprised to see the open hall, that excellent vehicle of familial hierarchies, making its appearance in the town; nor should we

---

[60] Goldberg, *Women, work and life cycle*; Smith (ed.), *Land, kinship and life-cycle*; Fleming, *Family and household*, pp. 72–6; Kate Mertes, *The English noble household, 1250–1600: good governance and politic rule* (Oxford: Blackwell, 1988), pp. 166–7.

[61] P. J. P. Goldberg 'What was a servant?', in Anne Curry and Elizabeth Matthew (eds.), *Concepts and patterns of service in the later Middle Ages* (Woodbridge: Boydell and Brewer, 2000), pp. 1–20.

necessarily assume that its urban function was appreciably different to that of its rural counterpart, in that it provided a recognisable *locale* for familiar social structures. If we see the open hall in such terms of *habitus* in the medieval town, then its apparent waste of useful economic space begins to make some sense, although, as Sarah Pearson notes, the question of the direction of influence is still not clear.[62]

There are undoubtedly some open halls in towns and I turn now to the evidence provided by the buildings of York, both surviving and excavated. Of over 139 surviving timber-framed buildings of the fourteenth to sixteenth centuries, unequivocal evidence for an open hall features in only twenty (about 14 per cent) of them, although excavated examples add a few more. The property at 28–32 Coppergate (Figure 5.8) is a clear example of Pantin's double-range parallel hall type.[63] In a plan that is remarkably similar to that of Pantin's principal exemplar of Tackley's Inn, Oxford, an open hall runs parallel to the street behind a row of shops, with an entrance to a screens passage through an internal passage between two of the shops. Although much altered at the rear, 41–45 Goodramgate (Figure 5.8) may originally have presented a similar layout, with a parallel hall in the position of the later-seventeenth-century structure that now lies to the south end of the complex. Alternatively, the 'hall-like' range that presently occupies the northern end and dates to the late fifteenth century may be an original right-angled hall.[64] A more certain right-angled hall may be found at 49–51 Goodramgate (Figure 5.8), where the hall range, interestingly, is of Wealden type construction.[65] Other examples can be found in York and I have discussed them elsewhere.[66] Space in the hall is restricted in the town compared to the countryside, but to either side there were often storied areas, as at 7 Shambles, which suggest that overall accommodation was of a similar order.[67] One-third of all the households in York in 1377 had servants, the mercantile trades employing over half

[62] Pearson, 'Urban and rural', p. 44.
[63] Royal Commission on the Historical Monuments of England [hereafter RCHME], *An inventory of the historical monuments in the city of York*, volume 5, p. 128; Pantin, 'Town-house plans', 217–223.
[64] RCHME, *York*, vol. 5, pp. 136–8.
[65] Ibid., pp. 138–40; Pantin, 'Town-house plans', 228–33.
[66] Grenville, 'Houses and households in late medieval England'.
[67] The area of the hall at 28–32 Coppergate is about 462 sq ft. The area of the replacement structure that may stand on the site of a parallel hall at 43–45 Goodramgate is 550 sq ft. That of the right angled hall at 49–51 Goodramgate is a mere 272 sq ft, although the area of the whole ground floor, excluding the shop, is 731 sq ft. At 7 Shambles the hall covers 170 sq ft, behind a shop of almost equal size and with a rear storied bay of similar dimensions, giving a non-commercial ground-floor area of *c*. 350 sq ft, perhaps compensated for in the construction of a third storey.

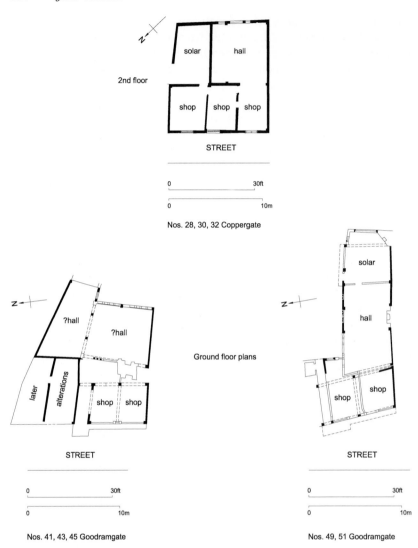

(After RCHME)

Figure 5.8 York: plans of the urban halls at 28–32 Coppergate, 41–45 Goodramgate and 49–51 Goodramgate (reproduced with permission of English Heritage–NMR).

of them and there being an average of two per household.[68] Merchant households were materially more comfortable and socially more complex – a complexity that seems to be reflected in the development of the plan to create increasing numbers of separate rooms, as at Bowes Morrell House in Walmgate.[69] Finally, this evidence is supported by the detailed study undertaken by the York Archaeological Trust on the Coppergate site, more famous for its early medieval finds, but equally important for the excavated remains of thirteenth- to fifteenth-century houses of open hall type, two of which may have been Wealdens of the same type as 49–51 Goodramgate and whose wealthy occupants supported houses and households which 'were clearly complex and able to provide accommodation for comparatively large numbers of dependents and "guests" of different kinds. Even more modest houses in the parish were typically headed by a married couple in 1381 and the majority housed at least one servant.'[70]

Sarah Pearson has argued that urban buildings form a distinctive and separate category, largely unrelated to rural houses. She comments on the importance of commercial and storage space on the ground floor of buildings in towns, 'along with a hall', but she also argues for a tight definition of a hall, looking for all the characteristics of the higher-status manor house: 'dais beam and bench, large windows, and service doorways', and these she notes are 'seldom present', making it perverse 'to view urban houses as adaptations of rural ones, as opposed to buildings which have developed specialized forms in their own right from the twelfth century onwards'.[71] But we have seen from the Wharram evidence that there is tellingly no evidence for the screens passage or dais of the 'classic' hall in the peasant croft, that locus of familial hierarchy. I am here proposing that the rural counterpart of the hall of the artisan or merchant house was not the manorial hall but the peasant croft, and probably that of the peasant who sent his teenage children into service in the town for training and socialisation and sent them to a household that, in its spatial syntax, resembled his own. In other words, peasants actively sought to place their children in households that reflected the values of their own, a fact we can see most clearly reflected not in the documentary evidence but in the buildings themselves, for, logically, there is little advantage to the urban entrepreneur in reserving so large a part of the ground space of his house for generalist purposes. Indeed the specific urban adaptations of commercial frontage and industrial or storage backland are testimony to

[68] Swanson, *Medieval British towns*, pp. 109–14; Goldberg, *Women, work and life cycle*, pp. 305–9.
[69] Grenville, 'Houses and households', pp. 317–21.
[70] Rees Jones, 'Historical introduction', p. 695.   [71] Pearson, 'Urban and rural', p. 53.

the requirements for specialised space, and domestic affairs could easily have been restricted to the upper floors, which were becoming increasingly significant through the fifteenth century.[72] There is no instrumental economic need for a hall in a town, and yet they are there. I argue that this can be explained by the requirement to provide a social *locale* that speaks of hierarchical structures and induces a degree of ontological security in strangers from the countryside: here is a house they can recognise, a safe house, and one in which they can confidently place themselves (or their teenaged sons and daughters). This would certainly support Pantin's view, *contra* Pearson, that in this house type, the town mimics the country.

Material conditions are here acting as an active agent in the reinforcement of conservative patriarchal power structures, which allowed the families of the migrating young to feel a degree of ontological security about the new world into which their offspring were venturing. A teenager from Wharram, placed in an artisanal household such as 7 Shambles, would quickly understand the social geography of the hall space. Sarah Rees Jones, in her work on women's influence in the design of urban homes, argues that, as a workplace, the hall represents 'safe' space in which occupations such as spinning, carding and some brewing might be located, as opposed to those industries requiring heat and/or strength, such as metal working or baking, which were normally located in external workshops.[73] This would, to an extent, reflect the situation in the peasant house, where the hall represents workspace as well as social space – and a similar degree of surveillance would be exercised over the young workforce. The direction of influence matters little here, although I would marginally favour a rural prototype; the important issue is that social space is deliberately constructed to create a specific set of social conditions, and family heads seem to agree, both in the countryside and in towns, about that material expression of social order. And if we were to look for the higher-status formal halls of the manor house in the towns, our search would cease at the guildhalls, which undoubtedly do demonstrate those elements of screens passage and dais so conspicuously absent from the domestic halls, and which function in much the same way as the rural manor hall for the dispensation of justice and the display of wealth and status.[74]

It would seem that in almost every other respect, the architecture of the town does indeed represent a new departure. The proliferation of shops on the commercial street frontage is one such innovation which has

---

[72] Grenville, 'Houses and households', p. 325.
[73] Rees Jones, 'Women's influence', p. 193.
[74] Giles, *Archaeology of social identity*, pp. 62–7.

received detailed treatment elsewhere.[75] It is perhaps worth noting that the most often cited reason for the long narrow shape of an urban burgage is that competition for space on the valuable commercial frontage demanded many narrow holdings. This does not look convincing when the plans of Wharram Percy and countless other late-medieval planned villages, equally dominated by oblong plots with their narrow side to the street, are taken into account. It might be the case that *habitus* again dictated the physical layout, rather than more functional economics.

Of more interest in this discussion of urban domestic accommodation is the issue of housing the poor and the marginal. Our Wharram teenager may have moved away from familial control into the sphere of an equally hierarchical artisan or merchant household, but equally, she may have moved to town with few prospects and ended up in a much more menial role as a labourer, a huckster or a prostitute. These footloose members of the urban underclass occupied cheap accommodation and by its nature, we probably see only the upper end of that market surviving. In York, the group of buildings collectively termed 'rents' are cheap two-storey cottages, with one room on each floor and no apparent means of heating or cooking.[76] Lady Row (Figure 5.9), built in 1316 on the churchyard of Holy Trinity Goodramgate to generate rents for the support of chantries, is the best-known example, but others are identifiable. A three-storey, double-jettied set of tenements at 85–89 Micklegate lies on the church-yard of the other York church dedicated to the Holy Trinity and was almost certainly built to generate rents, as were the Church Cottages at All Saints, North Street and 12–15 Newgate in the churchyard of St Sampson (for which a building account of 1337 survives in the Calendar of Patent Rolls); there was also the long-demolished, but well-documented row built by the parishioners of St Martin, Coney Street in 1335, 100 feet long, 18 feet wide at one end and 12 feet at the other.[77] It is

---

[75] Derek Keene, 'Shops and shopping in medieval London', in Lindy Grant (ed.) *Medieval art, architecture and archaeology in London*, British Archaeological Association Conference Transactions for 1984 (Leeds: Maney for British Archaeological Association, 1990), pp. 29–46; David Clark, 'The shop within? An analysis of the architectural evidence for medieval shops', *Architectural History* 43 (2000), 58–87; Grenville, *Medieval housing*, pp. 181–9.

[76] Short, 'The fourteenth-century rows of York'; Rees Jones, 'Women's influence', p. 194; Rees Jones, 'The household and English urban government', pp. 80–1.

[77] For Micklegate, see RCHME, *An inventory of the historical monuments in the city of York*, volume 3, *South-west of the Ouse* (London: HMSO, 1972), pp. 82–3; for North Street, see ibid., pp. 98–9; for the building contract for Coney Street, see L. F. Salzman, *Building in England down to 1540* (Oxford: Clarendon Press, 1952), pp. 430–2. An interesting example of a set of two-storey rents that had 'disappeared' has been recognised by Sarah Rees Jones at 87 Low Petergate, where a very narrow rear range at right angles to the street behind a pair of shops seemed to make no sense as a hall. She deduced that the

Figure 5.9   York: the rent, a distinctively urban type. Above: Lady Row, Goodramgate. Facing page: 54–60 Stonegate.

worth noting the pre-plague date of several of these examples and in that context, we should remember the dip in fortunes suggested by the documentary evidence for Wharram at this period. Migration may have been no less common before the Black Death than afterwards, and these building dates offer us concrete evidence for the accommodation of some of the migrants.

A further example of a purpose-built set of rental properties is 54–60 Stonegate (Fig 5.9), a property acquired by the vicars choral in 1278 and continuously let by them from that date until 1549. Fieldwork has established that the structure was built as a three-storey construction, and tree-rings from each storey cross match to give a felling date of 1322/3, suggesting a construction date very soon after that.[78] A curious anomaly is

property originally faced on to the now defunct Langton Lane which ran perpendicular to Petergate and marked the southern extent of the Liberty of St Peter, and so another set of rents has been identified.

[78] RCHME, *York*, volume 5, pp. 225–6; I. Tyers and K. Groves, 'Tree-ring dates from the University of Sheffield dendrochronology laboratory: York, 60 Stonegate', *Vernacular Architecture* 31 (2000), 127–8.

Figure 5.9 (cont.)

that there is no break in the rental accounts around this date. Where were the tenants while the previous structure was being demolished and the new one built? Certainly they continued to pay their rent and this remains a puzzle – one can only imagine that the vicars rehoused them temporarily, but omitted to clarify this in their records, presumably because there was no actuarial need to do so. This is an interesting building because it is clearly a set of single rooms, although the rental suggests a capital messuage with a hall in the centre on the plot enclosed by the L-shaped row. There was clearly a market for a 'bedsit' culture which the vicars choral exploited not only here but in other locations where the original buildings no longer exist.

These are buildings that are completely without parallel in the rural hinterland as far as the evidence of standing structures or excavated remains shows to date. They lack any resemblance to the principal social space of the established patriarchal social unit, whether that is seen as a rural nuclear family or an urban artisanal household with apprentices and servants as well as family members. These buildings represent the material response to a new social phenomenon, the urban poor, and it is a grouping that caused the city fathers endless concern, as the definitions of nuisance bear witness.[79] The buildings that survive almost certainly represent the upper end of this market; excavation, most recently in Walmgate, is beginning to provide us with a better understanding of the more ephemeral structures which existed in the suburbs.

It is beyond the scope of this chapter to consider in detail the living standards of this underclass, who probably worked away from their homes and subsisted on takeaways.[80] As a final speculative point, and one which requires further investigation, I raise the issue of counterbalancing forces, which provided an alternative to the patriarchal model I have suggested. In an article on urban real property, Rodney Hilton noticed that although there was a very brisk market in housing, particularly in subletting of property, there is little evidence to suggest that individual property accumulators saw their holdings as their principal source of income: 'presumably mercantile and industrial profits were such as to attract the bulk of urban capital. Some capital may have been invested in rent charges, though on nothing like the scale found in continental towns.' This is of interest, but what he says next, as a closing remark, seems to me to be completely central to the point I am trying to make about the conservative influence of men as heads of families: 'The main trend after the building expansion of the thirteenth century seems to have been towards institutional ownership of the bigger blocks of urban real property, safe investments, the income from which served the purposes of these institutions'.[81] Later work by Derek Keene supports some aspects of Hilton's observations, particularly the notion that ecclesiastical institutions formed major estates of rents in the medieval city.[82] In other words, the prevailing situation we have noted in York obtained elsewhere: the housing of the urban poor lay in the hands of the ecclesiastical institutions. Their own social structures were far away from the gender-dominated interactions of the secular middling sort. Could it be that, wittingly or unwittingly, it was the Church that acted to encourage the development of the truly urban housing culture, and in the name of profit to serve other purposes, undermined the deliberately reactionary links between town and country households that we can observe architecturally in the hall, so conspicuously absent from most forms of urban accommodation?

---

[79] Rees Jones, 'The household and English urban government', pp. 71–6; Pamela Hartshorne, 'The street and the perception of public space in York, 1476–1586', unpublished PhD thesis, University of York (2004), particularly Chapters 2.3 and 3.2.

[80] But see Goldberg, *Medieval England*, pp. 107–13; Carlin, 'Fast food and urban living standards'.

[81] Rodney Hilton, 'Some problems of urban real property in the Middle Ages', in *Class conflict and the crisis of feudalism*, revised 2nd edn (London: Verso, 1990), pp. 92–101.

[82] Keene, 'Landlords, the property market and urban development'.

In the development of the medieval town, the forces of conservatism were continuously pitched against the spirit of entrepreneurship. Material culture was used to signal these tensions in the ways described in the second section of this chapter: it reinforced the social *status quo* in the houses of merchants and artisans whose households contained those migrant servants from the rural hinterland, retaining a central open hall whose direct economic value in the town must have been marginal or even negative, but which enhanced the critical maintenance of social control. That control was sacrificed by institutional landlords in the housing of the new underclass of urban poor in rooming houses with no communal space. It may be significant that the merchant class did not invest heavily in this form of income – perhaps as much for ideological as economic reasons? The consequences of extreme wealth in close proximity to appalling poverty, both mediated by agents of exploitation that included not only the mercantile class but also the ecclesiastical institutions, create a tension in medieval towns that is apparent to the researcher and, with some help to tease it out, actually visible to the casual visitor to the modern city in the architecture, which is indeed explicitly urban. But that urban architecture, like the more nebulous urban culture with which we began, is constantly mediated and reformed by its rural context, and the study of the two together is illuminating and rewarding.[83]

---

[83] Many of the arguments I have presented in this chapter are congruent with those of Sarah Rees Jones in 'Women's influence' and 'The household and English urban government'. An interesting footnote to the methodological debate on interdisciplinarity is to note that we have arrived at broadly similar conclusions via different thought processes, using different theoretical approaches and – although our evidence base inevitably overlaps – taking our primary arguments from our own disciplinary areas of economic and social history and of archaeology. I would argue that the intrinsic likelihood that our conclusions are correct is enhanced by this.

6   The fashioning of bourgeois domesticity in later medieval England: a material culture perspective

P. J. P. Goldberg

The chapter that follows is predicated on the notion that peasant and bourgeois societies were characterised by different value systems and that these will be reflected in their material culture.[1] In order to explore this in respect of houses and household furnishings, I have drawn upon a collection of inventories, a source well known to early modern scholars, but somewhat neglected by medievalists, not least because of their comparative paucity.[2] Most of the 102 probate inventories in my sample were drawn up *post-mortem*, but nineteen from Lynn, probably dating to 1291–2, represent tax assessments.[3] A few others are also life-time inventories, for example that associated with the London merchant, Richard Lyons, whose estate was seized by the crown in 1376 and whose inventory can consequently be found in the National Archives.[4]

---

[1]   For a useful discussion of different patterns of consumption between peasants and towns-folk see C. Dyer, *Standards of living in the later Middle Ages: social change in England, c. 1200–1520* (Cambridge University Press, 1989), chapters 6 and 7.

[2]   Literature focusing on medieval probate inventories appears slight, but we may notice A. R. Myers, 'The wealth of Richard Lyons', in T. A. Sandquist and M. R. Powicke (eds.), *Essays in medieval history presented to Bertie Wilkinson* (Toronto: University of Toronto Press, 1969), pp. 301–29; J.-S. Deregnaucourt, 'L'inventaire après décès d'Ysabel Malet, bourgeoise douaisianne, en 1369: document pour server à l'histoire de la vie quotidienne de la bourgeoisie médiévale', *Revue du Nord* 64 (1982), 707–29. These are editions and discussions of one document rather than more ambitious studies. Richard Lyons's inventory is used in this present study. As will become apparent from the discussion that follows, it is noteworthy that the bourgeoise Ysabel Malet possessed numbers of cushions and significant amounts of silverware: Deregnaucourt, 'L'inventaire après décès d'Ysabel Malet', 708, 715–16. More ambitious, but focused on sixteenth-century Verona, is A. A. Smith, 'Gender, ownership and domestic space: inventories and family archives in Renaissance Verona', *Renaissance Studies* 12 (1998), 375–91. Smith notes that textiles and small decorative objects tended particularly to be owned by women (pp. 380–1).

[3]   The date of the Lynn assessments is not known for certain. I have followed arguments cogently put to me in a personal communication by John Hadwin for associating the Lynn material with the 1290 subsidy (hence the date 1291–2). I am indebted to Dr Hadwin for his advice on this and related matters. The individual inventories used in this chapter are all referenced in Table 6.1.

[4]   Myers, 'The wealth of Richard Lyons', pp. 301, 306–7.

The greater part of the sample represents urban households: sixty-six inventories relate to Beverley, Exeter, London, Lynn, Nottingham, Scarborough, Southampton, and York; a further five (and probably six) relate to the small market town of Northallerton. Thirty-one or thirty-two inventories, largely from the diocese of York, are specifically rural. This last group includes four early-sixteenth-century Nottinghamshire inventories. The remainder of the sample is dated before 1500. The majority belong to the fifteenth century though, as already noticed, Lynn provides a number of late-thirteenth-century inventories. In addition, there are peasant inventories dated 1293, 1329 and 1349–52, while several further fourteenth-century inventories pertain to Londoners and one to an Exeter woman. With three exceptions, I have consciously excluded from the sample both aristocratic inventories and clerical inventories, despite their comparatively good survival. The exceptions, which constitute comparative benchmarks, are Thomas Calstan, the builder of Bewley Court in Wiltshire; Roger de Kyrkby, the comparatively prosperous perpetual vicar of Gainsforth in County Durham; and William de Kexby, the precentor of York Minster.

In order to investigate possible patterns distinguishing rural and urban inventories which are not simply products of the very different levels of wealth found within the sample as a whole, I have focused on a small number of indicators. The first two comprise the numbers of cushions and (invariably silver) spoons recorded in each inventory. (The significance of these items will be more fully discussed in a later part of this chapter.) The next two indicators are measures of the proportion of the total value of household goods comprised firstly of beds and associated bedding (or sometimes solely bedding) and secondly of kitchen utensils or, where so distinguished, the contents of the kitchen.[5] The final two indicators are the proportion of the total assessed value of goods within each inventory, including cash but excluding debts owed or owing, that could be classed as belonging within the house proper – here labelled 'household' goods – and the equivalent proportion associated variously with stable, workshop, ship or fields, here labelled 'outside'.[6] This last distinction is of course a

---

[5] Beds are not always noticed, but bedding in the form of sheets, coverlets, pillows etc. invariably is. Mark Overton is critical of using the assessed values of specific items against the total valuation, 'not least because of the uncertain relationship between expenditure on consumption and the value of material goods in the inventory': Mark Overton *et al.*, *Production and consumption in English households, 1600–1750* (London: Routledge, 2004), p. 89. Overton's concern is justifiable, but my intention is to use these measures as no more than suggestive indicators.

[6] Numbers of inventories provide details of debts owed and owing in respect of the deceased's estate. This information, valuable though it is for establishing social and trading networks or for evaluating a person's wider economic standing, is marginal to our present purposes and so has been discounted from the present analysis.

little arbitrary, although it borrows a terminology used for example in some early sixteenth-century Nottinghamshire inventories.[7]

It would be possible to discuss at some length the problems inherent in the statistical evidence shortly to be presented, but my aim is not to present precise statistics – a purely illusory objective. Rather it is to suggest certain broader patterns with a view to contextualising them. I shall confine myself, therefore, to a few more important observations. First, the calculation of the value of kitchen utensils is often somewhat subjective, since not all the inventories in the sample distinguished rooms by name and hence differentiated the kitchen from other spaces. This is especially true of the inventories from Lynn dating to around the penultimate decade of the thirteenth century.[8] For a similar reason, it was at times difficult to assign goods under the headings 'household' and 'outside'. Some inventories appear particularly defective in that various supposedly essential household items, such as bedding, are not included; I tended to omit such inventories from the sample. It follows, however, that other inventories that are included here are nevertheless defective and hence misleading in ways that were not so immediately obvious. My rather crude methodology does, however, have one particular merit. Because I am concerned only with relative proportions of assessed values, neither broader changes in the cost of goods over the two centuries or more of the sample nor the likely undervaluation of goods for probate purposes will affect my data.[9] Comparison across time, across differing levels of society and wealth, and between town and country are thus possible.

From the three sets of measures, it is possible to suggest particular patterns that tend to characterise rural and urban inventories respectively. Thus the possession of cushions or silver spoons is, for most of the period observed, an urban phenomenon. Although cushions are not found in the

---

[7] The workshops and stock of merchants and other artisans are in fact likely to have been integral to the structure of the main dwelling house, so 'outside' is here a particularly abstract usage.

[8] It is likely that in numbers of less affluent houses 'the kitchen' did not even constitute a separate room. In a number of instances I have totalled the values of kitchen utensils, usually comprising brass pots, spits etc., which tend to be listed in close proximity within the inventory. This is, however, a necessarily crude measure.

[9] A measure of price inflation over the period is provided by the Phelps Brown and Hopkins index for a changing basket of consumables, though grain prices are the major influence. The index is based on the period 1451–75 (=100). The mean index value at the beginning of our period (1285–90) is 81. This had doubled to 164 by the period coinciding with our two most recent inventories (1529–30), though this last reflects comparatively new inflationary trends: E. H. Phelps Brown and Sheila V. Hopkins, 'Seven centuries of the prices of consumables, compared with builders' wage-rates', *Economica* n.s. 23 (1956), 311–12. This can only be a crude indicator; as price inflation varied among goods. Manufactured goods tended to become more expensive after the Black Death due to higher labour costs.

earliest inventories within the sample (those for Lynn in the last years of the thirteenth century) but are found in all four early sixteenth-century rural Nottinghamshire inventories, cushions would appear to be a predominantly urban phenomenon from at least the third decade of the fourteenth century until the second half of the fifteenth century.[10] Lucy de Collecote of Exeter, an apothecary's widow (d. 1324), possessed cushions, as did Hugh le Bevere of London thirteen years later.[11] The widow Katherine North of York (d. 1461), whose entire estate was valued at only 11s 8d, still owned four cushions, but William Litster of Wilton (d. 1417), who possessed household goods valued at nearly £6 and farm stock worth a further £11 or more, possessed neither cushions nor spoons. Silver spoons would appear already to be a marker of bourgeois identity by the later thirteenth century since all bar five of the nineteen Lynn inventories sampled here itemise them, though silver spoons probably also served as an indicator of wealth, since the Lynn inventories that fail to list spoons tend also to contain comparatively modest assets. A still more striking observation is that silver spoons are recorded in only one rural inventory within the entire sample.[12] In contrast silver spoons can be found in inventories pertaining to even quite modest urban households. For example, a set of six silver spoons is itemised in the inventory of the York shoemaker William Coltman (d. 1486), whose estate was valued at less than £8.

The second measure of the relative value of beds and kitchen utensils yielded slightly less sharply focused results, but these are still indicative of rather different priorities between peasant and bourgeois. The strongest indicator is the relative value of beds, bedding and kitchen utensils (or the contents of kitchens) combined as a proportion of the total assessed value of household items. These two items together represent more than half the entire value of household goods in only eight cases within the urban sample. Conversely they represent less than half the value in only six of the admittedly rather smaller proportion of rural cases.[13] It could be

---

[10] Seventeenth-century probate inventories for Kent suggest that by that period cushions were a comparatively common item of furnishing, though this was not true of the much less prosperous county of Cornwall: Overton et al., Production and consumption, table 5.1, p. 91. Overton's analysis does not distinguish urban from rural patterns.

[11] I owe identification of Lucy de Coldecote's status to Maryanne Kowaleski.

[12] I have excluded Roger de Kyrkby, the perpetual vicar of Gainsford, Co. Durham, and Thomas Calstan of Bewley Court from this rural sample. Kyrkby's spoons are noticed in his will, but not in his inventory. The exception is the 1451 inventory of Thomas Vicars of Strensall (near York). Vicars was a man of considerable wealth and should perhaps be classified as gentry rather than peasant.

[13] I have again excluded Roger de Kyrkby and Thomas Calstan of Bewley Court from this rural sample.

argued that since a significant number of the rural inventories were associated with estates that also comprised grain, livestock and farm equipment valued at two, three or even four times the value of the household goods, the values of beds and kitchen utensils as a proportion of the entire estate would be markedly lower. On that basis the rural and urban proportions would probably look rather more alike, but this is to miss the underlying point already suggested by my observations regarding cushions and spoons, namely that bourgeois homes tended to contain a wider range of furnishings – chairs, benches, chests, wall hangings and screens as well as eating utensils, bed linen and the like – than was true of their peasant counterparts and that this was not a simple product of relative wealth. The higher proportion of household assets vested in such essentials as beds and cooking utensils is surely indicative of a rather different system of values.

Peasant householders may have tended to invest primarily in household essentials compared to the more liberal spending of their bourgeois counterparts, but we need to ask if priorities, even between the essentials associated with sleeping and of eating, also differed by measuring the relative proportion of household assets associated with beds and bedding compared to those of the kitchen or kitchen utensils. This comparison is immediately problematic for those inventories that fail to distinguish rooms. There will be a tendency for valuations based on identified 'kitchen utensils', mostly cooking pots, to be too small, since kitchen inventories regularly comprise additional items such as cupboards and vessels that cannot otherwise be specifically assigned. On the other hand some wealthier households had brewhouses, pantries and the like itemised separately from the kitchen. Any conclusions must consequently be treated with circumspection, but the pattern that emerges seems clear enough. Peasant inventories suggest that rather more was invested proportionately in the needs of cooking than those of sleeping, whereas the reverse was true of bourgeois and mercantile households. There are only ten cases where urban probate inventories show rather more being invested in kitchen equipment than in beds and bedding. Of these, one is the case of John Gaythird whose designation of husbandman more properly identifies him as peasant than his residence in York. Three others are associated with the small market town of Northallerton.[14] In the case of rural persons, only six inventories show significantly more investment in beds than cooking

---

[14] For a useful account of this small episcopal town, the caput of the larger Liberty of Allertonshire, see Christine M. Newman, *Late medieval Northallerton* (Stamford: Shaun Tyas, 1999).

utensils.[15] Of these, two relate to the sample of four early-sixteenth-century probate inventories from Nottinghamshire.

The final measure is of the proportion of the total estate (excluding debts) associated with 'household' and 'outside' items respectively. Here it is possible to discern three different patterns. The characteristic 'peasant' pattern is for the 'household' part of the inventory to account for only a minority of the total value. This, for example, is true of the earliest peasant inventory in the sample, that of Reginald Labbe dated 1293.[16] Frequently it is found that 'household' possessions account for only a quarter or rather less of all goods accounted for. Thus William Atkynson (d. 1456), a husbandman of Helperby (Yorks., N.R.), possessed livestock worth well over £4 and grain valued at over £3, but household goods worth less than £2. The same peasant characteristics are found two years later in the case of John Crosby a few miles away at Tollerton. He possessed a crop of rye, a plough and four horses. His farming assets came to £1 9s, but his household goods were valued at only 6s 1d or about a sixth of the total. In only a couple of instances do peasant households depart from this model. John Scot of Acomb (d. 1456) and Emma Cowper of Dunnington (d. 1461) possessed 'out-side' assets worth only 38.3 and 44 per cent of their respective estates.[17] Scot owned a cow, a pig and some grain. Cowper had only a cow and three hens. Both Acomb and Dunnington were villages within easy walking distance of York. These then were smallholders rather than more substantial husbandmen who may even, as in the case of Emma Cowper whose modest possessions included a citole, have supplemented their livelihood in the city.[18]

To this peasant model it is possible to annex the case of the mariner Brian Sampall (d. 1479). He owned livestock and grain to the value of nearly £7, but his household goods were worth only £1. Implicitly his family livelihood depended, as did livelihoods in the nineteenth-century Danish island community of Fanø, on his seafaring coupled with peasant agriculture under his wife's supervision.[19] Both William

---

[15] Kyrkby and Calstan are excluded from the sample as before.

[16] T. H. Turner, 'Original documents: inventory of the effects of Reginald Labbe, d. 1293', *Archaeological Journal* 3 (1846), 65–6.

[17] The same is also true of Richard Sclatter of Elmley Castle, but his inventory lists neither livestock nor grain.

[18] A citole is a medieval stringed instrument, played by plucking the strings, and often associated with minstrels. It appears that the instrument was fast falling out of fashion by this date: Paul Butler, 'The citole project' www.crab.rutgers.edu/~pbutler/citole.html, site accessed 26 September 2005.

[19] This speculative observation cannot of course be substantiated by the probate inventory. For a brief discussion of women's by-employment in the fishing industry see Maryanne

Eryame and John Gaythird, husbandmen of Northallerton and York respectively, conform to this peasant model despite their urban locales. The peasant model is, however, specific to that level of society. It is not a general rural phenomenon. Neither Roger de Kyrkby nor Thomas Calstan, whose inventory is dated 1405, follow this model, both having much higher proportions of their wealth invested indoors than out.

Another pattern may be described as a bourgeois model. Here the great majority of goods can be classified as 'household'. Thus Robert Schylbotyll of Scarborough (d. 1416), whose inventory records considerable quantities of salt and wood in addition to two cows and a horse, nevertheless had the bulk of his property – over four-fifths – in household goods. The York weaver Thomas Catton (d. 1413) likewise possessed goods worth little more than £2 in his workshop, but nearly £31 within the main body of the house.

It could be argued that these differences are in part an artificial consequence of the urban consumer's greater dependence on goods purchased in the market place compared to the comparatively greater self-reliance of their rural cousins – hence inflating the value of possessions owned by townsfolk – but also of the tendency of urban appraisers to value household goods more highly (and perhaps more carefully) whereas rural appraisers would have a sharper eye for livestock and agricultural utensils. This may indeed be the case, but it serves to reinforce rather than to undermine the argument here: bourgeois society placed greater value (culturally and economically) on household goods whereas peasant society prioritised land, livestock and the working tools these required.

The third pattern observed I have dubbed a 'mercantile' model. This mirrors the peasant model in that much more is invested outside the 'household' than within, but otherwise follows the bourgeois pattern in that greater investment is made in beds and bedding than kitchens or kitchen utensils and these collectively account for a comparatively modest part of the total value invested in household goods. I would therefore suggest that the mercantile and bourgeois models can be seen as related. At one extreme is the fantastically wealthy Richard Lyons of London, whose richly furnished house in 1376 accounted for only a fraction of his

Kowaleski, 'The expansion of the south-western fisheries in late medieval England', *Economic History Review* 2nd series, 53 (2000), 446–7. For the more orthodox anthropological position on the sexual division of labour see P. Thompson, 'Women in the fishing: the roots of power between the sexes', *Comparative Study of Society and History* 27 (1985), 3–32; Dona L. Davis and J. Nadel-Klein, 'Gender, culture and the sea: contemporary theoretical perspectives', *Society and Natural Resources* 5 (1992), 135–47; R. B. Pollnac, 'The division of labor by sex in fishing communities', *Anthropology Working Paper* 44, International Center for Marine Resources Development, University of Rhode Island (1984). I am indebted to Maryanne Kowaleski for these references.

assessed wealth. Much more modest is the inventory of the York girdler Robert Tankard (d. 1439). Here the goods of the workshop accounted for fractionally over £3, but those in the remainder of the house for a little over £2. If a horse valued at 6s 8d is added into the calculation, then the proportion of 'outside' goods is 61.5 per cent. Numbers of wealthy Lynn merchants assessed for taxation in the late thirteenth century and whose stock variously comprised large quantities of herring, iron, timber, wool and wine likewise demonstrate this mercantile pattern.

The findings thus uphold the broad hypothesis that peasant and bourgeois patterns of consumption would differ. In fact the data suggest a further refinement in distinguishing a mercantile pattern from a more general bourgeois pattern. The particular cases of Roger de Kyrkby, the prosperous perpetual vicar, or William de Kexby, the precentor of the cathedral church of York, are akin to that of Thomas Calstan, the wealthy builder of Bewley Court, and probably represent a 'gentry' pattern.[20] Kyrkby's example is particularly striking, as it stands out from most of the other rural inventories in the sample using each of the four measures adopted: the vicar possessed both cushions and silver spoons; less than a tenth of the value of his household goods were represented by his beds, bedding and the contents of his kitchen; somewhat greater value was invested in beds than in cooking utensils; only a comparatively small proportion of his total assessed wealth lay outside the main house in his stable and granary.

Only a few other inventories display aberrant results from those that might be predicted on the basis of location, and in most instances only one of the three measures is aberrant. Thus the York brewer William Coltman (d. 1481) had more than 60 per cent of his household goods in the form of beds and, more conspicuously, kitchen utensils. The likelihood is, however, that his brewing business spilt over into his kitchen and that the measures consequently need revising. Robert Oldman, the reeve of Cuxham, invested to an unusual degree in clothing, so reducing significantly the relative proportion of household expenditure invested in bedding and kitchen utensils. He also invested somewhat more in sheets than in cooking pots. In a few instances, notably in the case of the later-thirteenth-century Lynn tax inventories, neither cushions nor spoons are noted within an urban context, though the Lynn evidence relates to a

---

[20] The 1488 inventory of Thomas Crayke of Beverley 'gentelman', for example, follows the pattern of listing silver spoons (39) and cushions (12). Beds, bedding and the contents of the kitchen account for only a small proportion of the total value of household goods, but beds and bedding are collectively worth more than items associated with the kitchen. The greater part of his estate is accounted for by household goods.

period before cushions appear to have been fashionable. Northallerton tends largely to correspond to the bourgeois model, but with some suggestions of a more mixed economy. John Smyth (d. 1499) fits the model in all respects despite having goods valued at a mere 18s 5d. However, the smith, John Stevynson (d. 1498), had nearly half his assets in the 'outside' category, over 40 cent being invested in agriculture. He also spent more on his kitchen than on his beds. James Lune (d. 1486), the owner of a dozen cushions and half a dozen silver spoons, nevertheless had some 56 per cent of the value of his goods in grain and livestock. He too had invested more in his kitchen than his beds.

The choice of cushions and silver spoons to constitute one of my three sets of measures is informed by a sense of the cultural meaning attached to these items. Cushions noted in inventories invariably come as parts of (presumably) matching sets, usually of three, four, six or twelve.[21] Quite often they are associated with an item known as a 'banker', a fabric covering or hanging. Thus Robert Talkan, a York girdler, possessed two sets each comprising dorsers (chair covers), costers (wall hangings), bankers, and (ten) cushions; the first set was of tapestry work, the second of red and blue. Cushions are thus an integral part of the décor of a room.[22] The inventory evidence suggests that they may have been found both in halls and in chambers, though the tendency is for most cushions to be confined to halls; only in more prosperous households are they located additionally in chambers.[23] Numbers of cushions represent a crude barometer of wealth. At one extreme is the phenomenally wealthy London merchant Richard Lyons, whose house boasted thirty-nine cushions between the hall and various chambers in 1376.[24] At the other, more than a century later, is Thomas Arkyndall of Allertonshire, whose total possessions both

---

[21] Cushions appear to have been specifically bequeathed in non-aristocratic wills only infrequently, but Maud Hyde (d. 1445) of the Suffolk cloth town of Sudbury left six cushions among various named furnishings to her son: P. Northeast (ed.), *Wills of the archdeaconry of Sudbury 1439–1474: wills from the register 'Baldwyne', Part I: 1439–1474,* Suffolk Records Society vol. 44 (Woodbridge, 2001), p. 161.

[22] Schofield, *Medieval London houses,* p. 132.

[23] For example John Cottom, mason, of York had four cushions (valued at 2d) in his hall and Robert Fawcette, pewterer, also of York, had six old cushions (valued at 1s) in his hall, but no further cushions are recorded in either case. The rather wealthier Beverley mason John Cadeby possessed a total of 15 cushions and these were as much associated with the bed chamber as the hall. The London draper Richard Toky had a large number of cushions in his hall, but he had a further two (valued at 2s) in his chamber.

[24] The inventory of Ysabel Malet of Douai (d. 1359) lists seventy-two cushions, a clear reflection of her considerable wealth, but possibly also of the greater material sophistication of the Low Countries: Deregnaucourt, 'L'inventaire après décès d'Ysabel Malet', 715–6.

farm and household were valued at little more than £1, but still included two cushions.

Arkyndall's inventory is significant as an indicator that the hitherto essentially bourgeois and aristocratic fashion for cushions had by the end of the fifteenth century been adopted within peasant society.[25] As already noticed, all four early sixteenth-century Nottinghamshire inventories within the sample mention cushions. Lyons's inventory and those of other fourteenth-century London merchants suggest, however, that cushions were then still as much a status symbol as a required item of furnishing. The cushion denoted wealth and leisure, itself in some ways a marker of wealth. Two texts from around the very end of the fourteenth century reflect this point. In Chaucer's *Troilus and Criseyde*, Criseyde, situated at the pinnacle of Trojan society, is described at one point sitting down 'upon a quysshyn gold-ybete'. In contrast, the author of *A Book to a Mother* pointedly observes that around Mary and her Child there were no gay coverlets, testers, curtains or cushions.[26]

Although it is implicit from inventories that cushions associated with chambers were probably part of the fittings of beds – alongside the coverlets, testers and curtains lacking at Christ's nativity – this is only really made explicit in wills. Thus early in the fifteenth century, Margaret de Courtnay left her son and daughter, respectively, sets of silk and damask cushions that were part of the furnishing of beds. A couple of decades later, John Stourton, another Somerset aristocrat, bequeathed his nephew various items for his chapel. These included, beside a psalter, vestments and a chalice, three cushions of silk.[27] It may be that these last were intended either for those kneeling at their devotions or to rest liturgical books upon. The resonances between these two examples go beyond simply wealth and leisure. They also encompass intimacy and the holy. I have elsewhere argued that both these qualities are in fact implicit in the bed and its fittings, but the example of the chapel cushions reinforces the point. In short, the distance between the domestic and the holy within bourgeois culture appears not to have been that great: their homes contained religious images and painted hangings and their parish churches were filled with material objects that had formerly functioned for domestic

---

[25] Arkyndall is described as 'of Allertonshire', a region rather than a specific location, but the assets associated with farming confirm his essentially rural and peasant identity.

[26] Geoffrey Chaucer, *Troilus and Criseyde*, in *The Riverside Chaucer*, ed. Benson, book 2, line 1129; McCarthy (ed.), *A book to a mother*, p. 49, l. 17. Nicholas Love likewise describes how Christ sat 'on the bare grounde, for there had he neither banker ne kuschyne': *The Mirrour of the Blessed Lyf of Jesu Christ*, ed. L. F. Powell (Oxford University Press, 1908), p. 98.

[27] F. W. Weaver (ed.), *Somerset medieval wills (1383–1500)*, vol. 1, Somerset Record Society 16 (London, 1901), pp. 50–1, 144.

use, whether wedding rings placed on images of St Anne, clothing given to make vestments or, to cite one particularly resonant bequest, a bed made over to the parish church to serve as an Easter sepulchre.[28]

Spoons are tangentially associated with the holy through their liturgical uses and, in some instances, their design, but are perhaps more immediately a symbol of status and wealth. Silver spoons are, for example, carefully shown on Sir Geoffrey Luttrell's high table in his famous psalter, a representation consciously modelled in the Last Supper.[29] John Olyver, a London draper, whose wealth in 1406 exceeded even that of Richard Lyons thirty years earlier, possessed five dozen silver spoons. (That only two appear in the Lyons inventory suggests that someone pocketed them from the disgraced merchant's home.) Any reading of wills readily demonstrates that silver spoons could possess something of the quality of an heirloom to be specifically bequeathed,[30] a perspective reinforced by the example of the four extant spoons originally given by Richard Whittington to his college and engraved with his arms. These spoons were comparatively plain in design, having only a 'knop' at the end, but from the end of the fourteenth century maidenhead spoons, supposedly symbolic of the Virgin, and by the later fifteenth century apostle spoons, headed by representations of Christ and his apostles, come to be found.[31]

[28] Borthwick Institute, Prob. Reg. 2 fol. 52v (Gateshed). See also P. J. P. Goldberg, 'Women in fifteenth-century town life', in J. A. F. Thomson (ed.), *Towns and townspeople in the fifteenth century* (Stroud: Sutton, 1988), p. 110. I discussed the cultural significance of beds in a paper given at the International Federation for Research in Women's History Conference, Belfast, August 2003 and hope to publish a version of this paper in due course. For a similar argument in respect of nuns see Marilyn Oliva, 'Nuns at home: the domesticity of sacred space', this volume.

[29] BL, MS Add. 43120, fol. 208v; Emmerson and Goldberg, '"The Lord Geoffrey had me made"', pp. 52–3.

[30] John Archer (d. 1452) of Lavenham, another Suffolk cloth town, bequeathed sets of six silver spoons to his widow, each of his two daughters and the wife of his cousin. His bequests to his son and his (male) cousin significantly do not include spoons. Although this example of gender-specific giving is probably unusual, it is tempting to suggest that the family spoons were bestowed here not strictly as heirlooms, but rather as mementos that would help women connected to the family and to John to preserve the memory of the same. A perusal of other mid-fifteenth-century wills from the Sudbury Archdeaconry provides a few other examples where women were preferred recipients of spoons (see the wills of John Waryn, sen., of Long Melford; John Howlot, sen., of Barnham; Joan Herberd of Yaxley; John Ponder of Waldingfield), though in other instances spoons were divided equally among all surviving children (see the wills of Robert Lister of Long Melford and John Fabbe, sen., of Burwell). This sample would also suggest that in this prosperous textile region, the ownership of silver spoons, though more conspicuous in urban wills, was beginning to spread into the countryside: Northeast, *Wills of the archdeaconry of Sudbury*, pp. 20, 33, 48, 143, 171, 184, 220, 228, 250, 268, 289, 330, 367, 381, 385, 392, 402, 438, 442, 444, 451, 509.

[31] Birmingham City Museum and Gallery has four maidenhead spoons dating from the first half of the fifteenth century (547'35 – 476, 515, 516, 518). An early extant example of an apostle spoon, hallmarked to London in 1504–5, is Boston Museum of Fine Art, Wilbour

Spoons thus served a variety of functions. They were conspicuous markers of wealth, but in common with other plate, they were also a form of savings, since plate could readily be converted to cash if need be. They symbolised good breeding reflected in good table manners, but implicitly for a level of society where eating within the home presented an opportunity for the household to perform and so demonstrate status and breeding.[32] Their liturgical resonances and the devotional references inherent in some designs take these implements beyond the purely mundane. Rather they come to embody distinctive cultural values that go some way to explain their presence in a good proportion of the artisanal and mercantile households in the sample, but in none of the peasant households in the sample.

The broader hypothesis, confirmed by the inventory evidence, that peasantry and bourgeoisie manifested essentially different value systems is strengthened by this closer consideration of cushions and spoons. Peasant priorities tended to lie outside the house as a domestic space. Though money might be invested in brewing utensils, it was farm equipment, grain and livestock that accounted for the most value. The house as a domestic space may have provided primarily for sleeping, for meal times, and for various supplementary economic activities such as brewing, spinning, carding, preparing flax. For at least the earlier part of the period it was even common for peasant houses to be shared with livestock.[33] Within peasant society much recreational activity, such as football and archery, was focused outdoors or at the alehouse.

The bourgeois house was likewise a place for eating, sleeping and supplementary economic activity, but these were not its sole functions. For artisans with their workshops and merchants with their stock and their counting houses, the home tended also to be the principal locus of *all* economic activity associated with the household. Place of residence and place of work essentially coincided. The house as a living and working

49.1710. For Whittington's spoons see Richard Marks and Paul Williamson (eds.), *Gothic: art for England 1400–1547* (London: Victoria and Albert Museum, 2003), pp. 276–7.

[32] This is reflected in the number of later medieval texts, such as 'The lytylle childrenes lytil boke' or 'Stans puer ad mensam', designed to instruct boys in etiquette and the art of waiting at table. Although ostensibly aristocratic in tone, these texts come to be found in mercantile manuscript collections and should perhaps be understood as essentially aspirational. See Nicholas Orme, *From childhood to chivalry: the education of the English kings and aristocracy, 1066–1530* (London: Methuen, 1984), pp. 136–9; Mertes, *The English noble household*, pp. 174–5, 179–80; Claire Sponsler, 'Eating lessons: Lydgate's "dietary" and consumer conduct', in Kathleen Ashley and Robert L. A. Clark (eds.), *Medieval conduct* (Minneapolis: University of Minnesota Press, 2001), pp. 1–22.

[33] J. Chapelot and Robert Fossier, *The village and house in the Middle Ages* (Berkeley: University of California Press, 1985), pp. 223–8; Dyer, *Standards of living*, p. 163; Grenville, *Medieval housing*, pp. 134–41.

environment was thus used continuously throughout the day and night. The bourgeois house also differed from its peasant counterpart in that it accommodated not just close kin, but other unrelated persons employed as servants (including apprentices) and journeymen. Though journeymen would only be present during working hours (but presumably including some meal times), servants were invariably unmarried adolescents of both sexes who lived in.

This last observation may help explain two related phenomena reflected in the inventory evidence, but equally apparent from other sources. The first is the tendency for bourgeois housing stock to comprise a greater diversity of living accommodation, particularly in terms of plural numbers of chambers, at least from the later fourteenth century.[34] This in part must have been a simple corollary of the need to house servants alongside the nuclear family, but also perhaps a desire to provide separate sleeping places for kin and non-kin, and a product of the need to separate unrelated adolescent males and females. The second is the increasing level of privacy allowed in particular to the master and mistress of the household, sometimes by the provision of separate chambers, but also by the fashion for bed curtains and screens.

The desire for greater privacy and to create intimate space within the bourgeois house must also be related to the relative permeability of houses that also functioned as the site of manufacture and trade, which received other folk's children as live-in servants, and received visitors as guests so as to consolidate friendship networks, business contacts or the household's social standing.[35] This again differs from the apparently much less permeable peasant house, which probably discouraged visitors other than immediate kin; no doubt it goes some way towards explaining the greater proportionate investment in household furnishings on the part of the bourgeoisie.[36] To this I wish to add one further crucial consideration.

---

[34] Dyer, *Standards of living*, pp. 202–4; Quiney, *Town houses of medieval Britain*, p. 237.

[35] The relationship between friendship and business networks is well illustrated by an early-fifteenth-century breach of faith case from York. Margaret Harman and her husband were invited to dinner and eat within the summerhall (otherwise parlour) of Robert Lascelles's house. Margaret and Robert were clearly business partners, but the case arose when the relationship turned sour: York, Borthwick Institute, cause papers, CP.F.174. The pertinent depositions are translated in P. J. P. Goldberg (ed.), *Women in England c. 1275–1525: documentary sources* (Manchester University Press, 1995), pp. 239–43. For live-in servants see Goldberg, *Women, work and life cycle*, ch. 4; P. J. P. Goldberg, 'Masters and men in later medieval England', in Dawn M. Hadley (ed.), *Masculinity in medieval Europe* (London: Longmans, 1999), pp. 56–70.

[36] Individual peasant dwellings appear to have been surrounded by banks, ditches, walls or hedges which may have served as a 'defence against human interference': Astill, 'Rural settlement: the toft and the croft', pp. 53–4.

Though the labour of wives (and other female members of the household) was essential to the functioning of both peasant and bourgeois household economies, there is reason to suspect that a marked gender division of labour effectively marginalised peasant wives. Women were, for example, debarred from such essential agrarian activities as ploughing, mowing and carting, but are associated with dairying, caring for poultry, brewing and spinning. This division of labour is given normative authority in the late fifteenth-century 'Ballad of a Tyrannical Husband'.[37] Bourgeois wives, in contrast, regularly assisted their husbands in the workshop, and were probably more directly involved in the market economy, whether selling the products of the shared workshop, engaged in commercial brewing or processing woollen yarn.[38] This, I suggest, gave them a more significant voice than their rural sisters in deciding priorities within the household budget.[39] Whereas expenditure on the hall and the parlour or summerhall,[40] the more public areas of the house, were probably as much priorities of the husband as the wife, expenditure on the chamber or, where there

---

[37] So far as these tasks were undertaken for wages, ploughing, mowing and carting commanded significantly higher levels of remuneration than dairying or spinning. 'The ballad of a tyrannical husband' (the title provided by its nineteenth-century editors) is published in Eve Salisbury (ed.), *The trials and joys of marriage* (Kalamazoo, MI: Medieval Institute Publications, 2002) and on-line at www.lib.rochester.edu/camelot/teams/thfrm.htm, site accessed 27 September 2005. There is a considerable literature on women and work in this period. An invaluable recent survey is Marjorie K. McIntosh, *Working women in English society, 1300–1620* (Cambridge University Press, 2005).

[38] See Goldberg, *Women, work and life cycle*, chapter 3.

[39] See Rees Jones, 'Women's influence on the design of urban houses', pp. 209–10. For a recent discussion of greater aristocratic artistic patronage by wives as well as widows see Loveday Lewes Gee, *Women, art and patronage from Henry III to Edward III: 1216–1377* (Woodbridge: Boydell, 2002).

[40] The root of the term *parlour* relates to speech, hence the parlour was a room that facilitated private conversation. Literary sources suggest the parlour functioned as a more intimate version of the hall. Langland, for example, writes:

> Elenge is the halle, ech day in the wike,
> Ther the lord ne the lady liketh noght to sitte.
> Now hath ech riche a rule – to eten by hymselve
> In a pryvee parlour for povere mennes sake,
>   (William Langland, *The vision of Piers Plowman: a critical edition of the B-text*, ed. A. V. C. Schmidt (London: Dent, 1978), passus 10, ll. 79–83.)

This understanding tends to be reinforced by Shannon McSheffrey's finding that the parlour sometimes served as an alternative venue to the hall for the witnessing of marriage contracts: McSheffrey, *Marriage, sex, and civic culture in late medieval London*, pp. 124–5. Matthew Johnson, however, in his study of the rural housing stock of a slightly later era, sees the later sixteenth-century parlour as essentially a lower-level bed chamber. By the later seventeenth century it had become usual to find parlours without beds, but with chairs, tables and stools, creating a more intimate space for entertainment: Johnson, *Housing culture*, pp. 123–8. A preliminary perusal of later medieval probate inventories

were plural chambers, the principal chamber represents investment in the most intimate space within the house. My tentative suggestion is that this represents the wife's priority and that the chamber – or even the bed itself – can also be seen to represent space particularly associated with the wife.[41] It was here that she could engage in private devotion, but it was perhaps here also, rather than in the more formal and public spaces of the hall or parlour, that she could entertain close female friends and relations. It was the nearest thing to a room of her own.

suggests a more complex picture: parlours may contain beds, but they may also contain seating and decorative hangings; several contain weapons and most appear to have been used at least in part for storage, a pattern that is often true of less used rooms. See also Schofield, *Medieval London houses*, pp. 66–7; Overton *et al.*, *Production and consumption*, pp. 131–3; and note 31 above.

[41] I have developed these ideas more fully elsewhere. See note 28 above.

Table 6.1 *Analysis of a sample of urban and rural inventories*

Name	Place/occupation	Date	1. No. of cushions	2. No. of spoons	3. Value of bedding/beds as % of total value of goods in house	4. Value of kitchen/cooking items as % of total value of goods in house	5. Value of goods in house as % of value of all moveables	6. Value of non-house goods as % of value of all moveables	Source
(a) URBAN									
1. William de Cranewyz	Lynn	1291–2	–	19	**12.4**	11.0	36.5	**63.5**	*Owen* (ed.), *The making of King's Lynn*, p. 235
2. Simon de Leverington	Lynn	1291–2	–	25	6.3	4.4	**62.0**	38.0	Ibid., pp. 235–6
3. Reginald the Taverner	Lynn taverner	1291–2	–	25	3.0	**6.3**	20.3	**79.7**	Ibid., pp. 236–7
4. Peter Dice	Lynn	1291–2	–	7	**13.0**	7.3	**55.7**	44.3	Ibid., p. 237
5. John Sterion	Lynn	1291–2	–	4	3.3	**4.5**	**T**		Ibid., pp. 237–8
6. Geoffrey le Franceys	Lynn	1291–2	–	8	**8.1**	6.1	**98.2**	1.8	Ibid., p. 238
7. Robert of London	Lynn	1291–2	–	24	**6.1**	4.4	**76.1**	23.9	Ibid., pp. 238–9
8. Robert le Barbur	Lynn barber	1291–2	–	–	12.7	**47.2**	**T**		Ibid., p. 239
9. Thomas de Weynflet	Lynn	1291–2	–	6	5.3	**10.1**	**67.4**	32.6	Ibid., pp. 239–40
10. Walter de Nichole	Lynn	1291–2	–	1	2.5	**3.1**	**68.0**	32.0	Ibid., p. 240
11. Peter de Birche	Lynn	1291–2	–	–	**29.9**	18.3	**T**		Ibid., pp. 240–1
12. John Quitloc	Lynn	1291–2	–	–	7.2	7.2	10.8	**89.2**	Ibid., pp. 241–2
13. Thomas de Holebech	Lynn taverner	1291–2	–	12	**6.4**	3.6	36.3	**63.7**	Ibid., p. 242
14. Hugh le Moygne	Lynn	1291–2	–	21	**8.5**	4.0	33.9	**66.1**	Ibid., pp. 243–4
15. Hugh le Iremonger	Lynn ironmonger	1291–2	–	22	4.0	**15.8**	14.5	**85.8**	Ibid., p. 245
16. Emma, wid. William Burel	Lynn	1291–2	–	9	1.9	2.0	44.2	55.8	Ibid., pp. 245–6
17. Richard le Barbur	Lynn barber	1291–2	–	–	**3.8**	2.4	**T**		Ibid., pp. 246–7
18. Philip de Bekx	Lynn	1291–2	–	x	**8.8**	4.2	15.3	**84.7**	Ibid., pp. 247–8
19. Ralph de Bretham	Lynn	1291–2	–	–	**5.4**	3.9	46.4	**53.6**	Ibid., pp. 248–9

Table 6.1 (*cont.*)

Name	Place/occupation	Date	1. No. of cushions	2. No. of spoons	3. Value of bedding/beds as % of total value of goods in house	4. Value of kitchen/cooking items as % of total value of goods in house	5. Value of goods in house as % of value of all moveables	6. Value of non-house goods as % of value of all moveables	Source
20. Richard de Blountesham	London citizen	1317	–	–	*	*	*		Riley (ed.), *Memorials*, pp. 123–5
21. Lucy de Collecote	Exeter	1324	4	8	7.6	8.1	**73.6**	26.4	Lépine and Orme (eds.), *Death and memory*, pp. 167–70
22. Hugh le Bevere	London	1337	5	–	13.7	13.8	**T**		Riley (ed.), *Memorials*, pp. 199–200
23. John Horne	Scarborough	1350	6	–	5.3	**6.0**	**T**		Stell, *Probate inventories*, p. 493
24. Thomas Kynebell[1]	London rector	1368	36	–	*	*	T		Thomas (ed.), *Cal. plea and mem. 1364–81*, pp. 91–2
25. Thomas Mockyng	London fishmonger	1373	11	12	**13.9**	11.3	16.3	**83.7**	Ibid., pp. 154–6
26. Emma Hatfield	London	1373	x	–	**[26.5]**	[13.5]	**54.2**	45.8	Ibid., pp. 158–9
27. Richard Lyons[2]	London merchant	1376	39	2	**8.7**	4.2	8.4	**91.6**	TNA, E 199/25/70; Myers, 'The wealth', 307–29
28. John de Hallam	Nottingham married clerk	1390	–	–	**15.4**	9.4+	T		Stephenson (ed.), *Records of Nottingham*, vol. 1, pp. 244–7
29. Henry de Whitley	Nottingham	1393	4	–	**49.1**	10.8	T		Ibid., pp. 252–5
30. Richard Toky	London draper	1393	19	13	**12.8**	6.1	**80.8**	19.2	Thomas (ed.), *Cal. plea and mem. 1381–1412*, pp. 209–13
31. Robert de Crakall	York mason	1395	6	12	3.9	**4.0**	**96.1**	3.9	Stell, *Probate inventories*, pp. 493–6
32. Simon Lastyngham	York clerk	1399	–	8	*	–	**T**		Ibid., pp. 496–7
33. Geoffrey Couper	York	1402	6	5	14.3	**36.7**	T		Ibid., pp. 507–8

No. & Name	Occupation/Place	Date	12	60	3.2	1.0	48.6	51.4	Source
34. John Olyver	London draper	1406	12	60	3.2	1.0	48.6	51.4	Thomas (ed.), *Cal. plea and mem. 1381–1412*, pp. 2–5
35. William de Kexby	York precentor	1410	6	12	1.9	2.7	T	64.5	Stell, *Probate inventories*, pp. 514–17
36. Hugh de Grantham	York mason	1410	12	17	4.2	5.2	44.8	6.5	Ibid., pp. 517–21
37. Thomas Catton	York weaver	1413	–	23	3.9	7.8	93.5		Ibid., pp. 521–3
38. Robert Talkan	York girdler	1415	20	36	3.9	2.8	T		Ibid., pp. 523–5
39. Robert Schylbotyll	Scarborough	1416	–	24	25.0	8.8	81.4	18.6	Ibid., pp. 525–7
40. John Cotom	York mason	1426	4	*	22.6	20.8	T		Ibid., pp. 549–50
41. Roger de Burton	York skinner	1428	*	*	*	13.8	19.5	80.5	Ibid., pp. 550–2
42. Thomas Baker	York stringer	1436	x	–	19.0	20.5	85.4	14.6	Ibid., pp. 552–4
43. John Bradford	York mason	1438	3	4	1.8	3.8	T		Ibid., pp. 554–5
44. Robert Takard	York girdler	1439	6	–	27.4	22.6	38.5	61.5	Ibid., pp. 557–8
45. John Cadeby	Beverley mason	1430s	15	40	3.9	10.0	87.3	12.7	Ibid., pp. 558–62
46. William Garton	?York	1430s	9	x	13.2	29.1	85.3	14.7	Ibid., pp. 562–3
47. John Danby	Northallerton	1444	–	–	13.2	28.1	59.7	40.3	Ibid., pp. 563–5
48. Thomas Overdo	York Baker	1444	12	x	9.1	8.8	72.7	27.3	Ibid., pp. 565–7
49. William Furnyvale[3]	London	1445	20	*	*	*	*		Jones (ed.), *Cal. plea and mem. 1437–1457*, pp. 78–81
50. Thomas Gryssop	York chapman	1446	6	11	8.3	4.7	21.3	78.7	Stell, *Probate inventories*, pp. 569–73
51. Richard Thomas	Southampton merchant	1447	16	–	30	26.9	9.8	90.2	*Southampton probate inventories*, pp. 2–9
52. John Stubbes	York barber	1451	18	13	27.6	13.6	69.2	30.8	Stell, *Probate inventories*, pp. 579–83
53. Thomas Peerson	York toller	1454	3	–	12.2	13.0	T		Ibid., p. 610
54. Robert Fawcette	York pewterer	1460	6	–	13.3	7.0	48.2	51.8	Ibid., pp. 613–15
55. Katherine North	?York	1461	4	–	32.1	16.4	T		Ibid., pp. 617–18
56. William Gale	York	1472	4	10	6.1	4.9	71.0	29.0	Ibid., pp. 630–4
57. John Brown	York	1474	20	7	36.1	21.1	73.6	26.4	Ibid., pp. 634–6
58. Brian Sampall[4]	?York mariner	1479	*	*	*	*	12.7	87.3	Ibid., p. 641
59. William Coltman	York brewer	1481	12	–	17.6	44.1	45.9	54.1	Ibid., pp. 645–6
60. John Carter	York tailor	1485	6	–	6.1	8.8	44.0	56.0	Ibid., pp. 648–52

Table 6.1 (*cont.*)

Name	Place/occupation	Date	1. No. of cushions	2. No. of spoons	3. Value of bedding/beds as % of total value of goods in house	4. Value of kitchen/cooking items as % of total value of goods in house	5. Value of goods in house as % of value of all moveables	6. Value of non-house goods as % of value of all moveables	Source
61. James Lune	Northallerton	1486	12	6	15.8	**26.3**	43.6	**56.4**	Ibid., p. 658
62. William Coltman	York shoemaker	1486	4	6	29.8	21.5	84.6	15.4	Ibid., pp. 658–9
63. William Eryame	Northallerton husbandman	1486	–	–	**46.6**	31.1	6.5	**93.5**	Ibid., pp. 659–60
65. John Gaythird	York husbandman	1494	4	–	12.7	**30.7**	14.1	**85.9**	Ibid., pp. 671–3
66. Matthew Salman	Southampton	1495	18	–	**17.7**	*	**T**		Southampton probate inventories, pp. 10–11
67. John Davey	Southampton	1516	–	–	**42.0**	14.7	**85.0**	15.0	Ibid., pp. 11–13
68. John Stevynson	Northallerton smith	1498	6	–	14.0	**21.3**	51.0	49.0	Stell, *Probate Inventories*, pp. 678–9
69. John Smyth	Northallerton	1499	3	–	**27.1**	12.7	**T**		Ibid., p. 681
70. Nicholas Withers	London citizen	late C15	22	20	**15.5**	3.3	**T**		TNA, E 154/2/15
71. W. Stede	London haberdasher	1499	12	26	**9.7**	6.7	**83.4**	16.6	TNA, E 154/2/7
(b) RURAL									
72. Reginald Labbe	[unknown]	1293	–	–	**44**	7	12.6	**87.4**	Turner, 'Original documents', *Archaeological Journal* 3, 65–6
73. William Lene	Walsham le Willows	1329	–	–	22.3	**36.3**	11.8	**88.2**	Lock (ed.), *Walsham le Willows*, pp. 133–5
74. Robert Oldman	Cuxham	1349–52	–	–	**15.9**	7.2	**29.6**	70.4	Harvey (ed.), *Cuxham*, pp. 153–5, 157–9
75. Thomas Calstan[5]	Bewley Court, Wilts.	1405	8	*	**7.1**	2.2	**82.6**	17.4	TNA, E 154/1/31

			12	[12]	5.4	3.2	85.6	14.4	
76. Roger de Kyrkby	Gainsford, Durham perpet. vicar	1412	12	[12]	5.4	3.2	85.6	14.4	Raine (ed.), Testamenta eboracensia, volume 1, p. 56
77. William Litster	Wilton	1417	–	–	34.0	33.3	34.5	65.6	Stell, Probate inventories, pp. 527–9
78. Robert Connyg	Helperby	1438	–	–	14.4	57.1	16.0	83.9	Ibid., pp. 555–6
79. Thomas Vicars	Strensall	1451	24	21	7.2	7.4	15.9	84.1	Ibid., pp. 583–9
81. John Scot	Acomb	1456	–	–	26.8	29.4	61.7	38.3	Ibid., pp. 612–13
82. Richard Sclatter	Elmley Castle	1457	–	–	25.6	33.5	88.6	11.4	Dyer, Standards of living, p. 170
83. John Crosby	Tollerton	1458	–	–	57.6	32.9	17.3	82.7	Stell, Probate inventories, p. 613
84. Emmota Cowper	Dunnington	1461	–	–	18.5	17.7	56.0	44.0	Ibid., p. 616
85. John Faysby	Huby	1463	–	–	34.8	34.8	5.4	94.6	Ibid., pp. 618–19
86. John Jackson	Grimston husbandman	1464	2	–	12.7	24.2	22.2	77.7	Ibid., pp. 620–2
87. John Hall	Holgate, York husbandman	1468	7	–	15.0	47.0	28.1	72.0	Ibid., pp. 624–5
88. William Haley	Lowdham, Notts.	1479	–	–	24.6	55.1	14.1	85.9	Ibid., p. 640
89. Thomas Smyth	Swinton	1479	–	–	39.8	32.5	10.1	90.0	Ibid., p. 641
90. William Akclum	Wharrom le Street	1481	–	–	14.4	43.7	24.2	75.8	Ibid., pp. 644–5
91. Thomas Kirkeby	[unknown, ?Yorkshire]	1482	16	–	?3.6	9.9	23.1	76.9	Ibid., pp. 647–8
92. Emmota Beveryngham	Brompton widow	1486	–	–	25.0	50.0	18.6	81.4	Ibid., p. 657
93. William Fox	Brompton husbandman	1486	–	–	39.4	60.6	10.3	89.6	Ibid., p. 660
94. John Robynson	Brompton	1490	–	–	35.8	44.7	22.9	77.1	Ibid., pp. 667–8
95. Thomas Smyth	West Rounton	1497	–	–	40.8	44.9	13.7	86.3	Ibid., pp. 676–7
96. Richard Barber	Allertonshire	1497	6	–	26.5	35.8	T		Ibid., pp. 677–8
98. Thomas Arkyndall	Allertonshire	1499	2	–	–	7.2	29.5	70.5	Ibid., p. 679
99. Thomas Robynete	Rampton, Notts.	1512	6	–	32.0	19.4	21	79	Kennedy (ed.), Nottinghamshire household inventories, pp. 6–7
100. William Howtchenson	Cropwell, Notts.	1515	6	–	22.2	42.6	18	82	Ibid., p. 8
101. William Rennar	Dunham, Notts.	1529	8	–	31.4	18.3	23.2	76.8	Ibid., pp. 8–9
102. John Leeke	?Notts.	c1530	6	–	20.7	25.9	42.2	57.8	Ibid., pp. 10–11

Key

Column 1 (Cushions) records total number of individual cushions itemised.

Column 2 (Spoons) records total number of silver spoons itemised.

Column 3 (bedding/beds) records the value of beds and bedding as a percentage of the total value of items inventoried within the main house (column 5).

Column 4 (Kitchen/cooking items) records the value of goods associated with the kitchen (or where no kitchen is specified, goods associated with cooking etc.) as a percentage of the total value of items inventoried within the main house (column 5).

Column 5 (House) records the value of goods associated with the main house as a percentage of the value of all moveable goods. Where only goods associated with the main house are recorded, this is represented by the letter **T** for totality of recorded goods.

Column 6 (Non-house) records the value of goods associated with property other than the main house (e.g. shop, merchandise, stables, barns, fields etc.) as a percentage of the value of all moveable goods.

In columns 3 and 4, the higher value of beds and bedding or kitchen items expressed as a percentage of the total value of items inventoried within the main house is shown in **bold** type. Likewise in columns 5 and 6, the higher value of goods associated with the main house or goods associated with property other than the main house expressed as a percentage of the value of all moveable goods is also shown in **bold** type.

    – no items recorded

    * insufficient or inadequate / damaged evidence

    x multiple items

    T totality of recorded goods

Sources

TNA, probate inventories, E 154; E 199. Dyer, *Standards of living*; P. D. A. Harvey (ed.), *Manorial records of Cuxham, Oxfordshire, circa 1200–1359*, Oxfordshire Records Series vol. 50 (London, 1976); P. E. Jones (ed.), *Calendar of plea and memoranda rolls of the city of London A.D. 1437–1457* (Cambridge University Press, 1954); P. A. Kennedy (ed.), *Nottinghamshire household inventories*, Thoroton Society Record Series vol. 22 (Nottingham, 1963); Ray Lock (ed.), *The court rolls of Walsham le Willows 1303–1350*, Suffolk Records Society vol. 41 (Woodbridge, 1998); David Lepine and Nicholas Orme (eds.), *Death and memory in medieval Exeter*, Devon and Cornwall Record Society n.s. vol. 47 (Exeter, 2003); Myers, 'The wealth of Richard Lyons'; D. M. Owen (ed.), *The making of King's Lynn*, Records of Social and Economic History n.s. vol. 9 (Oxford: British Academy, 1984); James Raine (ed.), *Testamenta eboracensia*, volume 1, Surtees Society vol. 4 (Durham, 1836); H. T. Riley (ed.), *Memorials of London and London life in the XIIIth, XIVth and XVth centuries* (London: Longman, Green, 1868); E. Roberts and K. Parker (eds.), *Southampton probate inventories, 1447–1575*, volume 1, Southampton Records Series vol. 24 (Southampton, 1992); Stell, *Probate inventories*; W. H. Stephenson (ed.), *Records of the borough of Nottingham*, volume 1 (London: Quarich, 1882); Thomas (ed.), *Calendar of plea and memoranda rolls of the city of London*; Turner, 'Original documents: inventory of the effects of Reginald Labbe, d. 1293'.

[1] The property had been attached as belonging to Margery, widow of Geoffrey de Dytton, but was claimed in court by the rector.

[2] Richard Lyons's ship and his two taverns have been excluded from the calculation.

[3] The inventory is defective and numbers of entries are now lost, but the value of beds/bedding listed exceeds that of kitchen utensils.

[4] The extant inventory fails to itemise household goods.

[5] Inventory in respect of Bewley Court only. Two-thirds of the jewellery inventories has been assumed to be associated with Bewley Court.

7 Nuns at home: the domesticity of sacred space[1]

Marilyn Oliva

The language, literature and rituals of medieval female monasticism are imbued with domestic imagery. Family ties, for example, are evoked when monastic superiors are enjoined to act as mothers to their spiritual daughters, the nuns in their convents.[2] A fifteenth-century English translation of the devotional work *The doctrine of the hert*, addressed to a community of nuns, allegorises household chores as spiritual exercises.[3] Even the image of the *Sponsa Christi* – Bride of Christ – and the symbols that thus inscribe a nun's vocation and profession – the veil, ring and salutations for her groom – though usually discussed in terms of a mystical union with Christ, nevertheless conjure the domesticity which marriage implies.

Imagery that includes household furnishings and domestic settings is also present in nuns' mystical visions, like those from the convent of Helfta in Germany in the thirteenth century, which include images of God's grace as a bed with pillows, of Christ's heart as a house, and of Christ's heart as a kitchen.[4] Ida of Neville, a Cistercian nun in the diocese of Liége in the Low Countries, describes how she passed from the 'refectory of the Eucharist' to a 'spiritual dormitory'.[5] Such visionary images of

---

[1] I would like to thank Mary Erler, Janet Jones, Jocelyn Wogan-Browne, William Stoneman and the editors of this volume for their valuable contributions to this chapter. As the chapter represents the first stages of a larger research project, it does not include a comparison with the interiors of male monasteries or canons' convents.

[2] Gertrude the Great, in fact, thought that abbesses and other holy women were 'virgin' mothers, like Mary: Sharon Elkins, 'Gertrude the Great and the Virgin Mary', *Church History* 66 (1997), 722.

[3] Denis Renevey, 'Household chores in *The Doctrine of the Hert*: affective spirituality and subjectivity', in Cordelia Beattie, Anna Maslakovic and Sarah Rees Jones (eds.), *The medieval household in Christian Europe c. 850–1550* (Turnhout: Brepols, 2003), pp. 167–85 for a recent discussion of this text. Christiana Whitehead, *Castles of the mind: a study of medieval architectural allegory* (Cardiff: University of Wales Press, 2003), pp. 123–4 also discusses this text.

[4] Rosalynn Voaden, 'All girls together: community, gender and vision at Helfta', in Diane Watt (ed.), *Medieval women and their communities* (Toronto: University of Toronto Press, 1997), p. 74 (pillows), pp. 80, 83 (Christ's heart as a house), p. 84 (kitchen).

[5] Jeffrey Hamburger, *Nuns as artists. The visual culture of a medieval convent* (Berkeley: University of California Press, 1997), pp. 144–5.

household arrangements and domesticity found further expression in one of the small paintings produced two centuries later by a nun at St Walburg Abbey, discussed and reproduced by Jeffrey Hamburger.[6] This painting shows a heart-shaped house with a closed front door securable by a lock and guarded by a dog. Visible through a large open window in the front wall of the house, a nun kneels at a table surrounded by the figures of the Trinity. The table is covered with a white cloth on which sits a chalice or drinking cup. The scene is one of domestic warmth and tranquillity with fittings that are simple but comfortable.

Literature, rituals and visions that sacralised domestic settings and household furnishings have been discussed by Hamburger as well as literary scholars and theologians interested in the development and promotion of the cults of the Eucharist and of the Sacred Heart.[7] Scholars have interpreted these allegories and iconography, however, solely as expressions of a mystical marriage, or as images that promoted an interactive, affective response from a viewer.[8] Scholars have not yet addressed the implicit domesticity of nuns' lives, nor has this imagery been contextualised with details of the material culture within their cloisters.

The purpose of this chapter is to show how English medieval nuns' spiritual domesticity was grounded in the actual physical elements of their medieval households, by looking at the decorations of their monastic interiors and at some of their domestic activities. Information drawn from thirteenth- and fourteenth-century household accounts and fifteenth- and sixteenth-century inventories of the English convents can anchor the spiritual, visionary and didactic expressions of nuns' devotional space to the physical surroundings of their cloistered interiors and to the domestic arrangements of, and activities in, their households. Details from these records can then show how nuns could in turn sacralise their domestic spaces.[9]

Though many of these records are unpublished and hence underutilised, they can tell us a great deal about nuns' household goods and

---

[6] Ibid., pp. 138–75 for a discussion of this imagery; Plate 12, facing p. 135, for this painting.

[7] For example, see Voaden, 'All girls together', pp. 72–91.

[8] Hamburger, *Nuns as artists*, pp. 137–75. Else Marie Wiberg Pederson, 'The monastery as a household within the universal household', in Anneke B. Mulder-Bakker and Jocelyn Wogan-Browne (eds.), *Household, women, and Christianities in late Antiquity and the Middle Ages* (Turnhout: Brepols, 2005), pp. 167–87 does discuss the monastic community, specifically the convent at Helfta, as a spiritual counterpart to and imitation of the divine, and notes the earthly family left behind by a nun upon profession.

[9] Jeffrey Hamburger, *The visual and the visionary. Art and female spirituality in late medieval Germany* (New York: Zone Books, 1998), pp. 454–6 notes the murals painted on the church and cloister walls of Katharinenkloster in Nuremberg that would have functioned in the same way for nuns passing from place to place.

their physical surroundings. Household accounts survive for twenty-six female houses, either singly or in runs of six to ten, and range in date from the late thirteenth to the sixteenth century.[10] These documents detail the income and expenses of a superior or officeholder and may include the purchase and/or repair of of bowls and other utensils, soft furnishings – like material for hangings – and pieces of furniture. While the accounts span a great deal of time, the inventories – which survive for twenty-one convents – date from the sixteenth century. These documents are a particularly rich source for these details of female monastic life in the later Middle Ages. Generated by agents of Henry VIII, who suppressed most of the English monasteries between 1535 and 1540, the inventories list and value a monastery's soft and hard furnishings, utensils and plate.[11] While some of the published inventories have been used very fruitfully by archeologists – Roberta Gilchrist, for example – to reconstruct the buildings and layouts of female monastic precincts (and by Eileen Power, who cited details from the inventories as evidence of the disarray of female houses at the end of their existence), neither the household accounts nor the inventories have ever been systematically analysed for the details they contain about the nuns' household furnishings and decorations.[12]

These documents are especially valuable because they survive for female monasteries large and small, wealthy and poor, of every order and affiliation, and from every geographical region in England. They therefore allow us to explore a variety of issues, including the relationship between the household possessions and ornamentation of these monastic communities and those of their secular counterparts, and the extent to which the nuns may have recreated the secular households they left to join

---

[10] The 26 (of the 132 female houses in medieval England) are: Amesbury; Blackborough; Bungay; Campsey Ash; Canonsleigh; Carrow; Catesby; Chestnut; Grace Dieu; Harrold; Marrick; Redlingfield; Romsey; St Helen's, Bishopsgate; St Mary Clerkenwell; St Mary de Pre; St Radegund; Stamford St Michaels; Stainfield; Swaffham Bulbeck and Wherwell priories; Barking; Lacock; Marham; Syon and Wilton Abbeys. For further information see Oliva, *The convent and the community in late medieval England*, pp. 132–4.

[11] A full discussion of these documents is beyond the scope of this chapter, but some information about them is warranted here. Inventories survive for approximately 16 per cent of the total number of female houses. Most of these have been published, but some in abbreviated form and some inaccurately, as will be seen below. Moreover, some of these records are much more detailed than others but even the most cursory of them provides important details of the nuns' domestic interiors.

[12] Gilchrist, *Gender and material culture, passim*; Eileen Power, *Medieval English nunneries c.1275–1535* (Oxford University Press, 1921; reprinted New York: Biblio and Tannen, 1964), *passim*. For more on this point, see note 72 below. See also Julian M. Luxford, *The art and architecture of English Benedictine monasteries 1300–1540: a patronage history* (Woodbridge: Boydell, 2007), esp. pp. 1–26, for a recent critical discussion of these and other sources that can inform us about the art inside monastic cloisters.

a monastic one. The documents also allow us to examine possible correlations between the quality of domestic fittings and a convent's wealth, and between the quality of goods and the status of the nuns who lived in these houses. While these sources yield inherently interesting details – given that we know so little about the material surroundings of female monastic life – they also provide evidence suggesting a collective female monastic material and visionary language and culture not limited by national or geographic boundaries.

Nuns' living quarters can be divided into four categories: (1) their cloistered rooms – including dormitories, dining areas, chapter rooms, inner halls and parlours; (2) utility rooms – like kitchens, brewhouses and bakehouses, various pantries; (3) guests' quarters – outer halls and parlours, bedrooms; and (4) rooms devoted to religious services – choirs, chapels and churches, many of which were shared with local parishioners. While the furniture and household goods in all of these rooms provide domestic details of female monastic life, this chapter looks specifically at the furnishings of the rooms in the cloistered areas: what the nuns saw and used every day as they passed from their dormitories through inner parlours and halls into chapter and dining rooms. The chapter also briefly surveys the ornamentation of the nun's choirs and chapels, where they spent at least eight hours a day in communal prayer and private meditation. The striking similarities between the nuns' domestic environment in the cloister and their places of worship in church or chapel suggest a permeable boundary between the two spaces. Placing chapel decorations in the broader context of a convent's mundane household furnishings also presents a more integrated and complete idea of the nuns' spiritual domesticity.

The floors and walls of the interior rooms of the English convents, like the accommodation of their secular gentry counterparts, were covered for warmth, decoration and cleanliness: floors with straw, walls with cloth or paper hangings.[13] Prioresses and officeholders at Carrow,

---

[13] For gentry practices in general, see Woolgar, *The great household in late medieval England*, pp. 70–3 for floors and wall coverings. In particular, see Ffiona Swabey, *A medieval gentlewoman: life in a gentry household in the early Middle Ages* (New York: Routledge, 1999), p. 79 for the use of rushes and wall decorations by Alice de Bryene (1413). Fragments of floor tiles have been found for Campsey Ash and Gracedieu Priories, but even tiled floors were probably covered with rushes or straw for warmth if not for cleanliness. Gilchrist, *Gender and material culture*, p. 82 (Campsey Ash), and TNA, E 315/ 172 (Gracedieu). This inventory is also printed in J. Nichols, *A history and antiquities of the county of Leicester*, 3 vols. (London: J. Nichols, 1804; reprinted in 1971 by S. R. Publishers, Ltd, in association with Leicestershire County Council), vol. 3, pt 2, pp. 653–65. Luxford, *Art and architecture*, p. 27 refers to the fragmentary remains of encaustic tiles at Shaftesbury Abbey as 'tips of lost icebergs'.

St Radegund's and Swaffham Bulbeck priories purchased rushes several times throughout the year.[14] At Marham Abbey, a small Cistercian house in north-west Norfolk, the abbess bought numerous bundles in preparation for the arrival and two-day stay of Henry VIII's ministers, there to inventory the abbey's estates, goods and personnel before closing it down.[15]

The walls of nearly every room in the English convents were covered in hangings: in both communal and individual sleeping quarters, as well as in halls, parlours and dining rooms. The hangings at Redlingfield, a small and poor house in Suffolk, were plain, unadorned linen.[16] But hangings at many other houses were made of high-quality material: usually sarcenet – a fine silk fabric – or, like four pieces hanging in the prioress's chamber at Kilburn Priory in Middlesex, red and green saye – an equally expensive fabric made of delicately woven silk or wool.[17] Some of the hangings, like the pieces of red and green saye at Kilburn, are laconically described as 'bordered with a story;' or as 'stained with work,' like those at Bruisyard Abbey.[18] Numerous other pieces, though, are described in greater detail.

Dormitory hangings at Chestnut Priory, a small Benedictine house in Hertfordshire, for example, were made of gold cloth stained (painted) with the image of St Giles.[19] At Castle Hedington, another very small and poor house in Essex, the nuns' draped banners on and around the crosses which hung in their dormitory: one of these banners was painted with a religious image and another banner was made of green silk.[20] The nuns' hall at Lillechurch Priory, a small Benedictine convent in Kent, was

---

[14] For Carrow Priory, see Norfolk Record Office [hereafter NRO], Hare 5955 227 × 1 for cellarer Isabell Wygon's account of 1520/21; this account has been edited by Lilian Redstone (ed.), 'Three Carrow account rolls', *Norfolk Archaeology* 29 (1946), 41–88, and p. 43 for Wygon's account. For St Radegund's, see the treasurers' accounts for the years 1449–1450 and 1450–51 in Arthur Gray, *The priory of St Radegund, Cambridge* (Cambridge Antiquarian Society, 1898), pp. 149, 166; for Swaffham Bulbeck, see W. M. Palmer, 'The Benedictine nunnery of Swaffham Bulbeck', *Proceedings of the Cambridge Antiquarian Society* 31 (1929), 43 for excerpts from Prioress Margaret Ratcliff's account of 1482.

[15] TNA, SP 5/2/246–8.

[16] Francis Haslewood, 'Inventories of the monasteries suppressed in 1536', *Proceedings of the Suffolk Institute of Archaeology* [hereafter *PSIA*] 8 (1894), 95–8.

[17] William Dugdale (ed.), *Monasticon anglicanum*, 8 vols. in 6 (London: Longman, Hurst, Rees, Orme, and Brown, etc., 1817–1830), vol. 3, p. 424.

[18] TNA, SP 5/3/126–7; this inventory, which was taken at the dissolution of Bruisyard Abbey, is printed in Francis Haslewood, 'Monastery at Bruisyard', *PSIA* 7 (1889/91), 322.

[19] J. E. Cussans, *A history of Hertfordshire*, 3 vols. (London: Chatto & Windus, 1870–81), vol. 2, *Hitchin, Hertford, and Broadwater*, p. 268.

[20] R. C. Fowler, 'Inventories of Essex monasteries in 1536', *Transactions of the Essex Archaeological Society* n.s. 9 (1906), 290.

adorned with several hangings of saints, including one with the image of St John.[21] The prioress's chamber there had a cloth hanging embroidered or stained with a prayer to the Virgin.[22] At Minster, a Benedictine house on the Isle of Sheppey in the Thames estuary, three painted cloths of the crucifix and the Virgin Mary hung in the parlour, and the walls of one of the nun's private rooms were hung with painted paper, not cloth, a detail which led the first editor of the sixteenth-century inventory from this house to suggest that this was the first instance of wallpapering a room.[23] While wall hangings were common in fifteenth-century secular gentry houses – like those of Thomas Fastolfe, for example – the iconography of those in the convents tended to be more specifically religious, adding a spiritual quality to the nuns' domestic settings which was perhaps less prevalent in secular households.[24]

In addition to the wall hangings and dormitory curtains which a nun would have seen every day as she made her way from room to room, bedding and ordinary household furnishings in rooms throughout the convent contributed to the decoration of these monastic interiors. Whether in common dormitories like those at Chatteris Abbey, Chestnut and Flixton priories, or in individual nuns' rooms at Minster, on the Isle of Sheppey, the nuns slept on feather beds, mattresses and pillows that were bolstered and canopied in white linen or buckram, a stiff material often used to line and give form to more flexible fabrics like

---

[21] R. F. Scott, *Notes from the records of St John's College* (Cambridge University Press, 1913), pp. 404–5.

[22] Ibid., p. 405.

[23] Mackenzie E. C. Walcott, 'Inventories of St Mary's Hospital, Dover, St Martin New-Work, Dover, and the Benedictine priory of S. S. Mary and Sexburga in the Island of Sheppy for nuns', *Archaeologia Cantiana* 7 (1868), 298, 296.

[24] See 'A letter from Thomas Amyot, Esq. F. R. S. Treasurer, to the Earl of Aberdeen, KT. President, accompanying a transcript of two rolls, containing an inventory of effects formerly belonging to Sir John Fastolfe', *Archaeologia* 21 (1827), 256–7 for painted cloths and tapestries, 263 for one painted with an image of shepherds; Woolgar, *The great household*, p. 67 for the highly decorated hangings with exclusively secular images. See also the inventories in Stell and Hampson, *Probate inventories, passim*. The hangings in these probate inventories are usually described simply as painted, or of a certain fabric, but in three cases the images on the hangings are described in detail: one had the image of the four evangelists (p. 509); another had the arms of St Peter (p. 573); and the third had an image on it of the Blessed Mary of Mercy (p. 665). In these rare instances the probates were for clerics: a prebendary, a canon and a chancellor, respectively. For the transformation of domestic rooms into sacred spaces wherein religious devotions and rituals were carried out in both English and continental European medieval secular households, see Webb, 'Domestic space and devotion in the Middle Ages'; Nuechterlein, 'The domesticity of sacred space in the fifteenth-century Netherlands', both in Spicer and Hamilton, *Defining the holy*. I am grateful to Maryanne Kowaleski for bringing this collection of essays, and these insightful articles, to my attention.

cotton and linen.[25] Nuns' bedding included blankets – some woollen, some lined – and pairs of sheets made of linen or diaper, a linen cloth embossed with a repeated pattern of small, often diamond, shapes. At Redlingfield, the nuns distinguished between the 'coarse' pairs of sheets for the servants and finer ones reserved for guests.[26] At Hampole Priory, a very small and poor house in Yorkshire, the *hostilaris* oversaw the details of such hospitality: thus in 1411 Dame Alice Lyte made up the guests' beds and delivered the soiled sheets and blankets to the porter at the priory's lower gate after their departure. The porter returned them to her at the same place – presumably laundered or at least aired.[27]

Nuns also slept under coverlets, which could be plain, or, like those at Lillechurch, highly decoratefd. Coverlets there were made of silk: one was red with an image of Christ, another yellow printed with flowers, and a third was green stained with crowns. The nuns' six pillows were embroidered with berries; the nuns at Flixton had four pillows similarly decorated and slept under lined blankets.[28] At Minster, Sheppey, the prioress had a coverlet painted with a religious image in her sitting room, and one

---

[25] For Chatteris Abbey in Cambridgeshire, see Claire Breay (ed.), *The cartulary of Chatteris Abbey* (Woodbridge: Boydell, 1999), p. 415; for Chestnut Priory, Cussans, *Hitchin, Hertford*, pp. 268–9; for Flixton, Haslewood, 'Inventories of monasteries', 89; for Minster, Walcott, 'Inventories', 294–97. This inventory suggests that some of the nuns slept in a common dorter, while others had chambers of their own. Walcott suggests that these separate rooms were cells separated by screens or partitions, but the wording of the inventory suggests otherwise, as the rooms are called chambers, not cells as they are in other inventories, and a name is attached to each. Most of the inventories suggest that nuns slept in a common dormitory in individual cells, separated from each other by hangings or screens, and this arrangement has been misinterpreted by historians as constituting separate bedrooms. This issue deserves revisiting elsewhere. In addition to the nuns' communal sleeping quarters, most English convents had at least one sleeping chamber for guests and frequently identified them by specific names: 'St Edmund's chamber' and the 'blue chamber' at Carrow Priory, in the city of Norwich, for example; see TNA, SP 5/1/111r. At Bruisyard Abbey, they were 'Yaxley's chamber' and a guest chamber: see Haslewood, 'Monastery at Bruisyard', 322; for the 'white chamber' at Redlingfield Priory, see Haslewood, 'Inventories of monasteries', 96; Norman J. G. Pounds, *Hearth and home: a history of material culture* (Bloomington: Indiana University Press, 1989), p. 198 suggests that dormitory curtains, also evident in gentry houses, were used for warmth rather than privacy.

[26] Haslewood, 'Inventories of monasteries', p. 97. See also Walcott E. C. Mackenzie, 'Inventory of St Mary's Benedictine priory at Langley, Co, Leicester, 1485', *Transactions of the Leicestershire Architectural and Archaeological Society* 4 (1872), 121 for the two feather beds and five 'febull' mattresses at this small convent.

[27] William Page (ed.), *The Victoria history of the county of Yorkshire*, vol. 3 (London: Institute of Historical Research, 1974) [hereafter *VCH*], p. 164. Similarly at Swine Priory, a Cistercian house also in Yorkshire, two nuns served as *janitrices* whose duties included passing food and drink through a window to attendant canons and *conversi*: Page (ed.), *VCH, York*, vol. 3, p. 179.

[28] Scott, *Notes from the records of St John's*, pp. 405–6 (Lillechurch); Haslewood, 'Inventories', 89; BL, Stowe Charter 336 (Flixton).

of the nuns there, Anne Loveden, had two coverlets, one of which belonged to the chapel of St John, which was probably one of the two there painted with images from the life of that saint.[29] In addition to the simple quilts catalogued at St Mary's Priory in Langley were two coverlets decorated with religious symbols: one with crosses and roses, and another with a crowned image of the Virgin Mary.[30]

The existence of feather beds, pillows and the attendant bedding is evidence of a level of comfort the nuns shared with the gentry class, and maybe even with some wealthy peasants.[31] Nuns may not have possessed as many feather beds, decorated coverlets and linen sheets as members of the upper gentry had – like Margaret Paston's numerous down pillows and pairs of fine sheets, or the many beds and fine-quality hangings belonging to Fastolfe, for example.[32] Nevertheless, the dormitory furnishings in these late-medieval convents are consistent with those found in the chambers of the lesser gentry, like those of Fastolfe's yeomen's chambers at Caister Castle, which included a few feather beds and mattresses, and plain sheets and blankets.[33]

---

[29] Walcott, 'Inventories', 300.

[30] Walcott, 'Inventory of St Mary's', 121–2 for the coverlets and bedding there, some of which were specifically for the labourers to use.

[31] For the finer quality of materials used by the wealthy, see Georges Duby (ed.), *A history of private life*, vol. 2, *Revelations of the medieval world* (Cambridge, MA: Belknap Press of Harvard University Press, 1988), p. 60, and especially p. 492 where he distinguishes between the beds and bedding of the very wealthy and those found in monasteries faithful to the ideal of poverty which were 'simple frames, no curtains, certainly no sheets'. Duby goes on to say, however, that 'Some monastic beds were beautiful and still yet austere', and he cautions against assuming that fancy fabric meant lax living. He cites Christine de Pisan, who wrote that the nuns at Poissey, where her daughter was a nun, 'slept fully dressed, without sheets, and on flocked rather than down mattresses', but that 'nevertheless, their beds were covered by elegant woven spreads'; these coverings were simply for decoration as the beds 'are hard and filled with flocking'. Along this same line of observation, see Janet Jones, 'The nunneries of London and its environs, 1100–1400', unpublished MPhil thesis, University of London (2008), p. 15 for a description of the spare fittings of the sleeping chamber at Kilburn Priory – which did include a feather bed – where the 'few nuns seem to have shared two beds in one room'. For wealthy peasants, see Sarah M. McKinnon, 'The peasant house: the evidence of manuscript illumination', in J. A. Raftis (ed.), *Pathways to medieval peasants* (Toronto: Pontifical Institute of Mediaeval Studies, 1981), pp. 301–9; and the inventory of John Hamme, bailiff and farmer of the Stonor family, in Christine Carpenter (ed.), *Kingsford's Stonor letters and papers, 1290–1483* (Cambridge University Press, 1996), p. 43.

[32] For Margaret Paston, see James Gairdner (ed.), *The Paston letters, a.d. 1422–1509*, 6 vols. (London: Chatto & Windus, 1904), vol. 6, pp. 50–3; these are among the items she bequeathed in her will. For Fastolfe, see 'Letter from Thomas Amyot', 258–9 and Woolgar, *The great household*, pp. 67, 78 for the abundance and high quality of bedding that characterised upper gentry and aristocratic households.

[33] 'Letter from Thomas Amyot', 264 and Woolgar, *The great household*, p. 67, where the differences between what Fastolf had and the possessions of his yeomen are obvious.

Much of the nuns' bedding was stored in chests or cupboards – pieces that, along with tables, chairs, benches and cushions, were mainstays of the convents' furniture.[34] The hall and parlour contents of Brewood Priory, a small Benedictine house in Staffordshire, are typical of many houses: several tables, both trestle and folding types, two benches and chairs.[35] Such unadorned furniture was typical also of wealthy farmers like John Hamme.[36] At Thetford Priory in Suffolk, dormitory furniture also included several tables, but all of them were painted or engraved with crucifixes or images of saints.[37] The tables in the nuns' individual sleeping quarters at Minster, Sheppey, had wooden crucifixes attached to them.[38] Some of the nuns there, Dame Anne Clifford, for example, had tables that were further decorated with a painted image of the Virgin.[39] Other furnishings at this convent included tables in the Great Parlour: one was painted with an image of the Epiphany, and another was a 'counting table' used for rendering household accounts and writing.[40] At the end of this hall stood two cupboards, each with locks and almeryes (drawers or cabinets securable with locks and keys for the nuns' valuables – books, deeds, pieces of silver or gold) and also for neighbours' goods deposited there for safe-keeping.[41]

'Evidence chests' like these were found in several of the English convents.[42] At Wherwell Priory in Hampshire, the abbess kept her seals inside two of these chests, for which she had two sets of three keys: two for the outer chest and one for the inner. She carried one set, the sacrist carried the other. [43] The nuns at Chestnut Priory also kept chests, one of which

[34] See, for example, the chests at Chestnut wherein the nuns stored their bedding: Cussans, *Hitchin, Hertford*, pp. 268–9.

[35] TNA, E 315/172. This inventory is printed by Gerald Mander, 'The priory of the Black Ladies of Brewood, Co. Stafford', in Isaac Herbert Jeayes *et al.* (eds.), *Collections for a history of Staffordshire*, 3rd series, Staffordshire Record Society vol. for 1939 (Bishop's Stortford, 1940), p. 217. Mander's transcription is more accurate and complete than Francis Hibbert's in *The dissolution of the monasteries as illustrated by the suppression of the religious houses of Staffordshire* (London: Pitman, 1910). The furniture at Kilburn Priory in London was similar in type and design: Jones, 'The nunneries of London,' p. 15.

[36] Carpenter, *Kingsford's Stonor letters*, p. 43.   [37] TNA, SP 5/1/119.

[38] Walcott, 'Inventories', 296–7.   [39] Ibid., 297.

[40] Counting tables appear in other inventories as well. At Flixton, for example, there was one in the buttery: Haslewood, 'Inventories', 89.

[41] Walcott, 'Inventories', 298.

[42] Robert Dunning, 'The muniments of Syon Abbey: their administration and migration in the fifteenth and sixteenth centuries', *Bulletin of the Institute of Historical Research* 37 (1964), 105–6 discusses the records and their storage at this large and wealthy house. For similar chests in secular houses see: Duby, *Revelations*, p. 502.

[43] William Page (ed.), *VCH, Hampshire and the Isle of Wight*, vol. 2 (London: Institute of Historical Research by Dawson of Pall Mall, 1973, reprinted from the 1900 edition), p. 135; the date for this is 1501.

was full of deeds.[44] Like many other pieces of furniture, the chests were covered with cloths or tapestries.[45] The cupboards in various rooms at Redlingfield, for example, were draped with cloths painted with images.[46] While tables, chests and cupboards were, like wall hangings and dormitory curtains, also part of gentry households, the nuns' furniture – like their softer furnishings – tended to be decorated with religious images rather than the floral designs or heraldry that adorned pieces of furniture in secular households.[47] Benches and chairs, pieces often associated with prosperous merchant households, were in these monastic ones often padded with cushions or carpets, which in several convents also served to cover windows.[48] The benches at Carrow Priory were engraved.[49] And the windows at Campsey Ash and Redlingfield were draped with carpet coverings.[50]

Smaller household fittings like andirons, tallow and wax candlesticks (often with branches), or forms in which to fit them, attest to the flames and fires that lit and warmed these priories.[51] Other smaller items included bells – mostly silver, some chained – which called the nuns to table for meals. Once the nuns were seated, the bells signalled quiet so they could listen to the reading while eating. At Carrow Priory, such reading was done from a lectern made of ash and engraved, appropriately, with an eagle, a symbol of St John the evangelist.[52] Cupboards in the refectories contained pieces of silver or silver-plated utensils, typically fire forks, candles, candlesticks, chafing dishes and basins, mostly of pewter or latten, which was a mix of yellow metals forged together into thin sheets. Pewter and latten basins were likely used, as they were in gentry houses, to wash one's hands during and after a meal.[53] The nuns at St Radegund's

---

[44] Cussans, *Hitchin, Hertford*, p. 270.

[45] As they were in gentry households: see Girouard, *Life in the English country house*, p. 53; Woolgar, *The great household*, p. 149.

[46] Haslewood, 'Inventories', 96.

[47] For the equivalent pieces in secular gentry and aristocratic houses, see Stell, *Probate inventories, passim*; Duby, *Revelations*, esp. pp. 406–7, 414, 463, 502.

[48] Cushions, especially the possession of several, were similarly markers of wealthy and usually urban households: see P. J. P. Goldberg, 'The fashioning of bourgeois domesticity in later medieval England: a material culture perspective', pp. 126, 132, this volume. Goldberg also cites examples of rural households in possession of cushions. He notes that they were most frequently found in halls, but in wealthy houses, cushions decorated both halls and other chambers. Cushions can be found in the inventories for both rural and urban convents, and they are almost always in halls, suggesting that these monastic households would conform to Goldberg's identification of less wealthy urban ones.

[49] NRO, Hare 5924 227 × 1 (1503/04).

[50] Haslewood, 'Inventories', 97 for Redlingfield; 115 for Campsey Ash.

[51] For these smaller items in both peasant and gentry houses, see Pounds, *Hearth and home*, p. 195.

[52] TNA, SP 5/1/111.   [53] Pounds, *Hearth and home*, p. 199.

purchased 'earthen' plates, dishes and cups – made of wood but glazed inside – and also a pair of bellows for the *fraytor*, or refectory.[54] At other convents drinking horns, goblets, cups – horn, silver or pewter – or masers (maple bowls or cups) were common, many of then bound or rimmed with bands of silver or gilt or set on stems decorated with flowers or images of saints.[55] Other utensils included spoons, mostly silver, like the eight counted at Flixton and the eleven at St Mary's, Langley.[56] Bruisyard Abbey had two dozen silver spoons in 1536.[57] At Lillechurch, the handles of one set of the nuns' spoons were decorated with acorns.[58] The handles of the thirteen-piece set of spoons with which the nuns at Minster, Sheppey ate were engraved, one with the face of Christ and the other twelve with the faces of the apostles.[59] Eating and drinking utensils like these – in both earthenware and metal – were increasingly common and plentiful at the tables of gentry families in the later Middle Ages – silver spoons, perhaps surprisingly, being the least expensive and most common in both sacred and secular households.[60]

Linens were also common household possessions. Those at Wintney Abbey are typical of what other, even smaller, convents had. These included fifteen table napkins; four tablecloths of Paris work; two linen tablecloths; and ten hand towels.[61] Nuns' linen supplies also included houselling towels, found either among their other linens or in the convent's sacristy.[62] These cloths served at least two functions: they were used as drapery over the Eucharist chalice, and/or as a sort of handkerchief or napkin within which the nuns carried their missals, psalters, bibles and

[54] Gray, *The priory of St Radegund*, pp. 150, 166 (1449/50, 1450/51).
[55] Pounds, *Hearth and home*, pp. 208–9 describes these small utensils, napkins and tablecloths as 'the niceties of eating', and notes how in the early Middle Ages they were the perquisite of wealthy households only; by the end of the period, though, use of these items had migrated down the social ladder to the houses of 'petty burgesses and yeoman farmers'.
[56] Haslewood, 'Inventories', 90. Spoons are also counting among the items at Castle Heddington (Fowler, 'Inventories of the Essex monasteries', 292) and at Brewood: TNA, E 315/172; Walcott, 'Inventory of St Mary's', 121 for these and for another eleven of 'another sort'.
[57] Haslewood, 'Monastery at Bruisyard', 323.
[58] Scott, *Notes from the records of St John's*, p. 405.
[59] Walcott, 'Inventories', 300.
[60] Consider, for example, the incredible number of silver basins, dishes and standing cups owned by William Paston: Gairdner (ed.), *The Paston letters*, p. 18. Pounds, *Hearth and home*, p. 209; Woolgar, *The great household*, p. 157. See also, Goldberg, 'Fashioning of bourgeois domesticity', pp. 126–7 above, for silver spoons in even moderately wealthy urban households.
[61] Page (ed.), *VCH history of Hampshire*, pp. 150–52 and also Diana Caldicott, *Hampshire nunneries* (Chichester: Phillimore, 1989), p. 81 (1420).
[62] Houseling towels appear among the possessions of several convents, including Chestnut: Cussans, *Hitchin, Hertford*, p. 268; Lillechurch: Scott, *Notes from the records of St John's*, p. 406; and Minster in Sheppey: Walcott, 'Inventories', 294.

other service books to church or chapel, a use that of course recalls linen used at mealtimes. This latter use also conjures the idea of The Meal – the Eucharistic banquet – and reinforces the notion that the word of God was food that nourished the soul.

The choirs, churches and chapels into which the nuns carried their prayer books were decorated, perhaps not surprisingly, with hangings and furniture of similar material and iconography, providing a link between the domestic and sacral spaces of these convents, making the chapels and churches extensions of the nuns' domestic space. In the vestry at Campsey Ash was stored a pair of silk curtains, one with the image of Jesus, the other embroidered with flowers, hangings for the nuns' chapel.[63] The nuns' choir at Lillechurch was adorned with several cloths, one of silk and gold, another stained with a gold cross in the middle, and a third painted with the Crucifixion in the centre.[64] The white diaper lenten cloths at this priory had rings sewn into the top border so the nuns could easily pull the curtains across a rod to shut off the high altar from view in the penitential season.[65]

Other church goods included altar cloths, tables and statuary. Many altar cloths were plain linen – and some by the 1530s old and worn – but others were made of expensive material and in good condition, like the gold-threaded ones the canonesses at Gracedieu in Leicester owned.[66] At Chestnut the nuns had several: a gold one painted with the image of St Giles; another of gold cloth unadorned; and another of satin bruges.[67] Furniture included alabaster, wood and ivory tables, like those at Redlingfield and Bruisyard which were engraved or painted with images of the Virgin or other religious figures.[68] In addition to these, the nuns could meditate on 'images great and small' like the statues of the Virgin and St George which adorned the chapels at Chestnut and Sopwell Priory in Hertfordshire.[69] The very small and poor house of Rothwell had two statues, one of St John and one of the Virgin.[70]

---

[63] Haslewood, 'Inventories', 114.

[64] Scott, *Notes from the records of St John's*, pp. 406–7.   [65] Ibid., p. 407.

[66] For an example of plain altar cloths, see TNA, SP 5/1/110, fol. 124v for those at Flixton Priory in Suffolk; TNA, E315/172 for Gracedieu.

[67] Cussans, *Hitchin, Hertford*, p. 268.

[68] Haslewood, 'Monastery at Bruisyard', 322 (Bruisyard); Haslewood, 'Inventories', 95 (Redlingfield). In fact, nearly every house for which we have evidence had alabaster tables in its chapel; see, for example, Mackenzie E. C. Walcott, 'Inventories and valuations of religious houses at the time of the dissolution, from the Public Record Office....' *Archaeologia*, 43 (1871), *passim*.

[69] Cussans, *Hitchin, Hertford*, p. 267 (Chestnut); Walcott, 'Inventories and valuations', 234 (Sopwell).

[70] Walcott, 'Inventories and valuations', 241. See R. B. Dobson and Sara Donaghey, *The history of Clementhorpe nunnery* (London: Published for the York Archaeological Trust by the Council of British Archaeology, 1984), p. 25 for

Chapel decorations at these English convents, then, were similar to those that adorned the nuns' domestic quarters in quality, design and iconography. And while the nuns' domestic, cloistered rooms included both ordinary and extraordinary furnishings, painted, embroidered and engraved images of saints, Christ and the Virgin adorned their walls and surrounded their beds and decorated the covers they slept under, the seats they sat on, the tables they attended and, at one convent at least, the spoons with which they ate, providing an environment of devotion throughout their households, not simply confined to chapel or church. The continuity of religious themes and images presents a more persistent and permanent pattern of design in the female religious houses than historians identify in secular gentry and aristocratic ones.[71]

The type and quality of the nuns' household and church furnishings and ornaments raise some interesting issues and questions. First, what can we say about the overall character of the domestic fittings of these monasteries? In most respects, they were more consistent with gentry households than with peasant ones: the nuns slept on feather beds and mattresses, with blankets and sheets, and also had wall hangings and tableware.[72] A gentry context for these household goods is consistent with Roberta Gilchrist's theory that architecturally female monastic houses resembled gentry houses; it is also consistent with the social status

Clementhorpe Priory, a small and poor house in Yorkshire, which had three statues in the nuns' chapel: one of St Sitha, one of St Bridget, and one with the dual figures of St Mary and St William.

[71] Webb, 'Domestic space and devotion', pp. 45–7 and Nuechterlein, 'The domesticity of sacred space', pp. 49, 78 discuss the prevalence of private devotional practices in secular households, but note that the exact locations of the religious paraphernalia – portable altars, painted panels, statuary and even books of hours – that transformed secular spaces into sacred ones are unknown, except for perhaps bedrooms, and that these decorative icons were locked away, kept apart from other household fittings, and brought out at specific times, making the fluidity of sacred and domestic space less permanent than I suggest was the case in female monastic households. See also Woolgar, *The great house-hold*, p. 73, for the combination of classical, heraldic and religious iconography of tapestries and hangings in wealthy secular households.

[72] Though the earthenware utensils at St Radegund's and elsewhere suggest a likeness to wealthy peasant households as mentioned above, p. 155. The nuns' households and possessions resemble secular households in another interesting way. One of the defining characteristics of gentry and aristocratic households was the portability of furniture (because households were itinerant at least until the thirteenth century, and because pieces were often used for different purposes) and how often valuable assets (silver cups and plates, for example) were kept in sleeping chambers for security; see Duby, *Revelations*, pp. 407, 502; Girouard, *Life in the English country house*, pp. 53–4. Some of the convents seem to have done the same since, not infrequently, the inventories describe pieces of silver in some of their dormitories, and also note seemingly misplaced furniture. Though Power, *Medieval English nunneries*, p. 319 and *passim*, cites these as examples of the disarray and a breakdown of the monastic ideal within the English convents on the eve of the Dissolution, it is also possible that the nuns were just doing what they knew how to do: keeping treasured items in a safe place and using furniture for various purposes.

of most of the nuns in these late-medieval convents, who were from lesser gentry and upper yeoman families.[73] The pattern of interior design presented here suggests that to a certain extent these nuns were recreating the household settings they had left behind, though with a more specifically religious theme. For a significant number of English nuns, however, their monastic households were likely more comfortable than their natal ones.

Within this general context of gentry households and society, however, nuns' domestic settings reveal some interesting variations. For example, there does not appear to have been a connection between a convent's wealth and the quality of its household furnishings. Minster, Sheppey was a wealthy house – worth at least £129 at the time of its suppression in 1535 – and so it is not surprising that the nuns there ate with silver spoons with the handles of Christ and the apostles.[74] Conversely, though, some of the wealthier houses – Campsey Ash (£182) and Chatteris Abbey (£100) – had some of the least fancy and least expensive furnishings.[75] And while some poorer convents did have the relatively cheap utensils found in commoners' households – the earthenware cups and plates at St Radegund's, for example, or the plain hangings at Redlingfield – many of the poor monasteries also had highly decorated and expensive furnishings. Chestnut, Lillechurch and Kilburn Priories – worth £14, £26 and £74 respectively at the Dissolution – owned some of the most highly decorated (and expensive) hangings and furnishings of any of these female houses.[76]

This incongruity could have reflected the tastes of a particular superior, community or benefactor, or represent a specific spiritual concern of the nuns. The nuns at Redlingfield, for example, may have shunned fancy

---

[73] Gilchrist, *Gender and material culture, passim*; for the social status of medieval nuns see Oliva, *The convent and the community*, pp. 52–61, 105–9. Goldberg, 'Fashioning of bourgeois domesticity', p. 133 above, notes that by the end of the fifteenth century 'the bourgeois and aristocratic fashion for cushions' had been adopted by peasant society, a pattern that can be seen in the possession of cushions by the poorer and rural convents covered here. Nuechterlain, 'The domesticity of sacred space', pp. 72, 75–6 associates the consumers and commissioners of art and illustrations in books of hours portraying the Madonna in domestic settings in the fifteenth-century Netherlands with urban burghers or members of a middle class who had easy access to urban markets, but that women and members of religious orders also bought 'domestic Madonna images'.

[74] Dugdale, *Monasticon*, vol. 2, p. 49.

[75] J. Caley and Joseph Hunter (eds.), *Valor ecclesiasticus*, 7 vols. (London: G Eyre and A. Staham, 1810–1834), vol. 3, pp. 499, 416, Chatteris Abbey and Campsey Ash respectively.

[76] Dugdale, *Monasticon*, vol. 4, p. 328 (Chestnut); David Knowles and R. Neville Hadcock, *Medieval religious houses: England and Wales* (London: Longman, 1971), p. 254 (Lillechurch); Dugdale, *Monasticon*, vol. 3, p. 424 (Kilburn).

furnishings because of a commitment to austerity. But what about the possession of expensive goods by small and poor convents? Where did the poor nuns get these wall hangings and decorated pieces of furniture? Did they buy them? Were they donated? Purchases of simple pieces of furniture appear in household accounts, but hangings rarely do. Often donations of high-quality items to monastic houses were recorded in benefactors' wills. Testamentary bequests to medieval English nuns included a variety of goods: money, books, clothing and furniture. In the fifteenth and sixteenth centuries, for example, bequests to individual nuns at Clementhorpe, the convent as a whole, and the nuns' church included a pair of linen sheets, cushions, a bed-cover decorated with flowers and birds, an 'iron-bound chest' – one of the evidence chests described above – towels and bronze pots.[77] Isabella Corp, a wealthy London widow, bequeathed expensive silver pieces, including a dozen spoons, as well as emerald, sapphire and diamond rings, to Margaret Heyroun, a nun at Barking.[78] Margaret also received from Isabella a blanket which she was to share with two other nuns there.[79] Elizabeth Yaxley bequeathed to the nuns at Carrow 'a clothe of tappestry worke, scored with the Nativity, Resureccion, and Epiphany, to hange in theyre church at solempne feestes', in memory of her soul and that of her husband.[80] It is also possible that the nuns themselves made at least some of the hangings or embroidered some of the bedding. Embroidery, spinning and sewing are three activities for which we do have some evidence: a nun at Bruisyard Abbey embroidered the cover of a psalter dated to the sixteenth century; in the fifteenth century, the nuns at Carrow wove the cloth for their habits and liveries, and may perhaps have sewn them as well.[81] Household accounts from Bungay, Campsey Ash and

---

[77] Dobson and Donaghey, *The history of Clementhorpe*, pp. 13–16.

[78] Reginald Sharpe (ed.), *Calendar of wills proved and enrolled in the Court of Hustings, London AD 1258–1688: preserved among the archives of the corporation of the city of London, at the Guildhall*, 2 vols. (London: J. C. Francis, 1889), vol. 1, p. 688; I am indebted to Janet Jones for this reference. Power, *Medieval English nunneries*, p. 328 also cites this will.

[79] Sharpe, *Calendar of wills*, vol. 1, p. 688.

[80] Walter Rye and Edward A. Tillett, 'Carrow Abbey', *The Norfolk Antiquarian Miscellany* 2 (1883), 475.

[81] For Bruisyard: Oliva, *Convent and community*, p. 68; for Carrow, Redstone (ed.), 'Three Carrow account rolls', 52. Caldicott, *Hampshire nunneries*, pp. 83–5; Power, *Medieval English nunneries*, p. 255; Valerie Spear, *Leadership in medieval nunneries* (Woodbridge, Boydell, 2005), p. 121 for instances of needlework, silkwork and sewing by nuns. For tapestries woven by Dominican nuns in southern Germany, see: Jane L. Carroll, 'Woven devotions: reform and piety in tapestries by Dominican nuns', in Jane L. Carroll and Alison G. Stewart (eds.), *Saints, sinners, and sisters. Gender and northern art in medieval and early modern Europe* (Burlington, VT: Ashgate, 2003), pp. 182–20. I am grateful to Maryanne Kowaleski for this reference.

St Radegund's include purchases of substantial amounts of thread and cloth, suggesting that sewing was an activity in which the nuns in these priories also engaged. Margaret Cotur, cellarer at Bungay in 1407, for example, bought 9½ rolls of patterned or striped cloth; 8 twelve-yard pieces of silk, 36 ells of wool cloth, ordered and cut, and 17s worth of thread.[82] Might some of this material and thread have been used for wall hangings and bed curtains?

And finally, if we look at the nuns' household decorations along with those in their churches and chapels, we might wonder if they consciously created a domestic setting with devotional elements that led them from and through their living quarters right into the choir and chapels where they prayed, thus creating a continuum of sacred/domestic space.[83] The idea that familiar objects and activities functioned for monastics and lay-people as tools for devotional and spiritual exercise and as topics for medieval allegory is nothing new.[84] We know, for example, that at least some English nuns heard a sermon that allegorised their religious dress piece by piece as tools to use on their path to personal salvation.[85] And we know that nuns were familiar with several devotional treatises which used the 'allegory of the edifice;' stories of buildings constructed with spiritual devices and virtues to instruct and inspire both monastics and laypeople.[86] The nuns' real, tangible household decorations and

[82] Suffolk Record Office, Ipswich Branch, HD 1538/156/7.

[83] The conscious pursuit and patronage of art by nuns has been identified in medieval Italian, French and German convents: see, for example, Hamburger, *The visual and the visionary, passim*; Mary-Ann Winkelmes, 'Taking part: Benedictine nuns as patrons of art and architecture', in Geraldine Johnson and Sara Mathew Grieco (eds.), *Picturing women in Renaissance and Baroque Italy* (Cambridge University Press, 1997), pp. 91–110; Joan Naughton, 'Books for a Dominican nuns' choir: illustrated liturgical manuscripts at Saint-Louis de Poissy, c.1330–1350', in Margaret Manion and Bernard Muir (eds.), *The art of the book – its place in medieval worship* (Exeter: University of Exeter Press, 1998), pp. 67–110. See also June L. Mecham, 'A northern Jerusalem: transforming the spatial geography of the convent of Wienhausen', in Spicer and Hamilton, *Defining the holy*, p. 152; Mecham notes that the observation of the Stations of the Cross by Cistercian nuns in Lower Saxony excluded the 'mundane' rooms – dormitories, kitchens, refectories – but the exclusion may have pertained specifically to this ritual and not to a broader design pattern of religious art.

[84] See Whitehead, *Castles of the mind*, especially chapter 7, for a recent analysis of how buildings and rooms provided a framework for spiritual exercises and private devotions.

[85] A fifteenth-century sermon addressed to a group of nuns, probably at Carrow Priory in the city of Norwich, for example, uses every piece of a nun's habit metaphorically as a tool or virtue necessary for spiritual growth and purification. See V. M. O'Mara, *A study and edition of selected Middle English sermons*, Leeds Texts and Monographs n.s. vol. 13 (Leeds, 1994), pp. 141–221. I am indebted to Mary Erler for reminding me of this.

[86] Whitehead, *Castles of the mind*, esp. pp. 117–39. See also Beryl Smalley, 'Use of the spiritual senses of scripture in persuasion and argument by scholars in the Middle Ages', *Recherches de Théologie Ancienne et Médivale* 52 (1985), 44–63, esp. 47. See also

furnishings – embroidered, painted, engraved with images of Christ, the Virgin Mary and a variety of saints – throughout their cloistered rooms and halls suggest that they did. We might also ask about the extent to which their domestic fittings inspired the writers of devotional texts; certainly the details of their furnishings would have at least reinforced their messages. However these details might be read, what they do reveal is that the nuns' household furnishings and ornamentation provided them with a domestic/devotional environment, like that which is so evident in the paintings from St Walburg. Knowing the furnishings and fittings of the English convents allows us an intimate and immediate view of the domesticity of the nuns who lived in them and shows exactly how their domestic details could translate so easily into devotional objects.

Nuechterlein, 'The domesticity of sacred space', pp. 65–6 for how details in domestic representations of the Annunciation – lilies, for example – functioned for secular viewers as both decor and symbols of the sacred.

8 'Which may be said to be her own': widows and goods in late-medieval England

Janet S. Loengard

This essay is about *things* – tangible things – and their ownership. It is concerned with personal items like clothing and jewellery, and with the goods that a household used in the course of its day-to-day routine, like beds and tablecloths and brass kettles. The ownership in question is that of the woman who lost her husband: what personal property might she expect to own following his death? In late-medieval England, the short answer has to be 'Maybe almost none' because at English common law before the nineteenth-century Married Women's Property Acts, a woman's chattels – and her money – became the absolute property of her husband on their marriage.[1] When he died they did not automatically return to her; he was free to bequeath them to anyone he chose and if his will did not bequeath them specifically they went to his executor.[2]

The longer answer, of course, is more complicated. Widowhood might make a woman wealthy if her husband had been well to do and loving: some men left their wives everything. Many more, probably overall a majority throughout the later medieval period, made their wife executrix or co-executrix, often effectively giving a surviving widow control of the residue of the estate. The percentage fluctuated from time to time and place to place, but by way of example, of seventy-three Oxfordshire men whose wills were probated in the Prerogative Court of Canterbury between 1393 and 1510, sixty-one made their wife sole or joint executrix;

---

[1] See the 1496/7 letters of Edward Plumpton to Sir Robert Plumpton, explaining that he hoped to marry a woman who had coin, debts, plate and 'other goods of great valour' so that she was said to be worth £1000 besides her land. However, he needed money for an adequate jointure, promising that if Sir Robert provided it and the marriage took place, 'whatsoever you doe for me in word, cost, and wrytting, yt shalbe mine, when we be maryed, to relesse and unbynd'. Thomas Stapleton (ed.), *The Plumpton correspondence: a series of letters, chiefly domestick, written in the reigns of Edward IV, Richard III, Henry VII and Henry VIII*, Camden Society vol. 4 (London, 1839; repr. with introduction by Keith Dockray, Gloucester: Alan Sutton Publishing Ltd., 1990), pp. 123, 128.

[2] This chapter uses the terms 'will' and 'testament' interchangeably, as is current practice, although strictly speaking a will referred to land and a testament to chattels.

among seventy-four wills of married men probated in the consistory court of London between 1492 and 1547, sixty-six named a wife either executrix or co-executrix; and of thirty-one wills of married aristocratic men in post-plague Sussex, nineteen named wives as an executrix.[3]

Moreover, a widow in the ecclesiastical province of York and some cities, among them London, was entitled to a third share of her husband's chattels – which of course included those which had been hers – as had been the custom throughout England until it died out in the fourteenth century.[4] (Generally, however, she could not choose which she would have unless her husband's will gave her that right.) Additionally, a surviving wife's interests could be arranged before the wedding by agreement; marriage settlements could and did limit a husband's testamentary freedom.

But even leaving aside such restraints on testators as customary thirds and pre-marital settlements, men's wills suggest that many husbands took into account chattels on which their wives might be thought to have at least a moral claim, if not one enforceable at common law. Such chattels fell into three broad categories: paraphernalia; items which a woman had brought to the marriage, especially those from a previous husband; and things women had inherited or been given even after their wedding. While husbands might – and did – treat such items as their own during the marriage, many men mentioned them as 'her' things in wills, specifically bequeathing them to the surviving spouse.

Then to rephrase the question: what goods might a woman in later medieval England hope to retain or get back, by way of 'her' personal property, if she survived her husband? There is no lack of theory. From *Bracton* in the thirteenth century through the early modern period, treatises repeated the rule that a married woman lacked possessions, often in the context of her inability to make a will. *Bracton* is the voice of moderation: because it is only proper, a woman is sometimes allowed to bequeath 'especially things given and granted her for personal adornment, as robes and jewels [*sicut de robis et iocalibus*], which may be said to be her own'.[5] Post-medieval writers were not so generous. The anonymous

---

[3] J. R. H. Weaver and A. Beardwood (eds.), *Some Oxfordshire wills proved in the prerogative court of Canterbury, 1393–1510*, Oxfordshire Record Society vol. 39 (Banbury, 1958); Ida Darlington (ed.), *London consistory court wills 1492–1547*, London Record Society vol. 3 (London, 1967); Mavis Mate, *Daughters, wives and widows after the Black Death* (Woodbridge: Boydell, 1998), p. 105 n. 53.

[4] Other cities had similar customs: for example, in fifteenth-century Lincoln a childless widow received half her late husband's goods. See Mary Bateson (ed.), *Borough customs*, 2 vols., Selden Society vols. 18, 21 (London, 1904, 1906), vol. 2, p. 127. The widow's share of chattels had nothing to do with her right of dower, also often a third; dower referred only to land.

[5] 'propter honestatem tamen receptum est quandoque quod testari possit … maxime de rebus sibi datis et concessis ad ornamentum, quae sua propria dici poterunt sicut de robis

seventeenth-century author of *The lawes resolutions of womens rights* remarked that 'the prerogative of the Husband is best discerned in his dominion over all ... things in which the wife by combination [marriage] devesteth her selfe of propertie ... and casteth it upon her governour ... The very goods which a man giveth to his wife are still his owne ... A wife how gallant soever she be glistereth but in the riches of her husband. ...' [6]

But such theory does not take into account the long-term day-to-day relationship of a husband and wife who share a kitchen and a bedroom as well as worries and griefs, pleasures and successes. Nor, when the relationship is ended by the husband's death, does it consider the necessity of providing at least a bed for the survivor, let alone keeping her decently clad. Widows could not reasonably be left without garments and a place to sleep. Nor were they. Wills, case law, correspondence and probate inventories taken together offer a rough outline of what possessions a new widow might receive – for one reason or another – when her husband died. The result is, of course, uncertain and incomplete. But it is a start.

Paraphernalia

Paraphernalia stands in a class by itself. Canon law and common law agreed that a widow had the right to her paraphernalia, defined as those goods so personal to a woman that they remained to her on her husband's death, rather than going to his executor – assuming they were still in her husband's possession at that time, since he had control over them so long as he lived and could alienate them freely. But canon law and common law disagreed sharply as to what those items were. The common lawyers' often-stated position in late medieval England was that paraphernalia included necessary and convenient clothing and no more – and that the judges would determine what was necessary and convenient. There are dark hints in a Year Book case of 1454 that it might mean the clothes on a woman's back: three gowns might be excessive. Fortunately, that was by way of dictum, not the actual holding of the case. [7] Custom in the province

---

et iocalibus ...' George Woodbine (ed.), *Bracton on the laws and customs of England*, trans. with revisions and notes by Samuel E. Thorne, 4 vols. (Cambridge, Mass: The Belknap Press of Harvard University Press, 1968–77), vol. 2, p. 179.

[6] T. E., *The lawes resolutions of women's rights* (London, 1632; repr. Norwood, NJ: Walter J. Johnson, Inc., 1979), Liber III, Section VIII, p. 129. The treatise is in general sympathetic to women.

[7] Year Book Mich. 33 H.6 31 b. *The Year Books ... with notes to Brooke and Fitzherbert's abridgements*, 11 vols. (London, 1668–80; repr. with introductory notes and tables by David Seipp with Carol F. Lee, Clark, NJ: The Lawbook Exchange, 2007). See also Henry Rolle, *Un abridgment des plusieurs cases et resolutions del common ley* [hereafter *Rolles abridgement*], (London, 1668), vol. 1, p. 911 §7.

of York, the city of London and some other areas also gave a woman her bed and a chest.[8] The letter books and plea and memoranda rolls of London speak of granting her the 'widow's chamber', defined in the 1391 acquittance by Alice Ancroft to the executors of her husband's will as being 'all the clothes belonging to her chamber, to wit, linen and wool for the beds and all the clothing for her body'.[9] The grant of bedroom furniture may actually have been observed fairly widely in the southern province: *Rolles Abridgement* remarks that 'les petits Customes de Normandie' include in paraphernalia at least a bed and coffer [*son lict ... et son coffre*] and that it appears those provisions 'agree altogether with paraphernalia in our [common] law'.[10]

Canon law was more generous. Not only did it include all a widow's clothing, it also granted her the things she used about her person, her array – a usefully ambiguous term. Both canon and civil law consistently gave women wider power over *parapherna*,[11] and the Church had gone so far as to argue that married women should be able to will their paraphernalia freely. It lost that battle. Archbishop John Stratford's 1342 canon decreeing excommunication of those who inhibited such testaments was evidently a dead letter; Edward III acceded to the commons' protest that women's freedom to make wills would be an unreasonable custom.[12] Nonetheless, in its capacity as the sole venue for probate of

---

[8] The custom persisted at least into the seventeenth century; see C. Jackson (ed.), *The Autobiography of Mrs. Alice Thornton of East Newton, Co. York*, Surtees Society vol. 62 (Durham, 1875), p. 246: 'my brother Denton ... said That it was the law and usually don, the widdow was to have her widdow-bed first out of all her husband's goods choose where she would.'

[9] Thomas and Jones, *Calendar of select plea and memoranda rolls of the city of London*, vol. 3, p. 177. There is also an early reference to the widow's chamber in Letter Book A; see Reginald Sharpe (ed.), *Calendar of letter books preserved among the archives of the city of London: at the guildhall* (London: J. E. Francis, 1899), pp. 137–8, 142–2 payment of 9½ marks to a widow (and her new husband) following a lawsuit for a trespass against her 'and this touching the chamber of the aforesaid Dionisia.' The language of the 1427 will of John Wyssyngsete of London seems almost formulaic: his widow is to have her whole chamber without diminution 'ut in lectis, robis et aliis ornamentis': E. F. Jacob (ed.), *The register of Henry Chichele, archbishop of Canterbury 1414–1443*, 4 vols., Canterbury and York Society vols. 42, 45–7 (Oxford: Clarendon Press, 1938–47), vol. 2, p. 365.

[10] *Rolles abridgement*, vol. 1, p. 911, §2.

[11] See, for example, the *Corpus juris civilis*, Cod. 5. 14. 8 and Dig. 23. 3. 9. 3. (Ulpian, *On Sabinus*, book 21).

[12] William Lyndwood, *Provinciale* (Oxford, 1679) liber III, title 13, *De testamentis*; he wrote an extended gloss on the topic, discussed by Charles Donahue Jr., 'Lyndwood's Gloss propriarum uxorum: marital property and the ius commune in fifteenth-century England', in Norbert Horn, Klaus Luig and Alfred Söllner (eds.), *Europäisches Rechtsdenken in Geschichte und Gegenwart: Festschrift für Helmut Coing zum 70 Geburtstag* (Munich: C. H. Beck'sche Verlagsbuchhandlung, 1982), pp. 19–37. The parliamentary response to the decree and the king's answer are in *The parliament rolls of medieval England*, 16 vols., ed. Chris Given-Wilson et al. (Woodbridge: Boydell, 2005, repr. 2007), available also on optical disc (Leicester:

testaments – bequests of personal property – the Church went on protecting the paraphernalia of widows when it could. In 1504, for example, in the Chancellor of Oxford's court – effectively the commissary court of Oxford – the executor of the will of John Fosbrook was told under penalty of £10 to return two gowns, a cap, a mantle and a silver girdle to Fosbrook's widow because they were her paraphernalia and therefore not Fosbrook's to bequeath.[13] Nor, apparently, were the churchmen standing in opposition to the general opinion of testators. Whatever they thought about women's lack of testamentary capacity, most men appear to have agreed with the canon law on the goods that comprised paraphernalia. Husbands' wills almost never used the term, but over and over they reiterated that wives were to have all their attire and apparel, ornaments and necessaries, and often they specified that beads, collars, girdles, borders and so on were included. It is not difficult to believe that they were simply ensuring their wives' paraphernalia against the claims of executors and heirs and the rulings of common law courts.[14]

Married women's testaments are rare but significant here, because presumably married women left only what what they thought was theirs. More importantly, they left only what their husbands thought was theirs, since otherwise, in the absence of a marriage settlement, a husband could deny his wife permission to make a will or, even if he gave it, refuse to probate the will after her death.[15] Women assumed that their clothing was theirs to give. They carefully itemised bequests: gowns (plain or furred), kirtles, cloaks, smocks, neckerchiefs, aprons. They made the same assumption about their girdles; bequests of girdles were second only to bequests of clothing. Girdles, both men's and women's, were worn low on the hips, often with a tab for attaching something like a small decorated

---

Scholarly Digital Editions in association with The National Archives, The History of Parliament Trust, and Cambridge University Press, 2005), vol. 2, pp. 149, 150 (Parliament 18 Edward III). The citations correspond to the pagination of the edition of Strachey, *Rotuli parliamentorum*. There is a detailed discussion of the Church's effort to secure testamentary capacity for women in Michael M. Sheehan, 'The Influence of canon law on the property rights of married women in England', *Mediaeval Studies* 25 (1963), 109–24.

[13] W. T. Mitchell (ed.), *Registrum cancellarii, 1498–1506*, Oxford Historical Society n.s. vol. 27 (Oxford, 1980), pp. 66, 227.

[14] Issues concerning paraphernalia came to common law courts collaterally, as in an action brought against a widow for detaining her husband's goods. A widow whose stepson was her husband's executor was particularly vulnerable.

[15] He could also simply delay distribution of goods until his own death, as in the will of Richard Smyth *alias* Panther (1554) in Dorothy O. Shilton and Richard Holworthy (eds.), *Medieval wills from Wells deposited in the diocesan registry, Wells, 1543–1546 and 1554–1556*, Somerset Record Society vol. 40 (London, 1925), p. 175: testator's son and older daughter were each to get a spoon and 6s. 8d. given to them by their mother, his late wife, at her death with his consent.

prayer book or keys. Some were silk. Some were harnessed with silver, some with silver gilt. Some were made of woven metal. Some were set with pearls. Some were half silk, half metal – the dymysent. When she made her will in February 1485, Agnes Lytton left her young daughter, her only child, no fewer than four: one gold set with stones and pearls, one harnessed with silver and gilt, one white damask with silver and gilt, one purple damask with silver and gilt.[16] Very few women could have matched that, but it seems clear that for most women, their girdles were their most precious possessions.

Beyond clothing and girdles, the question of paraphernalia becomes harder. What about jewellery, and what kind of jewellery? Or, to use a term which proved more ambiguous, what counts as *jocalia*? There is no comprehensive definition. In his 1456 will, John Aysshboy directed that his wife was to have all 'jocalia mea', enumerated as cups, bowls, girdles, spoons, 'et alii jocalibus meis quibuscumque'.[17] Both men's and married women's wills talk about beads: a widow is to have her beads, my daughter is to have my beads. Very often, 'beads' probably means 'rosaries', but not invariably. When Margaret Paston said she could not for shame go into the company of fashionable ladies wearing her beads – she was obliged to borrow something for her neck – she surely meant a necklace.[18] Latin wills may speak of *par precularum*, making the meaning clear, or even defining the Latin term further as in 'omnia precatoria mea wlgariter dicta beydes'.[19] But English wills overwhelmingly refer only to 'beads'. Very rarely they are specific: 'a set of prayer beads'[20], or 'my beads with the silver crucifix', or 'a pair of amber pater nosters'.[21] But usually, just 'my beads', of amber or coral or jet or silver. To judge from wills, many women and men must have seen beads as paraphernalia; they are included in so many men's catalogues of apparel or array and they appear so often in

---

[16] TNA, PROB 11/7/173. The will was probated in April, 1486, two months after it was made.

[17] Will of John Aysshboy (1464), TNA, PROB 11/5/29v.

[18] Davis, *Paston letters*, Part I, pp. 148–50, Margaret Paston to John Paston, 20 April 1453: 'I pray yow that ye woll do yowr cost on me ayens Witsontyd, that I may haue somme thyng for my nekke. When the Quene was here I borowd my cosyn Elysabet Cleris devys, for I durst not for shame go with my bedys among so many fresch jantylwomman as here were at that tym.'

[19] Jacob, *The register of Henry Chichele*, vol. 2, p. 188. Also Lawrence R. Poos (ed.), *Lower ecclesiastical jurisdiction in medieval England: the courts of the dean and chapter of Lincoln, 1336–1349 and the deanery of Wisbech 1458–1484*, Records of Social and Economic History n.s. vol. 32 (Oxford: British Academy, 2001), pp. 356, 358, 448, 478, 559.

[20] Will of Marione, wife of William Bette (1466), in Arthur Hussey (ed.), 'Milton Wills (next Sittingbourne) – I', *Archaeologia Cantiana* 44 (1932), 83.

[21] Raine, *Testamenta eboracensia*, vol. I, p. 282.

married women's wills. This is particularly understandable if rosaries are meant; who would seize a new widow's rosary?

A wedding ring would seem to be the most personal of jewels, but only a few men's wills specifically bequeathed their wives' wedding rings to them; in 1464, John Boton of London left his wife her 'array' and helpfully defined it to include clothing, two girdles and her wedding ring.[22] More often, married women's wills mention the ring, often leaving it to a cathedral or an altar in the church from which they would be buried, sometimes to a son or even a daughter in law.[23] But beyond that, there is no evidence that jewellery – chains, pendants, brooches – was seen as paraphernalia in the fourteenth or fifteenth centuries. Jewels are rarely mentioned in married women's wills – but then, perhaps most women did not have a gold chain to wear or to bequeath. The first case I have seen in which a court – and it was a secular court – gave a widow jewellery specifically as paraphernalia is post-medieval, the Viscountess Bindon's case in 1585.[24]

Goods brought to a marriage by a wife

Most men did not stipulate that they were returning such goods to their widows, but enough did to make it a noticeable theme. Barbara Harris in her study of aristocratic women between 1450 and 1550 put the figure at 8 per cent.[25] Mavis Mate, referring to Sussex after the Black Death, thought that in practice, most late-fourteenth-century Sussex widows received what they had brought to the marriage.[26] Because of variations from place to place and time to time, it may be impossible to calculate a percentage, but certainly many men's wills ordered the return.

---

[22] TNA, PROB 11/5/43v. In another instance, William Cordell's wide-ranging bequest to his widow included sheep, goods she had brought to the marriage, silver spoons, hooks, a harness girdle of silver, a wedding ring and a standing bed. Three of those items could have been paraphernalia. F. G. Emmison (ed.), *Elizabethan wills of south-west Essex* (Kylin Press: Waddesdon, Bucks., 1983), p. 21.

[23] Weaver, *Somerset medieval wills*, p. 312 (Our Lady in the priory church), p. 320 (Our Lady of Cleve); J. W. Clay (ed.), *North Country wills*, Surtees Society vol. 116 (Durham, 1908), p. 102 (daughter in law), p. 171 (son); T. C. B. Timmins (ed.), *The register of John Chandler, dean of Salisbury*, Wiltshire Record Society vol. 39 (Devizes, 1984), p. 147 (cathedral). Agnes Hanbram, on the other hand, left her best wedding ring to one person not identified as a relative and 'my wedding ring which I had at the marriage of her father' to a daughter: Shilton and Holdsworthy, *Medieval wills from Wells*, p. 153.

[24] *La Viscountess Bindon's case*, 2 Leonard, p. 166, 74 E[nglish] R[eports], p. 447 (1584); Moore K[ing's] B[ench] p. 213, 72 E[nglish] R[eports] 538 (1585).

[25] Barbara J. Harris, *English aristocratic women 1450–1550* (Oxford University Press, 2002), p. 133.

[26] Mate, *Daughters, wives and widows*, p. 195.

I have discussed the practice elsewhere;[27] the concern here is with the actual goods involved. Too often the provision is general; men spoke of 'all the plate and goods I hadde with her', 'all goods hers before she became my wife' or, like John Crowton of London in 1464, 'omnia iocalia et ustilamenta domus' which his wife Margaret had brought at the time when a marriage had been celebrated between them.[28] Frequently they must have contemplated an inventory which no longer exists, as when Thomas Sawer of Thelnetham provided in 1458 that his widow was to have 'all the chattels and utensils which she brought to me when we first married, according to what is seen to be hers and what mine'.[29] And sometimes the inventory is explicitly referred to, as in the 1503 will of Robert Arnolde which speaks of 'the stuff ... specified in bill annexed'.[30] Unfortunately, it is no longer annexed. A generous husband might even provide that there be replacement for well-used objects, as John Trollop of Thornley did in 1522 when he wrote that if his wife's napery or bedding were decayed, they were to be amended with as good of his own.[31] A less generous man might think like Thomas Skofyn, who in 1527 returned to his wife all her goods, 'my costs and charges deducted and paid'.[32] A return could except certain items, some as mundane as the cart and shod wheels mentioned by John Elyce in 1513,[33] although a confident husband could carve out valuable possessions to leave as he chose, like Thomas Mussenden in 1402, who returned her goods to his wife excepting a bed covered with ermine, which he left to his son, and another to be sold for the good of his soul.[34] Occasionally, testators hedged: they were

---

[27] Janet Senderowitz Loengard, '"Plate, good stuff, and household things": husbands, wives, and chattels in England at the end of the Middle Ages', in *Tant d'emprises – so many undertakings: essays in honour of Anne F. Sutton*, ed. Livia Visser-Fuchs (Bury St Edmunds: The Richard III Society, 2003), pp. 328–340.

[28] Register of Thomas Kempe, bishop of London 1450–1489, London Guildhall MS 9531/7, no folio number.

[29] Northeast, *Wills of the archdeaconry of Sudbury*, p. 343.

[30] Margaret McGregor (ed.), *Bedfordshire wills proved in the prerogative court of Canterbury, 1383–1548*, Bedfordshire Historical Society vol. 58 (Bedford, 1979), p 60.

[31] James Raine (ed.), *Wills and inventories illustrative of the history, manners, language, statistics etc. of the northern counties of England from the eleventh century downward*, 4 vols., Surtees Society vols. 2, 38, 112, 142 (London, 1835–1929), Part [vol.] I, p. 106. Also the will of William Nell (1418): Jacob, *The register of Henry Chichele*, vol. 2, p. 150. But there were conditions attached.

[32] C. W. Foster (ed.), *Lincoln wills registered in the district probate registry at Lincoln*, vol. II *(1505–1530)*, Lincoln Record Society vol. 10 (London, 1918), p. 58. He left nothing else to his wife and she was not an executrix.

[33] A. F. Cirket (ed.), *English wills 1498–1526*, Bedfordshire Historical Record Society vol. 37 (Streatly near Luton, Beds., 1957), p. 50. The 'English' refers to the language of the will. A number of wills in the volume explicitly provide for return of a woman's goods.

[34] Nicholas Harris Nicolas (ed.), *Testamenta vetusta*, 2 vols. (London: Nichols and Son, 1826), vol. 1, p. 161.

not to be held liable for goods long since used up or sold. Thus the widow was to get 'All the stuff she brought to me at our marriage that remains unspent at this time';[35] or 'now being in my possession'.[36] It was the rare husband who repaid a wife for goods which he had alienated, as did Sir Thomas Littleton in 1481 when he left his wife £20 in recompense of a silver basin which had been her first husband's and which he had presumably sold.[37] He may simply have been kind, or he may have been acting to meet the terms of a marriage settlement. Many of the new widows who got back what they had brought to a marriage had been married before. The goods they brought were often those left them by a first husband and were probably the subject of a (second) marriage settlement.[38] Richard Bronde in 1501 explained that he was returning to his wife goods 'specified in the inventory of Edmund Tatesburgh, late her husband'.[39] Almost certainly his testament was conforming to the terms of an agreement. It is true that there is no way of being sure whether a settlement is involved in any case unless it is referred to, but it looms in the background where a husband's testament returns to a woman everything she had when she entered the marriage together with everything she had acquired since that time,[40] or when all the goods returned are specified to have been a first husband's bequest,[41] or of course where a married woman makes a testament leaving exceptionally valuable possessions away from her husband. One of the most spectacular of those must be the will of Mercy, wife of Arthur Ormesby, probated in 1451. It includes folios of charitable bequests and valuable gifts to women – silver, jewels, clothing, a gilded girdle, books, money – but her only bequest to her

---

[35] Will of Richard Scowle (1491), TNA, PROB 11/8/310 and PROB 2/40, for will and inventory.

[36] Will of Sir Edward Knyvet (1528): Nicolas, *Testamenta vetusta*, vol. 2, p. 635. He also excepted whole categories of goods including plate.

[37] Will of Sir Thomas Littleton, ibid., vol. 1, p. 362.

[38] Recent literature on marriage settlements is typically concerned with the early modern period; see, for example, Amy Louise Erickson, *Women and property in early modern England* (London and New York: Routledge, 1993), and her earlier article, 'Common law versus common practice: the use of marriage settlements in early modern England', *Economic History Review* 2nd series 43 (1990), 21–39.

[39] TNA, PROB 11/13/42v. The will has been printed as an appendix in Henry Ansgar Kelly, 'Bishop, prioress, and bawd in the stews of Southwark', *Speculum* 75 (2000), 342–88.

[40] As in the will of Richard Beauchamps, Earl of Warwick (1435): Nicolas, *Testamenta vetusta*, vol. 1, p. 231. His wife was the heiress of Thomas, Lord Berkeley, and would have had a significant marriage portion and inheritance.

[41] Will of Sir Piers Edgcomb (1530): ibid., vol. 2, p. 647. 'All the plate in her keeping which was Sir Griffin Rice's, her first husband, with all her apparel and stuff of household left by him.'

husband was a gold ring with a flat diamond in it and he was not an executor.[42]

What were those things which women had brought to their husbands? Almost no inventories of married women's property exist; in the absence of a marriage settlement there would be none and any annexed to wills have disappeared. A rare survivor, the incomplete inventory of the widowed Agnes Wyslade – probably made in 1480, the year she married Sir William Stonor and presumably brought her things with her – suggests that she had a well-furnished, if not extravagant, house: beds and their coverings, pots, pans, a ladle, a hand mill, a pepper mill and various other kitchen equipment, tankards, trenchers, tablecloths, napkins, table boards, chairs, the furnishings for a chapel, a mass book, iron coffers, barrels and so on – and, more unexpectedly, a hand gun, a cauldron full of grease, and four more guns.[43]

Men's testaments are somewhat more helpful. Even though many husbands were not specific about the goods which they were returning, there are enough examples to offer hints. Probably only a minority of women had plate, but it appears periodically, sometimes referred to generally and sometimes piece by piece: 'the plate which is her own, a standing gilt cup, three bollyd pieces swagged with oon kover to the same',[44] 'a piece of plate with the cover having thereon her arms';[45] 'all such plate as was late Sir Francis Cheyney, my predecessor's'.[46] It is much more common to find references to brass, pewter and latten – presumably kitchen utensils and tableware, the hustilments of household that figure in so many testaments.[47] Robert Wareyn of Great Ashfield in 1460 left his wife 'The best cooking pot, a brass pot, two brass pans, a peel and a spit, which were hers previously.'[48] Even more modest were the goods brought by the unnamed wife of William Chappell, who was to have back 'ij little pans and the greatest

---

[42] London, Lambeth Palace Library, Registrum Johannis Kempe, fol. 298v. The volume is bound with the register of Archbishop John Stafford (1443–1452); fols. 207r to 347v are Kempe's, but there is some misbinding.

[43] Carpenter, *Kingsford's Stonor letters and papers*, vol. 2, supplementary letters and papers, p. 14. The two volumes are bound together as a single volume.

[44] Will of Henry Burnell (1490): Weaver (ed.), *Somerset medieval wills*, p. 290. She could use the rest of his plate so long as she did not remarry or 'leve unclene'.

[45] Will of Edmund Brudenall, Esq. (1425): Nicolas, *Testamenta vetusta*, vol. I, p. 207.

[46] Will of Sir William Compton, Knt. (1522–23), ibid., vol. 2, p. 591.

[47] Emmison (ed.), *Elizabethan wills of south-west Essex*, pp. 37 ('the brass and pewter which she brought') and 87 ('the pewter I had with her ... such brass and latten as she brought ... three pairs of sheets she brought and one new pair and all other such implements of house as she brought with her').

[48] Northeast, *Wills of the archdeaconry of Sudbury*, p. 434.

pan save one, her coffer and in pewter, because it is altered, the half thereof'.[49]

Women often brought beds and bedding, a not inconsiderable addition to a family's possesssions since a fully equipped bedstead was one of the most valuable articles in many houses.[50] Agnes Wyslade, for example, had a feather bed, a mattress, two coverlets, two blankets, five pillows and sheets.[51] Sheets – pairs of sheets, good sheets, less good sheets, new unused sheets, gentleman's sheets – were common currency in both men's and women's testaments. Wives got sheets, daughters got sheets for when they married, sons got sheets when they came of age. A good supply of bedding was important enough that it was often enumerated, as in Robert Blackwall's will when he returned to his wife 'All other bedding as sheets blankets coverlets counterpanes mattresses featherbeds pillows and napery' which she had brought to their marriage.[52]

Reasonably, then, for the most part married women's testaments bequeath the same kinds of household goods. The commonest items are coverlets, sheets, blankets, brass pots and pans, tablecloths, and other equipment for the kitchen or bedroom[53] – although even then, a husband might refuse to deliver a legacy, as Thomas Drynkwatere did in 1405 when his wife left their son a coverlet, a pair of best sheets, a pan and six gallon-vessels.[54]

Gifts and bequests to a woman

Both the personal possessions a woman brought to her marriage and the things she received after it might come from one of several sources. The bequests of former husbands tend to be visible because they were specifically noted, but former husbands were not the only grantors of women's

---

[49] Shilton and Holworthy, *Medieval wills from Wells*, p. 169 (1554).

[50] Beds were almost always described individually rather than being lumped with other possessions: 'To my wife all her apparel, the bed she brought with her, with the appurtenances belonging thereunto, and all our household stuff that she brought with her own money ...' ibid., p. 128 (1546).

[51] Carpenter (ed.), *Kingsford's Stonor letters and papers*, supplementary letters and papers p. 14.

[52] Will of Robert Blakwall (1515): McGregor, *Bedfordshire wills 1383–1548*, p. 108.

[53] Will of Joan Thole (1497): A silver ring, a folding table, a brass pot and clothing Weaver and Beardwood (eds.), *Some Oxfordshire wills*, p. 57; will of Margaret Whythede (1451): chests, towels, tablecloths, (together with clothing, a girdle, beads and cloth for a tunic) – but also a calf, sheep, fleeces and barley, presumably from her messuage with six acres arable and meadow, which she left her husband for life: Northeast (ed.), *Wills of the archdeaconry of Sudbury*, p. 232; and Agnes Capell (1452–3): a basin, ewer, and cauldron together with silver girdles and clothing, ibid., p. 276.

[54] Timmins, *The register of John Chandler*, p. 9. He was cited, but there was no prosecution.

goods. Both before and following marriage, women were given gifts or inherited chattels from a parent or a sibling or an unidentified third party, perhaps a more remote relative, a godparent or a friend. It is difficult if not impossible to know when the gift or bequest was made, but a reader is struck by the kind and number of things given or bequeathed to women who were or would be married, even with the donor's knowledge that husbands – present or future – could claim the books and plate and bedding and kitchen utensils and furniture. Testators and donors must have expected that their daughters and sisters and friends would get the benefit of the legacies and presents, and often enough it seems they did, if perhaps only at the end of the marriage. Dying husbands carefully explained that their widows were to have 'a small book with silver gilt covers with a diamond, which was late her father's',[55] 'a featherbed which was her mother's',[56] 'a silver pot with cover which her own father gave her',[57] 'a goblet of silver and gilt ... the which goblet was her mother's',[58] and so on, and the women in turn identified inherited items in their own bequests: 'the seal left to me by the will of my brother Nicholaus',[59] 'beads which were my sister's',[60] 'the primer lately my father's'.[61]

Some donors had an unspecified relationship with the women to whom they gave gifts; presumably they were not close family since husbands' bequests of such items do not identify the givers as parents, siblings or even the more ambiguous 'cousins'. John Sothill of Dewsbury in 1500 left his wife a 'flat pees [presumably plate] that Dame Ales gave her',[62] while Isabell Eyre got a gilt goblet which Lady Scrope had given her.[63] Thomas Burgoyne, auditor of the duchy of Lancaster, left his wife – among many other things – three silver and gilt spoons given her by two named but otherwise unidentified women, Mistress Peryent and Mistress Colles.[64]

---

[55] Will of Michael de la Pole, third Earl of Suffolk (1415): Clay (ed.), *North Country wills*, p. 8. His wife's father was Hugh, Earl of Stafford.

[56] Will of Thomas Morcoot (1523): McGregor, *Bedfordshire wills 1383–1548*, p. 119. It seems to have been given grudgingly; she also got a coverlet and tester 'with all appertaining', £10 in money, £10 a year for life and no more, 'she not meddeling with noon of my moveables'. She was not executrix.

[57] Will of Thomas Burgoyn, auditor of the Duchy of Lancaster (1546): ibid., p. 170.

[58] Will of Humfrey Starkey, chief baron of the Exchequer (1486): TNA, PROB 11/7/195.

[59] Will of Alice, wife of Richard Cary (1349): Alfred Gibbons (ed.), *Early Lincoln wills: an abstract of all the wills & administrations recorded in the episcopal registers of the old diocese of Lincoln ... 1282–1547* (Lincoln, 1888), p. 39.

[60] Will of Ann, wife of John, Lord Scrope (1498): Nicolas, *Testamenta vetusta*, vol. 2, p. 435. She may have been a widow; her will and that of her husband were proved on the same day but his is dated earlier.

[61] Will of Mercy, wife of Arthur Ormesby, knight (1451): Registrum Johannis Kempe, fol. 298v.

[62] Will of John Sothill (1500): Raine, *Testamenta eboracensia*, vol. 4, p. 168.

[63] Will of Roger Eyre (1515): ibid., vol. 5, p. 65.

[64] McGregor, *Bedfordshire wills 1383–1548*, p. 170 (1546).

Elizabeth, the second wife of the fourth Earl of Shrewsbury, rather less elegantly got two oxen given her by Thomas Eton, [65] and in 1509 Isabell Amyas's husband left her 'oon nut which John Alan gafe to her' [66] – there is actually a number of bequests of nuts, perhaps coconuts set into silver and made into cups.

The cirumstance where sentiment most often enters these generally unsentimental property arrangements is in the gift given by a husband to his wife. Legally, of course, there could be no such gift, as the treatise writer T. E. pointed out in such detail. Under the doctrine of coverture, husband and wife were one person at law and one cannot give a gift to oneself. In practice, it is clear that husbands and wives gave each other gifts at their marriage, at New Year, and on other unspecified occasions;[67] wills speak of '[a] certain silver cup with cover which I gave her on the day of our marriage',[68] 'a cross of diamontes which I gave to hir',[69] 'two gyrdils silver and gilte, and one salte percer gilte, and sex of my best silver sponys' given as a gift two years previously,[70] a great primer which 'before daies I gave to my wif',[71] 'ii silvar dishes that my wife did give me'.[72] Girdles are very often mentioned. They must have been a common wedding present from a bridegroom to a bride. The anxious Thomas Betson, about to wed his beloved Katherine Rich in 1478, wrote to Katherine's mother, Elizabeth Stonor: 'she [Katherine] must have gyrdilles, iii at the leyst, and how they shalbe made I know nat'. He needed advice, he said, as he was like a blind bear in such matters.[73]

Katherine was not alone in having a multiplicity of wedding girdles; in 1545 Agnes Hanbram, widowed, left a daughter her *best* wedding girdle.[74] Earlier, Alice Love, wife of Giles, left her elder son by her first husband

[65] Will of George Talbot, fourth Earl of Shrewsbury (1537): 'xiiii draught oxen whereof ii were given unto her by Thomas Eton': Clay (ed.), *North Country wills*, p. 144.
[66] Will of William Amyas (1509–10): Raine, *Testamenta eboracensia*, vol. 5, p. 17.
[67] A wife's gifts and the occasions for them are set out in detail in the will of Richard, Earl of Arundel (1392), Nicolas, *Testamenta vetusta*, vol. 1, p. 129: 'My dear wife gave me at our marriage a red vestment … I will that my said wife retain the vestment for her life if she particularly wishes to have it … To my dear wife … two salt cellars of silver which she gave me for my new years present at Castle Philipp …'
[68] Will of Thomas Witham, senior (1481): Raine, *Testamenta eboracensia*, vol. 3, p. 264.
[69] Will of Sir William Fitzwilliam (1534): Clay, *North Country wills*, p. 135.
[70] Will of Robert Lascelles (1507–8): Raine, *Testamenta eboracensia*, vol. 4, p. 269.
[71] Will of Robert Ffabyan, citizen and draper of London – and chronicler (1511): Nicolas, *Testamenta vetusta*, vol. 2, p. 498.
[72] Will of George Talbot, fourth Earl of Shrewsbury (1537): Clay (ed.), *North Country wills*, p. 144.
[73] Carpenter, *Kingsford's Stonor letters and papers*, vol. 2, p. 54.
[74] Shilton and Holworthy, *Medieval wills from Wells*, p. 153.

'my best gilt gyrdell that my husband Thomas Oxenbridge bought me to my Weddyng'.[75] Joan Powdych of Wisbech in her 1471 will left her brother the silvered blue girdle with which she was married to her spouse.[76] Doubtless this helps explain the strong sense among both men and women that girdles rightly belonged to a widow. Men's wills almost never attempted to leave a living wife's girdle away from her, although occasionally there was an effort to give a widow a life interest with a reversion to a daughter; in such case the wife donee may well have been a second wife and the girdle – and daughter – the first wife's.[77]

The sense of the wife's ownership was strong enough that it could survive even her death. Where a married woman died with no will probated, her husband's later will very often left her girdle to her daughter or granddaughter, or to another person she had specified. So one reads that a girl is to receive 'a harness girdle with a buckle and a pendant of silver and gilt … which was her grandmother's bequest'[78] or a daughter is to have 'a girdell that was here mother's wedding girdell and a payur of bedes'[79] or a named woman is to get 'j sylver harnest girdill whuch my first wiff gave unto hir at hir last day'.[80]

In an area filled with theory, perhaps girdles could stand for reality. Common lawyers could draw all the distinctions they chose, they could fret over 'our law' as opposed to 'their law', the canon law; they could – theoretically – deny newly widowed women more than one gown. Treatise writers could emphasize to the point of brutality a married woman's inability to own chattels, to leave anybody anything. The evidence suggests that to some extent at least, the Church and husbands did not agree with them. For many or even most men, the legal meaning of 'mine' was broader than its practical meaning. How much broader varied. When he briefly mentioned paraphernalia and speculated on its origin, Maitland remarked that 'In the end a small, but a very small, room was found' for

---

[75] Will of Alice Love (1506): TNA, PROB 11/15/123.

[76] Poos (ed.), *Lower ecclesiastical jurisdiction in late medieval England*, p. 537.

[77] As was clearly the case in the will of Robert Willett (1543–4), who left his daughter a girdle garnished with silver which had been her mother's, but she was not to have it so long as his current wife lived: Shilton and Holworthy, *Medieval wills from Wells*, p. 13.

[78] Will of John Coke the Elder (1544), ibid., p. 46. The donee also received beads of amber and other gifts including clothing and livestock, some of which may not have been part of her grandmother's bequest.

[79] Will of Thomas Everston (1521): E. M. Elvey (ed.), *The courts of the archdeaconry of Buckingham 1483–1523*, Buckinghamshire Record Society vol. 19 (Aylesbury, 1975), p. 387.

[80] Will of Maurice Biront of York, organ maker (1510): Raine, *Testamenta eboracensia*, vol. 4, p. 22.

the idea that ornaments of a woman's person were her own.[81] He gave no examples. But it might not be imprudent to suggest that at the very least, like a gown – maybe like a rosary and a wedding ring and in some places a bed and a chest – a girdle was safely a woman's own and even with a singularly unloving husband, she could hope to keep it when the marriage ended.[82] Beyond those things, though, her expectations – her hopes – had to vary, depending on where and when she lived, on the prudence of her father or her own bargaining position when she remarried, and of course, above all, on her husband.

---

[81] Frederick Pollock and Frederic William Maitland, *The history of English law before the time of Edward I*, 2nd edn with introduction and bibliography by S. F. C. Milsom, 2 vols. (Cambridge University Press, 1968), vol. 2, p. 430.

[82] This assumes, of course, that either the dead husband's estate had no outstanding debts or his chattels were sufficient for their payment. A widow's paraphernalia, barring her necessary clothing, was subject to claims of her late husband's creditors. Moreover, unless a will specifically so instructed, a court would not order the use of real property for payment of debts until all funds accruing from the sale of chattels – including paraphernalia – had been exhausted.

9 Weeping for the virtuous wife: laymen, affective piety and Chaucer's 'Clerk's Tale'

Nicole Nolan Sidhu

In a letter to Giovanni Boccaccio, written in 1373, Francesco Petrarch explains his motivation for translating the last tale of Boccaccio's *Decameron*, the legend of Griselda, from Italian into Latin. The desire springs, Petrarch writes, from a notion that others, ignorant of the Italian language, would appreciate this 'sweet tale' 'dulcis historia'.[1] He was not mistaken. The remarkable international popularity of the Griselda story through the later Middle Ages is now as legendary as the tale itself. Petrarch's translation sparked off a veritable Griselda frenzy, inspiring versions in French, Spanish, German and a variety of other European vernaculars.[2] Its most famous redactor in the English-speaking world was, of course, Geoffrey Chaucer, whose Clerk tells a version of the legend in the *Canterbury Tales*.

Chaucer's 'Clerk's Tale' draws heavily on Petrarch's redaction, preserving its tone of solemn religiosity and its Christian moral that a man ought to endure 'without complaint and for God what this little country wife endured for her mortal husband' 'pro deo suo sine murmure paciatur quod pro suo mortali coniuge rusticana hec muliercula passa est'.[3] English audiences received Griselda as enthusiastically as those on the Continent. Judging from the number of times it appears as a separate item in manuscript anthologies, the 'Clerk's Tale' was Chaucer's most popular fiction in the fifteenth century.[4]

[1] Francesco Petrarch, 'Historia Griseldis Epistolae seniles xvii.3', in Robert M. Correale and Mary Hamel (eds.), *Sources and analogues of the Canterbury Tales I* (Cambridge: D. S. Brewer, 2002), p. 110. Translation mine.

[2] For a catalogue of the transmission of Petrarch's Griselda story in Europe, see Raffaele Morabito, 'La diffusione della storia di Griselda dal xiv al xx secolo', *Studi sul Boccaccio* 17 (1988), 237–85, and Judith Bronfman, *Chaucer's Clerk's Tale: the Griselda story received, rewritten, illustrated* (New York: Garland, 1994). The other vernaculars include Catalan, Czech, Dutch, Polish, Portuguese and Hungarian.

[3] Petrarch, 'Seniles xvii.3', pp. 128–9.

[4] The 'Clerk's Tale' appears six times as a separate item in manuscript anthologies, making it the most frequently copied of the Tales. For documentation of the 'Clerk's Tale's'

The tale has been markedly less favoured by modern audiences, who typically find its central idea to be, in the words of one critic, 'too revolting for any skill in description to make it palatable'.[5] At the core of the modern distaste for the 'Clerk's Tale' is its apparent sponsorship of abhorrent domestic values. Celebrating a wife so acquiescent in the face of her husband's depravity that she even gives over her children to be murdered, the 'Clerk's Tale' has been a perennial challenge for those wishing to interpret Chaucer and his culture for modern audiences. Most scholars of the tale have felt obliged to offer some explanation as to why late-fourteenth-century writers and readers would have so delighted in a narrative that many in the present day regard as a deeply troubling account of perverse cruelty on the one hand and near-criminal passivity on the other. More disturbing still is the fact that Chaucer seems even more interested than Petrarch in sanctifying Griselda's acquiescence, augmenting his own version with a number of original allusions associating Griselda with Christ, the Holy Virgin, Job, the Crucifixion and the Nativity.

A long tradition of scholarship on the 'Clerk's Tale' has attempted to explain the repugnant Griselda–Walter relationship as a matter of faith rather than domesticity. According to these readings, Walter and Griselda represent not so much husband and wife as God and the human soul.[6] The celebration of Griselda's submission to Walter thus reflects medieval culture's belief in the necessity for human beings to exhibit an absolute and unquestioning faith in God. A closely related school of thought reads Griselda as an exemplary figure who is, in the words of one critic, 'a type of Christ himself, whose suffering and sympathy are not only exemplary but redemptive'.[7] Both of these readings have, however, been persuasively

---

appearance in manuscript anthologies, see John M. Manly and Edith Rickert, *The text of the Canterbury Tales studied on the basis of all known manuscripts*, 8 vols. (Chicago: University of Chicago Press, 1940), vol. 2, pp. 243–65; Daniel S. Silva, 'Some fifteenth-century manuscripts of the *Canterbury Tales*', in Beryl Rowland (ed.), *Chaucer and Middle English studies in honour of Rossell Hope Robbins* (London: George Allen & Unwin, 1974), p. 155; Seth Lerer, *Chaucer and his readers: imagining the author in late-medieval England* (Princeton University Press, 1993), p. 31.

[5] Thomas R. Lounsbury, *Studies in Chaucer: his life and writings*, 3 vols. (1892; reprint London: Russell & Russell, 1962), vol. 3, p. 341.

[6] Elizabeth Salter, for instance, writes of Griselda that 'a great general lesson about Christian endurance and fidelity is conveyed through a particular, vivid instance of the operation of those virtues'. Elizabeth Salter, *Chaucer: the Knight's Tale and the Clerk's Tale* (London: Edward Arnold, 1962), p. 37. Jill Mann concurred in 1991, proposing that the tale 'forces us to experience just what is asked of human beings in their submission to divine will' and 'finds an imaginative form within which [suffering] can be apprehended as a mystery': Jill Mann, *Geoffrey Chaucer* (Atlantic Highlands, NJ: Humanities Press International, 1991), p. 156.

[7] Linda Georgianna, 'The Clerk's Tale and the grammar of assent', *Speculum* 70 (1993), 817.

questioned by David Aers, who notes that they assume a kind of unitary homogeneity in medieval Christian thought and ignore 'those strands of Christian tradition which provided powerful resources for resisting tyranny and evil commands'.[8]

Recent years have seen a spate of readings that credit Chaucer with a more critical political consciousness than the one suggested by arguments for medieval culture's absolute injunction to obedience. These analyses frequently set aside the problem of piety – and of the more abhorrent ideologies implied in the Clerk's sponsorship of Griselda – by assuming that Chaucer's attitude to the tale's piety is primarily ironic.[9] Feminist scholars have been particularly prominent amongst these new readings, emphasising Chaucer's critical distance from the perverse relations of the Walter–Griselda household in order to present the 'Clerk's Tale' as a sophisticated reflection upon medieval notions of gender, marriage and class.[10] An influential new historicist analysis of the tale – which argues that it issues a critique of Petrarch's support for authoritarian forms of government – also has to set aside the possibility of sincere piety in order to credit the tale with analytical rigour.[11] While these recent readings

---

[8] Aers provides an excellent critique of arguments advocating Griselda's exemplarity or similarity to Christ, observing that Griselda does not die a political death or offer redemption to anyone and also noting that the tale does not show her living within the liturgy or the sacraments of the Church. See David Aers, 'Faith, ethics, and community: reflections on reading late medieval English writing', *Journal of Medieval and Early Modern Studies* 28 (1998), 360, and *Faith, ethics, and church: writing in England 1360–1409* (Cambridge: D. S. Brewer, 2000), pp. 30–2.

[9] One exception to this tendency to alienate the political from the pious is Lynn Staley, who takes both the political and spiritual meanings of the tale seriously, proposing that their convergence is an opportunity for Chaucer to explore what happens when political power is alienated from cultural authority. However, while Staley productively draws our attention to the political valences of Griselda's spiritual authority, the ethical problem of Griselda's submission to unjust commands remains unresolved. See Lynn Staley, *Powers of the holy: religion, politics and gender in late medieval English culture* (University Park, PA: Penn State University Press, 1996), pp. 233–59.

[10] See for instance, Gail Ashton, 'Patient mimesis: Griselda and the Clerk's Tale', *The Chaucer Review* 32 (1998), 232–38; Susan Crane, *The performance of self: ritual, clothing, and identity during the Hundred Years War* (Philadelphia: University of Pennsylvania Press, 2002); Carolyn Dinshaw, *Chaucer's sexual poetics* (Madison: University of Wisconsin Press, 1989); Elaine Tuttle Hansen, *Chaucer and the fictions of gender* (Berkeley: University of California Press, 1992); Lesley Johnson, 'Reincarnations of Griselda: contexts for the "Clerk's Tale"', in Ruth Evans and Lesley Johnson (eds.), *Feminist readings in Middle English literature: The Wife of Bath and all her sect* (London and New York: Routledge, 1994), pp. 195–220; and Sarah Stanbury, 'Regimes of the visual in premodern England: gaze, body, and Chaucer's "Clerk's Tale"', *New Literary History* 28 (1997), 261–89.

[11] David Wallace, *Chaucerian polity: absolutist lineages and associational forms in England and Italy* (Stanford University Press, 1997), pp. 261–300. Larry Scanlon's reading, on the other hand, asserts that the tale sanctions secular authority: *Narrative, authority, and power: the medieval exemplum and the Chaucerian tradition* (Cambridge University Press, 1994), pp. 322–50.

rightly draw our attention to Chaucer's complex engagement with questions of gender and public authority in the 'Clerk's Tale' – a facet that is wrongly overlooked in scholarship on the tale's piety – the problem of Griselda and Walter's relationship to Christian spirituality persists. In spite of Chaucer's analytical disposition, the fact that he wrote the 'Clerk's Tale' in his high style – and declaimed it in a language almost entirely devoid of the ironic inflections that we see in many of his other works – suggests that, on some level, his was indeed taking the tale's religious meaning seriously.

It is the argument of this chapter that we need not disregard the tale's sincere expressions of piety in order to credit it with a political consciousness. In what follows, I continue the feminist interest in the 'Clerk's Tale's' treatment of gender by examining how the tale engages with notions of domesticity, in particular the hierarchies and values that later medieval culture associates with the successful operation of the household. The domestic is clearly central to the 'Clerk's Tale', given its persistent focus on spouses, parents, children, servants and even household chores (closer attention is paid to cleaning and cooking in the 'Clerk's Tale' than in any other fiction in the Canterbury collection). In the foreground of the tale's domestic scenario is the Walter–Griselda marriage, and the strong disturbance that this relationship provokes – even among the tale's later medieval admirers – indicates that questions regarding the prerogatives and limits of domestic hierarchies are among the most compelling problems that the legend confronts.

The tale's piety is closely related to its interest in the domestic, but not in the way that previous feminist analyses – with their focus on women and femininity – might predict. In what follows, I argue that in spite of its female protagonist and its great concern with appropriate female behaviour, when it comes to matters of spirituality the Griselda legend's primary appeal is to men. If we examine the Griselda legend in light of medieval notions of successful masculinity, we can see that it has a remarkable capacity to fuse domestic ideology with pious rhetoric in ways that are very attractive to laymen. This, I propose, is the chief reason for the legend's remarkable Europe-wide popularity in the late fourteenth century, and a major source of Chaucer's interest in it.

Key to my argument is the notion that the Griselda legend's appeal does not lie in its didactic capacity to offer lessons to readers who passively receive its instruction, but in its ability to provoke a powerful emotional experience. By featuring a vulnerable young woman trapped in a bad marriage, the tale invites its lay male audiences to intervene imaginatively in the Walter–Griselda household as protectors and defenders of the quasi-saintly Griselda. The legend's distinctly masculine appeal makes it unique in the late fourteenth century, a time when the religious aspirations of middle-rank laymen far exceeded the capacity or willingness of the institutional Church to produce pious works fitted to their needs. The chapter is divided into four sections. The first section will examine the appeal to masculinity, piety and emotion evident in the legend's late-fourteenth-century career from Petrarch to Chaucer. The second will discuss the socio-historical dynamics behind these features. The third and fourth sections will then examine Chaucer's version in detail, first delineating Chaucer's emphasis on the Griselda legend's appeal to middle-rank men, then discussing Chaucer's interest in the political ramifications of laymen's attempts to fuse the domestic and the religious.

Griselda from Petrarch to Chaucer: masculinity, piety and emotion

The various redactions of the Griselda legend produced in Europe after Boccaccio consistently exhibit four features: an appeal to a male audience; an interest in eliciting intense emotional reactions from that audience; a persistent commitment to characterising the tale as a pious one; and, finally, a decidedly lay orientation, both among writers and audiences. All of these features are particularly evident in Petrarch's version of Griselda, the principal source for most late-medieval versions of the legend, including the 'Clerk's Tale'.[12]

Petrarch discovered the Griselda story in Boccaccio's *Decameron*, the first known written version of the legend. Averring in his prefatory letter to Boccaccio that he did not read the whole of the *Decameron*, 'since it was very lengthy and written in vernacular prose for the masses' 'siquidem ipse magnus valde, ut ad vulgus et soluta scriptus oratione', Petrarch nevertheless professes his delight at having found in Boccaccio's Griselda

a story that so pleased and engaged me that, amid enough duties to make me almost forget myself, I wanted to memorise it, so that I might recall its pleasures as often as I wished and retell it in conversation with my friends.

(que ita michi placuit meque detinuit ut, inter tot curas pene mei ipsius que immemorem me, illam memorie mandare voluerim, ut et ipse eam animo quociens vellem non sine voluptate repeterem, et amicis ut fit renarrarem).[13]

---

[12] J. Burke Severs finds that the two principal sources for the 'Clerk's Tale' are Petrarch's *Historia Griseldis* and an anonymous French rendition, *Le Livre Griseldis*, which cleaves very closely to Petrarch. See Severs, *The literary relationships of Chaucer's Clerk's Tale* (New Haven: Yale University Press, 1942), pp. 3–37.

[13] Francesco Petrarch, 'Seniles XVII.3', in *Letters of old age: Rerum senilium libri* I–XVIII, trans. Aldo S. Bernardo, Saul Levin and Reta A. Bernardo (Baltimore: Johns Hopkins University Press, 1992), pp. 108–11.

Unlike Boccaccio's vernacular, secular version, Petrarch's Griselda features a high Latin rhetorical style, weighty biblical and classical allusions, and a serious religious moral urging 'readers to imitate [Griselda's] womanly constancy, so that they might dare to undertake for God what she undertook for her husband' ('ut legentes ad imitandem saltem femine constanciam excitarem, ut quod hec viro suo prestitit, hoc prestare deo nostro audeant').[14]

For the modern reader keenly attuned to the monstrousness of Walter's abuse and Griselda's endurance, surely one of the most startling aspects of Petrarch's letter is the intense pleasure he takes in the story. Petrarch does not just like or admire the Griselda, he *savours* it, even going so far as to memorise it in order to have easy access to its 'pleasures'.[15] His delight does not dissipate with time, for, as Petrarch informs Boccaccio, the story 'had consistently pleased me for many years after I first heard it' ('michi semper ante multos annos audita placuisset').[16]

The reason for that pleasure is revealed in Petrarch's second letter to Boccaccio, written several years after the first. Here, Petrarch recounts the experience of a Paduan friend, 'a man of the highest intellect and broad knowledge', upon first reading Petrarch's Latin version.[17] The Paduan scarcely makes it past the middle of the tale before he is overcome with weeping and must stop. Composing himself and taking the text in hand again, the man is overwhelmed with a second fit of weeping, confesses that he cannot proceed, and hands it back to another member of his company to read. This Petrarch regards with great approval, praising the Paduan's 'sensitive' heart, and quoting the words of Juvenal as a testament to the nobility of sorrow:

> Nature admits
> She gives the human race the softest hearts;
> She gave us tears – the best part of our feelings.[18]

A second friend, from Verona, earns Petrarch's contempt when he reads the tale dry-eyed. But this, Petrarch is careful to note, is only due to the fact that the Veronese finds Griselda's exceptional consistency unbelievable. Otherwise, the man says, 'I too would have wept, for the touching subject and the words fit for the subject prompted weeping.'[19] Heightening

---

[14] Ibid., pp. 128–9.
[15] Anne Middleton calls this 'Petrarch's paradoxical delight in the tale's sadness': 'The Clerk and his tale: some literary contexts', *Studies in the Age of Chaucer* 2 (1980), 139.
[16] Petrarch, 'Seniles XVII.3', pp. 110–11.
[17] Petrarch, 'Seniles XVII.4', p. 669.   [18] Ibid.   [19] Ibid.

the emotional experience of the story, then, seems to have been one of Petrarch's primary objects in translating it.[20] Equally important is Petrarch's reconfiguration of Boccaccio's audience. The *Decameron* as a whole is addressed to women and, within the fictional frame narrative, Boccaccio's narrator remarks that the tale 'occasioned considerable discussion among the ladies'.[21] Petrarch, on the other hand, clearly intends the tale for an all-male audience, not only because of his concluding directive that the legend ought not to be used as an exemplum for women, but also by the very terms of his translation of the tale from the vernacular 'mother tongue' ('nostro materno eloquio') into Latin, the language of a masculine intellectual community.[22]

Petrarch's religious moral is almost universal in later versions of the legend. Indeed, as the tale's appearance in numerous collections of religious treatises indicates, many members of its audience regarded it primarily as a pious work.[23] This dedication to the legend's pious facets is surprising, given that the Griselda legend lacks most of the elements we expect from a holy tale: it features no miracles, no visions, no extensive prayers, and no appearances by God, Christ, Mary or the saints. And yet interest in the tale's piety is evident even in those versions that flout Petrarch's dictate against using the tale as a model for female behaviour. The author of the anonymous French *Livre Griseldis* deftly inverts Petrarch's pronouncement on women, declaring that the tale has been told '*not only* so that I might stir the wives of today to imitate this patience and constancy' ('non pas tant seulement que les femmes qui sont aujourd'uy je esmeuve a ensuir ycelle pacience et constance').[24] But the author still retains Petrarch's injunction that all readers should adopt Griselda as a model for their own relationship with God. Philippe de Mézières recommends Griselda's example to women in *Le Livre de la vertu du sacrement de mariage*, but he does so in a work that is, above all, a very passionate

---

[20] Thomas Farrell, 'The style of the "Clerk's Tale" and the function of its glosses', *Studies in Philology* 86 (1989), 301–4. Farrell notes that Petrarch seems pleased to have produced 'an essentially emotional response' to Seniles XVII.3 and observes that the intersection of high style with a concern for affective response in medieval rhetorical theory can be traced back to Cicero.

[21] Giovanni Boccaccio, *The Decameron*, ed. Jonathan Usher, trans. Guido Waldman (Oxford University Press, 1993), p. 678.

[22] Petrarch, 'Seniles XVII.3', pp. 108–9.

[23] For a discussion of the inclusion of Petrarch's *Griselda* in religious collections, see F. N. M. Diekstra, *A dialogue between reason and adversity: a late Middle English version of Petrarch's De remediis* (Assen: Van Gorcum, 1968), pp. 29–31.

[24] 'Livre de Griseldis', in Correale and Hamel (eds.), *Sources and analogues*, trans. Amy Goodwin, pp. 166–67.

expression of masculine piety. De Mézières is even more fulsome than Petrarch himself regarding Griselda's holiness, remarking that

the constancy and loyalty, the love and obedience of the aforementioned Marquise in the sacrament of her marriage to the Marquis her husband – after the saints and martyrs and others in the Christian faith – surmounts both nature and that of all virtuous married women mentioned in any of the ancient histories and chronicles

(la constance et loyaulté, amour et obedience de la dicte marquise ou sacrement de son mariage envers le marquis son mari, aprés les sains [et] martirs et autres en la foy crestienne, surmonte et nature et toute femme marie vertueuse dont les histoires anciennes et croniques faissent aucune mention.) [25]

Many redactions also reflect Petrarch's appeal to a lay male audience and his interest in eliciting emotional responses, recording intense male expressions of anger and sadness on behalf of the downtrodden Griselda. Philippe de Mézières, for instance, is passionate in his defence of Griselda and regularly interrupts the narrative to issue harsh criticisms of Walter's cruelty. The Ménagier de Paris – who includes the Griselda story in his collection of advice to his young wife – remarks at the tale's conclusion that he would never demand such obedience from her, noting that he is not a Marquis, 'nor am I so mad, so presumptuous, nor so immature that I don't well know that it is not for me to assault or to try you thus or in a like manner'. Moreover, he adds, the story recounts 'a cruelty too great, beyond reason in my opinion'.[26] Even Dioneo, the cynical narrator of Boccaccio's version of the legend, condemns Gualtieri's 'cruelties' and the 'utterly incredible ordeals' he forces on Griselda.[27]

Amidst all of this masculine feeling, there is little evidence of a correlative interest or emotion amongst other audiences or writers. There is no evidence that women were drawn to Griselda in the way they were to other figures of married female sanctity, like St Birgita of Sweden or the virgin martyr Saint Cecilia (who proved so inspiring to her female audience that ecclesiastical writers were prompted seriously to discourage women from following Cecilia's example of celibate marriage).[28] Christine de Pizan includes Griselda in the *Livre de la cité des dames*, but her attitude to the

---

[25] Philippe de Mézières, *Le livre de la vertu du sacrement de mariage*, ed. Joan B. Williamson (Washington D.C.: Catholic University of America Press, 1993), p. 356.

[26] 'ne je ne suis si fol, si oultrecuidié, ne si jenne de sens que je ne doye bien savoir que ce n'appartient pas a moy de vous faire telz assaulz ne essaiz ou semblables'; 'de trop grant cruaulté, a mon adviz plus que de raison': Georgina E. Brereton and Janet M. Ferrier (eds.), *Le Mesnagier de Paris*, trans. (modern French) Karin Ueltshci (Paris: Librairie Générale Française, 1994), p. 232. English translation mine.

[27] Boccaccio, *Decameron*, p. 678.

[28] Dyan Elliott, *Spiritual marriage: sexual abstinence in medieval wedlock* (Princeton University Press, 1993), p. 107.

patient heroine is rather cool. Christine does not praise the piety of Griselda's wifely suffering. Rather, she includes Griselda as an example of a woman of strong character (II.50) and lauds Griselda's excellence as a daughter to the aged Giannucolo (II.11.2).[29] The legend's career among churchmen is similarly unspectacular. Anne Middleton has drawn our attention to the fact that, in spite of its pious overtones, the Griselda tale is absent from clerical traditions, not appearing 'in homiletic, confessional, or exemplum literature, or in pulpit speech'.[30]

Chaucer's Griselda

Writing at the close of the fourteenth century, and cresting the international Griselda wave that had already seen the wide dissemination of the two French versions of Petrarch's tale and their inclusion in other collections like the *Ménagier de Paris* and *The book of the knight of La Tour-Landry*, Chaucer was well positioned to observe the dynamics of the tale's transmission after Boccaccio. His redaction amplifies the piety and appeal to masculine emotion that are characteristic of the Griselda legend's late-fourteenth-century career. Chaucer's ascription of the tale to the Clerk may at first seem to deny the lay appeal of the Griselda legend. But here we must note that the 'Clerk's Prologue' constructs the tale as what Seth Lerer has termed a 'patronized performance'.[31] This performance is given for exactly the kind of middle-rank layman who had historically proven so receptive to the Griselda legend. Before the Clerk begins to speak, the Host, Harry Bailly, instructs him to put away his 'sophyme' (5) and produce instead a 'myrie tale' (9) that will entertain the pilgrims and not put them to sleep.[32] The Clerk does not argue with the Host's demands, acknowledging that he is under the Host's 'gouvernance' and promising to 'do yow obeisance' (24).

In the tale itself, Chaucer's numerous pious allusions connect Griselda to Christ, the Holy Virgin and Job much more aggressively than the more subtle intimations of Petrarch's version. Petrarch's remark that the existence of the beautiful and virtuous Griselda in a peasant family is evidence

---

[29] Christine de Pizan, *The book of the city of ladies*, rev. edn, trans. Earl Jeffrey Richards (New York: Persea Books, 1998).

[30] Middleton, 'The clerk and his tale', 125.

[31] Lerer, *Chaucer and his readers*, p. 31. It is worth noting that the rhetorical flourishes of Petrarch's *Griselda* are antithetical to the Clerk's Aristotelian leanings. For a discussion of the conflict between Petrarchan rhetoric and Aristotelian logic, see Wallace, *Chaucerian polity*, pp. 292–3.

[32] Unless otherwise stated, all citations from Chaucer are taken from Benson, *The Riverside Chaucer*. All subsequent references to Chaucer's poetry will be cited by line numbers in parentheses in the text.

of 'heavenly grace, which sometimes lights on even the poorest dwellings' ('sed ut pauperum quoque tugurria non numquam gratia celestis invisit') is a subtle gesture towards the Nativity.[33] Chaucer's version makes the reference more explicit by replacing Petrarch's 'poorest dwellings' with a more explicitly New Testament mention of 'a litel oxes stalle' (207). Chaucer adds another, more heavy-handed figural parallel when – in a scene clearly reminiscent of the Annunciation – he features Griselda (again 'in an oxes stalle', 291) falling on her knees and trembling before Walter as he arrives to propose marriage. Chaucer later adds a direct reference to Job when the Clerk exclaims that while men speak of Job's humbleness, no one can match a woman's humility (932–8). The tale concludes with a pietà-like scene when the weeping Griselda grasps her long-lost children in a tight embrace before swooning to the ground.[34]

Also remarkable is the self-conscious emphasis Chaucer places on the legend's appeal to masculine emotion when he has the Clerk interrupt his own telling of the tale several times with emotionally charged praises of Griselda and condemnations of Walter. Other authors may exhibit an intense masculine response, either through their own interjections or their reports of reader reaction, but Chaucer's telling of the legend within the frame narrative of the pilgrimage allows him to inscribe the interaction of audience, tale and narrator within the boundaries of his own fiction.

The Clerk's responses reflect with remarkable accuracy the Continental reactions I have described above. In the course of his account of Walter's decision to test Griselda, the Clerk pauses to deliver a critique of the Marquis's needless 'assaye':

> … as for me, I seye that yvele it sit
> To assaye a wyf whan that it is no nede,
> And putten her in angwyssh and in drede.   (460–2)

This is very distant from Petrarch's own remarks in the tale proper (he simply reports Walter's test and leaves it 'to the more learned ones to judge' whether it is right or wrong), but it is very similar to Ménagier de Paris's tone of disapproval. Other remarks, like the Clerk's condemnation of Walter's 'wikke usage' (785) after the removal of Griselda's son, echo the outrage of Philippe de Mézières. Still others reproduce the weepy sentimentality of Petrarch's Paduan friend, as when the Clerk exclaims

---

[33] Petrarch, 'Seniles XVIII.3' , pp. 114–15.

[34] For a full account of the biblical and figural parallels of the 'Clerk's Tale', see John Speirs, *Chaucer the maker* (London: Faber and Faber, 1951), pp. 151–55; Derek Pearsall, *The Canterbury Tales* (New York: Routledge, 1985), p. 269; and Dolores Frese, 'Chaucer's Clerk's Tale: the monsters and the critics reconsidered', *Chaucer Review* 8 (1973), 133–46.

over the affecting nature of Griselda's reunion with her children in the tale's final scene: 'O which a pitous thyng it was to se / Hir swownyng, and hire humble voys to heere!' (1086–85).[35]

Fourteenth-century piety: the disjuncture between official religious culture and lay male activity

An important context for the late-fourteenth-century success of the Griselda legend is the disjuncture between the rapid growth of lay male piety in the decades following the Black Death and the models of religiosity promoted by the Church. While the later fourteenth century saw more and more laymen attempting to unite piety with the domestic and community roles of their daily lives, the Church was slow to provide a textual culture of analytical and imaginative works to support them. The disjuncture – which was most acute at precisely the time of the Griselda legend's first rush of Europe-wide popularity – is important to our reading of Chaucer's 'Clerk's Tale'. As I shall propose in the second half of this chapter, Chaucer's attempt to amplify the masculine emotion and piety of the Griselda legend is not just a mindless repetition of his sources but rather part of a self-conscious reflection upon the socio-historical conditions that fuelled the legend's immense popularity.

Chaucer's host and lay male spirituality

For later medieval laymen, respectable adult masculinity was governed by a few key principles. As well as the basics common throughout the history of the West – pithily summarised by Vern Bullough as 'impregnating women, protecting dependents, and serving as provider to one's family'[36] – medieval culture placed particular emphasis on a man's supervision of the household. This responsibility involved both discipline, to ensure that household members' behaviour met religious and community standards, and nurture, to safeguard the welfare of household members. Weak men are the objects of ridicule in comic literature like the Old French fabliaux of the thirteenth century, which often include morals advising men to assert control over their households. The historical and transnational persistence of this belief is illustrated in the fifteenth-century Englishman

---

[35] Farrell, 'Glosses', 300. Although it is not certain whether Chaucer had access to Petrarch's prefatory letters, Farrell thinks it is conceivable that Chaucer would have had access to Petrarch's prefatory remarks in the *Seniles*.

[36] Vern Bullough, 'On being male in the Middle Ages', in Clare A. Lees (ed.), *Medieval masculinities: regarding men in the Middle Ages* (Minneapolis: University of Minnesota Press, 1994), p. 34.

Peter Idley's advice to his son to chose a good wife but 'yeve hir not the maistrie'.[37]

Insight into the emphasis on nurture as well as control can be found in the early-fifteenth-century campaign of University of Paris chancellor Jean Gerson to renovate the image of St Joseph. In asserting Joseph's exemplarity, Gerson characterises him as a responsible patriarch who administers the household, promotes its fortunes and rules with loving authority over Mary and Jesus.[38] Other thinkers of the period also stress the householder's duty to nurture and to socialise those under his command. St Catherine of Siena urges fathers to 'notricare, reggere e governare la famiglia vostra con santo timore di Dio'.[39] Saint Bernardine describes a husband's four chief duties to his wife: to instruct her, correct her, live with her and support her.[40] In his own behaviour, the adult layman was expected to justify his authority by exhibiting the reason, disinterested judgement and sobriety that was thought to stand in opposition to women's supposed irrationality, weakness and indulgence of the body. Like the injunctions to command, the emphasis on male nurture also exhibits transnational and transhistorical persistence throughout the later Middle Ages, appearing in fifteenth-century English sources as well as those from fourteenth and early fifteenth-century France and Italy.[41]

---

[37] For instance, the fabliau *De Sir Hain et de Dame Anieuse* ('Sir Hate and Lady Hateful') advises that if a man has a domineering wife, he should beat her. See Raymond Eichmann and John Du Val (ed. and trans.), *The French fabliau: B.N. MS. 837*, 2 vols. (New York: Garland, 1984), p. 61; *Peter Idley's instructions to his son*, ed. Charlotte D'Evelyn (Boston: D. C. Heath and Co., 1935), p. 102.

[38] David Herlihy, 'The family and religious ideologies in medieval Europe', in Anthony Molho (ed.), *Women, family, and society in medieval Europe: historical essays 1978–1991* (Providence, RI: Berghahn Books, 1995), p. 172.

[39] St Catherine, *Epistolario di santa Caterina da Siena*, ed. Eugenio Dupré Theseider (Rome: Tipografia del Senato, 1940), p. 573. Also cited in Herlihy, 'Santa Caterina and San Bernardino on the family', in *Women, family, and society*, p. 187.

[40] San Bernardino, 'De matrimonio regulato, inordinato, et separato', in *S. Bernardini senensis opera omnia*, 9 vols. (Florence, 1950), vol. 7, pp. 57–9. Also cited in Herlihy, 'Santa Caterina and San Bernardino on the family', p. 191.

[41] Shannon McSheffrey's research into marriage in fifteenth-century London shows a similar expectation that the householder ought to be in command of his wife and dependents: 'Place, space, and situation', 972. Similarly, Stephanie Tarbin proposes that in late-medieval London, the identification of rationality as a male characteristic and carnality or wilfulness as a female trait inspired community leaders' interest in punishing male sexual infractions, since these crimes were seen as a violation not only of morality but also of manliness, which required one to rule one's own body. Tarbin, 'Moral regulation and civic identity in London 1400–1530', in Linda Rasmussen, Valerie Spear and Dianne Tillotson (eds.), *Our medieval heritage: essays in honour of John Tillotson for his 60th birthday* (Cardiff: Merton Priory Press, 2002), p. 132.

The rapid growth of religious fraternities in Italy, England, Germany and France in the 150 years following the Black Death led to laymen creating models of piety that accorded with these principles of masculinity.[42] John Henderson's study has shown that members of religious confraternities in fourteenth-century Florence fused the devotional and the social through the Pauline concept of charity, which 'fosters vertical devotional links through the love of God and also more horizontal social links through love of one's neighbor'.[43] In so doing, Florentine men extended their domestic roles as caretakers and providers of the household into the broader community and infused those roles with pious meaning. A similar interpenetration of sacred and secular identity is found in English fraternities of the later fourteenth century. Studies have shown that these spontaneous and voluntary associations were primarily the product of middle-class artisans who made the fraternity the centre of their spiritual and social world.[44] While English religious fraternities included women as well as men, their activities accorded particularly well with the masculine domestic role of providing leadership, discipline and financial support to the household. Fraternity activities included a number of initiatives aimed at unifying devotion and community work. Members of English religious fraternities provided funds to keep altar lights burning, ensured proper burials for their members, gave charity to sick and indigent members, maintained good behaviour among members and presented dramatic re-enactments of biblical stories.[45] As Miri Rubin remarks, these activities reflected fraternity members' belief that salvation

---

[42] In England, the post-Black Death growth of religious guilds is marked. There are records of only five London fraternities before the Black Death of 1348–49. Five fraternities were founded in the years 1349 to 1350 and a further seventy-four were founded between 1350–1400. See Caroline M. Barron, 'The parish fraternities of medieval London', in Caroline M. Barron and Christopher Harper-Bill (eds.), *The church in pre-reformation society: essays in honour of F. R. H. Du Boulay* (Woodbridge: Boydell, 1985), p. 23.

[43] John Henderson, *Piety and charity in late medieval Florence* (Oxford: Clarendon Press, 1994), p. 9. Similarly, Richard C. Trexler's study of ritual activities and public life in Florence has shown the interdependency of medieval urban secular identity and 'public sacred behaviour': *Public life in Renaissance Florence* (New York: Academic Press, 1980).

[44] However, in a finding that demonstrates the blurring between bourgeois and gentry identity during this period, one study of the Holy Trinity Guild in St Botolph Aldersgate found that of the 243 guild members who could be identified, 119 were royal servants, lawyers, clergy or gentry and the remaining 124 belonged to London craft guilds or companies. See Barron, 'Parish fraternities', p. 29.

[45] Ibid., pp. 24–6; Miri Rubin, 'Corpus Christi fraternities and late medieval piety', *Studies in Church History* 23 (1986), 97–109. Manuscripts of the cycle drama date from the mid to late fifteenth century. However, other evidence suggests that such presentations date from the fourteenth century. For instance, Chaucer's 'Miller's Prologue and Tale' contain several references to presentations very similar to the cycle drama. See the 'Miller's Prologue' (3124) and 'Miller's Tale' (3384).

could be achieved 'by safeguarding the community, of the quick and the dead, intact'.[46] Moreover, the social-networking aspects of the religious fraternities, which often gathered together members of similar occupational groups, created a contiguity between the layman's work life and his devotions.[47]

While fourteenth-century laymen were adept at merging faith with acceptable masculine behaviour in their daily lives, the Church was slow to provide a textual or imaginative culture to support them. Campaigns by Gerson and San Bernardino to renovate Joseph's image marked the beginning of attempts on the part of official religious culture to tailor piety to the domestic roles of laymen.[48] But these occurred in the very late fourteenth century and fifteenth century, several decades after the growth of religious fraternities. Throughout the fourteenth century, most Church-sponsored models of lay holiness were defined by ascetic, charismatic and mystical notions of spirituality that were often better suited to laywomen than to laymen.[49]

Affective piety, the form of medieval spirituality increasingly popular with lay people in the later Middle Ages, also accords better with the social roles of women than with forms of behaviour considered admirable in men – a fact that is perhaps not surprising given that its major text, the late thirteenth-century *Meditationes vitae Christi*, is addressed to a nun. The *Meditationes* pays special attention to scenes involving women or containing feminine activities like cooking or needlework.[50] Its imaginative prompts urge readers to imagine themselves in a servile position relative to the Holy Family, performing tasks like caring for the Christ child and cooking. An early passage in the *Meditationes*, for instance, encourages readers to participate imaginatively in the Nativity: 'Beg his mother to offer to let you hold Him a while. Pick Him up and hold Him in your arms ... Then return Him to the mother and watch her attentively as

---

[46] Rubin, 'Corpus Christi fraternities', 107.

[47] In early English parish fraternities, the boundary between professional life and pious observance was so permeable that a religious fraternity founded to maintain a light before the cross in a chapel in 1342 had morphed into a craft fraternity of brewers by 1389. Barron, 'Parish fraternities', pp. 13–14.

[48] Other promoters of Joseph include St Vincent de Ferrer and Peter D'Ailly. Herlihy, 'Making of the medieval family', p. 151.

[49] André Vauchez, *Sainthood in the later Middle Ages*, trans. Jean Birrell (Cambridge University Press, 1997), p. 264; Caroline Walker Bynum, *Holy feast and holy fast: the religious significance of food to medieval women* (Berkeley: University of California Press, 1987), pp. 21, 262. Bynum's work includes an extensive discussion of how models of holy behaviour were feminised in the later Middle Ages.

[50] Isa Ragusa and Rosalie B. Green, 'Introduction', *Meditations on the life of Christ: an illustrated manuscript of the fourteenth century*, ed. Isa Ragusa and Rosalie Green, trans. Isa Ragusa (Princeton University Press, 1961), p. xxxi.

she cares for Him … and remain to help her if you can.' Another passage advises the reader to 'Accompany [the Holy Family] and help to carry the child and serve them in every way.'[51]

Affective piety's emphasis on interpreting New Testament events through the prism of the Holy Family was also problematic for medieval men because the humble and often comical status of Joseph in popular medieval religious culture rubbed uncomfortably against prevailing notions of desirable male behaviour. The interventions of Jean Gerson and Bernardino notwithstanding, medieval art, literature and drama reveal a consistent tendency to belittle the holy foster father.[52] Popular medieval images of the Holy Family often characterise Joseph as an impotent and doddering old man. Given God's important familial relationship with Mary and Jesus, medieval portrayals of the Holy Family also often place God in the dominant masculine position and relegate Joseph to an ancillary role.[53] The *Meditationes* itself refers to Mary's husband as 'the saintly old Joseph' and characterises him as markedly lower in stature to the Virgin. When considering Joseph's dream of an angel who warns him to flee to Egypt, the author of the *Meditationes* remarks that the episode very aptly illustrates that visions are not a sign of spiritual superiority, 'since the angel made the revelations to Joseph and not to the Lady, although he was much inferior to her'.[54]

The starkest indication of the disjuncture between the Church's vision of spirituality and the growth of piety among middle-rank men is found in

---

[51] Ragusa and Green (eds.), *Meditations*, pp. 38, 68. Another passage advises the reader on how to comfort the grieving Virgin after the Crucifixion: 'If you will use your powers, you too will know how to obey, serve, console, and comfort her, so that she may eat a little, and comfort the others in doing so, for they have all fasted up to now', p. 347.

[52] Even Gerson's self-conscious attempt to renovate Joseph's image had trouble combating these cultural difficulties and Joseph did not gain a high stature among the faithful until the sixteenth and seventeenth century. Herlihy, 'The family and religious ideologies', p. 172.

[53] For discussions of Joseph's inferior and ridiculous status in later medieval religious culture, see Pamela Sheingorn, 'Joseph the Carpenter's failure at familial discipline', in Colum Hourihane (ed.), *Insights and interpretations: studies in celebration of the eighty-fifth anniversary of the Index of Christian Art* (Princeton University Department of Art and Archeology, 2002), pp. 156–167; Johan Huizinga, *The autumn of the Middle Ages*, trans. Rodney J. Payton and Ulrich Mammitzsch (Chicago: University of Chicago Press, 1996), pp. 193–6; Louise Vasvari, 'Joseph on the margin: The Merod tryptic and medieval spectacle', *Mediaevalia* 18 (1995), 163–89.

[54] Ragusa and Green (eds.), *Meditations*, pp. 38, 67. This image of Joseph is remarkably persistent throughout the later Middle Ages. The diptych of Melchior Broederlam at Dijon (1393–9), which depicts the presentation of Christ in the Temple and the Flight into Egypt, represents Joseph as a coarse old peasant. In the cycle drama, Joseph frequently appears as a ludicrous and jealous old man fussing over his pretty young wife and dubious about her rather wild story of being impregnated by God: 'Troubles of Joseph', in Martin Stevens and A. C. Cawley (eds.), *The Towneley plays*, EETS SS vols. 12, 13 (Oxford, 1994).

the Church's pattern of canonisation. Layman were not popular models of sanctity at any time during the Middle Ages. This remained true even as Church recognition of lay piety increased in the thirteenth and fourteenth centuries. In his comprehensive study of medieval sainthood, André Vauchez notes that after 1305, more than 71 per cent of newly canonised laity were female.[55] Laymen of the middle rank, moreover, were almost never recognised. During the whole of the Middle Ages, the Church canonised only one layman who did not belong to a princely or royal family.[56] This bias left married men and heads of households with little officially sponsored guidance on pious behaviour appropriate to their station. As David Herlihy has remarked, 'Patriarchy did not rule the ranks of the blessed, at least not in the late Middle Ages.'[57]

The 'Clerk's Tale' and laymen: adapting spirituality to lay masculinity

For laymen, the Griselda legend provided an attractive alternative to other pious texts because it reproduced their invitation to veneration and emotional engagement, but in a way that was much better adapted to accepted notions of lay masculinity. Indeed, many of the legend's most eccentric and difficult elements make much more sense when viewed in terms of their capacity to create a viable spiritual experience for middle-rank laymen. Chaucer's own version both amplifies the legend's invitation to lay male engagement and meditates upon its consequences.

Our first indication that Chaucer is highly conscious of the socio-historical dynamics that underlay the Griselda legend's popularity occurs in the 'Clerk's Prologue', in Harry Bailly's directions regarding what sort of tale the Clerk should tell. Here, Chaucer touches upon the conflict between Church-sponsored spirituality and the lay male piety that I have described above. The Host begins by rejecting the contemplative, learned model of piety, ordering that the Clerk reject his 'sophyme' (5). Such a model suggests femininity in Harry Bailly's world, as he indicates when he describes the clerk sitting on his horse 'coy and stille as dooth a mayde' (2). Equally repugnant to the Host is the penitential model; he warns the Clerk against preaching like the friars at Lent, 'to make us of oure olde synnes wepe' (13). Lay male alienation from the conventions of religious narrative is indicated by the Host's reference to boredom in his further injunction to the Clerk 'that thy tale make us nat to slepe' (14). Instead,

---

[55] Vauchez, *Sainthood*, p. 268.
[56] This is the twelfth-century Homobonus, merchant of Cremona. See Vauchez, *Sainthood*, pp. 356, 362–3.
[57] Herlihy, 'The family and religious ideologies in medieval Europe', p. 171.

the Host directs the Clerk to tell 'som murie thyng of aventures' (15), a request that we may think is not fulfilled by the Clerk's rather miserable tale of Griselda until we recall the pleasure that Petrarch and his audience took in the legend. Also remarkable is the Host's very explicit reference to social rank in his directive to the Clerk. Not only is the Clerk supposed to forgo the sorts of tales that appeal to learned clerics, but he should also direct his rhetoric at a middle-rank audience, putting away the 'termes', 'colours', 'figures' and 'heigh style' that the Host associates with writings directed at kings and instead speak plainly enough 'that we may understonde what ye seye' (19–20).

Chaucer's interest in a text that reconstructs piety according to middle-rank lay male domestic values very likely goes beyond an objective interest in the religious lives of members of the urban bourgeoisie like the Host. While Chaucer was a member of the late-fourteenth-century gentry with a long career of service to the most powerful aristocrats of the day, he was born into a middle-rank household and spent much of his life in contact with London's merchant and artisan classes. As G. K. Chesterton has remarked, 'Chaucer was chivalric, in the sense that he belonged, if only by adoption, to the world of chivalry and armorial blazonry ... Chaucer was none the less *bourgeois*, in the sense that he himself was born and bred of the burgesses.'[58] The very little we know about Chaucer's own domesticity suggests that he adopted a stance towards his family very much in line with the bourgeois *pater familias*' role of leadership and nurture. By his own report, Chaucer wrote *A Treatise on the Astrolabe* in response to the 'besy praier' of 'lyte Lowys, my sone'. The work displays Chaucer's intimate knowledge of the ten-year-old's education (he realises Lewis cannot yet read much Latin) and level of ability (Chaucer writes his own simplified treatise for Lewis because other treatises 'ben to harde to thy tendir age of ten yeer to conceyve').[59]

Given the current consensus in Chaucer studies that most of Chaucer's writing is directed at social equals and is only sporadically addressed to the higher echelons of society, we may assume that many in Chaucer's primary audience would have shared his domestic values.[60] The provenance of several of the six fifteenth-century manuscript anthologies in which the 'Clerk's Tale' appears alone (thereby attesting to its popularity separate

---

[58] G. K. Chesterton, *Chaucer* (London: Faber and Faber, 1932), p. 39. Also cited in Paul Strohm, *Social Chaucer* (Cambridge, MA: Harvard University Press, 1989), p. 10.

[59] Chaucer, 'A Treatise on the Astrolabe', p. 662.

[60] Although most of the 'inner circle' of friends and associates that Paul Strohm identifies as Chaucer's principal literary audience would have claimed 'gentle' status, 'each shared with his fellow merchants, citizens and burgesses of the middle strata the fact of non-aristocratic status or social rank': *Social Chaucer*, p. 10.

from the general popularity of the Canterbury collection) suggests a continuing interest in the tale amongst members of the middle rank.[61]

Griselda

For modern readers, one of the oddest elements of Petrarch's version of the legend (and those of later redactors) is the fact that that it claims on the one hand to offer a very profound pious meaning, and on the other features a protagonist (Griselda) whose behaviour and experiences do not accord with the conventions of holy heroism. Those who read the legend according to exemplary paradigms often face difficulties explaining how we might regard as admirable a woman who is so passive in the face of tyrannical authority that she lets her children go when she believes they will be taken away and murdered. Further problems with the exemplary model arise when we consider the exact nature of Griselda's suffering. Griselda's primary trial is to lose her children temporarily and to endure a bad (but not fatal) marriage. This sort of affliction is both qualitatively and quantitatively out of keeping with the agonies of other holy figures to whom she is compared: Christ died a political death whose ultimate function was to redeem suffering; the Holy Virgin suffered the harrowing loss of her son; Job lost everything he held dear – a loss that was remedied, but not replaced. Nor does Griselda suffer in the spectacular, embodied manner of the virgin martyr saints. Indeed, aside from eating a sparse diet and sleeping on a hard bed in her early days as a peasant, Griselda endures very little physical distress at all. This disjuncture is particularly acute in Chaucer's 'Clerk's Tale', which, as I have noted above, plays up Griselda's holy associations to a much greater extent than any other redaction.

---

[61]   HM 140 (1450–80), which also includes passages of advice to children and young men and a work entitled 'Six Masters' opinion on how to please God', was aimed at a mercantile audience. For a description of HM 140, see Manly and Rickert, *The text of the Canterbury Tales*, vol. 1, pp. 433–38. Seth Lerer also describes the manuscript's audience as mercantile. See Lerer, *Chaucer and his readers*, pp. 87–112. Rawlinson c 86 (post 1483) includes signatures that suggest either a mercantile or gentry ownership. For a description, see Manly and Rickert, *The text of the Canterbury Tales*, vol. 1, pp. 472–5. The fifteenth-century provenance of another manuscript, Naples xiii.b.29 (c. 1457) is not known. However, by the sixteenth century it had found its way into the hands of Tommasco Campanella, a Dominican philosopher and poet, who then passed it on to the di Leonardis, a distinguished Calabrian family of lawyers. Manly and Rickert, *The text of the Canterbury Tales*, vol. 1, pp. 379–80. Another manuscript, Longleat 257 (1425–75), which bears the signature of Richard III, was clearly intended for an aristocratic owner; interestingly, it also reveals a strong interest in lay piety. It includes the *Middle English metrical paraphrase of the Old Testament*, an ambitious retelling of the Bible for lay people. For a description, see Manly and Rickert, *The text of the Canterbury Tales*, vol. 1, pp. 339–42; and Charles Owen Jr., *The manuscripts of the Canterbury Tales* (Cambridge: D. S. Brewer, 1991), p. 109.

Chaucer's odd combination of holy reference and less-than-holy heroine makes much more sense, however, if we read the 'Clerk's Tale' as a narrative aimed at inviting lay male readers into a more domesticated experience of affective piety. In the sense that Griselda's patience and humility make her resemble Christ, Mary and the saints, her story is invested with an air of holiness. In the sense that her sufferings are more domestic than political or spectacular, she allows laymen a greater access to that holiness than is permitted by those other religious narratives.

Griselda's social position makes her particularly amenable to the imaginative intervention of Chaucer's audience. Young, female and vulnerable, Griselda is precisely the kind of person whom medieval English men were charged with protecting from harm.[62] Guild records show that senior men often took responsibility for young women, even when the latter were not members of the man's household. Several guild ordinances allow for the provision of dowries to daughters of deceased or impoverished guild members.[63] As a young girl from a peasant background, isolated geographically from her family and taken into a wealthy household, Griselda also fits the profile of the servant girls so often employed in the bourgeois households of later medieval England.[64] This was a group towards whom middle-rank men also felt a particular duty. Historically, housemaids were the responsibility of their male employers. Many employers acted as surrogate fathers to their female servants, negotiating the young women's marriages and ensuring that they did not partake in unsavoury relationships.[65] The similarity between Griselda

---

[62] Griselda's attractiveness in this respect might also account for the popularity of virgin martyr saints among later medieval laymen. Evidence from fourteenth and fifteenth-century England suggests that young, vulnerable virgin martyrs like St Katherine of Alexandria were very popular. While most saints are credited with no more than eight extant lives in medieval English manuscripts, the life of St Katherine is recorded in at least fourteen different Middle English versions, as well as twelve Latin lives and three Anglo-Norman ones. There are eleven extant lives for another virgin martyr, St Margaret. Guild returns also give evidence of a marked preference for St Katherine. The returns of 1389 record twenty-two guilds of St Katherine; the only more popular saint is John the Baptist, with forty-nine dedications. Katherine Lewis, *The cult of St Katherine of Alexandria in late medieval England* (Woodbridge: Boydell & Brewer, 2000), pp. 2, 163.

[63] Toulmin Smith and Lucy Toulmin Smith (eds.), *English gilds: the original ordinances of more than one hundred early English gilds*, EETS OS vol. 40 (London, 1870), pp. 194, 340.

[64] Goldberg, 'Masters and men in later medieval England', p. 68.

[65] Shannon McSheffrey, 'Introduction', in Shannon McSheffrey (ed. and trans.), *Love and marriage in late medieval London*, TEAMS Documents of the Practice Series (Kalamazoo, MI: Medieval Institute Publications, 1995), p. 18; McSheffrey, '"I will never have non against my faders will": consent and the making of marriage in the late medieval diocese of London', in Constance M. Rousseau and Joel T. Rosenthal (eds.), *Women, marriage and family in medieval Christendom: essays in memory of Michael M. Sheehan, C.S.B.* (Kalamazoo, MI: Medieval Institute Publications, 1998), p. 160.

and the later medieval servant girl is frequently emphasised in the 'Clerk's Tale', which often features Griselda performing the duties of a house-maid, cleaning, cooking and preparing Walter's household for a gathering. The identification is further supported by Griselda's own profession to Walter on the day he exiles her from his house, when she remarks to her former husband that she had never believed herself worthy enough to be his 'chamberere' (chambermaid) and had always regarded herself as 'But humble servant to youre worthynese' (819; 824).

Although it is beyond the scope of this chapter to explore the full range of the legend's impact in other national contexts, it is worth noting that this aspect of the legend may well have held a similar appeal for Italian men. As a poor girl who lacks a strong father figure, and, later, as a pregnant woman and a mother of small children, Griselda occupies two positions that would have rendered her a popular object of charity among confraternities in fourteenth-century Florence. In the years following the Black Death, Florentine charitable confraternities developed a particular interest in dowerless girls, giving greater amounts of money to those individuals than to orphaned boys or recently widowed women as part of an attempt to make up for 'the loss by girls of the financial and legal support of their fathers during a particularly vulnerable stage in their life-cycle'.[66] Pregnant women and mothers with small children were also popular objects of charity in the Florentine confraternities. The insignia for the charitable confraternity of Orsanmichele included two lame and blind men, and a pregnant woman. Records of the fraternity reveal that throughout its history, it provided considerable support for pregnant women and women with small children.[67]

Walter's flaws

The fact that Griselda's suffering is psychological rather than physical – so perplexing if her role is to stand as a holy exemplar – is also conducive to the intervention of the lay male audience. As Elaine Scarry has observed, physical pain has the distinction among other forms of suffering of being entirely internalised, experienced by the individual alone and incapable of being shared collectively.[68] Thus, the embodied suffering of Christ and the saints may be worthy of admiration, but it presents a challenge to the kind of piety that demands close emotional identification. Charismatic piety manages to solve this problem by replicating the suffering of the

---

[66] Henderson, *Piety and charity*, pp. 274, 320.   [67] Ibid, p. 274.
[68] Elaine Scarry, *The body in pain: the making and unmaking of the world* (New York: Oxford University Press, 1985), p. 5.

divine in the worshipper. But this, as I have noted in my discussion above, was not easily accessible to most bourgeois laymen in later medieval England. Griselda's familial suffering, on the other hand, is entirely externalised and public and thus imminently available to engage her lay male audience.

Like his characterisation of Griselda, Chaucer's portrait of Walter is not easily assimilated to a typological or exemplary reading of the 'Clerk's Tale'. Those who wish to read the Walter–Griselda marriage as a stand-in for the soul's relationship to God have always found it difficult to explain why Chaucer should have chosen to make Walter more heartless and less inscrutable than he appears in the sources. Chaucer's alterations to Petrarch's original systematically eliminate the compassion Walter occasionally shows to Griselda. For instance, in the climactic moment of Walter's torture, when he demands that Griselda leave his house to make room for a new wife and she responds stoically, asking only for a shift to wear on her way home, Petrarch's version shows a softer side of Walter, describing him as being so overcome by tears that he must turn his face away from Griselda to hide them ('Habundabant viro lacrime, ut contineri ampliusiam non possent. Itaque faciem avertens…'). He then leaves weeping ('et sic abiit illacrimans').[69] In Chaucer's version, Walter sheds no tears but rather finds he must leave Griselda's presence, 'for routhe and for pitee' (893). Elizabeth Salter regards this choice as an artistic failure, because it renders Chaucer's Walter too flawed and too human to stand for God.[70] The inconsistency seems particularly acute in light of Chaucer's references to the Book of Job, a narrative whose primary purpose is to illustrate the absolute incommensurability between the ways of God and those of humanity.

Once again, however, if we examine the character of Walter in terms of its capacity to facilitate male imaginative participation in the tale, Chaucer's choice makes much better artistic sense. Walter's humanity and flaws are precisely what allow laymen to intervene legitimately on Griselda's behalf. Unlike God, Walter does not embody an awesome, inscrutable masculine power whose mysteries are not open to interrogation. Readers of the tale need not adopt a deferential stance towards Walter – as they must towards God the Father in tales of Mary or the virgin martyr saints – because his flaws as a human being are so obvious.

This same interest in demoting Walter is evident in the reluctance of Chaucer (and of Petrarch before him) to portray the full extent of Walter's military power. As the Marquis of Saluzzo, Walter is a mighty aristocrat,

[69] Correale and Hamel (eds.), *Sources and analogues*, pp. 124–5.
[70] Salter, *Knight's Tale and Clerk's Tale*, p. 59.

and yet we never see him participating in combat or in the fearsome martial processionals that define a figure like Theseus in the 'Knight's Tale'. Instead, Walter is almost exclusively figured in domestic settings that are not much different from the ones in which an average bourgeois man might find himself. Even the betrothal scene in Griselda's humble village – ostensibly a moment in which Walter's power as an aristocrat over his peasant subjects is most in evidence – looks very much like the betrothals of the London middle classes.[71] Nor, for all his dictatorial arrogance, do Walter's actions with Griselda and her children require more authority than an average bourgeois householder would have at his disposal. Sending away his children to be raised by an aunt was surely not beyond the powers of the average man. Ejecting one's wife from the household without a divorce was illegal (and Walter's aristocratic status may explain why he is not immediately punished for this infraction), but as an action in and of itself, the ejection of Griselda requires nothing more than the average man's usual control over his household. This stands in contrast to the military capacity and political authority required, for instance, of Theseus for the invasion of Thebes in the 'Knight's Tale'.

Once again, it is difficult to make these details fit into a typological or exemplary interpretation. If the point of the 'Clerk's Tale' is to illustrate a pious woman's sufferings under tyranny, then surely images of Walter's political and military power would only increase our admiration of Griselda. The lack of interest in Walter's military power does, however, make sense if the end is to encourage imaginative intervention, since Walter's domesticity renders him all the more susceptible to the judgement of a bourgeois male audience.

In the Continental redactions, the Griselda legend's call to active participation, and its similarity to the texts of affective piety, is implicit. In Chaucer's 'Clerk's Tale', these features become aggressively explicit. The Clerk's frequent celebrations of Griselda's patience and condemnations of Walter's cruelty invite readers to join him in an emotionally engaged experience of the narrative. Moreover, the Clerk refers to his addition to the Canterbury collection not as a tale, but as an 'excercise' (1156), the same term that the *Meditationes vitae Christi* uses to describe its spiritual activities.[72]

Social conditions in late-fourteenth and fifteenth-century England accentuated the legend's invitation to male intervention, helping to explain Chaucer's interest in it and its continuing popularity in the hundred years

---

[71] McSheffrey, 'Place, space, and situation', 974. McSheffrey notes that it was common for London betrothals to occur in the woman's home.

[72] Ragusa and Green (eds.), *Meditations*, 1.

after his death. Of particular importance in the English social context is the fact that Griselda's afflictions occur within a marriage. In later medieval England, marriage was central to the adult identity of bourgeois laymen, demarcating a man's passage from adolescence to adulthood.[73] Charles Pythian Adams has observed that, among medieval craftsmen and merchants, 'marriage was the single most important step in an individual's career', moving men into a socially superior age group and a new domestic unit.[74] In his community, a man's identity was rooted in his relationship to the household. A man's 'reputation for honesty, good fame, and status depended on his ability to protect and control his dependents'.[75] Recognising that a functioning marital partnership was essential in all but the highest levels of society, authors of late-medieval advice manuals for men inevitably devote a good deal of time to the matter of marriage and the choosing of a wife.

Scholarship on the 'Clerk's Tale' has not sufficiently appreciated how profoundly Walter's behaviour towards Griselda violates late-medieval criteria for a good husband. The strict sense of hierarchy that pervaded medieval marriage theory – in which the husband was in command and the wife was obliged to obey him – did not mean that a husband was entitled to treat his wife in whatever way he chose. Medieval culture did not allow the father life or death power over his family in the manner of the Roman *patria potestas*.[76] Rather, it was deeply influenced by the words of Paul's letter to the Ephesians, which advises that the husband is ethically bound to love his wife as his own body.[77] Medieval advice manuals for men frequently reflect this doctrine, citing Paul's letter and recommending affectionate treatment of wives, even as they insist that men should always have 'the maistrie'. In the Middle English *How the Goode Man Taght Hys Sone*, a father advises his son to be affectionate and kind towards his wife, noting that

> Thogh sche be sirvunt in degree,
> In some degre sche fellowe ys.[78]

Of particular concern to the middle-rank men of later medieval England would have been Walter's desire to tempt Griselda. Convictions regarding

[73] Ruth Mazo Karras, *From boys to men: formations of masculinity in late medieval Europe* (Philadelphia: University of Pennsylvania Press, 2003), p. 16.

[74] Charles Phythian-Adams, *Desolation of a city: Coventry and the urban crisis in the late Middle Ages* (Cambridge University Press, 1979), p. 86.

[75] Shannon McSheffrey, 'Jurors, respectable masculinity, and Christian morality: a comment on Marjorie McIntosh's *Controlling misbehavior*', *Journal of British Studies* 37 (1998), 272.

[76] Herlihy, 'The family and religious ideologies', p. 159.   [77] Eph. 5.21–29.

[78] 'How the goode man taght hys sone', in Eve Salisbury (ed.), *The trials and Joys of marriage* (Kalamazoo, MI: Medieval Institute Publications, 2002), pp. 131–2.

women's weak nature meant a husband was charged with protecting his wife from temptation, not putting it in her path. Poems of advice frequently express a keen sense of the husband's responsibility to super-intend the moral weaknesses and susceptibility of his wife and not to test her. The Middle Scots poem *Ratis Raving* advises a husband to 'leid hir wysly with fauore', if he wishes to have his wife honour him. Later, the poet implies that communities often blamed unruly wives on a husband's mistreatment, advising the husband to treat his wife well so that no one will blame him if she misbehaves:

> Bot do pow sa thine awne part,
> That nane reprufe the efterwart,
> Na sa tha scho was cauß in the
> That suld amove It fo to bee.[79]

Similarly, in the Middle English *Myne Owne Dere Sone*, a father advises his son not to be 'jelous' of his wife, lest his suspicions and accusations push her into an infidelity she should never have considered otherwise.[80]

Walter's mistreatment of Griselda encourages laymen to intervene imaginatively because medieval English culture advocated senior male intervention in pathological marriages. A number of recent studies have shown how, during the fourteenth and fifteenth centuries in England, senior middle-rank men were increasingly being given the responsibility for policing community morals, including sexual behaviour.[81] Marjorie McIntosh's study of the leet courts in late-medieval English villages and market towns has led her to conclude that, due to the breakdown of the manorial system and the unwillingness of larger bodies of government to

---

[79] *Ratis Raving*, in J. Rawson Lumby (ed.), *Ratis Raving and other moral and religious pieces in prose and verse*, EETS OS vol. 43 (London, 1870), pp. 52–53 [lines 943, 965–68].

[80] Tuano J. Mustanoja (ed.), 'Myne awen dere sone', *Neuphilologische Mitteilungen* 49 (1948), 145–93.

[81] McSheffrey, 'Introduction'; and 'Jurors, respectable masculinity, and Christian morality'; also her 'Men and masculinity in late medieval London civic culture: governance, patri-archy, and reputation', in Jacqueline Murray (ed.), *Conflicting identities: men in the Middle Ages* (New York: Garland Press, 1999), pp. 243–78; Marjorie K. McIntosh, 'Finding a language for misconduct: jurors in fifteenth century local courts', in Barbara A. Hanawalt and David Wallace (eds.), *Bodies and discipline* (Minneapolis: University of Minnesota Press, 1996), pp. 87–122, and *Controlling misbehavior in England, 1370–1600* (Cambridge University Press, 1998); Cordelia Beattie, 'Governing bodies: law courts, male house-holders, and single women in late medieval England', in Cordelia Beattie, Anna Maslakovic and Sarah Rees Jones (eds.), *The medieval household in Christian Europe c. 850–1550: managing power, wealth, and the body* (Turnhout: Brepols, 2003), pp. 199–220; Rees Jones, 'The household and English urban government in the later Middle Ages'; Ben R. McRee, 'Religious guilds and the regulation of behavior in late medieval towns', in Joel Rosenthal and Colin Richmond (eds.), *People, politics, and community in the later Middle Ages* (New York: St. Martin's Press, 1987), pp. 108–122; Tarbin, 'Moral regulation'.

regulate community matters, responsibility for maintaining order increasingly fell on householders of middling rank.[82] In London, the mayor and aldermen supervised the regulation of morals within their jurisdiction. Juries in local ward mote assemblies were required to report suspected sexual infractions. Ward officers, assisted by leading householders, detected and imprisoned couples accused of adultery and fornication.[83] Older men were entitled to tell those engaging in adultery or bigamy to desist, and to put pressure on couples engaged in a sexual relationship with no apparent intention of marrying.[84] Shannon McSheffrey's study of fifteenth-century London legal records has led her to conclude that medieval patriarchy extended much wider than a father's governance of his household:

paternal power was echoed and buttressed by the paternalistic authority exercised generally by respectable older men, the fathers of the community. Senior men had the duty and the privilege to govern and to ensure the proper working of social relationships within their sphere of action. The maintenance of community and the marital bond that, in many ways, was at its heart, was their responsibility.[85]

For these men, controlling male behaviour was as important as controlling female behaviour. The ordinances of the Guild of St Anne, in the church of St Lawrence, Jewry, London, for instance, warned guild members that:

If any of the company be of wicked fame of his body, and take other wives than his own, or if he be a single man, and be hold a common lechour or contekour, or rebel of his tonge, he shall be warned of the Warden three times; and if he will not himself amend, he shall pay to the Wardens all of his arrearages that he oweth to the company, and he shall be put off for evermore.[86]

The ordinances of the Guild of the Holy Trinity and St Leonard of Lancaster warned that a guild member would be exiled if he lived in adultery, or took anyone into his house who had been an adulterer.[87] These same regulations also encouraged guild members to protect one another's dependents, declaring that 'No one of the guild shall wrong the wife or daughter or sister of another, *nor shall allow her to be wronged* so far as he can hinder it'[88] (italics mine).

Chaucer's 'Clerk's Tale' dramatises precisely the kind of senior male intervention I have been discussing when it features a committee of 'the

[82] McIntosh, 'Finding a language', 88. See also *Controlling misbehavior*.
[83] Tarbin, 'Moral regulation', p. 127.
[84] McSheffrey, 'Introduction', p. 19 and 'Men and masculinity', p. 251.
[85] McSheffrey, 'Introduction', p. 19.   [86] Smith and Smith, *English gilds*, p. xl.
[87] Ibid, p. 163.   [88] Ibid.

peple' choosing a spokesperson 'that wisest was of loore' to advise Walter to secure his succession by marrying. One might say that Walter's noble status would have stymied such notions of intervention, but here we must once again note how unwilling Chaucer is to display Walter in all his noble military power. The tale's initial description of the 'yonge' Walter hunting and hawking to the detriment of all other cares makes him appear less like a leader and more like the kind of hot-blooded post-adolescent that senior men were frequently called on to discipline in late-medieval English communities.[89]

The reader as character: Griselda's passivity and readers' resistance

Placing Chaucer's Griselda in the context of marriage theory in later medieval England can also help us to understand the logic behind one of Griselda's most notorious features: her extreme passivity in the face of Walter's cruelty. Many readers have been troubled by the suggestion that Griselda's passivity amounts to an affirmation of total obedience to political authority, regardless of the consequences. In this section, I want instead to suggest that the Chaucer's tale *does* encourage resistance, not by example, but by creating an emotional vacuum that the reader himself is obliged to fill.

Griselda's passivity is problematic for many readers because they at once sense a tremendous pressure in the tale demanding some kind of resistance to Walter's cruel behaviour and yet cannot square this pressure with Chaucer's endorsement of Griselda. In considering this situation, most critics have assumed that the responsibility for resisting Walter lies with Griselda. Thus, those who believe the tale encourages us to resist tyranny must condemn Griselda as a monster. Conversely, those who wish to retain Chaucer's pious notion of the character have denied that the tale exhibits any pressures of this kind, arguing that it only reflects medieval convictions about the necessity of obeying authority, no matter how unjust.

The problem here is not with the idea of resistance but with assumptions as to who is responsible for resisting. Medieval marriage theory

---

[89] Walter's carefree behaviour reflects Barbara Hanawalt's description of the medieval 'wild and wanton' adolescent who must be disciplined by 'sad and wise' adults. That senior men would often be called on to enforce such discipline is evidenced in Stephanie Tarbin's description of apprenticeship contracts that instruct apprentices not to marry or commit fornication during their period of service. Hanawalt, *Growing up in medieval London: the experience of childhood in history* (New York: Oxford University Press, 1993), pp. 108–13; Tarbin, 'Moral regulation', p. 133.

required that Griselda obey her husband. While medieval culture placed certain restrictions on *patria potestas*, it did not entitle women to resist unfair treatment. Very few models of honourable female resistance were available in a culture that closely identified wifely disobedience with misrule, disorder and social breakdown. As Paul Strohm has recently noted, the 1352 Statute of Treason in England names a wife's murder of her husband and a servant's murder of his master (also relevant, given Griselda's rank) as acts of treason.[90] But as we have seen from my discussion above, this does not mean that medieval culture was without a notion of a husband's responsibilities. Bad husbands did indeed exist, but the duty of correcting them lay not with the wife but with other men in the community.[91]

Thus, the problem in the 'Clerk's Tale' is not with Griselda, but with the absence of men who might come to her defence. Griselda's complete isolation in the face of Walter's tyranny is remarkable – the fact that she has no mother, no brothers or cousins, to defend her. The result is the poetic equivalent of eliminating the invisible 'fourth wall' in theatre: it results in a breakdown of the separation between characters and audience. Because Griselda remains undefended, the pressure to resist Walter becomes a vacuum, pulling the tale's audience in to play the role that is required but that no character is willing to take.

If that vacuum is present in other versions of the tale, it is significantly increased in Chaucer's version. As I have noted above, Chaucer's alterations to Petrarch's original eliminate the compassion Walter occasionally shows to Griselda, making him harder and more cruel. Chaucer also exaggerates Griselda's pathos, making her appear more pitiful than she does in his sources. Griselda's leave-taking of her first child, for instance, is expanded to include a speech in which Griselda sadly bids the little girl farewell and remarks that 'this nyght shaltow dyen for my sake' (560). Similarly, the tranquillity of Petrarch's Griselda during her exile from Walter's house is interrupted somewhat in Chaucer by a brief moment of nostalgia in which Griselda remembers the happy early days of her marriage:

> O goode God! How gentil and how kynde
> Ye semed by your speche and your visage
> The day that maked was oure mariage!   (852–4)

---

[90] Paul Strohm, *Hochon's arrow: the social imagination of fourteenth-century texts* (Princeton University Press, 1992), p. 125.

[91] Medieval culture also allowed for women to correct their husbands. My intent here is not to deny this, but rather to note that such council is not strictly required of women in marriage in the way that obedience is. In spite of advice to women to admonish their husbands, medieval culture retained a great deal of antipathy to female challenges to male authority.

This drive to open the tale up to the participation of its audience also accounts for what would otherwise be a very strange oversight in a pious tale – Griselda's rather distant relationship with God. God does not appear to Griselda, nor is she presented as being in his particular care in the way that Mary and the virgin martyr saints are. Nor is Griselda shown seeking out this relationship. She certainly prays, but she does not do so with anything like the frequency of Chaucer's other religious heroines, such as Custance in the 'Man of Law's Tale' or Cecilia in the 'Second Nun's Tale'. But this does not suggest that she is ungodly. Clearly, Griselda is virtuous and good. But she is not so holy that her male audience need be discouraged by God's dominant masculine presence.

Piety, politics and domesticity

Politically, the 'Clerk's Tale' has often been regarded as a conservative, even regressive, work. This is not surprising given the tale's conclusion. Griselda returns to Walter, thereby affirming his authority and the tyrannical ideology he represents, both as a husband and as a ruler. Meanwhile, Walter's people, who begin the tale in an authoritative advisory role, are decried in the narrative's concluding sections as unprincipled and fickle.

I have no wish to argue that the 'Clerk's Tale' does not ultimately affirm the status quo in Saluzzo. However, the final, climactic sections of Walter's torture of Griselda – consisting of her departure from his household and her return to it as a servant – are remarkable both for the intense critique they contain of Walter as a husband and also for how they manage to extend that critique into a political statement that promotes the middle ranks of society as a source of political wisdom and stability. Even as Griselda continues through these passages in complete submission to Walter, her passivity inspires the Clerk and, by extension, the tale's audiences to deliver a critique of the domestic and political system that allows for her degradation. Readers of this tale who have looked for movements of resistance and regression have tended to focus on the contrast between the tale proper and Chaucer's Envoy. According to these readings, the comical wifely rebellion recommended in the Envoy acts as a release valve for the oppressive domestic politics of the tale's conclusion. In the following section, I wish to suggest that the real political watershed in the 'Clerk's Tale' occurs when Walter welcomes Griselda back into the marriage, thereby initiating a regression back to the status quo that continues *through* the Envoy which – in spite of its apparent promotion of wifely rebellion – is just as affirmative of the status quo as the Walter–Griselda reunion.

The first episode of these final passages, Griselda's exit from Walter's house, is both the tale's most distasteful exhibition of a wife's degradation and, ironically, its moment of most articulate resistance to the theory of feminine inferiority that creates it. Bareheaded and barefoot, stripped down to her shift, Griselda proceeds to her father's home, leading a parade of 'folk' who follow her, 'wepynge in hir weye' (897). Before this moment, the Clerk has criticised Walter's poor treatment of Griselda, but this passage is the first time he extends his critique beyond the particulars of the Walter–Griselda relationship to question the notions of female inferiority that inform Walter's suspicion of Griselda and his need to test her. Making a passionate tribute to Griselda's 'pacient benyngnytee' (929), the Clerk goes on to note that while clerks often praise Job for his humbleness, their work is primarily concerned with men. This, the Clerk objects, is wrong, since women far exceed men in the virtues of humbleness and loyalty:

> Though clerkes preise wommen but a lite,
> Ther kan no man in humblesse hym acquite
> As womman kan, ne kan been half so trewe
> As wommen been, but it be falle of newe.   (932–5)

The passage is also notable for its very explicit rejection of an oppositional model of gender relations – which sets men and women at odds in an interminable battle of the sexes – in favour of a model that emphasises male–female reciprocity. The reciprocal model has been encouraged throughout the tale by Chaucer's invitation to readers to intervene on Griselda's behalf which, as I have noted above, emphasises those facets of medieval patriarchy that call on men to nurture women, rather than discipline them. This passage sees the most explicit articulation of that reciprocal model. The Clerk's identification with Griselda, his critique of Walter and his critique of clerical misogyny suggest that strict gender divisions do not always apply and that men can side *with* women *against* other men.

This interrogation of misogyny and the move from an oppositional to a reciprocal model of gender relationships also appears in the 'marriage group' fictions that frame the 'Clerk's Tale' in the Canterbury collection. The Clerk's critique of clerical misogyny takes up the Wife of Bath's objections to clerks who never 'speke good' of wives ('Wife of Bath's Prologue' 689), and the Wife herself shifts from opposition to reciprocity when her fifth marriage to Janekin changes from a pitched battle between misogynist and shrew to a new alliance based on a mutual release of power.[92] This same opposition also appears in the 'Merchant's Tale' when the combative January–May

---

[92] Janekin gives the Wife 'the governance of hous and lond' (WBP 814) and the Wife in turn becomes 'to hym as kynde / As any wyf from Denmark unto Ynde' (WBP 823–4).

relationship is set against that of Pluto and Proserpina, who initially fight but then negotiate a truce after both admit they no longer wish to oppose each other.[93]

The 'Clerk's Tale', however, is remarkable for being the only one of these fictions to explore the links between domestic politics and the power relationships of the wider community. In the final episodes of the tale, outrage over Griselda's plight metamorphoses briefly into a larger critique that identifies the pious Griselda closely with middle-rank lay people and positions that group as the source of reason and justice in a world gone mad. This middle-rank critique is crystallised in the speech against the 'peple' delivered at the nadir of the tale's political and domestic relations. Griselda has been dismissed from Walter's household, then reintegrated as a domestic servant; Walter's new young 'bride' arrives and the people, formerly heartbroken at Griselda's exile, now begin to praise Walter's wisdom in choosing a new wife. At this moment, in an addition to the text that is entirely Chaucer's own, the people are condemned for their changeability and unreliable judgement:

> 'O stormy peple! Unsad and evere untrewe!
> Ay undiscreet and chaungynge as a fane!
> Delitynge evere in rumbul that is newe,
> For lyk the moone ay wexe ye and wane!
> Ay ful of clappyng, deere ynogh a jane!
> Youre doom is fals, youre constance yvele preeveth;
> A ful greet fool is he that on yow leeveth.'   (995–1001)

On the surface, this condemnation may seem to affirm Walter's authority, but in fact it makes a very interesting distinction that subtly promotes a certain subset of Walter's subjects. The passage is spoken not in the voice of the author, but by 'the sadde folk in that citee' (1002). Who exactly these 'sadde folk' might be is never explicitly stated. But the fact that they are 'folk' rather than 'gentils', and the fact that they are located in the city, suggests an urban bourgeois identity. Moreover, as spectators who decry the mad goings-on of Saluzzo, these folk are closely aligned with the tale's audience, who also watch and decry the tale's events.

It is also in these passages that the link between Griselda's quasi-pious heroism and the urban bourgeoisie is made most explicit. Sobriety and seriousness – the two qualities that earn Griselda praise and celebration

---

[93] After fighting over who is in the wrong in the January–May marriage, Pluto and Proserpina both give up ground in order to achieve peace. Pluto tells Proserpina, 'be no lenger wrooth; / I yeve it up!' (MerT 2311–12). Proserpina responds similarly by saying 'Lat us namoore wordes heerof make; / For sothe, I wol no lenger yow contrarie' (MerT 2314–15).

throughout the tale – are in this passage linked to those same members of the urban bourgeoisie who decry the people's fickle behaviour.[94] The Clerk describes them as 'sadde folk of that citee', an adjective that denotes seriousness and sobriety in Middle English and that is used to describe Griselda nine different times through the course of the tale.[95] The nature of Griselda's journey from Walter's home to that of her father also evinces a middle-rank identity. While in religious terms Griselda's journey recalls Christ's walk to Calvary, in cultural terms, the procession of 'folk' that she leads looks very much like the religious processions that Charles Phythian-Adams and Mervyn James have identified as a core expression of late-medieval bourgeois urban identity.[96]

Thus in these climactic moments of the tale, the tyranny of Walter and the irrational responses of his people are contrasted not only with the sober and steady behaviour of Griselda herself, but also with a group of middle-rank subjects. While this group's critique of the people's fickleness is ostensibly separate from the Clerk's ongoing objections to Walter's domestic politics, the two are, in fact, closely aligned because Griselda, the 'sadde folk of the city' and the members of the tale's audience who take up the Clerk's invitations to object to Walter's behaviour as a husband are all unified according to a common set of practices and values that were closely identified with the middle ranks in later medieval England. Moreover, the conflation of the domestic and the political in these final passages is accentuated by the fact that Griselda's exile and return are both public events, observed by all members of Saluzzian society and involving political, as well as domestic, consequences.

Regression

The alliance between Griselda and the 'sadde folke' is quickly dissipated by the Walter–Griselda reunion, which reintegrates Griselda into the aristocratic household. This reintegration accomplishes two things. In

---

[94] Sobriety and seriousness were highly valued in the bourgeois culture of later medieval England. Barbara Hanawalt and Ben McRee describe the sober, responsible behaviour that guilds required of their members. Similarly, Shannon McSheffrey describes how fifteenth-century civic and ecclesiastical documents often use words like 'boni et graves' to denote respectable members of the community. Hanawalt and McRee, 'Guilds of *homo prudens* in late medieval England', *Continuity and Change* 7 (1992), 163–79; McSheffrey, 'Men and masculinity', p. 256.

[95] Griselda is described as having 'sad courage' (220), a 'sad contenance' (293), a 'sad face' (552), and a 'sad visage' (693). She is 'sad stedfast' (564), 'sad and kynde' (602), 'sad for everemo' (754) and 'sad and constant as a wal' (1047). She holds her children 'sadly' (1100).

[96] Phythian-Adams, *Desolation of a city*, pp. 112–22; Mervyn James, 'Ritual, drama and social body in the late medieval English town', *Past and Present* 98 (1983), 3–29.

domestic terms, it justifies Walter's abuse of Griselda by asserting that such treatment can result in a happy and successful marriage. In political terms, it justifies Walter's authority by demonstrating that he can recognise and appropriate the bourgeois values that formerly stood in stark opposition to his tyranny in the climactic procession scene.

One of the most remarkable features of the tale's conclusion and the Envoy is the way that they continue to align domestic politics with power relations in the broader community. If, in the climactic final episodes of the tale, resistance to Walter is linked with a reciprocal model of gender relations, the reinstatement of Walter is correspondingly linked through the Envoy to a reinstatement of the combative model. Griselda, the Clerk tells us in the Envoy, 'is deed, and eek hire pacience' (1177) and so, presumably, are the cross-gender alliances she inspires. In its place, the Envoy promotes the familiar battle of the sexes. Dedicated to the Wife of Bath and drawing on the tropes of misogynist tracts and obscene comedy, the Envoy's ironic advice to women fully to indulge themselves in nagging and answering back to their husbands emphasises those elements of medieval culture that figured relations between the sexes as a struggle for power in which men must fight to assert control over women's disruptive and anti-social behaviour. The masculine sympathy that exerts such a powerful force over the 'Clerk's Tale' proper is denigrated throughout the Envoy, but most particularly in its evocation of the tale of Bycorne and Chichevache (1188). Featuring a grossly obese cow that feeds on patient husbands and a lean one that feeds on patient wives, the story makes a laughing stock of masculine sympathy, characterising it as a weakness that leads to female rebellion against established hierarchies.

In spite of the regressive movement of the Envoy, however, the tale retains its power to evoke strong emotions in its readers, to bind that emotion to religious faith, and to use that fusion to enhance a new bourgeois identity. Historians have noted that, particularly in the towns and cities of England in the second half of the fifteenth century, merchants and craftsmen created a lay-centred, civic-minded style of Catholicism.[97] According to this model, civic elites viewed their attempts to regulate their communities as pious work that ensured the preservation of Christian society. Thus, laymen sanctified the execution of their secular duties as acts of religious devotion. As a literary work that invites its audience to an adult male experience of piety, Chaucer's 'Clerk's Tale' is a literary avatar of this historical trend.

---

[97] McSheffrey, 'Jurors, respectable masculinity, and Christian morality', 277; H. F. Westlake, *The parish guilds of mediaeval England* (London: Society for Promoting Christian Knowledge, 1919); Susan Brigden, 'Religion and social obligation in early-sixteenth-century London', *Past and Present* 103 (1984), 67–112.

10 On the sadness of not being a bird: late-medieval marriage ideologies and the figure of Abraham in William Langland's *Piers Plowman*[1]

Isabel Davis

Introduction

In the C-text revision of *Piers Plowman*, Langland saw fit to sanitise and moderate his poem in a number of areas. As a result the B-text, the earlier version, is seen by scholars as a more daring piece of political commentary. Part of the picture about Langland's poetic negotiations of contemporary ideologies, one which has not yet been fully drawn, concerns his partiality to marriage, which is strategically, although incompletely, written out in C. In striving to be more judicious, the C-text interiorises a cultural anxiety surrounding marriage in the period just after the Peasants' Revolt. Indeed, it has been suggested by Ralph Hanna that the absence of material on marriage from the later C-text, just like the omission in C of B's apparently incendiary discussion of labour politics, was a direct reaction to the use that was made of *Piers Plowman* in that rising.[2] This chapter investigates Langland's strategic contribution to the marriage debate in the last decades of the fourteenth century, looking

[1] I am grateful to the editors of this volume, Jeremy Goldberg and Maryanne Kowaleski, the audience of the Medieval Domesticity conference at Fordham, Emma Mason and Richard Rowland for their constructive comments on earlier versions of this chapter and the conference paper from which it originated.

[2] Ralph Hanna, *William Langland*, Authors of the Middle Ages 3 (Aldershot: Variorum, 1993), p. 148. The B-text and the C-text are dated to before and after the Peasants' Revolt respectively, allowing this speculation on Langland's response to the rising. For a discussion of the political importance of the C-text revisions, see Kathryn Kerby-Fulton, 'Langland and the bibliographic ego', in Steven Justice and Kathryn Kerby-Fulton (eds.), *Written work: Langland, labor, and authorship* (Philadelphia: University of Pennsylvania Press, 1997), pp. 69 and 74–6; James Simpson, 'The constraints of satire in *Piers Plowman* and *Mum and the Sothsegger*', in Helen Phillips (ed.), *Langland, the mystics and the medieval English religious tradition: essays in honour of S. S. Hussey* (Cambridge: D. S. Brewer, 1990), pp. 11–30 (*passim*) and Andrew Cole, 'Trifunctionality and the tree of charity', *English Literary History* 62 (1995), pp. 16–17.

at what exactly some of his rewrites do to the case for marriage in his poem and how they might be read as evidence for sexual attitudes in this period.

To say, as some critics do, that marriage is only a metaphor for William Langland is akin to arguing that he is only interested in plough-men as a figure for the labour of the soul; the work of scholars, like Christopher Dyer, who have used *Piers Plowman* in their economic histories of the period forestalls any such claims.[3] Indeed, Langland's imagery regularly and evasively fails to indicate whether the tenor or the vehicle of his figures of speech is his subject; he deftly switches between treating the stuff – the body, the action, the social valences – of his imagined dramas and treating the abstract theological things that he makes them signify. This is true too of his treatment of marriage, which is, I suggest, a primary Langlandian subject. What is more, *Piers Plowman* is a complex and conflicted reaction to socio-economic events and patterns that can be read – as, say, Dyer's work on ploughmen has shown – as a crucial piece of evidence for the significant political debates taking place in post-Black Death England. Langland's poetics are posi-tioned at the site of an impasse between competing ethical assessments of the states of virginity and marriage; his poem, then, is an invaluable witness to a contemporary re-evaluation of the moral possibilities of conjugality. Although matrimony is a theme that occupies several sec-tions of the poem, in this chapter I shall look particularly at Langland's use of the figure of Abraham and *his* discussion of marriage. Abraham, who is also identified as Faith, acquires an extraordinary plasticity in *Piers Plowman* and is bound up with a kind of mournfulness, a mournful-ness that I suggest is characteristic of the bourgeois defence of marriage both in this poem and in the culture within which it was produced. This mournfulness is the 'sadness of not being a bird' of my title, an unhappy contrast between the avian and human worlds that points up the anxiety surrounding marriage and domestic practice in the last decades of the fourteenth century. The differences between the B and C-text versions of Langland's poem show a reluctant and begrudging return to the ortho-dox preference for chastity over marriage.

---

[3] M. Teresa Tavormina, in particular, in the only book on Langland and domesticity, argues that marriage is part of Langland's repertoire of images but that it is not as significant in the poem as theological concerns: *Kindly similitude: marriage and family in Piers Plowman* (Cambridge: D. S. Brewer, 1995), p. xiii. Christopher Dyer, 'Piers Plowman and plow-men: a historical perspective', *Yearbook of Langland Studies* 9 (1994), 155–76.

Abraham and marriage metaphors

Typically the relationships between the body and the soul, between the Church and Christ, between the enclosed religious and Christ, were imagined as conjugal ties. The bridal imagery of the Song of Songs and Revelation was interpreted allegorically by exegetes, most famously Bernard of Clairvaux, and was made to lend an ardent and erotic charge to the choice to remain a virgin or to become celibate.[4] Sometimes the figure could be used the other way too: to legitimate secular marriage; indeed, St Augustine uses nuptial imagery like this.[5] Often, though, the comparison between spiritual and earthly marriage was one which ranked them, invariably preferring the former and, sometimes incidentally and sometimes viciously, denigrating the latter; St Jerome is inclined to such hierarchies in *Adversus Jovinianum*.[6] The nuptial motif was also, following the Church Fathers, an enduring one in later, medieval writing on virginity. John Bugge has charted the fortunes of this theme in the misogamist virginity treatises of the high Middle Ages; the twelfth-century *Hali Meidenhad*, for example, follows Jerome in demeaning the institution of marriage and in recommending and glamorising the virginity option in juxtaposition.[7]

Marriage, then, was an abiding metaphor for spiritual subjects in the Christian tradition; but it is instructive to contrast its use in *Piers Plowman* with its use in other texts whose indifference or antipathy to marriage is palpable. The contrastive example I shall use is from the generation just after Langland, from the 'hyper-orthodox' pen of Thomas Hoccleve in the early fifteenth century.[8] Hoccleve is much more convinced than is Langland of the pre-eminence of chastity and virginity over marriage. When Hoccleve uses a marriage exemplum he always turns it into an abstract metaphor; the story of Jereslaus' good and faithful wife in *The series*, for example, is rendered as a dualist allegory, a debate between body and soul with no significance for marriage *per se*.[9] Although Langland does

---

[4] John Bugge, *Virginitas: an essay in the history of a medieval ideal* (The Hague: Martinus Nijhoff, 1975), pp. 90–6. Sensibly, however, Sarah Salih cautions against the modern assumption that such texts are surely sexual rather than religious: 'When is a bosom not a bosom? problems with "erotic mysticism"', in Anke Bernau, Ruth Evans and Sarah Salih (eds.), *Medieval virginities* (Cardiff: University of Wales Press, 2003), pp. 14–32 (*passim*, esp. p. 14).

[5] See, for example, Augustine, *De nuptis et concupiscentia*, *PL* vol. 44, cols. 0419-20, I, X, xi.

[6] See, for example, Jerome, *Adversus Jovinianum*, *PL* vol. 23, cols. 0251D–0254A, I, xxx.

[7] Bugge, *Virginitas*, esp. p. 89.

[8] Hoccleve's hyper-orthodoxy is discussed in Richard Firth Green, *Poets and princepleasers: literature and the English court in the late Middle Ages* (Toronto: University of Toronto Press, 1980), pp. 183–6.

[9] Thomas Hoccleve, *Hoccleve's works: the minor poems*, eds. F. J. Furnivall and I. Gollancz, rev. edn J. Mitchell and A. I. Doyle, EETS ES vols. 61, 73 (Oxford, 1970), p. 176.

use marriage as a metaphor, and typically to represent the intimacy between his personified abstractions like Study and Wit, he always also betrays a 'friendliness' to marriage for its own sake.[10] Furthermore, he tellingly seeks to cover, in his revised c-text, the naked partiality of the b-text to conjugality. The suppression in the later 1380s revision not only highlights the enthusiasm for marriage in b but also testifies to a cultural pressure to be more moderate and circumspect about the value of matrimony than the earlier, 1370s poem had been.[11]

When Hoccleve, in the 1420s, uses the example of Abraham he does so in a decidedly bizarre manner, and this is instructive about the way that his work interiorises a similar embarrassment about marriage to that conveyed by the reviser of *Piers Plowman* some thirty or forty years earlier. His narrator of *The Regiment of Princes* intends, or so he claims, to caution against fornication, and yet he uses the stories from Genesis 12.11–20 and 20.1–13, in which Abraham pretends that Sarah is his sister rather than his wife; it is unclear exactly how the Abraham example relates to or proves the intended moral point.[12] It does, however, point up a significant anxiety about admitting to marriage. Like Abraham, Hoccleve's narrator is uncomfortable about being married; his use of the patriarch reveals a wishfulness that his wife were his sister, and is a subjective articulation of a sexual shame attendant upon the institution of secular marriage. There is no such chariness in the encounter between Abraham and the dreamer Will in the b-text of *Piers Plowman*. Abraham, who is also identified as Faith, uses marriage ostensibly as an image to untangle and explicate the doctrine of the Trinity. And yet, in this b-text rendition, there is also an enthusiasm for marriage which would be unnecessary if it were only a convenient simile:

---

[10] The idea of Langland's 'friendliness' to marriage comes from F. R. H. Du Boulay, *The England of 'Piers Plowman': William Langland and his vision of the fourteenth century* (Woodbridge: Boydell and Brewer, 1991), p. 26.

[11] Although the conventional dating of the c-text of *Piers Plowman* is the mid-1380s, Anne Middleton has suggested that it postdates the 1388 Cambridge Statute on vagrancy. There is, as Middleton has shown, a discursive proximity between Langland's poem and the 1388 Statute, but this does not necessarily prove a direct borrowing, especially given that concerns about vagrancy predate the 1388 statute. Further we should not necessarily assume that legislative productions always set, and that literary texts always follow, the political agenda: 'Acts of vagrancy: The c version "autobiography" and the statute of 1388', in Justice and Kerby-Fulton, *Written work*, p. 214. For a discussion of the preoccupation with vagrancy prior to the 1388 statute, see Chris Given-Wilson, 'The problem of labour in the context of English government, *c*. 1350–1450', in Bothwell, Goldberg and Ormrod (eds.), *The problem of labour in fourteenth-century England*, pp. 88–9.

[12] Thomas Hoccleve, *The regiment of princes*, ed. Charles R. Blyth (Kalamazoo: Medieval Institute Publications, 1999), lines 1695–745.

Might is in matrimoyne, that multiplieth the erthe,
And bitokneth trewely, telle if I dorste,
Hym that first formed al, the Fader of hevene.
The Sone, if I it dorste seye, resembleth wel the widewe:
Deus meus, Deus meus, ut quid dereliquisti me?
That is, creatour weex creature to knowe what was bothe.
As widewe withouten wedlok was nevere yit yseyghe,
Na moore myghte God be man but if he moder hadde.
So widewe withouten wedlok may noght wel stande,
Ne matrimoyne withouten muliere is noght muche to preise:
Maledictus homo qui non reliquit semen in Israel.
Thus in thre persones is parfitliche pure manhede –
That is, man and his make and mulliere hir children.

(B, XVI, lines 211–23)[13]

There are three trinities being overlaid in this passage. First there is the conventional Trinity of Father, Son and Holy Ghost. Secondly there is the one, mentioned here at the end, of the man, his wife and their children. Thirdly there is the triad of sexual states: marriage, widowhood and virginity. There is something a little contrived about the way that the first and the third relate here: widowhood can only be understood in relation to the Son if Christ's feeling of abandonment at the Crucifixion is read as a kind of bereavement. The relationship between virginity and the Holy Ghost is not stated and only implied by the connections between the other two. The force of this passage is directed at marriage and its association with God the Father, as shown in the powerful first half line of this excerpt with its muscular alliteration: 'Might is in matrimoyne'.

Abraham disrupts the apparently conventional and vertical hierarchy of the grades of chastity – with virginity at the top and continence and marriage below it – that occurs in more usual discussions about sexual status. Indeed he disrupts the figure of the tree of Charity with its three kinds of fruit – married, vidual and virginal – that appears earlier in the same Passus of *Piers Plowman*.[14] That disruption is acknowledged in the redactions and clarifications made in the C-text rendering of Abraham's speech. The correlation between the three grades of chastity

---

[13] I use the following editions of *Piers Plowman*: William Langland, *The vision of Piers Plowman*, 2nd edn, ed. A. V. C. Schmidt (London: Everyman, 1987); William Langland, *Piers Plowman: the C-text*, 2nd edn, ed. Derek Pearsall (Exeter University Press, 1994). Unless otherwise stated I shall be referring to the B-text. The Abraham episode is not included in the earlier A-text and so I have not used it here.

[14] See B, XVI, lines 67–85. However, I do not think that this section is wholly conventional in its account of the three grades of chastity either, avoiding mapping the tree's fruit directly onto the Pauline hierarchy of virginity, widowhood and marriage. The equivocal C-text redactions of this passage are also suggestive of Langland's desire to improve the position of marriage in this comparison.

and the Holy Trinity is excised and another trinity – of Adam, Eve and Abel – is substituted. Abraham's discussion of marriage in the c-text is given more limited and concise approval:

> 'In matrimonie aren thre and of o man cam alle thre
> And to godhede goth thre, and o god is all thre.
> Lo, treys encountre treys,' quod he, 'in godhede and in
>   manhede.'   (c, xviii, lines 237–9)

The Holy Trinity and the human institution of the family are separated much more efficiently in c. The force of Abraham's b-text 'Might is in matrimoyne' is strikingly absent along with the phrase itself. The c-text keeps the b-text's 'Matrimonye withoute moylere is nauht moche to preyse' (c, xviii, line 221) but on its own it becomes begrudging, dulling the positive zeal of the passage from the earlier poem. The c-text shifts the weight of emphasis more fully and exclusively from the vehicle to the tenor of the marriage figure: in b Abraham is at least as interested in marriage as he is in the Trinity, in c he has sloughed his preoccupation with marriage to concentrate more single-mindedly on the triple nature of God.[15] In the C-text, then, matrimony is more clearly a didactic figure used in the dreamer's theological education.

The c-text reviser needs, it seems, to moderate the message on marriage that comes from the authoritative persona of Abraham. And yet, because Abraham's authority on marriage in particular is dubious, he might have relied on the persona device to delimit the impact of these assertive claims for wedlock. Indeed, the dreamer is anxious to verify Abraham's authority after the patriarch, in the next Passus, flees the scene where a man is wounded, becoming the priest in Langland's version of the parable of the Good Samaritan (b, xvii, lines 49–125). This flight leads Will to question what Abraham/Faith has told him about the Trinity, which he feels competes and conflicts with other advice that he is given by the figure of Hope. Charity – who doubles as the Good Samaritan in Langland's accretive personification – assures him that Faith and Hope are both correct. What Abraham/Faith says about the doctrine of the Trinity *is* authoritative. Charity then asks the dreamer to excuse the failure of Hope and Faith to stop on the road to Jerusalem, on account of their being from a different time and because they are therefore limited through no fault of their own. Abraham exists before the Incarnation and so is not yet in possession of

---

[15] Tavormina prefers the c-text version for exactly this reason: M. Teresa Tavormina, 'Kindly similitude: Langland's matrimonial Trinity', *Modern Philology* 80 (1982), 126–7 and *Kindly similitude*, p. 220.

the necessary ointment ('the blood of a barn born of a mayde', B, XVII, line 95) to minister to the injured man.

Abraham is indeed sound on the Trinity. Augustine, in *De Trinitate*, had developed the idea that Abraham's use of the singular form to address God and the two angels on the plains of Mamre (Genesis 18.1–3) was an indication of his special understanding of the difficult three-in-one logic.[16] Langland uses this association, as many late-medieval texts do, giving Abraham the special commission of expounding the doctrine of the Trinity.[17] However, whilst Abraham has a prescience about Christ's coming – according to John 8.56, another text often cited in relation to Abraham – and whilst Langland represents him as a herald of Christ (B, XVII, line 247 and B, XVII, line 133), his place in time restricts his understanding of other things. On marriage in particular, the Church Fathers were insistent that Abraham could offer no example to Christians. For example, Jerome and Augustine, in their writings on marriage and virginity, were adamant that the virginal example of Christ obviated that of the married man Abraham and others who lived under the old law rather than the Gospel.[18] This may explain why in *Piers Plowman* Abraham doesn't fully include virginity in his account of the Trinity in the B-text: he is not yet in full possession of the ethical options offered under the new covenant established by Christ.

Augustine uses Abraham extensively in his discussions of marriage. Indeed, Augustine's overdetermination of the example of the patriarch testifies to the strength that he lent to the adversaries that Augustine attacks in his writings on marriage. Augustine gives virginal men and women the answer they need to counter the question 'What then, are you better than Abraham or Sarah?', but in doing so he preserves intact the accusation about the conceitedness of the virginal.[19] He argues not only that Abraham is of a different time, under a different law, commanded by God and driven by the need for a population increase, but also that Abraham should be compared to the sexually continent rather than the

---

[16] Augustine, 'De Trinitate', *PL* vol. 42, col. 0858, II, x, ixx. Clifford Ando has noted that Augustine pays a lot of attention to the use of singulars and plurals in an effort to assemble more evidence to explain the difficult idea of the Trinity: 'Signs, idols, and the incarnation in Augustinian metaphysics', *Representations* 73 (2001), 34.

[17] B, XVI, lines 225–30. For other medieval examples, see e.g. the Barbers' Play in R. M. Luminansky and David Mills (eds.), *Chester mystery cycle*, EETS SS vol. 3 (Oxford, 1974), play IV, and *Mirk's Festial*, ed. Theodore Erbe, EETS ES vol. 96 (London, 1905), p. 76.

[18] Jerome, *Adversus Jovinianum*, cols. 0243A–0243D, I, xxiv and Augustine, 'De bono conjugali,' *PL* vol. 40, col. 0392, XXII, xxvii.

[19] Ibid., col. 0392, XXII, xxvii.

married of Augustine's day. Abraham was compelled only by God and never by personal lust. Further, Augustine reads Abraham's compliance with God's injunction to sacrifice Isaac as proof of his willingness to pass up the procreative function of marriage in order to be faithful to God. Augustine finds in that act a kind of chaste practice.[20]

Probably because Abraham was so roundly discounted as a possible model for the married by authorities like Augustine, he is not often used in robust defences of marriage that are prepared to claim anything for the primacy of marriage over virginity. The Wife of Bath, in her aggressive defence of her multiple marriages, uses Abraham like this:

> I woot wel Abraham was an hooly man,
> And Jacob eek, as ferfoth as I kan;
> And ech of hem hadde wyves mo than two,
> And many another holy man also.
>
> ('The Wife of Bath's Prologue', lines 55–8)[21]

But the point of Abraham's deployment in Chaucer's poem is to undermine the Wife's arguments: she invokes the patriarch's polygamy to justify her remarriage, not to defend marriage as a regular category when polygamy, outside of the Old Testament, is surely outrageous and indefensible. Not even Jerome makes an explicit connection between polygamy and remarriage, although he implies it.[22] Because it was common and not anathema for widows and widowers to remarry, Alison would do better to invoke contemporary practice rather than the example of the patriarch, Abraham. Furthermore, 'The Wife of Bath's Prologue' is comically constructed out of, in part, the failed and satirised arguments of St Jerome's targets as they are represented in *Adversus Jovinianum*; St Jerome had already dismissed the idea that Abraham was a role model who made marriage ethically superlative. Indeed, in its use of Abraham, the Wife's

---

[20] Ibid., col. 0388, XVIII–XIX: 'quandoquidem filium immolare jussus Abraham, intrepidus ac devotus, quem de tanta desperatione susceperat, unico non pepercit, nisi eo prohibente manum deponeret, quo jubente levaverat. /... Restat ut videamus utrum saltem continentes nostri conjugatis illis patribus comparandi sint' (forasmuch as Abraham, being bidden to slay his son, fearless and devoted, spared not his only son, whom from out of great despair he had received save that he laid down his hand, when He forbade him, at Whose command he had lifted it up; it remains that we consider, whether at least continent persons among us are to be compared to those Fathers who were married). Translation: 'On the good of marriage', in Augustine, *On the Holy Trinity, doctrinal treatises, moral treatises*, ed. Philip Schaff, A Select Library of the Nicene and Post-Nicene Fathers series I vol. 3 (Edinburgh: T&T Clark, 1887; Grand Rapids, MI: William B. Eerdmans, 1956), p. 22.

[21] *The Riverside Chaucer*, ed. Benson. All references will be to this edition.

[22] Jerome, *Adversus Jovinianum*, cols. 0232B-0234A, I, xiv; cols. 0243A–0243D, I, xxiv.

Prologue confirms nothing except Chaucer's equivocation over Alison and her lifestyle. Because a medieval audience knew that Abraham couldn't be used like this, her words persuade them only of her credibility as a vulnerable and desiring subject, doing nothing for the cause of marriage itself.

Abraham is also regularly used to recommend marriage in texts that repeat and, unlike the Wife of Bath, respect the usual Pauline hierarchy from 1 Corinthians 7.37–8. For example, the virginity tract *Speculum virginum* figures Abraham, along with Noah and the other patriarchs, as fruit on a tree, beneath the fruits of continence and virginity, in a way that is reminiscent of Langland's hierarchy of the fruits on the tree of charity that the dreamer-narrator has been shown prior to meeting Abraham.[23] Such tracts have no problem with recommending Abraham's example – in a limited sense Abraham does legitimate the institution of marriage – but then they do not seek, either, to commend it over the state of continence or virginity. Identifying with Abraham, according to the virginity trees, was no shame for those who couldn't otherwise contain themselves and follow the example of the Apostle Paul (1 Corinthians 7.8). Morton Bloomfield maintains that Langland's treatment of the three sexual states and Abraham's discussion of the Trinity are a combination of the arboreal imagery in virginity tracts, like the *Speculum virginum*, and Joachim de Fiore's schematic representations of time as a tree. The Joachite *figurae* show a tree in which the age of the Father, the Old Testament – on which the patriarchs grow as fruit – gives way to the age of the Son, the New Testament – which bears the fruit of Christ and Mary – which in turn anticipates a future, third age of the Holy Ghost. Notwithstanding the problematic reception history of Joachite writings, Langland's temporal structure does suggest similarities.[24] However, both the Joachite and the virginity trees are concerned to pass over Abraham: they are not principally interested in his example and iconographic meanings. A true combination of these trees would project a utopian future inhabited by the pure and chaste, which is precisely not the concern in *Piers Plowman*; if it were, Abraham would certainly *not* be the best authority to select.

Langland appropriates the Abraham of the mystery cycles – where he also has a speaking part but speaks to quite different ends – to avoid the pitfalls in which the Wife of Bath is ensnared. In the mystery plays

---

[23] The whole of this paragraph engages with Morton W. Bloomfield, '*Piers Plowman* and the three grades of chastity', *Anglia* 76 (1958), 227–53 (esp. pp. 247–8 and plates I and II).

[24] On the reception history of the Joachite *figurae*, see Marjorie Reeves and Beatrice Hirsch-Reich, *The figurae of Joachim of Fiore* (Oxford: Clarendon Press, 1972), p. 314.

Abraham is not a spokesman on marriage but on the importance of faith and obedience to God; and the story of his willingness to sacrifice Isaac operates as prolepsis for the Crucifixion at the cycles' climax.[25] In using the Abraham persona familiar from the cycle drama, with a nod to his role elsewhere in the marriage debate, Langland can explore Abraham's partial view – a world in which virginity was not yet an option – and he can do so without contradicting exegetical authority, without adopting the position of a quintain like Chaucer's Wife of Bath. Furthermore, in this section of *Piers Plowman* there are some characteristically Langlandian equivocations which resist consigning Abraham's example, as the exegetes do, to the Old Testament past. As David Aers has noted, Langland's temporal structure is not as clear as that in, say, Joachim de Fiore's theology;[26] Langland allows Abraham's example to bleed into the values of the present. When the dreamer questions Abraham's authority in the Good Samaritan Passus, he tellingly never doubts his wisdom on marriage; when Charity confirms Abraham's insight on the Trinity he tacitly buttresses his claims about matrimony. Langland subtly modifies the iconography of Abraham by combining the different ways in which he is usually discussed in exegetical and medieval literature. Abraham's special connection with the Trinity and his status as a married man, those aspects which I have discussed so far, are two separate iconographic strands which Langland twists together to create something new. Indeed, Abraham's status as a husband does not usually impinge on his other iconographic significances. As I shall go on to discuss in the next section of this essay, his importance in the early Christian formulation of sexual and conjugal ethics is oddly – and conveniently for a celibate but patriarchal clergy – separate from his role as a father, a role which was much more readily allegorised and abstracted than that of husband. In stressing his marriedness and reattaching it to his paternity Langland includes marriage in the idea of Abraham. The effect is to promote him as a symbol of secular piety – as a fleshly, and not just a spiritual or surrogate father, as he had been most often used in his more clerical manifestations.

---

[25] The Chester Barbers' Play in particular offers Abraham and Isaac as types of God and Christ respectively. In other plays, such as the Towneley version of the Abraham story, the accent upon the innocence of Isaac leaves his similarity to Christ implicit. Luminansky and Mills (eds.), *Chester mystery cycle*, p. 78, lines 468–75: 'By Abraham I may understand / the Father of heaven … By Isaack understande I maye / Jesus …'. See, for a discussion of the differing emphases within this typology, Stevens and Cawley, *The Towneley plays*, vol. 2, pp. 454–5.

[26] David Aers, '*Piers Plowman*' and Christian allegory (London: Edward Arnold, 1975), pp. 92–3.

Abraham the father

Christian commentators, of course, needed to extend God's covenant beyond Abraham's literal lineage, to define the elect community not as a racial category but as a community of the faithful. St Paul in particular, in his Epistles, grouped allegorical significances around the Genesis narrator's account of Abraham's genealogy. Augustine's idea of the two cities was derived, in part, from St Paul's allegorical treatment at Galatians 4.22–30 of the two dynasties descending from Abraham's sons: Ishmael (whose mother was a bond maiden) and Isaac (the son of the free woman Sarah).[27] Paul points out the use of the singular 'seed' rather than 'seeds' in God's original promise, which, he says, signifies the one Christ rather than Abraham's multiple offspring (Galatians 3.16). Following suit, the genealogical emphasis in medieval sermons was not upon Abraham and his immediate offspring – Abraham's literal fatherhood supplied stories which served to illustrate other points – but upon an agnatic line from Abraham, through Joseph to Christ. Indeed, these genealogies were influential in the medieval sermon tradition, which as we know is closely attached to Langland's poetics, and which was concerned to define the Christian community as a spiritual family, using familial language – brothers, sisters, fathers and mothers – to describe faith as relatedness. This tradition was not interested in the idea of Abraham as a husband – the aspect of Abraham that exercised the marriage and virginity tracts – but rather in his other iconographic and doctrinal significances – such as his special understanding of the Trinity, for example. In the sermon on the Epiphany from *Mirk's Festial*, for instance, an unqualified belief in the Trinity and the 'werkes' associated with that belief are prerequisites for entry into the Christian family in whose dynastic heritage Abraham has a special place:

[...] ʒe schull beleue þat here ben þre persons and on *God yn Trynyte*. [...] Wherfor he þat byleueth and doth þe werkes of þe byleue wythout dowte, he schall be sauet; and he þat beleueth not, he schall be dampnet. The werkes of þe byleue byn mekenes and charyte. For wythout þes two schall þer no man be sauet; and he þat hath þes two, he ys wrytten yn þe geanology of Cryst. Wherfor, yn wytnes of þys geanology þat ys red yn mydwyntyr-nyght, begynnyth aboue at *Abraham*, and so comyth downe to Ioseph, and soo to our lady Mary, in schouyng þat ys most mekest of hert, ys next to oure Lorde; and seche he avaunset. And þerfor þe geanology þat ys red this night, begynyth at Ihesu Cryst, and goth vp to Adam, and so ynto God, yn schewyng þat he þat hath perfyte loue to hys eme-crysten, ys

---

[27] Augustine 'De civitate Dei,' *PL* vol. 41, cols. 0523-6, xvii, i–iii. Galatians 4.22–30 was also the text of the sermon on 'Mid-lenten Sunday', the day the dreamer says he meets Abraham in *Piers Plowman*.

wryttyn yn þe geanologe of God yn Heuen; and schall be as cosyn and dere derlyng to God þer wythouten ende.[28]

Moreover Abraham was a type of God the father in more ways than one.[29] He is the father who would sacrifice his son, Isaac, just as God sacrifices Jesus; but he is also the benevolent father who lovingly draws the souls of the faithful into the haven of his bosom after death. In the parable of Lazarus (Luke 16), Christ says that after death the poor man Lazarus is admitted to the bosom of Abraham; it is Abraham that the rich man, in hell, begs for mercy, asking him to send Lazarus to relieve some of his suffering. This place – Abraham's bosom – was richly imagined in medieval art, as Jérôme Baschet and Pamela Sheingorn have shown.[30] Langland also dramatises this idea as the dreamer looks into the folds of Abraham's clothes and sees a tiny figure of a 'lazar' – a leper, but also Lazarus – resting there:

> I hadde wonder of hise wordes, and of hise wide clothes;
> For in his bosom he bar a thyng, and that he blissed evere.
> And I loked in his lappe: a lazar lay therinne
> Amonges patriarkes and prophetes pleyinge togideres.
> 'What awaitestow?' quod he, 'and what woldestow have?'
> 'I wolde wite,' quod I tho, 'what is in youre lappe.'
> 'Lo!' quod he – and leet me se. 'Lord, mercy!' I seide.
> 'This is a present of muche pris; what prynce shal it have?'
> 'It is a precious present,' quod he, 'ac the pouke it hath attached,
> And me therwith,' quod that wye, 'may no wed us quyte,
> Ne no buyrn be oure borgh, ne brynge us fram his daunger;
> Out of the poukes pondfold no maynprise may us fecche
> Til he come that I carpe of: Crist is his name
> That shal delivere us som day out of the develes power,
> And bettre wed for us wage than we ben alle worthi –
> That is, lif for lif – or ligge thus evere
> Lollynge in my lappe, til swich a lord us fecche.'   (B, XVI, lines 253–69)

This charming passage imagines the narrator, pointing into Abraham's bosom, asking wide-eyed, as a child might, to see what thing he is comforting inside the folds of his clothing. The word 'pleyinge' – which is

[28] Erbe (ed.), *Mirk's festial*, pp. 51–2. My emphasis.
[29] See, for example, ibid., p. 77 and Luminansky and Mills, *Chester mystery cycle*, p. 78, lines 468–75.
[30] Jérôme Baschet, 'Medieval Abraham: between fleshly and divine father', *Modern Language Notes* 108 (1993), 738–58 and Pamela Sheingorn, 'The bosom of Abraham Trinity: a late medieval All Saints image', in Daniel Williams (ed.), *England in the fifteenth century: proceedings of the 1986 Harlaxton symposium* (Woodbridge: Boydell, 1987), pp. 273–95.

particularly associated in Middle English, as in modern, with children – captures the paternal tone of this iconographic tradition that regularly depicts the souls in Abraham's cloth as infants that he gathers to him.[31] 'Lollynge' too, especially without the censure that usually accompanies the language of indolence in Langland's poem, suggests the helplessness of a dependant. Baschet has noted, however, that the iconographic tradition of Abraham's bosom and cloth of souls was principally a clerical one that figured Abraham as a spiritual rather than a fleshly ancestor, investing Abraham with a non-carnal kind of paternity that privileged spiritual over actual kinship.[32] The children that he swaddles, after all, do not include Isaac but are rather the community of the faithful, who are all unindividuated equals – in Langland, the 'lazar' plays happily with the prophets and the patriarchs – without the generational distinctions of a family group; the figure of Abraham's bosom is not about blood kinship. The question for medievals was whether Abraham's bosom still existed or whether it became redundant on the death of Christ and the establishment of the new covenant.[33] Langland, with his characteristic idiosyncrasy, imagines Abraham carefully guarding his bosom while its precious resident, incarcerated like a stray animal in Satan's pound, waits to be released by Christ, picturing hell as some sort of municipal facility. This maintains the uncertainty about the present status of Abraham's 'lappe', which may be either suspended or remain as a place within a place. Regularly in medieval systems of representation, though, Abraham stands in for the Father God, fostering in the limbo of his bosom the souls that will eventually be saved through the sacrifice of Christ and delivered to their true Father. Again, this is part of a Christian chronology and Abraham surrenders his responsibility for the human soul at the Crucifixion. In this way, medievals regularly interpreted Abraham as a surrogate father and this was an iconographic tradition that did not usually coincide with the discussions, which took place elsewhere, about Abraham in relation to marriage and biological fatherhood.

Late-medieval culture, much more so than our own, understood systems of surrogacy, fosterage, fraternity and social relatedness – life cycle service, guild fraternities, monastic communities and so on – that replicated or resembled, but weren't in fact, family ties and structures.[34] And,

---

[31] The *Middle English dictionary* notes that 'pleyinge' is always insulting when used of adults.
[32] Baschet, 'Medieval Abraham', p. 758.
[33] Sheingorn, 'The bosom of Abraham Trinity', p. 281.
[34] See the work done by P. J. P. Goldberg on life-cycle servants and other fostering arrangements in *Women, work and life cycle in a medieval English economy*, esp. pp. 212, 227 and 231 and 'Orphans and servants: the socialisation of young people living away from home in the English later Middle Ages', in M. Corbier (ed.), *Adoption et fosterage* (Paris: Editions de Boccard, 1999), pp. 231–46.

after all, spiritual kinship was not only part of an abstract theology but a widespread, although now under-researched, aspect of medieval social practice.[35] A spiritual family was constructed around the child at baptism. A brief look at the ritual significance of this spiritual family shows the ways that medieval culture celebrated the idea of spiritual surrogacy. In baptism, presided over by the clergy, Christians were reborn to their real father: God. This ritual rebirth was necessary because of the dangerous stain of original sin to which their biological parents unwittingly exposed them at their conception. At baptism, they were spiritually fostered by earthly godparents. There is good evidence that these figurative ties were fervently practised and socially efficacious. No doubt the spiritual families that these ceremonies instituted were implicated in, and complementary to, natural families. However, they could also present an alternative, offering individuals support in the absence of, or even in opposition to, their parents. Indeed, it would not seem that spiritual kinship was necessarily considered lesser and artificial in relation to natural blood ties. Rob Lutton has described spiritual ties as 'figurative' but not as 'fictive', anxious not to impose a twenty-first-century preoccupation with genetics and biology on a culture that valued theology more than our own, a culture that accepted, after all, that the substance of bread and wine could transform into flesh and blood on consecration, even while its accidents remained bread-like and wine-like.[36] Baptism was another sacrament which made substantial things that we might think of as only symbolic. The discussions about where and if Abraham's bosom existed, for example, indicate the 'peculiar substantiality' of allegorical and abstract concepts.[37] Contemporary injunctions on incest prohibited marriage between persons related spiritually, making godparenthood 'real' and significant.[38] Indeed, non-biological but nevertheless familial ties had to be *material* in order to explain other potential problems in the Christian

[35] But see John Bossy, 'Blood and baptism: kinship, community and Christianity in western Europe from the fourteenth to the seventeenth centuries', *Studies in Church History* 10 (1973), 129–43; Rob Lutton, 'Godparenthood, kinship, and piety in Tenterden, England 1449–1537', in Davis *et al.*, *Love, marriage and family ties*, pp. 217–34.

[36] Lutton, 'Godparenthood, kinship, and piety', p. 219. For the Aristotelian theory behind transubstantiation see, for example, Diarmaid MacCulloch, *Reformation: Europe's house divided, 1490–1700* (London: Allen Lane, 2003), p. 25.

[37] Marie-Louise von Franz, cited in Sheingorn, 'The bosom of Abraham Trinity', p. 276.

[38] See, for example, R. H. Helmholz, *Marriage litigation in medieval England* (Cambridge University Press, 1974), p. 78 and the early-fifteenth-century *Jacob's well*, ed. Arthur Brandeis, EETS OS vol. 115 (London, 1900), p. 50. Helmholz notes, however, that in two ex-officio cases where spiritual affinity was cited the men involved were permitted to purge themselves *proprio iuramento*, suggesting that the Church courts considered the impediment of spiritual kinship 'less dangerous than actual consanguinity', p. 71, n. 159.

story, like the otherwise problematic paternity of Joseph.[39] Similarly there
was a materiality to the structures of divine kinship and the genealogies
that I was discussing above in relation to Abraham.

Spiritual ideas, of course, extruded into literary and rhetorical theory
and inflected the way in which figurative language was applied, affecting
what was considered to be fiction and what truth. Augustine's treatise
De doctrina Christiana begins with semiotics and the definitions of a thing
and a sign; Christianity, and especially Augustine's Platonic version of it,
requires a thoroughgoing understanding of how symbols relate to abstract
and material truths.[40] So, for example, sacrifice – the idea closest to the
heart of the Christian story – was a kind of semantic figure, the substitution of one thing for another. However, this does not mean that either was
considered less 'real' than the other, nor that the relationship between
them was in any way 'untrue': the scapegoat *does* literally carry the sins of
the follower. Paul describes the way in which God *did* receive, albeit in the
form of a 'parabola' (parable), the sacrifice of Isaac even though a ram was
substituted in his place (Hebrews 11.19).[41] Further, Augustine argues
that what Paul does at Galatians 4.22–30 should most properly be
described not as an 'allegoria' (allegory) but rather as an 'aenigma'
(riddle).[42] Abraham *did*, after all, actually have two sons; his having sons
was not an image or idea but a fact. Thus Paul illustrates the spiritual truth
that resides not in a form of words, not in a fiction, but in a fact.
Augustine's aim, when he discusses this in the *City of God*, is to prove
that paradise might exist, that Eden was not only an idea. Whilst the Old
Testament prefigures the New, and while Genesis can be read allegorically, such readings do not preclude the physical reality of the places and
the people that it describes. Langland too has an interest in things and their
signs and an ability to produce a subtle and compelling combination of the
two, stressing as 'real' both theological meaning and the physical form that
stands in for it. He does this neither to justify nor, indeed, to deny the
importance of theological substance but to re-emphasise the accidents –
the domestic facts – of the Abraham story, realigning Abraham's figurative
and somatic connotations, making his spiritual meanings germane to
his role within the alternative tradition of the marriage debate. Imagery

---

[39] Augustine, 'De nuptiis et concupiscentia,' *PL* vol. 44, cols. 0420–1, xi, xii.
[40] Augustine, 'De doctrina Christiana,' *PL* vol. 34, cols. 0019-20, i, i–ii. For further
discussion on Augustine's semiotics, see R. A. Markus, *Signs and meanings: world and
text in ancient Christianity* (Liverpool University Press, 1996), esp. pp. 106–7 and Ando,
'Augustinian metaphysics', pp. 32–8.
[41] See also, Augustine, 'De doctrina Christiana,' cols. 0019-20, i, ii.
[42] Augustine, 'De Trinitate,' cols. 1068-9, xv, ix, xv; Augustine, 'De civitate Dei,' col. 0394,
xiii, xxi.

is always inseparable from, and organically related to its meanings, but Langland does more than most to validate both the visible and invisible truths of his figures; his use of Abraham is no exception.

Langland partially reclaims Abraham from clerical reckoning, which leaves him looking awkward in arguments like the Wife of Bath's that try to read him as a straightforward exemplum. This feat of reconciliation, I suggest, testifies both to the seriousness of this poem's aims and also to the delicate social position that *Piers Plowman* occupies in terms of the milieu from which it originated and in which it was read. It has long been thought, from evidence both within and without it, that the poem has one foot in the clerical and one in the secular world.[43] There is an attempt, in *Piers Plowman*, to mediate between the opposed discourses of secular conjugality and clerical misogamy, those discourses which are placed in direct confrontation in the 'Wife of Bath's Prologue'. Thomas Hoccleve, my other point of comparison with Langland, also displays his vulnerability to these tensions in his self-conscious and embarrassed use of the Abraham stories and, although his narrator unflinchingly recommends chastity over married sex, he does so to resolve the same ethical dilemma that faces Chaucer's Wife: about the contemporary perception of marriage as a compromised and lesser sexual identity. This anxiety about the moral inferiority of wedlock is also exhibited in *Piers Plowman*, and explains the poem's investment in Abraham and in making him an authoritative bridge between secular and clerical world-views: a man who can both have a family and successfully explain the Trinity.

Being faithful and the sadness of not being a bird

Abraham was specially associated with faith before Langland, especially in readings of Hebrews 11 where he was, along with Noah and others, made an example of unquestioning allegiance to God and a devout believer in the substance of promises and other unseen things. There were also other reasons why Abraham was considered as a model of pious obedience: his willingness, in the Genesis account, to journey to the land of promise at God's command, his circumcision of his male offspring, his acceptance of Sarah's conceiving even in old age and, in the commentary tradition, his acknowledgement of the triple nature of God. The story, though, of Abraham and Isaac's dreadful walk to the sacrificial altar, the image of the father's knife raised above his own boy lain face down to spare some

---

[43] See, for example, J. A. Burrow, 'The audience of *Piers Plowman*', *Anglia* 75 (1957), 373–84 (esp. pp. 379–83) and, more recently, Steven Justice and Kathryn Kerby-Fulton, 'Langlandian reading circles and the civil service in London and Dublin, 1380–1427', *New Medieval Literatures* 1 (1997), 59–83 (esp. pp. 65, 83).

of his fear, was one of the most extraordinary in the Christian story, encapsulating the central Christian themes of sacrifice and humility before God, and was affectingly depicted on the guilds' pageant wagons throughout the late Middle Ages. In *Piers Plowman* Abraham reports the baptism of Jesus by John the Baptist and, in repeating the Baptist's words: 'Ecce Agnus Dei' (B, XVI, line 252a), reminds the reader of the angel's last-minute substitution of a ram for Isaac.[44] He thus celebrates Christian salvation by exploiting in his own story the relief the reader feels at the miraculous intervention that stays Abraham's hand. Augustine contrasts Abraham, in his obedience, with the disobedient Adam, arguing, finally, that Adam's insubordination is greater than Abraham's submission because Adam was not asked for as painful a price as Abraham; his rebellion was capricious and *wil*ful and an un*reason*able attempt to acquire powers of *rationality* reserved for God himself.[45] The power of Abraham and Isaac's story comes from Abraham's being able, because of the intensity of his *faith*, to suspend his own *will*, without questioning the workings of God, even in the apparent absence of *reason*.

In *Piers Plowman*, the narrator receives a lesson in having faith before the entry of Abraham; this lesson is also a negotiation between Will and Reason. The dreamer, Will – who is also, of course, a personification of the interior faculty of will – attacks Reason, in Passus XI of the B-text, for his apparent absence from human relationships and patterns of conduct; again, the subject of the lesson is domestic and sexual ethics. He observes the orderliness with which the birds and animals go about their procreative lives:

> Reson I seigh soothly sewen alle beestes
> In etynge, in drynkynge and in engendrynge of kynde.
> And after cours of concepcion noon took kepe of oother
> As whan thei hadde ryde in rotey tyme; anoonright therafter
> Males drowen hem to males amornynge by hemselve,
> And femelles to femelles ferded and drowe.
> Ther ne was cow ne cowkynde that conceyved hadde
> That wolde belwe after bole, ne boor after sowe.
> Bothe hors and houndes and alle othere beestes
> Medled noght with hir makes that mid fole were.
> Briddes I biheld that in buskes made nestes;
> Hadde nevere wye wit to werche the leeste.
> I hadde wonder at whom and wher the pye

---

[44] This is the sort of disruption within Langland's Christian chronology that resists Joachite temporal figures in the way that Aers describes: '*Piers Plowman' and Christian allegory*, pp. 92–3.

[45] Augusine, 'De civitate Dei,' col. 0423, XIV, XV.

Lerned to legge the stikkes in which she leyeth and bredeth.
Ther nys wrighte, as I wene, sholde werche hir nest to paye;
If any mason made a molde therto, muche wonder it were.

(B, XI, lines 334–49)

After this passage the dreamer sees a more in-depth vision of the birds in particular, and marvels at the way in which they build their nests, keep their eggs safe, have sex and look after their progeny high up in trees and conceive by breathing through their beaks (B, XI, lines 350–61). It is a standard Langlandian tactic to establish a morally appropriate grouping in one alliterative line and to indicate the seemliness of its segregation from others contained in other lines, and it occurs in the quotation above to show, through formal pattern, the dreamer's satisfied observation of the good conduct of the animals and birds.[46] The juxtaposition with human behaviour annoys and saddens Will, who says to Reason: 'I have wonder of thee, that witty art holden, / Why thow ne sewest man and his make, that no mysfeet hem folwe' (B, XI, lines 373–4). Both Reason and, in the next Passus, Ymaginatif remonstrate with the dreamer for his insolence: for daring to question God and for his lack of patience. The dreamer is told, indeed, that he is like the fallen Adam, striving to know God's inner self and he is expelled, like Adam from Eden, from his dream of 'Myddelerthe' (e.g. B, XI, lines 415–17); this, of course, intensifies rather than ameliorates his sadness. Ymaginatif includes the avian theme in his disciplining of Will's prurience, telling him, for example, that only 'Kynde' – that is God/nature – knows how the peacock to 'cauken in swich a kynde' (B, XII, line 229) and 'no creature ellis' (B, XII, line 226).

The later encounter with Abraham, which I have been discussing hitherto, develops some of the themes that are raised here, and the two episodes are intricately connected. Although other sources have been suggested for the long quotation above, it comes, I think, from Augustine's *De nuptiis et concupiscentia*:

Copulatio itaque maris et feminae generandi causa, bonum est naturale nuptiarum: sed isto bono male utitur, qui bestialiter utitur, ut sit ejus intentio in voluptate libidinis, non in voluntate propaginis. Quanquam in nonnullis animalibus rationis expertibus, sicut in plerisque alitibus, et conjugiorum quaedam quasi confoederatio custoditur, et socialis nidificandi solertia, vicissimque ovorum dispertita tempora fovendorum, et nutriendorum opera alterna pullorum, magis eas videri faciunt agere, cum coeunt, negotium substituendi generis, quam explendae libidinis.

---

[46] See also B, IX, lines 175–6.

[The union, then, of male and female for the purpose of procreation is the natural good of marriage. But he makes a bad use of this good who uses it bestially, so that his intention is on the gratification of lust, instead of the desire for offspring. Nevertheless, in sundry animals unendowed with reason, as, for instance, in most birds there is both preserved a certain kind of confederation of pairs, and a social combination of skill in nest-building; and their mutual division of the periods for cherishing their eggs and their alternation in the labor of feeding their young, give them the appearance of so acting, when they mate, as to be intent rather on securing the continuance of their kind than on the gratifying of lust.][47]

Langland makes his narrator into a Will-ful and partial reader in his rendition, omitting the phrase 'rationis expertibus' and so failing to specify the exact relationship between reason and the birds – to distinguish, as Augustine does, between rational action and the appearance of the same. What is similar, though, is the interest in the domestic labours and sexual behaviour of the animals and especially the birds. The birds mate and rear their young in a seemly but, crucially, not in a rational way. Augustine's point here is, of course, not about birds but about people and how they can resemble the decorous but unreasoning birds. It is a blessing of nature, Augustine says just after this passage, for men and women to be united as associates for procreation but, outside of a marriage of the faithful, this blessing can be turned into evil and sinful lust.[48]

The narrator of *Piers Plowman* is an inadequate reader and he observes the birds and animals without apprehending the full point of their example, hence his distressed outrage. Faith, that quality of which the dreamer displays a distinct lack in his importunate questioning, is crucial in helping people to replicate the example of the unreasoning birds. Although the contrast between avian decorum and human impropriety makes Will sad, Abraham, in his guise as Faith, recommends marriage as a positive human alternative to the birds' instincts. Abraham, though, is a bit like the birds himself. Indeed, he often comes up in Augustine's work in the same places

---

[47] Other suggestions about the source can be found in Joseph S. Wittig, '*Piers Plowman* B, Passus ix–x: elements in the design of the inward journey', *Traditio* 28 (1972), 211–80 (pp. 241–2) and John A. Alford, 'The idea of reason in *Piers Plowman*', in Edward Donald Kennedy, Ronald Waldron and Joseph S. Wittig (eds.), *Medieval English studies presented to George Kane* (Cambridge: D. S. Brewer, 1988), pp. 199–215. Augustine, 'De nuptiis et concupiscentia,' cols. 0415-16, i, iv, v. Translation: Augustine, 'On marriage and concupiscence', in *Anti-Pelagian writings*, ed. Philip Schaff, A Select Library of the Nicene and Post-Nicene Fathers of the Christian Church series I vol. 5 (Edinburgh: T&T Clark, 1887; repr. Grand Rapids, MI: William B. Eerdmans, 1956), i, v, [iv].

[48] 'Eo modo ergo et illam concupiscentiam carnis, qua caro concupiscit adversus spiritum, in usum justitiae convertunt fidelium nuptiae.' Augustine, 'De nuptiis et concupiscentia,' col. 0416, i, iv, v. (In like manner, therefore, the marriage of believers converts to the use of righteousness that carnal concupiscence by which 'the flesh lusteth against the Spirit': translation in Schaff, ed., *Anti-Pelagian writings*, i, v, iv.)

as the bird motif.[49] Abraham is like a bird because, and again on account of his place in time, he has fewer choices than the modern Christian: he has the choice only to obey or disobey God: the choice to marry or not, have children or not, give them up or not. The Christian, though, has the added, more perfect but complicating option of virginity. The dreamer cannot, then, be entirely cheered up by Abraham; the sadness of not being a bird is part of the modern Christian condition.

Interestingly the sadness of not being a bird comes up elsewhere too. Consider, for example, this little lyric:

> Foweles in the frith,
> The fisses in the flod,
> And I mon waxe wod.
> Sulch sorw I walke with
> For beste of bon and blod.[50]

> [Birds in the wood,
> Fishes in the river,
> And I must grow mad.
> I walk with such sorrow
> For (either 'on behalf of' or 'as') the best / a beast of bone and
>   blood.]

Decidedly affecting, this compact verse describes the condition of fallen man – the beast of bone and blood – contrasting his despondent derangement with the order and propriety of the birds and fishes in their apposite elements.[51] The word 'beste', though, is a neat pun and can also mean the best of 'bon and blood', that is Christ; the Eucharistic connotations of 'bon and blod', indeed, alert us to that sense. Trying to follow Christ is an alienating, homeless experience, one which is movingly contrasted with that of the birds and fishes at home in their natural habitats. Indeed, Jesus warns a man who would follow him: 'vulpes foveas habent et volucres caeli tabernacula; Filius autem hominis non habet ubi caput reclinet' (The foxes have holes, and the birds of the air nests: but the son of man hath no where to lay his head, Matthew 8.20). The figure of Need uses this verse to bring the narrator into line in the final Passus of *Piers Plowman* (B, xx, lines 44–7); in the shadow of Antichrist's imminence, the narrator is still inappropriately looking for a nest.

---

[49] See, for example, Augustine, 'De bono conjugali,' col. 0388, xix.

[50] Carter Revard, 'Foweles in the Frith', *Notes and Queries* n.s. 25 (1978), 200.

[51] For a full analysis of this little lyric and its ambiguities, see Thomas C. Moser Jr, '"And I mon waxe wod": the Middle English "Foweles in the frith"', *Proceedings of the Modern Language Association* 102 (1987), 326–37.

This heart-rending homelessness demonstrates the way that Christian sacrifice was partly about, and indeed was made more powerfully poignant because, it was a denial of familial bonds and homely comforts. This is most clearly demonstrated, of course, in God's willingness to sacrifice his son and, as we have seen, that sacrifice is anticipated in the Old Testament story of Abraham's willingness to do the same. The Abraham and Isaac plays without exception make appeal to the sentiment in the family drama. In the Chester Barbers' Play Abraham repeatedly says that his heart is going to break, and the dialogue is punctuated with endearments – 'Deere sonne' and 'O deere Father' – and exclamations of grief – 'Wele-Awaye'.[52] The Towneley Abraham movingly wonders: 'What shall I to his mother say?'[53] Indeed, the story is inherently sad: Gregory of Nyssa could not, he claimed, look at the tableau of Abraham about to kill Isaac without being overcome with grief.[54] To read Abraham's compliance as a chaste gesture, as Augustine does, describes Abraham as a proto-Christian, yes, but it also invests his chasteness with the emotional cadences, the sorriness of his paternal grief. Chastity, the preferred sexual ethic of the Middle Ages, is a very mournful sacrifice.

Suggestively January, in Chaucer's 'Merchant's Tale', in contemplating his own ill-advised marriage, also uses the same bird motif:

> That bachelleris have often peyne and wo;
> On brotel ground they buylde, and brotelnesse
> They fynde whan they wene sikernesse.
> They lyve but as a bryd or as a beest,
> In libertee and under noon arreest,
> Ther as a wedded man in his estaat
> Lyveth a lyf blisful and ordinaat
> Under this yok of mariage ybounde.
>
> ('The Merchant's Tale', lines 1278–85)

The editor's punctuation – the full stop at the end of the third line cited here – has clarified a moment of ambiguity at line 1281: who is it, the married man or the bachelor, who lives in freedom like a bird or a beast? The syntax alone does not make it clear. The passage is punctuated in this way, though, to maintain January's intended distinction between the sorrowful and unstable single life and the free and blissful married life – the same associations that we have seen in Langland; January complains

---

[52] Luminansky and Mills, *Chester mystery cycle*, e.g. pp. 72, 75, lines 350, 413.
[53] *The Towneley plays*, I, 55, line 225. Even the York play of Abraham and Isaac, which is a lot more emotionally restrained, includes some poignant notes: Richard Beadle (ed.), *The York plays* (London: Arnold, 1982), pp. 98–9, lines 229, 311.
[54] Cited in Baschet, 'Medieval Abraham', p. 743.

that unlike the birds, the unmarried have nowhere to lay their heads. Chaucer exploits the figure for its full comic potential, though; the ambiguity here raises doubts about January's high expectations of married life, setting him up for his fall. Indeed the bachelor life, for January, has not been a period of Christ-like virginity but a time during which he might more truly be said to have lived, if not exactly like a 'bryd' then certainly like a 'beest'; the Merchant says, indeed, that he 'folwed ay his bodily delyt' (line 1249), living 'In libertee and under noon arreest' before, rather than after, his marriage. What is sad here is not the lack of a bolt hole or nest in January's bachelor life but rather his delusion: his perverse manipulation of right thinking on marriage. Chaucer clearly expects his audience to be aware of the 'proper version' of the bird theme and how it more usually appeared in discussions of marriage; for the joke to work, the avian image must be very familiar.

Although in 'The Merchant's Tale' Chaucer makes a comedy out of this melancholy, elsewhere in the marriage debate taking place in the literature of the late fourteenth and early fifteenth centuries, this sadness is more faithfully reproduced; again, Chaucer's 'Wife of Bath's Prologue' and Thomas Hoccleve's poetry are instructive. The Wife of Bath's contribution to the *Canterbury Tales* is comically exuberant, but its comedy is offset by and deepens Alison's tragic subjectivity. Alison's fifth marriage, to cleric Jankyn, is also an account of her dealings with clerical misogamist values. Whilst both she and Jankyn compromise, and whilst there is accommodation made for the other on both sides, Alison's powerful attraction for her spouse ties her into a relationship with her worst enemy, and her final reconciliation with him is only reached after the terrible domestic violence that leaves her permanently disabled. The Wife craves the authority of, and cites those who recommend, the pearly aesthetics of virginity rather than marriage. Her Prologue teeters between an attack and a corroboration of, and ultimately represents an uncomfortable and decidedly unhappy engagement with, a discursive tradition that causes her ideological harm and labels her as fallen. In Hoccleve's autobiographical poems too, the narrator has interiorised, and hopes – with more grounds than Chaucer's Wife of Bath – to identify with, the clerical values which prefer virginity over marriage; consequently he only ever discusses his wife with a dejected regret and heaviness.[55] It is telling, then, that in *Piers Plowman* the celebratory power of Abraham's B-text speech is surrendered in C, which by contrast is more muted in its tone. This

---

[55]   See, for example, Thomas Hoccleve, *The Complaint and Dialogue*, ed. J. A. Burrow, EETS OS vol. 313 (Oxford, 1999), lines 739–42 and *The Regiment of Princes*, lines 1222–7, 1447–58.

self-censorship serves to deaden the eagerness of the younger poet and signals a snap back to the clerical ideologies in which he is also invested. The pathos in that reluctant return, though, only serves to emphasise the seriousness of the marriage theme in this poem and, I have tried to suggest, in its period. The poignant lyricism of Langland's poetics of marriage subtly contends with the clean aesthetics of the literature on virginity, attempting to negotiate a dignified, if tragic, place for wedlock within late-medieval society.

11   Fragments of *(Have Your) Desire*: Brome women at play[1]

Nicola McDonald

Understood as both a physical space and a social network, the household is readily identified by modern scholarship as *'the* privileged locus for medieval women'.[2] The equation between women, domestic space and the communities they support – evidenced in sources as diverse as court records, devotional manuals, private correspondence, lyric poetry and conduct literature – helps us to locate medieval women and to understand the narratives and material conditions of house and home that determined so many of their lives. Yet it is also an equation whose ideologies, whereby women are predominantly constrained, silenced and excluded, demand resistance. This can (and does) take various forms, but crucial to it is a reassessment of both primary sources (what *medieval* evidence suggests about the divergent roles, identities and desires of women) and critical certainties (what *modern* scholarship, for all of its heterogeneity, posits as somehow fundamental to medieval women's experience). The aim of this essay is to insert into current debates about women and the household, in particular about women's textual communities within the gentry household, the evidence provided by a single late-fifteenth-century manuscript (the so-called Brome commonplace book)

---

[1] This chapter is part of an extended project on women at play in late-medieval England and, tangentially, France; the material discussed here intersects with the more courtly evidence I examine in Nicola McDonald, 'Chaucer's *Legend of Good Women*, ladies at court and the female reader', *Chaucer Review* 35 (2000), 22–42 and 'Games medieval women play', in Carolyn P. Collette (ed.), *The Legend of Good Women: context and reception* (Woodbridge: Boydell & Brewer, 2006), pp. 176–97. I am grateful to Arlyn Diamond, Maryanne Kowaleski and Felicity Riddy for their comments on an earlier draft of this essay. All references to *A new index of Middle English verse* (hereafter *NIMEV*) are to Julia Boffey and A. S. G. Edwards (eds.), *A new index of Middle English verse* (London: British Library, 2005); all references to *A short title catalogue of books printed in England, Scotland and Ireland and of English books printed abroad* (hereafter *STC*) are to A. W. Pollard and G. R. Redgrave (eds.), *A short title catalogue of books printed in England, Scotland and Ireland and of English books printed abroad*, 3 vols., 2nd rev. edn (London: Bibliographical Society, 1976–91).
[2] Sarah Salih, 'At home, out of the house', in Carolyn Dinshaw and David Wallace (eds.), *The Cambridge companion to medieval women's writing* (Cambridge University Press, 2003), pp. 124–40 (p. 125).

for a culture of domestic play that demanded women's participation and, in turn, provided them with an unparalleled opportunity to articulate distinctly secular desires. My interest here is in both the material traces of women at play and the ways in which, as modern readers, we need to learn how to 'squeeze' (to borrow Steven Justice's tactics for discerning voices of rebellion) these 'taciturn records' – of textual culture, domestic order and female desire – 'until they talk'.[3]

There has to date been little interest in women at play either within or without the medieval household, and indeed play is not a concept we readily associate with medieval women. Although we know little about the cultures of play particular to the gentry, the household itself is readily identified as a vehicle of sociability. The role of games in domestic sociability is imperfectly understood and rarely examined, but it has not gone undocumented; women's participation in domestic play is repeatedly signalled. Gower's identification of both dice and *demandes d'amour* as suitable for women's entertainment is neatly matched by Margaret Paston's account of popular household 'disportys' (chess, cards and backgammon as well as 'lowde' pursuits like singing and disguisings).[4] Fashionable metropolitan women are singled out as the audience for an erotically charged game like *Ragman Roll*, while *Chaunce of Dice*, another courtly social game, addresses itself to both women and men.[5] And these are not isolated examples. If the household is, inescapably, an instrument of social control whereby women are taught right thinking and their conduct is policed, it is also a remarkably permeable space whose boundaries, real and metaphorical, are crossed and re-crossed countless times a

---

[3] Steven Justice, *Writing and rebellion: England in 1381* (Berkeley: University of California Press 1994), p. 9.

[4] John Gower, *Confessio Amantis*, in G. C. Macaulay (ed.), *The complete works of John Gower: the English works*, 2 vols. (Oxford: Clarendon Press, 1901), book 4, lines 2792–3; Norman Davis (ed.), *Paston letters*, vol. 1, p. 257. Dice games, regularly associated with social disorder, were a constant source of anxiety in later medieval England. Dicing, along with cards and ball games, was banned by Parliament and local authorities sought (with varying degrees of seriousness and success) to regulate the misconduct that gaming was thought to occasion. But as Marjorie McIntosh makes clear, the legislation and its enforcement, driven by a concern for public order (dicing was a common tavern sport) and economic security (betting could be financially crippling), was primarily aimed at the young and the poor. See Marjorie K. McIntosh, *Controlling misbehavior in England, 1370–1600* (Cambridge University Press, 1998), pp. 96–107. The kind of domestic diversions recommended by Gower and played by the East Anglian gentry seem to have escaped official censure.

[5] Andreas Freudenberger (ed.), *Ragman Roll: ein spätmittelenglisches Gedicht* (Erlangen: Junge & Sohn, 1909); E. P. Hammond, 'The Chaunce of Dice', *Englische Studien* 59 (1925), 1–16. For a discussion of the games and of the different emphases occasioned by a women-only and a mixed gender audience, see McDonald, 'Games medieval women play', pp. 185–6.

day.[6] It is an intimate sphere of mixed company (including women and men, sometimes of divergent social status) that is not limited to the nuclear or even immediate family. Whether as a function of the hospitality that is every householder's obligation, or simply as a result of the daily round of business, the household is mobile and fluid, a hub of traffic, in and out.[7] Alongside the fantasies of order, sobriety and restraint that figure so prominently in the records of late-medieval women, there is evidence, albeit ephemeral and circumscribed, that household games did not simply socialise women in conformity with dominant ideologies but rather afforded them a space in which to play with – to debate, nuance, challenge – those ideologies. *Mulier ludens* is accessible to us only sporadically and then in fragments, but her contribution to the complexity of medieval women's lives demands our attention. What follows is a detailed examination of the games (especially the anti-feminist cipher puzzles and the dice game *Have Your Desire*) that are recorded in the Brome manuscript and my attention is focused on what they might have meant to the women, rather than men, who played them. At first glance, the game texts are inescapably prosaic, even uninteresting – which no doubt accounts for

---

[6] For the policing function of the household see Felicity Riddy's, Preface to 'The moral household' and for its inherent permeability and resistance to definition see Sarah Rees Jones's, Preface to 'The public houshold and political power', both in Beattie *et al.* pp. 129–35 (especially p. 135) and pp. 11–18 (especially p. 11–12), respectively.

[7] A manuscript like the so-called 'Findern' anthology (Cambridge University Library MS Ff.1.6, edited in facsimile by R. Beadle and A. E. B. Owen, *The Findern manuscript, Cambridge University Library MS. Ff.1.6* (London: Scolar Press, 1978)), a collection of secular and courtly verse compiled in a gentry household in the North Midlands throughout the second half of the fifteenth-century, gives us a glimpse at the social dynamic, the regular toings and froings, of the late-medieval household and of especially women's sociability around the recreational text. In addition to the Derbyshire Finderns (with whom the manuscript is now identified), various, predominantly female, members of the Cruker, Cotton, Frauncis, Shirley and Hungerford families – all gentry neighbours of the Finderns and variously connected with them or with each other through marriage – copied items into the manuscript and wrote, or had their names written, in its margins. Other named scribes, all men, have been loosely identified as 'estate servants', here acting as amanuenses. One who signs himself 'Nicholas plenus amoris' ('Nicholas full of love', fol. 67v), may have had, whatever his rank, a distinctly intimate stake in the sociability that the manuscript and its texts promoted. What so distinguishes medieval households like those of the Finderns and their network of associates is the way in which women and men came and went, on business or for pleasure: to share news and deliver goods, to celebrate festive occasions, discuss the latest fashions in shoes and poetry, to make marriages and gloat over bad deals, for companionship, no doubt competition, and sometimes to play games. See John J. Thompson, 'Collecting Middle English romances and some related book-production activities in the late Middle Ages', in Maldwyn Mills, Jennifer Fellows and Carole M. Meale (eds.), *Romance in medieval England* (Cambridge: D. S. Brewer, 1991), pp. 17–38 (especially pp. 30–7) and Ralph Hanna, 'The production of Cambridge University Library MS Ff.1.6,' *Studies in Bibliography* 40 (1987), 62–70, for recent accounts of the manuscript's compilation.

the lack of scholarly attention – but they quickly prove to be enormously articulate, as productive of modern debate as of the medieval conversations they were designed to animate. At the end of this chapter I will come back to the model of the household, here encoded in the short set of precepts known as 'Arise Early', to think about ways in which domestic order, at Brome at least, acknowledges and seeks to accommodate women's desires.

The Book of Brome: fragments for a household at play

New Haven, Yale University, Beinecke Library MS 365, the so-called Brome commonplace book or Book of Brome, has long hovered at the periphery of debates about late-medieval household books, women's literacy and domestic piety.[8] A small, well-worn paper manuscript dating from the late fifteenth and early sixteenth centuries, it was compiled in two distinct phases by two different scribes and contains material relating to the divergent needs of a gentry household and its tenants. In its earliest form, comprising the largely pious verse[9] and model legal documents that

---

[8] The manuscript first came to public attention with Lucy Toulmin Smith's edition, *The book of Brome: A common-place book of the fifteenth century* (privately printed, 1886); a more recent, reliable description is found in Barbara Shailor (ed.), *Catalogue of medieval and Renaissance manuscripts in the Beinecke Rare Book and Manuscript Library, Yale University*, 3 vols. (Binghamton, NY: Medieval and Renaissance Texts and Studies, 2001), vol. 1, pp. 210–14. The manuscript features in surveys of what have come to be known as, variously, common-place books, household books, and miscellanies but, despite the insights it offers into fifteenth-century gentry culture, this puzzling volume has received no sustained critical attention. See Julia Boffey and John J. Thompson, 'Anthologies and miscellanies: production and choice of texts', in Jeremy Griffiths and Derek Pearsall (eds.), *Book production and publishing in Britain 1375–1475* (Cambridge University Press, 1989), pp. 279–315, especially pp. 293–4 and footnotes 85 and 86. Eamon Duffy, most influentially, uses it as an index to the East Anglian gentry's undistinguished taste for 'catechetical and moralistic material': *The stripping of the altars*, p. 74. Sharon D. Michalove, 'The education of aristocratic women in fifteenth-century England', in Sharon D. Michalove and A. Compton Reeves (eds.), *Estrangement, enterprise and education in fifteenth century England* (Stroud: Sutton, 1998), pp. 116–39, looks briefly at the contents that may have been of interest to women readers in the household (p. 127). For the complexities of manuscript taxonomy and the debate over nomenclature see: Julia Boffey, 'Bodleian Library, MS Arch. Selden. B.24 and definitions of the household book', in A. S. G. Edwards, Vincent Gillespie and Ralph Hanna (eds.), *The English medieval book: studies in memory of Jeremy Griffiths* (London: British Library, 2000), pp. 125–34'; Boffey and Thompson, 'Anthologies and miscellanies', *passim*.

[9] In addition to the *Abraham and Isaac* play for which the manuscript is most famous (Norman Davis, ed., *Non-cycle plays and fragments*, EETS SS vol. 1, Oxford, 1970), the Brome manuscript's original pious contents include an incomplete life of St Margaret (*NIMEV* 2673), a vision of purgatory (*Owayne Miles*), a catechetical dialogue (the Middle English *Ipotis*), the Fifteen Signs of Doomsday (*NIMEV* 1823) plus a few short prayers, monitory verses and an Annunciation lyric (*NIMEV* 3736).

fill, in fits and starts, about half of its five gatherings, it is associated with the household of John Cornwallis (d.1506), a middle-rank Suffolk squire whose manors, including his primary residence at Brome, were clustered along the Suffolk–Norfolk border just north of Eye.[10] Some time before 1499, the manuscript passed to Robert Melton, one of the executors named in Cornwallis's will and in all likelihood the family's steward, who used its blank leaves to record farm and domestic accounts as well as private expenditure, procedures for the local manorial courts (over which Melton probably presided), and short devotional and medical pieces. The intersection here of different textual cultures (predominantly pious and pragmatic) and different communities of readers (the men and women of the household as well as their employees) seems at first glance to map neatly on to what we already know about the strongly utilitarian reading practices of many gentry households and the kinds of discursive domains that were organised around, or managed by, the written word. In other words, although the manuscript points to a diversity of users, all of whom exploited or augmented it for a diversity of purposes, the bulk of its contents – the careful calculus of purgatory and the directions for a trental, the surveillance of tenants and management of their tenements, the documentation of rents paid, produce sold and bonnets bought – exemplify the ideologies of regulation, reckoning and hierarchical masculine authority that are regularly associated with a conservative late-medieval gentry and their books. And, indeed, it is almost exclusively as a record of a 'sober and conformist' gentry piety that the Book of Brome has excited what interest it has since it was (re)discovered, in the muniment-room of Brome Hall, near the end of the nineteenth century.[11]

---

[10] From the evidence of his will (TNA, PROB 11/15; PCC, 12 Adeane), the life of John Cornwallis (like his manor and his household) was circumscribed and parochial. Drawn up in English, perhaps by his steward Robert Melton, the will betrays his comparatively modest funds and resolutely local interests. His attachments are to the churches on his estate (he requests burial in the chancel of Brome church) or in its immediate vicinity, his close family (childless, his heir is his brother Edward; he makes modest bequests to the daughters of his youngest brother William and his sister Katherine, plus of course his wife Elisabeth, and he appoints, in addition to Robert Melton, both William and a third brother, Robert his executors), and most insistently his manor house Lyng Hall. The Hall's layout (chapel, hall, parlour and chamber plus a brewhouse and bakehouse) and contents are detailed with inventory-like specificity. Less than fifty years after John's death, when the family had successfully insinuated itself into the court, his great nephew, the recusant Sir Thomas Cornwallis (1518–1604), a member of Mary Tudor's Privy Council (whose wife was a lady of the queen's privy chamber), left Lyng Hall for the larger, more fashionable and newly built Brome Hall. I am grateful to Jeremy Goldberg for adding his expertise to my enthusiasm for John Cornwallis's will.

[11] Duffy, *Stripping of the altars* (1992 edn), p. 75; Michalove, 'Education of aristocratic women', p. 127.

That the manuscript testifies to the tastes of a household that was distinguished as much by its distance from the obsessions of the fashionable elite as for the thorough conventionality of its piety there is little doubt. The Cornwallises, for whom the so-called 'literary' contents were originally compiled, were either not interested in or had no access to the kind of courtly verse that animated aristocratic metropolitan circles or fashion-conscious provincial households like those of the Derbyshire Finderns and their neighbours.[12] Indeed, they don't seem to have cultivated a taste for secular poetry, whether narrative or lyric, at all. In their choice of devotional texts they likewise appear to have eschewed the emotional effusions characteristic of so much East Anglian popular piety, as well as the intricacies of theological debate and the reformer's zeal, opting every time for the kind of material that Duffy, in his survey of late medieval religion, dubs 'credulous' and 'orthodox'.[13]

My interest in the Book of Brome, and in the insights it can offer us into the textual cultures available to late-medieval gentry women, is predicated precisely on the apparent orthodoxy of the manuscript's contents and its

---

[12] Anthologies of courtly verse, like Oxford, Bodleian Library MSS Fairfax 16 and Bodley 638 (which include Chaucer's shorter poetry, alongside the works of his near-contemporaries and two English dice games), became popular in metropolitan circles in the second half of the fifteenth century. Both are available in facsimile: J. Norton-Smith (ed.), *Bodleian Library MS Fairfax 16* (London: Scolar Press, 1979) and Pamela Robinson (ed.), *Manuscript Bodley 638: a facsimile* (Norman, OK: Pilgrim Books, 1982)). Cambridge University Library MS Ff.1.6, the so-called Findern anthology (see note 7 above) comprises exclusively secular, polite literature and is regularly cited for the unusually extended reach of its courtly and metropolitan tastes. Indicative of its readers' interest in current ludic fashion, the Findern anthology includes, alongside amorous debate poems, a short narrative episode (the 'Alexander–Cassamus' fragment) based on the fourteenth-century *Voeux du paon* in which a party of would-be lovers play *demandes d'amours*, the most popular form of amorously-inflected, courtly entertainment (for a discussion of *demandes d'amours* as women's entertainment see McDonald, 'Games medieval women play', pp. 190–7). A recent article by K. A. Doyle, 'Thisbe out of context: Chaucer's female readers and the Findern manuscript', *Chaucer Review* 40 (2006), 231–62, provides a persuasive account of Findern's investment in and detailed understanding of the kind of ludic culture that was fashionable in metropolitan circles and at court. Doyle offers a timely reminder that we must not underestimate the capacity of gentry women to play with the terms of amorous debate. Likewise we must be careful not to make the distinction between metropolitan and provincial tastes (including those at Brome) too absolute. Two lines from Chaucer's 'Lak of stedfastnesse' (*NIMEV* 3140) plus Lydgate's 'Seven wise counsels' (*NIMEV* 576) are copied into the *Book of Brome*; and while John Cornwallis's affections may have been at Lyng Hall, his country seat, he was evidently no stranger to the city. He identifies a London property in his will (a 'place in London called Barones', according to his youngest brother William [TNA, PROB/11/19; PCC, 24 Ayloffe]) that was still in the hands of his widow Elisabeth in 1519.

[13] Duffy, *Stripping of the altars*, p. 75. The Brome *Abraham and Isaac*, for instance, concludes not with the detailed typology of Chester's expositor (the version with which it is most closely allied) but with the stern injunction to 'groche not aȝens owre Lord God' ('The Brome *Abraham*' in Davis, *Non-cycle plays*, p. 456).

ideologies. Evidence for women's readership of commonplace or household books is limited and often simply inferential.[14] Only on rare occasions does a manuscript record the names of medieval owners, women or men, let alone the readers who in so many different ways had access to its contents. When Sharon Michalove posits the Book of Brome as a 'spur to [women's] literacy', she uses the manuscript's devotional and didactic contents – 'the religious literature favoured in households' – to infer a woman reader eager to use the collection's prayers, saint's life and catechetical material for her own edification and for the education of her household.[15] Research on medieval women readers and on the kinds of textual communities in which they participated has, over the past few decades, worked hard to reassess the extent of women's literacy, a facet of their lives that has been markedly underestimated, and to chart the complexity and sophistication of women's reading practices. That research, in part reflecting the weight of extant evidence, has tended to focus on religious reading and on the kinds of female communities that were forged around devotional texts.[16] At its most interesting, it demonstrates the ways in which medieval women were not simply passive consumers of religious culture but rather enormously adept at exploiting the opportunities that piety afforded them for self-expression, independence and authority. Michalove's assumption – in effect an educated guess – that the Cornwallis women used the Brome manuscript for devotional and didactic purposes conveniently accords with what we already know about medieval women's reading practices; at the same time it works to reinforce our preconceptions about the textual cultures and associated codes of conduct available to medieval women. The image of the pious woman, attending to the spiritual needs of her well-ordered household, is as much a reflex of modern scholarship as a fantasy of medieval moralists. What Michalove, Duffy and others have missed in their attention to household piety and the devout woman is the evidence that the Book of Brome

---

[14] Julia Boffey and Carole Meale, 'Gentlewomen's reading', in Lotte Hellinga and J. B. Trapp (eds.), *The Cambridge history of the book in Britain*, vol. 3, *1400–1557* (Cambridge University Press, 1999), vol. 3, p. 536.

[15] Michalove, 'The education of aristocratic women', p. 127.

[16] Jocelyn Wogan-Browne, 'Analytical survey 5: "reading is good prayer": recent research on female reading communities', *New Medieval Literatures* 5 (2002), 229–89 provides an excellent summary of the history of anglophone scholarship on medieval women readers and their textual communities. Boffey and Meale, 'Gentlewomen's reading', seek to nuance the ideologically charged portrait of women 'workyng, praying, redyng' that emerges from didactic sources; they suggest that 'the reality, for gentlewomen, involved access to a range of books much wider than has been suspected' (pp. 526, 540). Mary Carpenter Erler, *Women, reading and piety in late medieval England* (Cambridge University Press, 2002) similarly cautions that the prevalence of religious texts – which are more likely to be preserved and their circulation to be recorded – may well 'overemphasize religious reading' (p. 3).

offers for a glimpse of a rather different community of women readers. Alongside the pious verse and humdrum domestic accounts, the manuscript provides startling if fragmentary evidence of a household at play, a distinctive ludic space, what Huizinga calls a play-ground and others after him a game-space, in amidst the daily demands of spiritual and economic reckoning, in which women and men came together to play games and solve puzzles, for laughter, merriment and conversation.[17]

I am particularly interested in *Have Your Desire*, an amorously inflected dice game for mixed company that is preserved (one of just four extant copies), albeit incomplete, in the Brome manuscript.[18] But in the discussion that follows, I make use of the full range of game texts available to the Brome householders.[19] As Boffey and Meale have recently proposed, women's 'reading habits' and 'tastes' were much more 'eclectic' than we had assumed;[20] the culture of play that the Brome manuscript documents helps us better understand a little-appreciated facet of women's lives as well as the opportunities they had to speak out. The evidence of *Have Your Desire* and similar social pastimes indicates not only that women did play games, in their own households as well as in those of friends, neighbours and family, but also that the games they played were remarkable for their deliberate disruption of order (both verbal and social), for their sexual licence (prompting precisely the kind of thoughts and behaviour that medieval authorities elsewhere sought to prohibit), and for the explicit opportunity, unmatched in surviving textual evidence, that they provided medieval women for the formulation and assertion of their own desires.

According to Julia Boffey and John Thompson, in what is the most convincing account of the manuscript's early history, the Book of Brome

---

[17] The classic accounts of the social significance of play remain Johan Huizinga, *Homo ludens: a study of the play element in culture*, trans. R. F. C. Hull (London: Routledge and Kegan Paul 1949) and Roger Caillois, *Man, play and games*, trans. M. Barash (New York: Free Press of Glencoe, 1961, first published in French 1958). Both play and games continue to receive considerable attention in many disciplines; most theorists identify a distinctive game-space that is both separate from and integral to everyday social practice. See Huizinga, *Homo ludens*, chap. 1, for his identification of the 'play-ground' (especially p. 28) and its intimate connection with 'ordinary life'. Also relevant here is Victor Turner's account of the liminality of play: *From ritual to theatre: the human seriousness of play* (New York: Performing Arts Journal Publications, 1982). For a recent summary of the rich scholarship on games and play, especially in relation to the 'debate about women' in late medieval literature, see Betsy McCormick, 'Remembering the game: debating the *Legend*'s women', in Collette, *Legend of Good Women*, pp. 105–31 (especially pp. 105–10).

[18] *NIMEV* 3694.3.

[19] Lucy Toulmin Smith edits the full set of game texts in *A common-place book of the fifteenth century*, pp. 11–18, although her edition of the dice game has been superseded by W. L. Braekman, 'Fortune-telling by the casting of dice: a Middle English poem and its background', *Studia Neophilologica* 52 (1980), 3–29.

[20] Boffey and Meale, 'Gentlewomen's reading', p. 537.

Figure 11.1 The opening of the 'Book of Brome'. New Haven, Beinecke Rare Book and Manuscript Library, Yale University, MS 365, fols 1v–2r. Reproduced with permission of The Beinecke Rare Book and Manuscript Library.

started out in the second half of the fifteenth century as a collection of unbound paper gatherings (some of whose leaves were removed early on and without detriment to the surviving texts) that were used for different purposes. Although it is incomplete and fragmentary, copied by a scribe who worked 'intermittently and haphazardly', an initial principle of organisation can still be readily discerned. Of the five extant gatherings, two (the third and fourth) were originally left blank; the first two gatherings were reserved for what Boffey and Thompson call 'edifying literature'; while the final one contains, predominantly, model forms of legal documents (in Latin with an English translation) relating to private and domestic law.[21] What this account of the manuscript's contents and organisation glosses over, however, is the material – a collection of puzzles, short verse and the incomplete copy of *Have Your Desire* – that occupies the first four folios and that on closer inspection clearly forms a coherent, if not fully realised, unit of recreational verse. The manuscript's first scribe broke off copying the dice game, the longest item in this opening section (it fills fols. 2r–3r), just half way through the complete text but he then left three pages blank (fols. 3v–4v), suggesting that he originally planned to go back and finish it, before he started copying his next item, the catechetical dialogue now known as *Ipotys* which effectively opens the devotional section of the manuscript. The disparate texts that fill the first two pages (the single folio that precedes the game), aligned by Boffey and Thompson with the 'random scribbles' that commonly feature on flyleaves,[22] include two so-called moral or conduct verses (now known as 'Man in Merthe' and 'Arise Early'[23]), a series of five anti-feminist cipher puzzles[24] and a four-line monorhyme[25] whose punch line, like the puzzles, draws on anti-feminist commonplace, this time the 'schrod' woman or 'qwen' who gets her way ('wyll'). Reproduced in Figure 11.1 is the first full opening of the manuscript's ludic unit (fols. 1v–2r). On the left, in the left-hand column, are the anti-feminist cipher puzzles and, in the right-hand column, 'Arise Early'; on the right are the first eight rolls (6.6.6. through to 6.5.4) of *Have Your Desire*.[26] It is on this unfinished and untidy evidence that my argument is built.

---

[21] Boffey and Thompson, 'Anthologies and miscellanies', pp. 293–4
[22] Ibid., p. 311, n. 86.   [23] *NIMEV* 2064 and *NIMEV* 324, respectively.
[24] *NIMEV* 3256.3.   [25] *NIMEV* 3372.6.
[26] Fol. 1v additionally includes a list, in cipher, of technical terms for resting by humans and animals (perhaps designed to familiarise players with the cipher) plus a two-line macaronic rhyme. The rhyme ('A! lord God, mercy qui verba cuncta creasti / Helpe! Kyng of cownefort, qui vitam semper amasti') either functions independently or, with its playful emphasis on love, creativity and words, as a coda to 'Arise Early', the cipher puzzles or both.

Whether the manuscript's original compiler ever intended to produce a whole gathering of game texts – a project that was sidelined when he started work on the devotional verse and then completely abandoned – we can of course never know. The layout and decoration of fol. 1v (the current second page, on which the puzzles are copied) – with the decorated capital, pen-work flourishes and careful hierarchy of scripts, exactly the same methods that are used elsewhere in the manuscript to mark the beginning of a major item – work hard to effect a deliberate and ambitious, if ultimately short-lived, start. Even the restraint advocated by the initial (and so-called) moralising verse ('Man in Merthe', on fol. 1r and unique to this manuscript), with its measured mirth, fortitude in the face of capricious fortune and lightly subversive promise of success, seems to be purposefully tailored to the requirements of the game material that follows. It does not, however, finally matter that the compiler's playful impulse was interrupted. Puzzles, dice games and comic sayings are the kind of ephemera that only rarely survive in anything more than fragments. In a household like that of the Cornwallises, where loose leaves of paper (like those taken from the gatherings before the manuscript was bound) were available and far more practical for the informal and impromptu demands of play, it is remarkable that traces such as these, of a fully fledged ludic programme, have survived at all.

Debating women: a culture of gendered play

Despite their apparent diversity (puzzles, sayings, versified precepts and a dice game), the bulk of the texts that make up Brome's ludic unit are informed by a culture of gendered play whose preoccupations are remarkably familiar: the 'matter of woman' and heterosexual desire. From the evidence of the preponderantly anti-feminist puzzles alone (the manuscript's only complete game), we might well conclude that there is little here to interest medieval women. All five puzzles draw on pervasive stereotypes – women as shrews ('schrewys'), for instance – and all exploit the same formula: players are given a list of nouns in cipher ('b stpkfksch', 'b mklstpn', 'b ffdkrbfd' and 'b xopmbn'), prefaced by an imperative that works as a clue to the puzzle's solution; the 'iiij things [that] take gret betyng' prove, with the reinsertion of missing vowels, to be 'a stokfisch', 'a milston', 'a ffedirbed' and, common to all five, 'a wooman'.[27] But to

---

[27] These puzzles use one of the simplest and most common forms of medieval cipher; all of the vowels (including 'w') have been replaced by the consonants that, in alphabetical order, follow them: so 'x' replaces 'w', 'p' replaces 'o', 'b' replaces 'a' and so on. Once deciphered the puzzles read in full: 'Take iii claterars: a pie, a iai [jay], a woman; take iii

dismiss the anti-feminist puzzles as necessarily inimical to female players (however much we might want them to be) is to misunderstand fundamentally the terms and structure of the medieval gender game in which they participate. The prevalence of often virulent misogyny is a familiar impediment to modern critics interested in recuperating medieval women. Loath to imagine them complicit in what, to modern sensibilities, can only be their own oppression, we prefer to maintain medieval women's exclusion from (or at the very least to deny their pleasure in) a community that not only disparages them but depends on the perpetual reiteration of that disparagement. The anti-feminism that structures the Brome cipher puzzles, that provides their distinctive lexis and comic charge, is incontestable, but that cannot be our conclusion. Misogyny pervades all aspects of medieval culture and, tiresome though it is, nothing we do will change it; misogyny is a productive starting point but it cannot always be where we end up. My contention is that the games found in the Brome manuscript, games that are located within a sharply delineated culture of gendered play (whose principal features are outlined below), provided the women who played them with a unique occasion to imagine and then articulate their own, specifically secular, desires. The challenge here is to think, in ways that do not patronise medieval women, about how a culture of play created opportunities for women to mock and manipulate misogyny's apparent hegemony and to assert their own, desiring voices. Refusing the logic of misogyny, whereby women's agency is foreclosed, we need instead to put women (back) at the centre of the game and, in doing so, we need to give full rein to the inherent disruption of play.

That the 'rhetorical formulae of misogyny' were regarded as a 'game' Alcuin Blamires makes clear, and not only for the 'intelligentsia'.[28] They underpin in particular the distinctive play of courtly poetry and its fashionable imitations, but also animate more mundane, often derivative productions like the lyrics, riddles, short narratives and games of chance (including the Brome puzzles) that are indexed in memorable profusion by Francis Utley.[29] My point here is not to argue that medieval women (or men, for that matter) were more amused than we are by women's alleged equivalence with millstones and stockfish or that they found the spectre of

---

lowrars: a ape, a owle, a woman; take iii schrewys: a waspe, a wesill, a woman; take iii angry: a ffrier, a fox, a woman; ther be iiii things take gret betyng: a stokfisch, a milston, a ffedirbed, a wooman'.

[28] Alcuin Blamires (ed.), *Woman defamed and woman defended: an anthology of medieval texts* (Oxford University Press, 1992), p. 12.

[29] Francis L. Utley, *The crooked rib: an analytical index to the argument about women in English and Scots literature to the end of the year 1568* (Columbus: University of Ohio Press, 1944); for Brome's anti-feminist puzzles see pp. 275, 287.

a good beating simply more funny (reductive stereotype and domestic violence are still potent comic forces). On the contrary, the whole point of the puzzles' extreme, one-sided rhetoric, framed explicitly (as it is here) as a game, was to provoke its inversion and, at the same time, to foment debate and conversation.

The late medieval popularity of the 'debate about woman' as a social diversion for mixed company, especially in courtly circles, has attracted considerable attention in recent scholarship.[30] We are now accustomed to thinking about fashionable women and men (to whom most of the evidence points) coming together to play a variety of text-based games, all preoccupied with questions about women and/or desire and designed to promote lively, contentious talk. What current research has most effectively underlined is the game's inherently binary structure, 'encompassing both anti-feminist and pro-feminist positions'.[31] Although both sides of the debate are only rarely detailed in full, that binary structure necessarily informs every formulation. Even without explicit articulation, one side always invokes the other. And both are, as rhetorical positions, wholly inflexible: women are either essentially good *or* inherently evil, worthy of praise *or* deserving of blame. But the purpose of the game lies not in the simple reiteration of irreconcilable poles, but in the dialectic, in the protests, fragmentary complicities and energetic discussion, that the clash of rhetorical extremes provokes. The debate's origin in clerical culture (with Blamires' 'intelligentsia') is clear and women's exclusion from that culture is no doubt responsible for its inherent asymmetry – there is no

---

[30] John Stevens, *Music and poetry in the early Tudor court* (London: Methuen, 1961) remains the seminal account of late medieval social entertainment; his reading of courtly poetry as a 'game of love' designed to encourage debate among women and men is outlined in chapter 9. See also Richard Firth Green, 'The *familia regis* and the *familia cupidinis*', in V. J. Scattergood and J. W. Sherborne (eds.), *English court culture in the later Middle Ages* (London: Duckworth, 1983), pp. 87–108 for a discussion of the culture of amorous play at the Ricardian court. More recently both Alastair Minnis and Florence Percival, delineating an interpretive context for Chaucer's *Legend of Good Women*, have sketched out the culture of debate around questions of 'woman' and amorous desire that animated fashionable metropolitan circles: Alastair J. Minnis, 'The world upside down: gender game as alternative art', in *Chaucer's shorter poems*, Oxford Guides to Chaucer (Oxford: Clarendon Press, 1995), pp. 443–54 and F. Percival, 'The *Legend* as courtly game', in *Chaucer's legendary good women* (Cambridge University Press, 1998), pp. 299–323. See also, McDonald, 'Games medieval women play'.

[31] McCormick, 'Remembering the game', p. 111. Alcuin Blamires's work on the pro- as well as anti-feminist traditions has effectively demonstrated the extent to which the two sides of the debate are interrelated. Both his *Woman defamed and woman defended* and his *The case for women in medieval culture* (Oxford: Clarendon Press, 1997) demonstrate the extent to which the debate is fundamentally symbiotic. See also the introduction to Thelma Fenster and Clare Lees (eds.), *Gender in debate from the early Middle Ages to the Renaissance* (New York: Palgrave, 2002), pp. 1–18.

corresponding case for or against men – but its extension into lay culture and the vernacular, where from at least the fourteenth century it became a form of domestic entertainment, fundamentally changed not only the make-up of the audience (now both men and women) but with it the game's dynamic and its stakes. Although the distinctive quality of the game-space – a purposefully delineated time and place that is both different from the daily routine and integral to it, where cultural imperatives are not only acted out but interrogated[32] – is well recognised, there has been little interest in teasing out what it might have offered the medieval women who participated in these games. Alastair Minnis has convincingly argued that Chaucer's *Legend of Good Women* (itself a product of this same culture of play) provided a 'site for actual dissent', for 'men and women alike to push at the hierarchical limits of what was possible'.[33] What is important here is that the radical potential of Chaucer's poem, posited by Minnis, is determined not by its courtly audience but by its ludic structure. It is a potential that the *Legend* shares with other manifestations of this inherently polemical game and one that demands that we think more seriously about what the Brome manuscript's games offered the gentry women who played them.

Stockfish and shrews: anti-feminist cipher puzzles

Read as a sequence, as their layout and rhetorical patterning suggest, the five cipher puzzles play out an anti-feminist comedy of retributive violence that works by way of its own neat inversion.[34] When 'woman' is successfully deciphered she is exposed, in the terms of popular stereotype, as what R. Howard Bloch has called 'a bundle of verbal abuse'.[35] As well as being

---

[32] For the 'spatial separation' of play and its 'absolute and peculiar' order, see Huizinga, *Homo ludens*, especially chapter 1 (pp. 38, 29) who also argues for its inherent seriousness: play is 'an integral part of life in general' and it serves a '*significant* function' (pp. 27, 19).

[33] Minnis, *The shorter poems*, p. 451.

[34] See note 27 for the text of the five puzzles.

[35] R. H. Bloch, *Medieval misogyny and the invention of Western romantic love* (Chicago: University of Chicago Press, 1997), p. 20. Women's speech, and in particular its excesses, was one of the most popular butts of misogynist humour, as the length of the 'speech, women's' entry in the index to Blamires (ed.), *Woman defamed* demonstrates (p. 325). As a strategy to diminish the value of women's words, this kind of humour did have a very real effect on the way in which what women said was perceived by contemporaries; women's voices were formally excluded from many spheres of medieval life, while speech defined as transgressive was punishable by law. But that does not mean that women did not contest stereotypical representations. Research on the early modern period has provocatively suggested some of the ways in which women successfully challenged the commonplaces of misogyny, including those that branded them gossips and shrews. See Pamela Allen Brown, *Better a shrew than a sheep: women, drama, and the culture of jest in early modern England* (Ithaca: Cornell University Press, 2003); Bernard Capp, *When gossips meet: women, family, and neighbourhood in early modern England* (Oxford University Press,

perennially 'angry', she is a 'claterer' (chatterer), 'lowrar' (scowler) and 'schrew' who, so the logic goes, fully deserves the physical abuse, the 'gret betyng', that is finally, in the last puzzle, meted out to her (by, we intuit, her victims). Some players may, of course, have stopped here, content with the substitution of vowels for consonants and the reiteration of familiar platitudes. But no doubt others, as much to keep a brief game going as to fundamentally question its rhetoric, would have contested both individual analogies and general conclusions. Put into the explicitly dialogic context of an entertaining debate, where the inert stereotypes demand both inversion and refutation, the puzzles work not simply to reinforce pernicious clichés or endorse violence against women but to open up the extraordinary prospect of women and men engaged in discussion about the power and effect of women's words, of their verbal dexterity and uncompromising directness of speech, of their ability to use language to question male authority and in doing so to 'have [their] wyll' (as the short rhyme, copied onto the bottom of the preceding page, puts it). Reducing women to uninflected categories, whether good or bad, fully participates in the misogynist enterprise, but it is only when we limit ourselves to the inflexible medium of the page, when we stop short of imagining the game in play (its palpably one-sided rhetoric the subject of debate), that the categories invoked by the Brome puzzles are uninflected. Games are inescapably serious (despite the laughter, comic gestures and levity that animate them); they are an enormously effective means of inculcating dominant ideologies. Many medieval women doubtless learned through the puzzles' rhetoric their subordination to male hierarchies of textual meaning and with it men's social and economic power. But we can also be sure that through the fracturing of hegemonic order that the game promotes some learned to speak out against that subordination – against their depiction as, inflexibly, nagging wives, scolds, gossips or shrews – and to define themselves in accordance with their own obsessions and in their own words. To argue that anti-feminist stereotype functions, through the dialectic of its inversion, to challenge, even subvert, misogyny (the very ideology that controls the terms of the

2003); Joy Wiltenburg, *Disorderly women and female power in the street literature of early modern England and Germany* (Charlottesville, VA: University Press of Virginia, 1992). Most recently, and with particular reference to late-medieval England, Sandy Bardsley has argued for a more nuanced understanding of how medieval audiences understood the popular correlation of women with troublesome speech: 'medieval people', she posits, 'read (or listened) both with and against the texts, producing for themselves individual and even contradictory interpretations of what it *meant* that women were so closely associated with excessive and usurpationary words'; 'some women may have interpreted representations of disorderly and defiant female speech … as affirming'. Sandy Bardsley, *Venomous tongues: speech and gender in late medieval England* (Philadelphia: University of Pennsylvania Press, 2006), pp. 66, 149.

debate) is not simply naïve wish-fulfilment. It is rather to give due credit to women's agency in the production of ludic meaning, just as, for instance, we have elsewhere credited their effectiveness (despite the relentless misogyny of clerical ideology and religious practice) in articulating personally satisfying forms of piety.

Have Your Desire: women at play

I want now to turn my attention to *Have Your Desire*, the dice game that follows on from the puzzles.[36] Although incomplete, it is the longest and most complex game text that the manuscript records and it provides incontrovertible evidence that its ludic programme was designed for the entertainment of women as well as men. *Have Your Desire* is a game of divination in which players draw fortunes by chance; the choice of fortune is determined by the roll of three dice and in its complete form the game consists of fifty-six four-line fortunes, or stanzas, that match each of the possible number combinations from 6.6.6 through to 1.1.1. The roll to which each fortune corresponds is indicated in the first line of each stanza ('you þat has castin iij sisses here' through to 'you has casted thre acys on raw'[37]) and, occasionally, in a diagram representing three dice in the margin next to the fortune. Since it was first published in its entirety in 1980, it has received virtually no critical attention and Braekman's edition leaves the game untitled, a feature which obscures its content and has no doubt contributed to its neglect. The title I provide here takes its authority, as is standard with medieval verse, from the first line – '[ʒow] schall haue ʒowr dessyer the same ʒere' ('You will have your desire this very year') – and effectively captures the overwhelming preoccupation of the

---

[36] *Have Your Desire* is preserved in four manuscripts dating from the fourteenth and fifteenth centuries, but is complete in only one, Boston, Public Library MS Med.q.101 (fols. 84v–87). The Boston manuscript serves as Braekman's base text ('Fortune-telling by the casting of dice'), although its current shelf mark differs from that recorded by Braekman; *NIMEV* cites yet a third shelf mark. Aberdeen, University Library MS 123 (fols. 149v–152v) contains rolls 6.6.6. to 3.3.3, while BL, MS Sloane 513 (fols. 98v–99) contains only seventy-four lines, from roll 6.6.6 to the mid point of roll 6.3.1. The Brome manuscript (fols. 2r–3r) preserves slightly less than half of the game, rolls 6.6.6 to 5.5.3. Wherever possible citations, indicated by roll number, are from the Toulmin Smith edition of the Brome version. There are two exceptions signalled by an asterisk following the roll number; both are from Braekman's edition of the Boston version. Citations from the second half of the game are likewise from Braekman's edition. Unless otherwise indicated, rolls 5.5.2 to 1.1.1 refer to the Boston version. Occasional citations are also taken from the Aberdeen version whose variants Braekman records in full; these are indicated by roll number and an A. In his edition of the Boston version, Braekman records 'y' for 'þ'; throughout I have substituted the Middle English orthography.

[37] The first line of *Have Your Desire*, indicating the roll, is missing from the Brome version, whose scribe carefully left space for both a rubricated title and decorated capital.

individual fortunes. Although the four extant versions do show some variation, there can be no doubt that the desire which the game seeks to arouse and, sporadically, to satisfy is amorous.

In the Brome manuscript only twenty-four fortunes, those for rolls 6.6.6 to 5.5.3, are extant, just less than half of the game. Yet we can, I think, be certain that the Cornwallises did have access to a complete version, most likely on loose leaves of paper that would have been more practical for actual use. The incompleteness of the Brome version does not result from the lack of an exemplar (unusable and of no intrinsic merit, it is highly unlikely anyone would start copying, part way into a gathering, a fragment of a game), but rather from the compiler's change of direction, signalled by the subsequent religious texts, from the playful to the devotional. His flagging interest is equally evident in the missing first word (where space has been left for an ornamented capital) and the unfinished rubrication (dice, for instance, are drawn into the margin of only one page, fol. 2v). In the analysis that follows, I treat *Have Your Desire* in its entirety, drawing my examples from all four extant versions and from rolls 6.6.6 to 1.1.1, a practice that apparently disregards the integrity of individual manuscript witnesses and, at first, seems inimical to my project. It is, however, only near the end (for rolls 4.4.1 to 3.3.3, which are preserved in only two of the manuscripts) that the extant versions show any significant variation; and, more importantly, that variation does little to affect the game's overall meaning: not because the players were insensitive to shifts in tone or register, but because, as I hope will become clear, the game text itself construes the written record as little more than a springboard for the social exchange and private rumination that is its purpose. We will never know what, exactly, the fortunes missing from the Brome manuscript (5.5.2 to 1.1.1) invited, promised or proscribed, but their effect would not, I am confident, have been markedly different from what we find, in all of their variety, in the other extant versions. The informal, inherently fragmentary nature of play is responsible for the scrappy remains of *Have Your Desire*, a feature which effectively reminds us of its vitality as a real game played by real people.

The range of fortunes that *Have Your Desire* comprises is extensive. Some charge the players with sexual misdemeanour: one lover is 'wanton and nysse' [5.2.2]), a second as 'comon' as 'þe cart way' (5.4.1). Others revel in comic insult (you know as much 'peramour' as a 'sow can sew silk' [5.4.2]) or promise divine intercession: Mary will 'schyld' you 'fro schame' (5.5.3). Some focus on manners, good (4.3.2) and bad (4.1.1), on physical comportment ('god beri[n]g' [4.3.1]) and the allure of beauty (2.2.1), or the disparity between outer and inner worth (a 'body gent and smal' conceals moral chaos, a 'gret strew' [2.2.2]). Most betray a keen awareness of rank ('you has sett þi hert in siche degre' that there is 'no profett ne wirchipe for þe' [4.2.2]), coupled with a persistent fantasy of social advancement: 6.5.5 promises a 'freynchepe' by which 'ʒe schall avanteyssyd be', while 3.3.3 extends the 'ioie' of newly won 'wyrchip' to the whole family ('all þi kyn'). Likewise, despite the inevitable prominence of luck, most seek to confirm the value of hard work: 6.6.2's insistence that success ('to haue ʒowr wyll') requires 'myche' 'travell', is matched by 6.5.2's assurance that those who work 'wysely' will achieve their 'purposse'. Most of the fortunes are insistently gender neutral (as we would expect in a game for mixed company that relies on chance), but the few that aren't – whether marked by reductive stereotype ('wo' is 'hym' who is 'seker of þe' because 'þou ert as anger as any harnet' [5.3.2A]) or simply pronoun ('he' 'schall spede of hys askynge' [6.3.1]) – not only confirm women's participation, alongside men's, but, more radically, suggest that players (again both women and men) may have been encouraged by the liminality of the game-space to experiment, however momentarily, with the performance of differently gendered identities or desires.

Comparison with its closest analogues, *Chaunce of Dice* and *Ragman Roll*, the only other amorously inflected games of chance that survive in English from the late Middle Ages, underlines *Have Your Desire*'s distinctive aesthetic and demonstrates how it too works to encourage a dialogue between women and men, gathered together for the purpose of social entertainment, around matters of secular, and especially sexual, desire. I have written elsewhere about *Chaunce of Dice* and *Ragman Roll*, both of which are explicitly located in a courtly milieu.[38] They depend for their effect on a close knowledge of the conventions of fashionable poetry and even individual lines of (especially Chaucerian) verse, and they exploit the ludic mode to draw attention to the kinds of things that, in polite discourse, are hidden or ignored (in particular the sexually available lover's body stripped down to its basic urges). I have argued that these explicitly conversational courtly games, in which some women were doubtless voluntary and enthusiastic participants, challenge our preconceptions about women's leisure habits and cultural tastes, demand that we think about women's active participation, in the game-space at least, in their own sexualisation, and provide us with a rare insight into a long overlooked sub-culture of women talking not about 'the things of God', but about their own libidos.[39]

---

[38] McDonald, 'Games medieval women play', pp. 180–9.
[39] Riddy, '"Women talking about the things of God"', offers a stimulating analysis of 'talk' as a key medium of cultural exchange; her valorisation of 'conversation', although focused on the devotional, is a model for my own understanding of the very real importance of the ludic conversations in which gentry women participated.

In all sorts of ways, *Have Your Desire* sets itself apart from the courtly games. There are no identifiable allusions to fashionable poetry, however indirect; there is no blatant obscenity and the humour is only ever mildly risqué; individual fortunes are too short to allow comic scenarios to develop or for the proto-renaissance 'portraits' some commentators find in *Ragman Roll*;[40] the versification is resolutely pedestrian (paired couplets as compared to Chaucer's continental imports, rhyme royal and the ababbcbc octave of the 'Monk's Tale' used in *Chaunce of Dice* and *Ragman Roll*, respectively); and the game's fragmentary preservation in commonplace books and manuscript miscellanies compares unfavourably with the textual stability of the well-ordered anthologies that record the courtly texts. And it is this distance from the hub of late-medieval literary production that has discouraged a serious modern readership. Yet, everything about *Have Your Desire* suggests its calculated appeal, as the practical basis for an easy-to-play game, to an extended audience with catholic tastes, diverse literacies and few cultural pretensions.

Whereas *Chaunce of Dice* and *Ragman Roll* use their very precise referencing of current literary fashion to confirm (or construct) their players' exclusivity, their distance from the uninitiated, *Have Your Desire* depends for its effect on, primarily, proverbial rhetoric, some attested ('no man can hold that wyll awey' [6.4.2], 'thynke on the hyndyng [ending] or that ʒe begynne' [6.4.1], 'to ber a horn and hit not blowe' [4.2.2a][41]), some not ('all that ys yll, let yt be styll' [6.3.3], 'as able as a sowe to syt at a kynges table' [4.3.3a]). Its vocabulary of amorous desire nods, occasionally, to courtly tropes (the lover's 'petyssyon' [6.3.2], good 'consayle' [5.5.1]) and romance or lyric convention ('gentil and mild of mude' [4.3.2], 'of body gent and smal' [2.2.2]), but it never requires insider knowledge. Similarly, although desire is construed as a function of the body and is understood to have physical consequences – success affords the lover 'gret dyssort [disport]' (6.4.3), while failure precludes the 'þe plai þat was your fader and your moder betuen' (4.3.3) – *Have Your Desire* does not depend for its effect on ribald innuendo or sexually charged double entendre. Desire is never 'hoote' and 'brennynge', men are not celebrated because they can thrust hard ('styfly sheyt'), and women don't invite just anyone to 'thressyn' in their 'berne[s]'.[42] For all that it is insistently amorous, its erotic is only rarely somatic and it never explores the kind of titillation

---

[40] Hammond, 'The Chaunce of Dice', 2.
[41] Bartlett Jere Whiting, *Proverbs, sentences, and proverbial phrases from English writings mainly before 1500* (Cambridge, MA: Harvard University Press, 1968), H413, E84, H488.
[42] Hammond, 'Chaunce of Dice', line 165; Freudenberger (ed.), *Ragman Roll*, lines 88, 53.

afforded by the dirty words or outrageous scenarios that distinguish *Chaunce of Dice* and especially *Ragman Roll*.

The pioneering work of scholars like Ruth Mazzo Karras and Kim Phillips has suggested the enormous importance of social status in the practice and perception of women's sexuality.[43] Late-medieval aristocratic women, especially those in the greater households, were, they argue, afforded a sexual freedom (encompassing but not limited to the kind of playful flirtation that Phillips calls 'parasexual interaction'[44]) that was unavailable to their social inferiors. And indeed, the differences that separate *Have Your Desire* from its courtly analogues seem to confirm the social exclusivity of sexually licentious play by and for women. But while there were, no doubt, real differences between the kind of conduct (verbal as well as physical) that was licit in fashionable metropolitan circles and the more modest households of the provincial gentry, we should not dismiss the very real audacity that, nevertheless, inheres in the amorous play that *Have Your Desire* facilitates. The fortunes that it comprises, like those of its analogues, function primarily as what John Stevens (writing about the courtly love lyrics) has called '*formulae*' for social exchange;[45] they reveal whatever depth of meaning they have only in action, when they are put into play by real people in real social situations. A game like *Have Your Desire* that prioritises talk, demands the participation of both women and men, and works to generate, and then play off, amorous intrigue not only provides an insight into the kinds of sociable activities popular in gentry households, but also works to construct the household (for the duration of the game at least) as an erogenous play-ground in which its members are socialised in forms of conduct that diverge from the dictates of authoritative discourse, in particular those that seek to efface female desire and its consequences.

The short, undeveloped texts that make up *Have Your Desire*, whether hinting at veiled fantasies or prosaic urges, were not designed for simple, uninflected recitation, nor a mute audience. They celebrate 'wit' (3.2.2) and 'sutell[ty]' (3.3.1); they pit players against their 'enmyes' (6.2.1, 5.5.2, 4.4.2) and hurl charges of pride and wanton[ness] (5.2.2); they warn against getting bogged down in 'synne' (6.4.1), and promise love at first sight (2.2.1) as well as 'gold and catille' (4.2.1). And we can only

---

[43] Ruth Mazzo Karras, '"Because the other is a poor woman she shall be called his wench": gender, sexuality and social status in late medieval England', in Sharon A. Farmer and Carol Braun Pasternack (eds.), *Gender and difference in the Middle Ages* (Minneapolis: University of Minnesota Press, 2003), pp. 10–29; Kim Phillips, *Medieval maidens: young women and gender in England, 1270–1540* (Manchester University Press, 2003), especially chapter 4.

[44] Phillips, *Medieval maidens*, pp. 153–4.   [45] Stevens, *Music and poetry*, p. 207.

begin to imagine the fractured conversation, accusations and futile defence, laughter or even red-faced silence that must have attended the social gatherings during which it was played. *Have Your Desire* may not be packed with lewd innuendo or racy puns, but nowhere does it prescribe the dialogue between women and men that it occasions. Depending on the identity and amorous interests of individual players, on the distinctive piquancy of different social configurations, there are few limits to the kind or, perhaps more subversively, tone of exchange it can sustain.

Have Your Desire purposefully positions itself at the intersection of text and performance, of the words on the page and the social exchange that those words engender. It locates its meaning in an interplay between desire and its articulation that is produced not by the text alone but by the improvised dialogue that it works to generate. The game's stake does not lie, as in *Chaunce of Dice* and *Ragman Roll*, in the overt flaunting of decorum (through the use of taboo words or the detailing of illicit sex in individual fortunes), but rather in the formulation and then probing of desires that are, at first, inchoate or at least unsaid. All games, of course, are only really significant in play. The game text, like a set of rules or instructions, functions to prompt and then delineate action; but some games are more (or differently) scripted than others. Unlike its courtly analogues which insistently render the erotic corporeal, *Have Your Desire* construes desire almost exclusively in terms of 'thowt' (sometimes under-stood as 'wyll', the 'hart' or 'entencion') which, in turn, functions only in relation to its utterance, what one fortune suggestively calls 'schawng' 'thoght' (6.5.4*). When amorous intent is defined as explicitly physical, this usually serves to signal its impossibility: 'þou canst as myche pera-mour, as a sow can slepe yn a ladyes boure' (5.4.2A); 'þe sal neuer haue hit, i wheyn, þe plai þat was your fader and your moder betuen' (4.3.3). Desire is instead understood to produce and to be fuelled by the words that are used to articulate it. The fortunes are full of references to 'wytt' (3.3.1, 3.2.2) and 'wordis fele' (5.3.3), to the lover's ability to 'florice and flater' (4.4.4); and satisfaction is itself understood in terms of achieving 'ʒour petyssyon' (6.3.2), 'hys askynge' (6.3.1). More remarkable, however, is the prominence of fortunes that identify desire as something that players 'dare not tell' (6.5.1). In fortune after fortune, they are teased with the 'schame' (6.5.3) and 'folly' (6.6.1) of the 'dredful' (6.5.2*) desires that they 'der neyther speke nor loke' (6.1.1).

But the driving force of *Have Your Desire* is the speaking, the telling of desire. For all of its insistence on 'priuynesse'(3.3.3A), on the unspeak-able, the game works with extraordinary single-mindedness to prompt disclosure, to force women and men to articulate for the assembled company the desires that they have heretofore sought to hide or repress.

'ʒe dare not sey all that ʒe thynkes' (5.5.5), challenges one fortune, whose only purpose is to make its recipients reveal their unexpressed, or inexpressible, thoughts, the 'all' that they think. Another warns of the 'schame' that exposure would entail, 'gyf þi dissire were knawn' (5.1.1), precisely to encourage illicit revelation. Because the desire the game seeks to arouse and/or satisfy is rarely defined (the text of individual fortunes is purposefully evasive), it demands its precision from the players whose responses lend the dialogue the energy that works to keep it going, to prompt further disclosures, which in turn prompt others. *Have Your Desire* gains its distinctive edge, one that was no doubt amplified in play, from its obsession with the articulation of desires that do not bear easy scrutiny. It dares its players to give voice to things that are 'wanton and nysse' (5.2.2), the uncontrolled or rebellious urges that are properly subject to restraint. And this is where it is most interesting. It works by inciting players to put all of their amorous desires (thoughts and intentions, including illicit ones) into words and, in doing so, it functions if not to sanction 'non lefful thyng[s]' (6.2.2) then at least, through inviting their articulation, to render them possible.

Despite the references to shame and sin, the injunction to repress dissolute desire and the assurance that transgressive demands will fail ('ʒe schall not spede of your askyng', 6.2.2), *Have Your Desire* works, as I have outlined above, to encourage the articulation of just such shameful, dissolute and transgressive desires, by women as well as men; and in doing so it purposefully puts them in a discursive space that is distanced from conventional regulatory practice. And I want to push this further still. As a game that was played within the purview of the late-medieval gentry household, there are necessarily very real limits to the kinds of desires that were conceivably admissible; its order, for instance, is resolutely heterosexual and, despite a fantasy of social mobility, it never countenances seriously debased couplings.[46] But within these limits, brushing up against them, is a conception not simply of desire as productive of or fuelled by its articulation, but rather desire *as* articulation, desire as utterance itself. The desire that this game promises ('[ʒow] schall haue ʒowr dessyer') is, at least partially, made manifest within the game-space itself, where it is subject to the (de)regulation of ludic (mis)rule. Because desire is here, explicitly, construed as a function of language ('askynge', 'petyssyon', 'wordis fele'), of the process through which 'thowt', 'wyll' and 'entencion' are put into discourse, the primary pleasure that it offers lies, I want to suggest, precisely in the discursive practices that playing the

---

[46] *Ragman Roll*, in contrast, imagines the fashionable women who are its audience coupling with 'yomen and gromes': Freudenberger (ed.), *Ragman Roll*, line 88.

game entails. Physical or material satisfaction, at some remove from the game-space, may well be a by-product, but it is not a necessary corollary of the verbal play that the game encourages.[47] Naming desire, giving it shape, contour and detail, effectively brings desire into existence and, within the carefully delineated boundaries of the game, the process of articulation serves as an end in itself. It is here that *Have Your Desire* provided the women who played it with their most significant opportunity, not only to 'haue [their] wyll', but to formulate, and experience, desires that ran counter to the dominant ideologies of gender and social conduct. Some women will not of course have taken up the challenge to give voice to their desires, or at least not to all of them. Part of the game's pleasure must lie in the fragmentary, elusive fashion in which the desires it seeks to arouse, some licit, others not, are or (just as importantly) are not spoken forth. Although desire requires articulation, it does not demand revelation. Desire exists and is enjoyed in all of its disruptive plenitude in incomplete formulations, shards of sensation, half-apprehended intimations and in private cogitation. As one fortune puts it: 'þoght is fre' (6.1.1A). Here, in a gesture that epitomises the game's latent potential, the proverbial is radical.[48]

Routine pleasures: desire in the household

In conclusion, I want to turn to 'Arise Early', the short list of 'precepts in – ly' (as they are formally known), that is copied onto the same page as the cipher puzzles and is, both visually (see Figure 11.1) and conceptually, inseparable from the Book of Brome's ludic programme. The longest of the extant versions of a popular advisory poem, Brome's 'Arise Early' is the only one that does not put the reader to sleep. I reproduce it here in full:

> Fyrst arysse erly
> Serve thy god deuly
> And the war[l]d besylly
> Do thy warke wyssely
> ȝyffe thy almesse sekyrly
> Goo be the wey sadly

---

[47] Writing about analogous continental games, Richard Firth Green, '*Le roi qui ne ment* and aristocratic courtship', in Keith Busby and Erik Kooper (eds.), *Courtly literature: culture and context* (Amsterdam: J. Benjamins Publishing Company, 1990), pp. 211–25, argues that they were used to promote courtship and marriage (p. 213). Although his hypothesis is no doubt valid, it effectively renders the experience of play secondary to the gains (material and social) that the game can, or is intended to, produce. Here, however, I am more interested in thinking about what the players experienced in the process of play and within the confines of the game-space.

[48] For the diffusion of 'þoght is fre', see Whiting, *Proverbs*, T238.

And awnswer the pepll curtesly
Goo to thy met happely
Syt therat discre[t]ly
Off they tong be not to lybraly
Arysse fro thy met tempraly
Goo to they sopper sadly
Arysse fro sopper soburly
Goo to thy bed myrely
And lye therin jocundly
And plesse and loffe they wife dewly
And basse hyr onys or tewyis myrely.[49]

Despite evidence that these 'barely poetic lists of basic advice' can be 'as short or as long as one prefers' without 'damage' to their 'sense' (or so *A manual of the writings in Middle English* contends[50]), the omission here of what is conventionally the final precept, 'and slepe surely', disturbs the ordered progression of narrative, defers closure and, unquestionably, affects this poem's meaning. 'Arise early' offers its addressee, here a married householder,[51] a clearly articulated code of daily conduct, from morning to night, that locates his well-regimented body in an ordered domestic space that is a place at once of labour, piety and intimacy. Advice on conduct away from home is perfunctory ('goo be the wey sadly') and extra-domestic sociability is severely circumscribed ('awnswer the pepll

---

[49] Both *A new index of Middle English verse*, p. 25 (*NIMEV* 324) and J. Burke Severs, Albert E. Hartung and Peter G. Biedler (eds.), *A manual of the writings in Middle English, 1050–1500*, 11 vols. (New Haven: The Connecticut Academy of Arts and Sciences, 1967–2005), vol. 9, p. 3367 ([105] Precepts in –ly (b)) list manuscript and early print versions of 'Arise Early' from the mid-fifteenth to early-sixteenth centuries; neither list is complete. At last count, there were seventeen extant copies of this version of 'precepts in –ly'. Two are only short extracts of four and five lines, respectively (BL, MSS Additional 37049, fol. 86, and Sloane 1360, fol. 232). The remaining fifteen copies, ranging from ten to seventeen lines, all construct a broad narrative of the householder's day, from morning to night. There are eleven manuscript copies: Cambridge, Magdalene College, MS Pepys 1047 (fol. 1; 16 lines); Dublin, Trinity College MSS 516 (fol. 27; 14 lines) and 661 (p. 62; 16 lines); BL, MSS Landsdowne 762 (fol. 16v; 16 lines), Sloane 747 (fol. 65v; 11 lines), Sloane 775 (fol. 56v; 16 lines) and Stowe 850 (fol. 1; 11 lines); Aberystwyth, National Library of Wales MS Porkington 10 (fol. 187v; 10 lines); New Haven, Beinecke Library MS 365, the Brome manuscript (fol. 1v; 17 lines); New York, Columbia University MS Plimpton Addenda 2 (fols. 4–4v; 9 lines); Oxford, Balliol College MS 354 (fol. 159v; 11 lines). A reader has copied a version into British Library, printed book 1B.49408 (fol. 34v; 16 lines). And there are three early prints: STC 3308 (sig. f.v; 11 lines [reprinted several times]); STC 4851 (fol. 36; 11 lines); STC 17030 (f.3+; 11 lines). I am grateful to Linne Mooney for palaeographical advice and to Andrew Ilsley for his careful transcription of the Dublin versions.

[50] Cameron Louis, 'Proverbs, precepts, and monitory pieces', in Severs *et al.*, *A manual of the writings in Middle English*, vol. 9, p. 2990.

[51] Only the Brome version makes its addressee explicitly male; all of the others carefully maintain gender neutrality.

curtesly'). Everyday life, in all of its diversity, is imagined within the confines of the household. Work and devotion are the preoccupation of the day, whose routine is structured around two communal meals (a midday 'met' and evening 'sopper'), and at every turn the householder is urged to conduct himself with moderation and restraint: to watch his tongue, his manners and his personal comportment, at home and away. At the end of the busy day, he is sent to bed.

It is at this point in the brief narrative that extant versions of 'Arise Early' diverge in a number of different and suggestive ways. Going to bed uniformly signals a radical change in tone. 'Myrely' ('merrily') breaks into the litany of restrictive precepts with a jolt of levity that is immediately extended as the householder is advised to 'lye therein jocundly' – joyfully or giving pleasure.[52] In most versions, sleep now intrudes and the burst of exuberance is abruptly cut short.[53] A further articulation of conjugal sexual relations as the householder's duty ('plesse and loffe they wife dewly'), akin to devotion to God (who is here also served 'duly'), features in just seven of the extant versions, where it both gestures to the theology of the marriage debt and seeks to bring the palpable energy of sex within some kind of acceptable limit.[54] In six of these versions, sleep 'surely' follows, bringing the night's brief pleasure to a conclusion. Here in the Book of Brome, however, where sleep never comes, the final precept – 'And basse hyr onys or tewyis myrely' ('and kiss her once or twice merrily') – functions not to close down erotic possibility but to fuel it, to extend the householder's sober, disciplined day (where his main meal was the only 'happy' prospect) into a nocturnal space of unregulated pleasure. Just as 'once or twice' ('onys or tewyis') hints at the potential for an endless cycle of reiteration, the final 'myrely' neither signals an end nor returns us to the beginning, to the early start of the householder's day when a good night's sleep would be most appreciated. 'Myrely' takes us back instead to his 'myrely' getting into bed, into what was by the end of the fifteenth century, when this poem was copied, an increasingly private, intimate space,

---

[52] See *Middle English dictionary*, under *jocŭnd(e)lī (adv.)* 'happily, cheerfully'; *jocŏund(e) (adj.)* 1b 'joyful, delighted, elated, exultant', 2a 'giving pleasure, pleasing' and 2b 'expressing pleasure, joyous'.

[53] All fifteen of the narrative versions of 'Arise Early' send the reader to bed 'mryely' and advise 'jocund' conduct therein; eight (Trinity 516, Sloane 747, Stowe 850, Porkington 10, Plimpton Ad.2, Balliol 354, STC 4851, STC 17030) then send the reader immediately to sleep, which is later glossed by Pepys 1047 as 'holi' 'ffesyk'.

[54] Pepys 1047 ('plese thy make dewli'); Trinity 661 ('ples thy love diewly'); Landsdowne 762 ('please thy loue duely'); Sloane 775 ('please thy loue duly'); BL.IB.49408 ('please thy love duly'); STC 3308 ('plese thy loue duly') and of course Beinecke 365, the Book of Brome ('and plesse and loffe they wife dewly). Note the gender neutrality of 'thy make' and 'thy loue' in contrast to Brome's 'they wife'.

formally sequestered, as are these lines of verse, from the everyday business of the household, where he pleases his wife: once, twice, and so the cycle continues.

The detailed provision in such a brief list of highly conventional advice of a distinctive time and place for sexual desire effectively marks it out as indispensable to the routine of the conjugal household. At the same time, the verse seems to acknowledge that, unlike other bodily regimes (eating or working), it is susceptible neither to easy regulation nor sober restraint. Located – formally, chronologically and ideologically – at the opposite extreme from the householder's religious duties, sexual desire is here allowed a space to flourish that is expressly outside of the restrictive codes that operate elsewhere in the verse. The gesture is complex and not altogether benign. The urge to order sexuality, for all of the enthusiasm of its representation, can never be innocent and we must be careful not to read it as simply advocating unrestrained conjugal pleasure. Circumscribed in time and place, sexual desire is licensed in some but not all of its variety. The householder is implicitly prohibited from going to bed in the middle of the day and with anyone other than his wife. Further still, a list of precepts cannot, of course, be read straightforwardly as evidence of social practice; it serves rather a primarily ideological function. Not only does 'Arise Early' urge a model of household conduct, it works to promote the household as the proper locus for the householder, who, so it contends, can be satisfied (spiritually, materially, physically) within its confines.

My interest in 'Arise Early' is not in the male householder to whom it is addressed but in his wife, the woman whom we first meet in bed. Although the precepts silence and confine her, in the service of her husband's sexual needs, she refuses, like the desire with which she coincides, to be formally circumscribed. The domestic economy which the precepts seek to regulate depends, just as much as the sexual one which it comprehends, on her activity and, indeed, if order is to be achieved, her complicity (in getting the family out of bed, its meals on the table, its devotions learned) is required. From the moment when she too awakes, no doubt just as early, her shadowy presence attends her husband's throughout the day, at home and abroad, at table and in devotion, in the management of the household and in promoting, and regulating, its sociability.

The dynamic adumbrated by 'Arise Early', whereby women and their desires are imagined, if at all, only as a function of masculine order is thoroughly conventional (and it is not simply a medieval phenomenon). But that does not mean that either women or their desires are effectively occluded. Although the short narrative does render the householder's wife an object of desire, at the same time it acknowledges, however incompletely, her own desires. The householder is directed not only to 'loffe' but to 'plesse' his wife, a gesture – like the preceding insistence on 'jocund' ('pleasure giving') conduct in bed – that proposes that her satisfaction is not simply desirable but necessary to the fantasy of sexual (dis)order the precepts promote. The narrative refusal to submit to bed-time discipline informs the conduct of both wife and husband and it works to delineate, within the household, an erogenous space that makes possible the playing out of women's, as well as men's, desires. Further still, it makes the wife's pleasure ('plesse and loffe they wife', 'basse hyr onys or tewyis') the standard by which her husband's conduct is measured. 'Arise Early', like the games with which it is paired, invites us to position women in the medieval gentry household as desiring subjects. And, again like the games, it constructs an imperfectly circumscribed space, in which the playing out of that desire is not only licit but positively encouraged.

12 Home visits: Mary, Elizabeth, Margery Kempe and the feast of the Visitation

Mary C. Erler

At the end of the fifteenth century the feast of the Visitation appears to have been everywhere in England. The Blessed Virgin's travel to Elizabeth's home in order to support her cousin's miraculous pregnancy, at a time when she too was divinely *enceinte*, provided a fascinating subject for both liturgy and iconography. London parish churchwardens' accounts, for instance, record multiple payments to have the Mass and office of the new feast copied,[1] and Low Countries books of hours imported into England, in their frequent illustrations of Mary and Elizabeth's meeting, seem intrigued by this tender connection between women, sustained across generations (see back cover).[2] It was Pope Sixtus IV's re-establishment of the feast in 1475, opening the last quarter of the century, that produced these affirming responses.[3] But there is evidence as well for earlier English devotion to the occasion of the Visitation, if not necessarily to the feast, and the enthusiastic late-fifteenth-century investment in this devotion had a prequel.

The earliest English interest in the Visitation spans a period of approximately sixty years, from Pope Boniface IX's first promulgation of the feast

---

[1] For instance in 1485/6 the parish of St Andrew Hubbard paid 2s to Thomas, stationer, 'for wrytyng of the Vesitacion [office] of our lady and the masse of the Same' (Guildhall Library MS 01279/1, fol. 51v). Between 1485 and 1487 the parishioners of St Nicholas Shambles spent 5s 'for ij qwayres of vellom wrytton & notyd with the servyce of our lady' (St Bartholomew's Hospital Archive, MS SNC 1, fol. 135). In 1497/8 St Stephen Colman St gave 4s to Thomas Knapp, stationer, 'for to sett the festes of the vysitacion of our lady and transfyguracion and the writyng and setting In to diuers bokus' (Guildhall Library MS 04457/1, fol. 77v).

[2] The image reproduced on the back cover of this volume comes from a book of hours of *c.* 1500 illustrated by the Master of the Dresden Prayer Book, an artist working in Bruges from *c.* 1465 to *c.* 1515 (BL, MS Egerton 1149, fol. 53v).

[3] Historian of the liturgy R. W. Pfaff, traces three stages in the development of the feast: Boniface IX's proclamation in 1389; the Council of Basel's decree of 1441; and Sixtus IV's promulgation in 1475, though he says 'certainly official observance of the Visitation in England really began only with Sixtus's decree'. Richard Pfaff, *New liturgical feasts in later medieval England* (Oxford: Clarendon Press, 1970), p. 47.

in 1389[4] until the middle of the following century – that is, the last decade of the fourteenth and first half of the fifteenth century. It is in this period that Nicholas Love produced his influential meditations on the gospels, *The Mirror of the Blessed Life of Jesus Christ* (*c.*1409), and it is at this time that Margery Kempe lived and travelled (*c.* 1413–38). During these years Love's meditations on the Visitation and Margery's living out of its narrative sprang from an atmosphere in which the spiritual centrality of family and home was strongly emerging. Recent work on the religious climate of the late Middle Ages has stressed the importance of small units – the locality, the parish, the neighbourhood, and above all, the family as the nourishing ground out of which this period's devotion sprang.[5] The occasion of the Visitation can be read as celebrating the culture of home, as its narrative focuses successively on the family visit, on the female mysteries surrounding birth, and on home ties of blood and affection. Margery's travels in particular recognise this domestic culture, one which in the early fifteenth century was popular and powerful enough to allow the traditional apostolic vocation of preaching to be imagined in alternative terms. Preaching and its desired outcome, conversion of heart, could now be reconceived – as conversation, a mode by definition private and personal.

Boniface's institution of the feast stimulated the composition of several Visitation offices. One of these was written by an Englishman, Cardinal Adam Easton, the Norfolk Benedictine and supporter of St Birgitta of Sweden.[6] Two occurrences of the devotion in England before the end of

---

[4] Anthony Goodman suggests that the 1389 institution of the feast, specifically as a corrective to the papal schism, may have been of especial interest to John of Gaunt, since this was 'an objective central to Gaunt's policies' and the feast was early recognised by the Carmelites (1393), with whom Gaunt had many connections. Anthony Goodman, *John of Gaunt: the exercise of princely power in fourteenth-century Europe* (New York: St. Martin's Press, 1992), p. 246.

[5] For one of the earliest attempts at an account of the spirituality of a region, see Gail McMurray Gibson, *The theater of devotion: East Anglian drama and society in the late Middle Ages* (Chicago: University of Chicago Press, 1989). During the last decade Clive Burgess's essays on parish life and spirituality in Bristol have offered something similar for the southwest: e.g. Clive Burgess (ed.) *The pre-Reformation records of All Saints', Bristol. Parts I and II*, Bristol Record Society vols. 46, 53 (Bristol, 1995, 2000). The subject of the parish has been treated by Beat Kümin, *The shaping of a community: the rise and reformation of the English parish, c. 1400–1560* (Aldershot: Scolar Press, 1996); he has also co-edited a collection on this topic: Katherine L. French, Gary G. Gibbs and Beat A. Kümin (eds.), *The parish in English life 1400–1600* (Manchester University Press, 1997). Analysing late medieval reading, Rebecca Krug has emphasised the centrality of family: *Reading families: women's literate practice in late medieval England* (Ithaca: Cornell University Press, 2002).

[6] James Hogg, 'Adam Easton's *Defensorium Sanctae Birgittae*', in Marion Glasscoe (ed.), *The medieval mystical tradition: England, Ireland, and Wales. Exeter symposium VI: papers read at Charney Manor, July 1999* (Cambridge: D. S. Brewer, 1999), p. 224, n. 45. Though Easton's office has been dated before 1385, Pfaff thinks it was composed for Boniface,

the fourteenth century suggest a degree of early liturgical familiarity. Pfaff notes that at the important Benedictine monastery of St Albans, the chronicler Thomas Walsingham registered the recent papal institution of the feast in 1392, three years after its initial announcement.[7] At St Albans too, almoner William Wintershill, 'eruditissimus', confessor to four abbots, and possibly the author of the historical compilation preserved as London, British Library MS Harley 3775 and of other St Albans histories,[8] founded an altar dedicated to the Visitation in the old infirmary while he was lying ill there.[9] The date was probably in the latter 1420s, since a St Albans will of 1428 leaves money to Wintershill and three other monks, all confined to the infirmary.[10] In addition John Amundesham says that Wintershill was responsible for introducing the office and Mass of the Visitation at the monastery in 1430,[11] when it was sung in the octave of St Amphibolus in the chapel of the Virgin. It seems clear that around the first quarter of the fifteenth century the feast of the Visitation was being observed at St Albans.

Equally suggestive is the establishment in 1396 of a Carthusian charter-house dedicated to the Visitation on the isle of Axholme (Lincolnshire). The founder was Thomas Mowbray, one of the lords appellant and close kinsman to Richard II.[12] Because Pfaff says that early devotion to the Visitation was manifested in Prague, 'probably from 1386',[13] it may be

hence after 1389. He calls it 'the office ... most widely accepted in the Roman books': *New feasts*, p. 44.

[7] John Taylor, Wendy R. Childs and Leslie Watkiss (ed. and trans.), *The St Albans chronicle: the Chronica Maiora of Thomas Walsingham*, vol I: *1376–1394* (Oxford: Clarendon Press, 2003), pp. 922–3.

[8] James G. Clark, *A monastic renaissance at St Albans: Thomas Walsingham and his circle c. 1350–1440* (Oxford: Clarendon Press, 2004), p. 123, though the editors of Walsingham's *Chronica maiora* (see above) disagree (p. xxxviii). Clark earlier suggested that the narratives attributed to Walsingham, the *Annales Ricardi Secundi et Henrici Quarti* and the *Gesta abbatum* continuation, may have been Wintershill's work: 'Thomas Walsingham reconsidered: books and learning at late-medieval St Albans', *Speculum* 77 (2002), 846, 859, disagreeing with V. H. Galbraith (see below, note 10). For Wintershill's biography, see A. B. Emden, *A biographical register of the University of Oxford to A.D. 1500*, 3 vols. (Oxford: Clarendon Press, 1957–59), vol. 3, no. 2127.

[9] H. T. Riley (ed.), *Annales monasterii S. Albani a Johanne Amundesham monacho ... (A.D. 1421–1440)*, vol. 1, Rolls Series no. 28 (London, 1870), Appendix D, p. 449.

[10] V. H. Galbraith (ed.), *The St Albans chronicle 1406–1420, edited from Bodley MS 462* (Oxford: Clarendon Press, 1937), p. lvi, n. 1.

[11] Amundesham, *Annales*, p. 52. Other passages in Amundesham suggest that Wintershill may have underwritten more than one Marian altar: Pfaff neatly analyses the several ways of interpreting this evidence, Pfaff, *New feasts*, p. 46, n. 5.

[12] See Christopher Given-Wilson, 'Thomas Mowbray, first duke of Norfolk (1366–1399)', in *The Oxford dictionary of national biography*, ed. H. C. G. Matthew and Brian Harrison (Oxford University Press, 2004); online ed., ed. Lawrence Goldman, October 2005, http://www.oxforddnb.com/view/article/12360.

[13] Pfaff, *New feasts*, p. 42.

that Mowbray's choice of dedication constituted a compliment to Anne of Bohemia, Richard's dead queen. Perhaps Pope Boniface IX was pleased to have his liturgical initiative confirmed by this new foundation only seven years later, since he granted the monastery a special plenary indulgence, the 'Portiuncula' (originally given visitors to St Francis of Assisi's church).[14] Penitents who went to Axholme on the feast of the Visitation and gave alms to maintain the fabric received remission of all sins, from baptism to that day. The feast was observed at the Bridgettine abbey of Syon between 1419 and 1426, where it is found in a processional manuscript,[15] and of course Margery Kempe's visits there are recorded, about a decade later, in 1434.

Devotion to the Visitation found early English visual expression as well, when it sometimes appears as one of the joys of Mary or illustrates the canonical hour of Lauds. In her survey of British illuminated manuscripts between 1285 and 1385, Lucy Freeman Sandler lists eighteen manuscripts with Visitation illuminations, mostly historiated initials. Two East Anglian books, however, feature the devotion more prominently: the Gorleston psalter from Suffolk *c.* 1310–*c.*1320, which Sandler calls 'a masterpiece of East Anglian art', and another psalter *c.* 1320–*c.*1330, probably from Norwich, now El Escorial Library MS Q.11.6, where fifteen framed miniatures, including the Visitation, accompany a poem on the name of the Virgin (in Anglo-French) and the joys of the Virgin (in Latin.)[16]

From the first half of the fifteenth century Kathleen Scott lists eight books with Visitation miniatures, the largest being a one-column miniature accompanying *La Estorie del Euangelie* in the Vernon manuscript (no. 1), while Oxford, Corpus Christi College MS 161, a text of the *Speculum Humanae Salvationis*, perhaps from York, is followed at the end by a series of small pen and wash drawings depicting the seven joys. Notable in this group is a Visitation miniature found in the book of hours belonging to Catherine of Valois, Henry VI's queen, produced for her, possibly between 1420 and 1422, probably in London (Figure 12.1).[17]

---

[14] Rose Graham, 'Axholme', in *The Victoria history of the county of Lincolnshire*, vol. 2, ed. William Page (London: Constable, 1906), pp. 158–60.

[15] Oxford, St John's MS 167 (processional) and also in BL, Royal 2.A.xiv, a Syon breviary c. 1400. Pfaff, *New feasts*, p. 57.

[16] Lucy Freeman Sandler, *Gothic manuscripts 1285–1385*, 2 vols., Survey of Manuscripts Illuminated in the British Isles, vol. 5 (London: Harvey Miller, 1986). The Gorleston Psalter is no. 50; the Escorial MS is no. 80. Visitation images appear as well in nos. 11, 38, 83, 87, 88, 98, 115, 117, 118, 122, 125, 130, 138, 140, 145, 146.

[17] The Visitation also appears in a historiated initial in the Neville hours, which Scott calls the most important book of hours from the first decade of the fifteenth century (no. 23). Other Visitation scenes are found in nos. 9, 47, 80, 108. Kathleen L. Scott, *Later Gothic manuscripts 1390–1490*, 2 vols., Survey of Manuscripts Illuminated in the British Isles, vol. 6 (London: Harvey Miller, 1996).

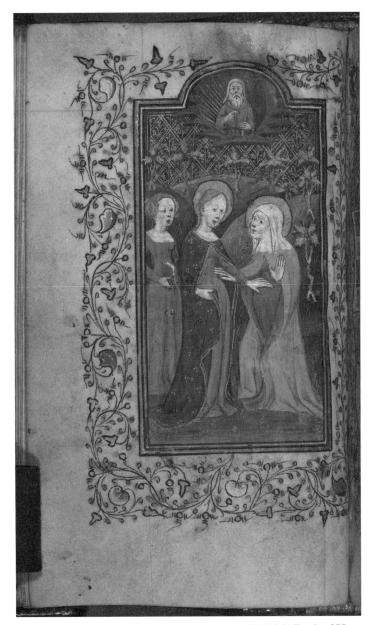

Figure 12.1 Visitation scene from Catherine of Valois's Book of Hours, possibly made between 1420 and 1422, probably in London. Reproduced with permission from British Library MS Additional 65100, fol. 53v.

The record of public Visitation art in Norfolk includes a number of early carvings or paintings that Margery Kempe might have viewed before we lose sight of her about 1438 – although Visitation art is richly abundant in the latter half of the fifteenth century.[18] Perhaps the earliest Norwich Visitation images are the roof bosses in the south cloister walk of the cathedral, carved between 1327 and 1329. Here Elizabeth's left hand rests on the Virgin's shoulder, her right on Mary's abdomen.[19] Art historians have found it difficult to date a retable from the Norwich church of St Michael at Plea that shows the heads of Mary and Elizabeth in a smaller panel above the Annunciation; most recently it has been assigned to the 1420s.[20] Meg Twycross has pointed out the visual similarity between the embrace of the Four Daughters of God (Mercy, Justice, Truth and Peace) and that of Mary and Elizabeth, both images placed together to accent their similarity in a 1440s stained glass window from the church of St Peter and Paul in Salle, Norfolk, northwest of Norwich.[21]

The best known of these East Anglian examples is the Visitation window in St Peter Mancroft, the main parish church in Norwich. It shows Elizabeth wearing a laced maternity gown that emphasises the physical nature of this sacred event (Figure 12.2). Margery had travelled in 1433

[18] In his 1463 will John Baret, a servant to the abbot of Bury St Edmunds and a well-off merchant, left money for an altarpiece of the story of the Magnificat, which was to include his own verses on the subject. In this he may have been inspired by the verse *Lyf of Our Lady* written by his friend the poet and monk of Bury John Lydgate (d. 1449). Samuel Tymms (ed.), *Wills and inventories from the registry of the commissary of Bury St Edmunds and the archdeacon of Sudbury*, Camden Society vol. 49 (London, 1850), pp. 19–30.

[19] Martial Rose and Julia Hedgecoe, *Stories in stone, the medieval roof carvings of Norwich cathedral* (New York: Thames and Hudson, 1997), pp. 37, 47. A recent listing of Norfolk art is provided by Ann Eljenholm Nichols, *The early art of Norfolk: a subject list of extant and lost art*, Early Drama, Art and Music Reference Series 7 (Kalamazoo: Medieval Institute, 2002). I am indebted to Dr. Nichols for much generous help on the topic of East Anglian Visitation art.

[20] The panel was assigned to 1420–35 by Pamela Tudor-Craig, 'Medieval panel paintings from Norwich, St Michael at Plea', *Burlington Magazine* 98 (1956), 333–4. David King agrees:*The medieval stained glass of St Peter Mancroft Norwich*, Corpus Vitrearum Medii Aevi (Oxford University Press, 2006), p. 17, and see his earlier article dating the panel *c.* 1420–40, 'The panel paintings and stained glass', in Ian Atherton *et al.* (eds.), *Norwich cathedral: church, city, and diocese 1096–1996* (London: Hambledon Press,1996), pp. 410–30. A later dating, 1450–75, is given by Marks and Williamson, *Gothic: art for England* no. 277, where the painting is reproduced in colour.

[21] Meg Twycross, 'Kissing cousins: the four daughters of God and the Visitation in the N-Town Mary Play', *Medieval English Theatre* 18 (1996), 99–141, plates 3 and 6. The glass has been much restored; as Twycross says, 'The motif [is] original though most of the glass is not' (p. 128). King, *Medieval stained glass*, p. 17 suggests that this image was inspired by the Council of Basel's promulgation of the feast in 1441 and he dates the glass to that year. See also his 'Salle Church – the glazing', *Archaeological Journal* 137 (1980), 334–35.

Figure 12.2 Visitation window in St Peter Mancroft, Norwich, 1450–55.
Reproduced with permission of English Heritage–NMR.

to Aachen where, like St Birgitta and her husband and the visionary Dorothea of Montau, she had viewed Our Lady's maternity smock, part of a treasure of relics exhibited every seven years,[22] and an object that explicitly, perhaps defiantly, shifts the familial to a public register.[23] Though the window has been recently dated 1450–5, probably a decade or so after Margery's death, the possible involvement of a Netherlandish glazier employed in a Norwich workshop reminds us of the power of such Low Countries influences in East Anglia, both visual and devotional.[24]

Pfaff is somewhat uncertain about the feast's real origins, calling it 'a rare example of a new liturgical observance established solely by the fiat of authority' and noting that unlike the other new feasts of the Transfiguration and the Name of Jesus, the Visitation seems not to have had the long preceding period of 'unofficial or popular observance' that would ordinarily have produced a new liturgical commemoration.[25] It may be, however, that these visual clues testify to the existence of a devotional interest preceding a liturgical one. In addition, at the level of custom, the Visitation opens out into the world of popular practice that lay below the formality of liturgical observance. *Mirk's Festial*, for instance, from the 1390s, offers a decidedly non-scriptural account, in which the suggestion of women's mysteries, and of the experiential training of mid-wives, is strong. He says that Our Lady 'dwellyd þer wyth hur cosyn tyll Seynt Ion was borne, and was mydwyff to Elilʒabeth, and toke Ion from þe erþe. And soo scho lernd all þat hur nedyd, forto come alʒeyne þe tyme

---

[22] Meech and Allen, *The book of Margery Kempe*. Subsequent references will be incorporated in the text as the 'Book' (of Margery Kempe). Johannes Marienwerder, *The life of Dorothea von Montau, a fourteenth-century recluse*, trans. Ute Stargardt, Studies in Women and Religion vol. 39 (Lewiston, NY: Edwin Mellen Press, 1997), p. 69.

[23] E. Jane Burns's recent article on Mary's chemise preserved as a relic at Chartres is illustrated with pilgrim badges showing the same dress-shape with horizontally extended arms: 'Saracen silk and the Virgin's chemise: cultural crossings in cloth', *Speculum* 81 (2006), 365–97. Carole Rawcliffe provides a photograph of a pilgrim badge from Cologne, found in Norwich, that depicts Mary's smock, the *sancta roba*: 'Curing bodies and healing souls: pilgrimage and the sick in medieval East Anglia', in Colin Morris and Peter Roberts (eds.), *Pilgrimage: the English experience from Becket to Bunyan* (Cambridge University Press, 2002), pp. 136–7. Noting the survival at the museum in Lynn of a pilgrim badge from Wilsnack's shrine of the Holy Blood, Caroline Barron says 'it is possible to imagine that this badge … was brought back by Margery to her home town': *Pilgrim souls: Margery Kempe and other women pilgrims*, Confraternity of St James Occasional Paper no. 6 (London, 2004), p. 11, citing Brian Spencer, *Pilgrim souvenirs and secular badges* (London, 1998), item 263b.

[24] King, *St Peter Mancroft*, p. cxlv, suggests the window comes from the local [John] Wighton workshop: '[Wighton] had the Netherlandish glazier William Mundeford working for him, and may have known the Franco-Flemish glazier Henry Pers'. King offers parallels between the Mancroft Visitation window and a Cologne panel painting of *c.* 1460, suggesting an early-fifteenth-century exemplar for both (pp. 17–18).

[25] Pfaff, *New feasts*, p. 40.

þat hur sonne schuld be borne of hur. Syþen scho was parfyt þerof[26] Mary went home.[26] The reference to Mary taking the infant John 'from þe erþe' is found also in the *Golden Legend*; in Love's *Mirror*, translated from de Caulibus' Latin; in the contemporary *Speculum devotorum*, where it is attributed to 'the Book of Rightful Men' (that is, Peter Comestor's *Historia scholastica*); and in Margery Kempe's Book.[27] Such 'raising rituals' were common all over Europe and had the aim of protecting the newborn child (or possibly of incorporating it into the family): an important person, usually the father, raised the infant toward the roof, symbolising its membership in the house with all its protective symbolism.[28]

Whatever the Visitation's unofficial and popular components, it is Nicholas Love, writing before 1409, who gives us the fullest account of the way the 1389 feast might have been understood by most people. Margery Kempe lists Bonaventure, long thought to have written the *Meditationes vitae Christi*, as one of the authors her priest read to her (143/25–29), perhaps beginning around 1413, although her editors differ as to which Bonaventurian work she means. Sanford Meech believes Margery refers to the *Stimulus amoris*, while Hope Emily Allen says, 'There can be no doubt that Margery knew the great work ... Probably she knew that [translation] by Nicholas Love ... but I have noted no coincidences (in vocabulary or otherwise) to prove such relation'.[29]

Love faithfully translates his Latin source, the *Meditationes*, and in doing so, brings into English a Franciscan emphasis on poverty, humility and human emotion. Thus for instance we are told that Mary made the trip without 'þe grete companye of houre maidenes & damyseles' (*Mirror*, p. 30), but accompanied instead by Poverty, Meekness and honest Shamefastness. (We might wonder whether pilgrimage practice is here

---

[26] Theodor Erbe (ed.), *Mirk's Festial: a collection of homilies*, EETS ES vol. 96 (London, 1905), p. 107.

[27] Jacobus de Voragine, *The Golden Legend: readings on the saints*, 2 vols., trans. William Granger Ryan (Princeton University Press, 1993), vol 1, p. 330; Michael G. Sargent (ed.), *Nicholas Love's Mirror of the Blessed Life of Jesus Christ* (New York: Garland, 1992), pp. 30–3; John Patrick Banks, S. J., '*Speculum devotorum*, an edition with commentary', unpublished PhD thesis, Fordham University (1959), p. 47; *Book of Margery Kempe*, pp. 191–4.

[28] Stephen Wilson, *The magical universe: everyday ritual and magic in pre-modern Europe* (London: Hambeldon Press, 2000), pp. 188–9. Enid Porter, *The folklore of East Anglia* (London: Roman and Littlefield, 1974), p. 18 says, 'A baby born at home used to be carried upstairs when it left its mother's room for the first time. This made certain that it would "rise in life"'.

[29] Meech notes that the text reads 'Bone-ventur, Stimulus Amoris' and says 'there is no instance in the *Book of Margery Kempe* of the designation of a writing by the name of its author standing alone' (p. 320), i.e. that Bonaventure's name here refers to the author of *Stimulus* rather than to an additional unnamed work. For Allen, see p. 333.

being reproved, particularly female trips to shrines accompanied by other women – female trips to pray for fertility, safe delivery and the recovery of children from their ills.)

The difference in worldly circumstances between Mary and Elizabeth is also stressed. When Mary returns home, her poor house is contrasted with Elizabeth's dwelling, which is called 'plentyuous', while Mary has neither bread nor wine. In 'hire owne pouerte & bare house', Love says, Mary needs 'to gete hire lyuelode with hir awne handes & bodily trauaile'. Humble poverty at home and women's part in that suffering is here recognised (*Mirror*, p. 32).[30]

But the pleasures of home are celebrated as well. After Mary uttered the Magnificat she and Elizabeth

> wenten to sitte to gedire … And þan asked oure lady of Elizabeth þe manere of hire conceyuyng, & she aȝeyn of þe maner of hire conceyuyng, & so þei tolden eiþere to oþere gladly þe grete gudenesse of oure lord, & lowedon & wirchipedon god of eiþer conception, & so in þonkyng god & gostly myrþ þei contynueden dayes & nyȝtes. (*Mirror*, p. 31)

The echoes of ordinary female conversation can be heard in this recounting of the realities of pregnancy and in the enjoyment of the pleasures of family – perhaps an anticipation of the domestic joys soon to be figured by another group of relatives in Mary's house, the Holy Family. Indeed, the house and what happened inside it as Mary and the angel spoke had been celebrated since the twelfth century at Walsingham[31] – the greatest English shrine, so near Lynn, whose souvenir badges often took the form of a little house.

In all the passages just quoted, Love's meditative exploration of the realities of house and home relays the thoughts of his Latin source. But at the conclusion of the Visitation story, Love breaks out into his own, original, glorification of domestic life. Commenting on the group gathered within Elizabeth's house he says, 'þis was a blessed companye of men & women & of children' (*Mirror*, p. 31). The patristic trope that compares monastic life to heaven is a familiar one. In Aelred of Rievaulx's

---

[30] That pilgrimage did offer an enlargement of women's horizons, and that it was continuously criticised for just this reason, is illustrated by a sermon from the end of Elizabeth's reign (1599), on the Queen of Sheba's journey to visit Solomon. The preacher, Thomas Holland, sums up the position: 'it is vnseemely for a woman to travell any long way without her husband and a thing iustly reproued, iustly misliked of our fathers, as namely the gadding abroad in pilgrimage, heretofore rebuked even by our learned satyricals of our owne nation' – by which he means Chaucer. Thomas Holland, 'A sermon preached in Paul's Church' (Oxford: J Barnes, 1600), STC 13596.5, sig. B4.

[31] J. C. Dickinson, *The shrine of Our Lady of Walsingham* (Cambridge University Press, 1956).

sermon on the feast of All Saints, for instance, he likens the community that the monk enters to the company of angels. 'The proper response of the monk, made one ... with his brothers, is to sing interiorly with joy.'[32] In Love's reference to an extended family as a 'blessed company', this traditional comparison is replaced by the suggestion that it is the home, rather than the monastery, that constitutes heaven for the assembled company.

It is the concluding moral Love offers, however – marked .N. marginally to signal his own contribution – that catches the significance of the Visitation for the fifteenth century. Here, he says,

> In þis forseid processe of þe visitacione of oure lady we hauen ensaumple þat it is leueful & oft spedful [permissible and often helpful] deuout men & women to vesit oþer for edificacion & gostly recreation, & namelich þe ȝongere to þe eldire , so þat it be done in dewe tyme, & with oþere leueful menes. (*Mirror*, p. 31)[33]

Love is here outlining what might be called a spirituality of the visit. It seems unlikely that he is defining a fresh practice; instead, he is more likely to be confirming and approving an existing pattern of behaviour, one which draws in equal parts on the fascination of travel and the pleasures of society. These gratifications, travel and society, stand in opposition to monastic life with its vows of stability and the restrictions of the cloister. Essentially secular pleasures, they are firmly spiritualised here. As with so many other fifteenth-century currents, it is Margery Kempe's life that allows us to see the specific ways in which this devout fashion of the spiritual visit was deployed.

Margery's family service as nursemaid, in her meditations, first to St Anne and then to the Virgin, is extremely well known. She plays a part in the Visitation as well, where she is commanded by Our Lady to come along, and carries with her a large two-quart container of spiced wine, for Mary and Joseph on the journey. In Margery's narrative, as in other accounts, Our Lady raises the baby John. The authorising figures are both female: Mary 'toke hym vp fro þe erthe wyth al maner reuerens & ȝaf hym to hys modyr' (19/2-3). Having earlier received an endorsement of her work from the Virgin, Margery now asks Elizabeth at the cousins' parting to recommend her to Mary's continuing service, and she receives a second endorsement from Elizabeth, who says 'þu dost ryght wel þi deuer'

[32] John R. Sommerfeldt, *Aelred of Rievaulx on love and order in the world and the Church* (New York: Newman Press, 2006), p. 40.
[33] Michael Sargent has suggested in conversation that Love may here have in mind a monastic model rather than a lay one, and may wish to authorise visits between religious (especially younger to elder for spiritual profit), where passage from one Carthusian cell to another might be particularly relevant.

(19/9-10). Standard family custom is visible in this vertical transfer of a long-serving, trusted, valued employee from mother to daughter, and then in the servant's horizontal recommendation by a cousin.

It is the secular practice of domestic visits, however, not the spiritual meditations on service, that provide the outlines of Margery's active life rather than her contemplative one. In travelling Margery recreated the gospel episode, not mentally as in her meditations, but physically. Like Mary's travel, Margery's was both joyful and fraught with difficulty. The contemporary author of the *Speculum devotorum*, who, like Nicholas Love translated the *Meditationes vitae Christi* and who identifies himself as a Carthusian of Sheen writing for a 'dear sister', commands his readers or hearers to focus on the hardship of Mary's trip: 'nowe here haue compassion of þe laboure þat [Mary] hath in goynge in and oute' (*Speculum*, p. 47).

This going and returning characterised Margery's spiritual life for several decades: not only, of course, in the famous pilgrimages abroad, but in her English travels, which in their narrower range we might see as more imitative of Mary's Visitation. The names are familiar: Bristol, Henbury, Hailes, Leicester, Boston, Melton Mowbray, Lincoln, York, Cawood, Bridlington, Hull, Hessle, Beverley, Ely, Norwich, Mentling, Ipswich, Walsingham, Canterbury, London, and more. To these places, often with John Kempe in a subsidiary Joseph-like role as companion and protector, she 'went ... forth ... & spokyn wyth Goddys seruawntys, boþen ankrys & reclusys & many oþer of owyr Lordys louerys' and 'þan was sche wolcomyd & mech mad of in dyuers placys' (25/19-22; 22/34).[34] 'Our lord's lovers' recalls Birgitta's frequent use of the phrase 'friends of God'.[35] This travel was divinely endorsed, if not divinely commanded: Christ told her that 'my seruawntys desyryn gretly to se þe', and it was in these journeys that her national reputation was established.

It seems likely that much of her local travel was accomplished by water. Lynn's location as a port at the mouth of the navigable river Ouse, as well as on the Wash, made it an important nexus for trade and shipping, and it continued to flourish 'as long as the Great Ouse remained the ordinary

---

[34] Samuel Fanous observes that 'the domestic travels are circumscribed by a high degree of selectivity' (for instance the single glancing mention of Walsingham, the famous shrine very near to Lynn): 'Measuring the pilgrim's progress: internal emphases in *The book of Margery Kempe*', in Denis Renevey and Christiania Whitehead (eds.), *Writing religious women: female spiritual and textual practices in late medieval England* (Cardiff: University of Wales Press, 2000), p. 160.

[35] Bridget Morris says that Birgitta probably intends 'the faithful who take up the reforming battle against those without faith or with a lapsed faith': Denis Searby (trans.), *The revelations of St Birgitta of Sweden*, vol. 1, *Liber caelestis, Books I–III*, introduction and notes by Bridget Morris (Oxford University Press, 2006), p. 169.

route along which six and more counties received and dispatched goods'.[36] Certainly the frequency with which Margery visited the Franciscan nuns of Denny, in the fenlands south of Lynn, was due to the ease of river travel on the Ouse from Lynn to a few miles south of Ely, where the abbey stood.[37] Lynn was connected by water with other important monastic houses like Ramsey and Crowland.[38] Margaret Aston records the many trips around his diocese taken via water by Margery's contemporary Thomas Arundel when he was bishop of Ely, commenting that 'in some areas of the fens and East Anglia waterways may often have been more frequent, as well as less hazardous than roads'.[39] Augustus Jessopp has called the area around the east–west river Nar which runs into the Ouse at Lynn 'the Norfolk holy land', since it contained nine religious houses, 'no one of which was five miles distant from the stream'.[40]

Lynn was conveniently placed, as well, for journeys to the north by either road or water, and river traffic involving the Humber and its tributaries was heavy. A survey of shipping references from the various state rolls through the year 1441 shows that about one-third allude to such northern navigation.[41] In fact the Humber estuary and East Anglia are the two areas where the English landscape made water travel most natural. An account of a trip in 1319 from London to York illustrates the land and water routes and the time each took. Two groups of Cambridge scholars travelled north: one took five days to complete the 150-mile journey by road, the other took nine days, mostly by water.[42] Margery would have begun her travel from Lynn, rather than London; if she were to have taken a boat from Lynn across the Wash to Boston (one writer calls this 'an afternoon's trip'),[43] the water journey to York from that city would have lasted four to five days. From Lincoln, somewhat north of Boston, the

---

[36] N. J. Williams, *The maritime trade of the East Anglian ports 1550–1590* (Oxford: Clarendon Press, 1988), p. 50.
[37] Coming home to Lynn from London around 1418, Margery was stopped three miles from Ely. Since this was near Denny abbey, it may be that this trip had included or intended a visit to the nuns and a return to Lynn by water (136/31-2).
[38] E. Carus-Wilson, 'The medieval trade of the ports of the Wash', *Medieval Archaeology* 6–7 (1962–3), 185.
[39] Margaret Aston, *Thomas Arundel, a study of church life in the reign of Richard II* (Oxford: Clarendon Press, 1967), pp. 218–19.
[40] 'Even in comparatively modern times the Nar was navigable as far as Narborough': Augustus Jessopp, 'On the edge of the Norfolk Holy Land', in *Studies by a recluse in cloister, town and country* (London: G. P. Putnam's Sons, 1893), p. 90.
[41] J. F. Edwards and B. P. Hindle, 'The transportation system of medieval England and Wales', *Journal of Historical Geography* 17 (1991), 126.
[42] F. J. Stenton, 'The road system of medieval England', *Economic History Review* 1st series 7 (1936–7), 20.
[43] Williams, *Maritime trade*, p. 139.

shortest route 'ran northwards by road for 32 miles to Burton Stather on the Trent, then by boat down the Trent to its junction with the Ouse, then up the Ouse to Howden, and so along 18 miles of level road to York'.[44]

The model that has long been used in discussing Margery's English travels is that of pilgrimage, and certainly she did visit many shrines. Recently however it has been suggested that in its frequency and multiplicity, short-range travel to shrines was substantially different from the experience of the grand overseas journeys, and indeed that it might better be considered a form of local experience. The editor of a collection of essays on pilgrimage points out that usually such trips 'involved a few days' travel at most. Over half the pilgrim badges that have been recovered from a deposit at Kings Lynn were from nearby Walsingham.' His description of such travel to shrines strongly suggests the Visitation: 'rather like [family] visits which became a part of family piety'.[45]

How unusual for women was travel to local shrines or travel on family visits? Attempts to quantify female travel come, again, from the literature of pilgrimage, and they do not tell us much about travel around England for women in the fifteenth century.[46] This was, however, perhaps not quite so restricted as we might think.[47] The diet accounts of Margery's contemporary, the Suffolk landowning widow Alice de Bryene, are discussed by Fiona Swabey for the year 1412/13. Margery's travels began just

---

[44] Stenton, 'Road system', 20. Carus-Wilson, 'Medieval trade', 195, describes a similar land and water combination trip. Cloth purchased at Boston for the monks of Durham in the late thirteenth century went to Lincoln, then by cart to Torksay, by boat down the Trent to the Humber, up the Ouse to York, Boroughbridge, then to Durham by cart.

[45] Colin Morris, introduction to Morris and Roberts, *Pilgrimage*, p. 6. See also Eamon Duffy's essay in the same volume, which follows others in suggesting that Victor Turner's characterisation of pilgrimage as a liminal experience should be modified: 'the single most important energy in late medieval English religious practice was its drive toward localism' (Eamon Duffy, 'The dynamics of pilgrimage in late medieval England', in Morris and Roberts, eds., *Pilgrimage*, p. 165). For further criticism of Turner's thesis, see Simon Coleman and John Elsner, 'Pilgrimage to Walsingham and the re-invention of the Middle Ages', in J. Stopford (ed.), *Pilgrimage explored* (York Medieval Press, 1999), pp. 189–214.

[46] Katrien Heene, 'Gender and mobility in the Low Countries: traveling women in thirteenth-century exempla and saints' lives', in Ellen E. Kittell and Mary A. Suydam (eds.), *The texture of society: medieval women in the southern low countries* (New York, 2004), 31), citing Norbert Ohler, *The medieval traveler* (Cambridge, 1989), p. 187, says women 'made up one-fourth to one-third of medieval pilgrims in general and even half of those visiting local places of pilgrimage. L. A. Craig has recently surveyed work on quantifying female pilgrimage travel in '"Stronger than men and braver than knights": women and the pilgrimage to Jerusalem and Rome in the later Middle Ages', *Journal of Medieval History* 29 (2003), 154–5.

[47] Terence Bowers emphasises the historic restrictions on travel for women, suggesting that travel was a way of conferring 'full personhood' and that consequently Margery's travel was subversive, reshaping the way 'contemporaries understood her and the world': 'Margery Kempe as traveller', *Studies in Philology* 97 (2000), 26.

about this time; it was in June 1413, coming back from York, that she and John Kempe made the mutual vow of chastity which to some extent catalysed her journeys. Alice de Bryene, though Margery's contemporary, was considerably more rural, more wealthy, and more elevated socially. Her accounts reveal a travelling population in which women constituted a larger element than did clergy (8 per cent versus 5 per cent), and in which women occasionally travelled alone. Somewhat surprisingly, Swabey concludes that 'women appear to have been as mobile as men at this time, if they were free from home-based responsibilities'.[48] Presumably such women, if married, had the spousal permission that John Kempe granted Margery (25/12-13).

Swabey reminds us that the reasons for travel were various: 'to supervise ... estates, negotiate business, maintain ... patronage, purchase luxury goods, visit friends and relations, go on pilgrimage, and for entertainment'.[49] Margery's text offers variations on the model of the home visit to friends and relatives presented in Mary's Visitation, and Love's description of the practice is frequently echoed in Margery's accounts: 'deuout men & women to viset oþer for edificacion & gostly recreacion' (*Mirror*, p. 31). In Margery's visit to York, for instance: 'many good men & women preyd hir to mete & madyn hir ryth good cher & weryn ryth glad to heryn hyr dalyawns, hauyng gret merueyle of hir speche for it was fruteful' (120/13-16). In Beverley her temporary guardian 'toke hir be þe hand & led hir hom to hys hows & dede hir sittyn wyth hym at mete & drynke, schewyng hir goodly cher. þedyr comyn many prestys & oþer men eftsonys to se hir & spekyn wyth hir, & meche pepil had gret compassion þat sche was so euyl ferd wyth' (133/3-7). In Norwich she was defended against a priest's charges by a woman who 'sithyn ... had hir hom wyth hir to mete & schewyd hir ful glad & goodly chere as long as sche wold abydyn þer' (148/21-23). Similar shared meals and conversations are recorded in Bristol (109/6-9), Melton Mowbray (117/23-26), Hull (129/10-11), London (136/29-31), even at home in Lynn (143/1-6). In Margery's travels, England is dotted everywhere with such men and women and what we would particularly like is a map of her visits, with names of her hosts.

The conclusion of Love's Visitation chapter – again, his own interpretation of the event – further recalls Margery's life. He is pointing out the spiritual profit to be had from domestic talk. 'Also if we take gude entent to þe wordes of Marie & Elizabeth, alle þei weren in lowyng of hem self, & to wirchipyng of god & magnifiying him in alle hese werkes, & tellyng his grete mercy shewed to mankynd to stire man to þe loue & þe wirchipe of

[48] Swabey, *A medieval gentlewoman*, p. 123.   [49] Ibid., p. 88.

god' (*Mirror*, p. 32). The purpose of cousinly conversation is growth in the spiritual life, through recognition of divine agency in ordinary events.

The author of the *Speculum devotorum* also stresses the importance of conversation. Describing life inside the home of Mary, Joseph and Jesus, he has Mary say,

> And he spoke to vs (vnderstondeth our Lady, and Ioseph separately, þat is to sey, departeth fro other) confortable wordes and words of diuinite, so þat we were fulfillede contynuantly with vnspekable ioye ... After þis he talked homely in þe house with his frendes þat com to hym of þe Lawe and of þe signyficacions and figure therof ... These bene þe wordes þat our Lady hadde to Seynte Brigette ... which I haue drawe here in Englesshe tonge almoste worde for worde, for þe more conuenyente forme and order of these simple meditacions, and to your edificacion or ony other deuoute creature þat kan not vnderstonde latyn ... (*Speculum*, pp. 102–3).[50]

The household can sustain both instructive conversation, in which Christ teaches Mary and Joseph separately, and also what appears to be the conversation of equals in a discussion of textual interpretation. So in these two translations, Love's and the unknown Carthusian's, perspectives both Franciscan and Bridgettine that stress the value of domestic connection and conversation are made available in English.

In her visits, as elsewhere in her life, Margery's relation to family is ambiguous. As she redefines and spiritualises marriage, so too the family visit becomes something larger and more lofty. Margery travels in order to include Our Lord's lovers everywhere in England, within a broadened definition of the intimate connection provided by family. In looking at Margery's active redefinition of the home visit, we might remember her parallel redefinition of preaching, in which she refuses the term, famously asserting, 'I preche not ... I come in no pulpytt, I vse but comownycacyon & good wordys, & þat wil I do whil I leue' (126/18-20).[51] Conversation and good words are, of course, exactly the activity endorsed by Nicholas Love for the home visit.

The model of the preacher, from which Margery excludes herself, is not the only one for which her travels qualify her. Perhaps the vocation of

---

[50] The text is indeed a word-for-word translation of St Birgitta's *Liber celestis*, Book 6, chapter 58: see Roger Ellis (ed.), *The Liber celestis of St Bridget of Sweden: the Middle English version in British Library MS Claudius B.i.*, EETS OS vol. 291 (Oxford, 1987), p. 447.

[51] Barry Windeatt suggests 'that in practice Margery Kempe took ... a more instructional role', citing what amounts to conventional preaching in the fields to a group of Englishmen abroad (*Book of Margery Kempe*, chapter 42): '"I use but comownycacyon and good wordys": teaching the *Book of Margery Kempe*', in Dee Dyas, Valerie Edden and Roger Ellis (eds.), *Approaching medieval English anchoritic and mystical texts* (Rochester, NY: D. S. Brewer, 2005), p. 117.

missionary might better describe her incessant travels – a vocation she would have known well from St Paul, to whom there are eight references in her Book. Paul attributes his own constant movement to his 'daily pressing anxiety' for all the churches. But Margery's travels are never supervisory, and we are never given the sense that she travels in order to oversee the progress of the devout communities or individuals she visits. Rather it is another element in missionary work, the inspirational, that she is mistress of. Still, Margery might with Paul list her impressive travels: 'in journeyings often, in perils from floods, in perils from robbers … in perils in the city, in perils in the wilderness, in perils from the sea, in perils from false brethren, in labor and hardships, in many sleepless nights, in hunger and thirst, in fastings often, in cold and nakedness'.[52]

Pauline weariness surfaces too in Margery's responses. After several summonses from the abbess of Denny, she thinks she will postpone the visit as she can barely make the effort ('sche myth euyl duryn þe labowr', 202/9-10). Subsequently Christ commands her to go, but again she resists, 'for it was pestylens-tyme, & hir thowt þat sche wolde for no good a deyd þer' (202/16-17). Finally, faced with what seems the last obstacle, an absence of boats to Cambridge, she receives a powerful divine assurance that 'sche xulde ben ordeynd for wel a-now' (203/5-6). Enacted on such a scale as Margery's, even domestic travel necessitates a response of hero-ism, and momentarily here the domestic visit, its scope enlarged, touches the demanding apostolate of more conventional messengers.

Most purely, though, these approved visits whose purpose was spiritual exchange emerge from a familial model and are legitimated by it. They thus allow the development of an apostolic vocation traditionally forbid-den to women. Margery was often explicit about the obstacles that family life provided to a version of sanctity still massively monastic. Yet this particular family-related secular practice, the visit, served her well, allow-ing the development of an instructive model whose central figure is not the prophet or the preacher or even the missionary, but the family member. In her discovery of the possibilities of spiritual authorisation within a domes-tic model, Margery was by no means alone. Indeed the triumph of the domestic took many contemporary forms. A recent writer, for instance, speaks of Catherine of Siena's 'exploitation of the informal domestic genre of the vernacular letter to communicate inspired messages'.[53]

Lately it has been suggested that the history of visiting awaits critical examination, particularly the role of visits in 'the evolution of domestic

---

[52] 2 Corinthians 11: 26–7.
[53] F. Thomas Luongo, 'Saintly authorship in the Italian renaissance: the Quattrocento reception of Catherine of Siena's letters', *Journal of the Early Book Society* 8 (2005), 4.

space and its material content'. The author says, 'aspects of domestic penetration [or] incorporation like visiting and commensality [shared meals] around life events have yet to be valued as significant ... scenarios of consuming'.[54] and hence she suggests that visiting should have a place in the historical account of material consumption. Surely visits must have been influential in shaping the definition of household space or the design of household objects, and hence they must powerfully have affected the physical experience of home life. The example of Margery Kempe might suggest that visiting has been part of the history of spirituality as well, in the visit's provision of a definitely lay strategy for the sharing of spiritual experience, and as domestic space becomes the venue for spiritual exchange. Throughout her life Margery enacted the New Testament narrative of the Visitation, newly recognised in the late-fourteenth-century liturgy and newly endorsed by Nicholas Love as a spiritual practice, in a way that makes us rethink travel, family and the home visit.

[54] Sara Pennell, 'Consumption and consumerism in early modern England', *Historical Journal* 42 (1999), 556.

Consolidated bibliography

PRIMARY SOURCES

'A letter from Thomas Amyot, Esq. F.R.S. Treasurer, to the Earl of Aberdeen, KT. President, accompanying a transcript of two rolls, containing an inventory of effects formerly belonging to Sir John Fastolfe', *Archaeologia* 21 (1827), 232–80.

Armitage-Smith, S. (ed.), *John of Gaunt's Register*, Camden Society, 3rd series, vol. 21, London, 1911.

Arnold, Thomas (ed.), *Select English works of John Wyclif*, 3 vols., Oxford: Clarendon Press, 1869–71.

Austin, David (ed.), *Boldon Book*, Phillimore: Chichester, 1982.

Baker, P. S., and Michael Lapidge (eds.), *Byrhtferth's Enchiridion*, EETS SS vol. 15, Oxford, 1995.

Ballard, Adolphus (ed.), *British borough charters, 1042–1216*, Cambridge University Press, 1913.

Banks, John Patrick, S. J., '*Speculum devotorum*, an edition with commentary', unpublished PhD thesis, Fordham University, 1959.

Barney, S. A., W. J. Lewis, J. A. Beach and O. Berghof (eds.), *The Etymologies of Isidore of Seville*, Cambridge University Press, 2006.

Bateson, Mary (ed.), *Borough customs*, 2 vols., Selden Society vols. 18, 21, London, 1904, 1906.

Beadle, Richard (ed.), *The York plays*, London: Arnold, 1982.

Beadle, Richard and A. E. B. Owen (eds.), *The Findern manuscript, Cambridge University Library MS Ff. 1.6*, London: Scolar Press, 1978.

Benson, Larry (ed.), *The Riverside Chaucer*, 3rd edn, Oxford University Press, 1987.

Bickley, F. B. (ed.), *The little red book of Bristol*, 2 vols., Bristol: W. C. Hemmons, 1900.

Blamires, Alcuin (ed.), *Woman defamed and woman defended: an anthology of medieval texts*, Oxford University Press, 1992.

Boccaccio, Giovanni, *The Decameron*, ed. Jonathan Usher, trans. Guido Waldman, Oxford University Press, 1993.

Braekman, W. L., 'Fortune-telling by the casting of dice: a Middle English poem and its background', *Studia Neophilologica* 52 (1980), 3–29.

Brandeis, Arthur (ed.), *Jacob's Well*, EETS OS vol. 115, London, 1900.

Breay, Claire (ed.), *The cartulary of Chatteris Abbey*, Woodbridge: Boydell, 1999.

Brereton, Georgina E. and Janet M. Ferrier (eds.), *Le Mesnagier de Paris*, modern French trans. Karin Ueltshci, Paris: Librairie Générale Française, 1994.

Brown, W. and C. S. Clay (eds.), *Yorkshire Deeds*, vols. 1, 2, 6, Yorkshire Archaeological Society Record Series vols. 39, 50, 76, Leeds, 1909, 1914, 1930.

Burgess, Clive (ed.), *The pre-Reformation records of All Saints', Bristol. Parts I and II*, Bristol Record Society vols. 46, 53, Bristol 1995–2000.

Calendar of close rolls preserved in the Public Record Office, 1234–37, London: HMSO, 1909.

Calendar of patent rolls preserved in the Public Record Office, 71 vols., London: HMSO, 1891–1982.

Caley, J. and Joseph Hunter (eds.), *Valor ecclesiasticus*, 7 vols., London: G. Eyre and A. Straham, 1810–1834.

Carpenter, Christine (ed.), *Kingsford's Stonor letters and papers, 1290–1483*, 2 vols. in 1, Cambridge University Press, 1996.

Catherine of Siena, *Epistolario di santa Caterina da Siena*, ed. Eugenio Dupré Theseider, Rome: Tipografia del Senato, 1940.

Chambers, R. W. and M. Daunt (eds.), *A book of London English, 1384–1425*, Oxford: Clarendon Press, 1931.

Chew, Helena M. and William Kellaway (eds.), *London assize of nuisance 1301–1431: a calendar*, London Record Society vol. 10, Leicester, 1973.

Cicero, *De oratore*, ed. E. W. Sutton, Heinemann: London, 1942.

Cirket, A. F. (ed.), *English wills 1498–1526*, Bedfordshire Historical Record Society vol. 37, Streatly near Luton, Beds., 1957.

Clay, J. W. (ed.), *North Country wills*, Surtees Society vol. 116, Durham, 1908.

Corpus juris civilis Cod. 5.14.8; Dig. 23.3.9.3.

Coss, P. R. (ed.), *The early records of medieval Coventry*, British Academy Records of Social and Economic History n.s. vol. 11, London: Oxford University Press, 1986.

Darlington, Ida (ed.), *London consistory court wills 1492–1547*, London Record Society vol. 3, London, 1967.

Davis, Norman (ed.), *Paston letters and papers of the fifteenth century*, 2 vols. Oxford: Clarendon Press, 1971–6.

Davis, Norman. (ed.), *Non-cycle plays and fragments*, EETS SS vol. 1, Oxford, 1970.

Dugdale, William (ed.), *Monasticon anglicanum*, 8 vols. in 6, London: Longman, Hurst, Rees, Orme, and Brown, etc., 1817–30.

Eichmann, Raymond and John Du Val, (ed. and trans.), *The French fabliau: B.N. MS. 837*, 2 vols., New York: Garland, 1984.

Ellis, Roger (ed.), *The Liber celestis of St Bridget of Sweden: the Middle English version in British Library MS Claudius B.i*, EETS OS vol. 291, Oxford, 1987.

Elvey, E. M. (ed.), *The courts of the archdeaconry of Buckingham 1483–1523*, Buckinghamshire Record Society vol. 19, Aylesbury, 1975.

Emden, A. B., *A biographical register of the University of Oxford to A.D.1500*, 3 vols. Oxford: Clarendon Press, 1957–59.

Emmison, F. G. (ed.), *Elizabethan wills of south-west Essex*, Kylin Press: Waddesdon, Bucks., 1983.

Erbe, Theodore (ed.), *Mirk's Festial: a collection of homilies*. EETS ES vol. 96, London, 1905.

Farrer, William and C. T. Clay (eds.), *Early Yorkshire Charters*, vol. 1, Edinburgh: Ballantyne, Hanson and Co., 1914.

Faull, Margaret L. and Marie Stinson (eds.), *Domesday Book*, vol. 30, *Yorkshire*, Chichester: Phillimore, 1986.

Fenwick, Caroline (ed.), *The poll taxes of 1377, 1379 and 1381*, vol. 3, *Wiltshire – Yorkshire*, British Academy Records of Social and Economic History n.s. vol. 37, Oxford University Press, 2005.

Fisher, John H., Malcolm Richardson and Jane L. Fisher (eds.), *An anthology of Chancery English*, Knoxville: University of Tennessee Press, 1984.

Foster, C. W. (ed.), *Lincoln wills registered in the district probate registry at Lincoln*, vol. ii (1505–1530), Lincoln Record Society vol. 10, London, 1918.

Francis, W. Nelson (ed.), *The book of vices and virtues*, EETS OS vol. 217, Oxford, 1942.

Freudenberger, Andreas (ed.), *Ragman Roll: ein spätmittelenglishes Gedicht*, Erlangen: Junge und Sohn, 1909.

Furnivall, F. J. (ed.), *Early English meals and manners*, EETS OS vol. 32, Oxford, 1868.

    The Babees Book: medieval manners for the young, done into modern English from Dr. Furnivall's texts by Edith Rickert, New York: Cooper Square Publishers, 1966.

    The fifty earliest English wills in the Court of Probate, London, EETS OS vol. 78, Oxford, 1882.

Gairdner, James (ed.), *The Paston letters, a.d. 1422–1509*, 6 vols., London: Chatto and Windus, 1904.

Galbraith, V. H. (ed.), *The St Albans chronicle 1406–1420, edited from Bodley MS 462*, Oxford: Clarendon Press, 1937.

Gibbons, Alfred (ed.), *Early Lincoln wills: an abstract of all the wills & administrations recorded in the episcopal registers of the old diocese of Lincoln . . . 1282–1547*, Lincoln, 1888.

Given-Wilson, Chris *et al.* (eds.), *The parliament rolls of medieval England, 1275–1504*, 16 vols., Woodbridge: Boydell, 2005, 2007 and (optical disc) Leicester: Scholarly Digital Editions in association with The National Archives, The History of Parliament Trust, and Cambridge University Press, 2005.

Goldberg, P. J. P. (ed.), *Women in England c. 1275–1525: documentary sources*, Manchester University Press, 1995.

Gross, Thomas and R. Schieffer (eds), *Hincmarus de ordine palatii*, Monumenta Germaniae Historica, Fontes Iuris Germanici Antiqui, vol. 3, Hanover, 1980.

Grosseteste, Robert, *Templum Dei*, ed. J. Goering and F. A. C. Mantello, Toronto Mediaeval Latin Texts vol. 14, Toronto: Pontifical Institute of Mediaeval Studies, 1984.

Hale, William Hale (ed.), *The Domesday of St Paul's of the year 1222*, Camden Society vol. 69, London, 1858.

Hammond, E. P., 'The Chaunce of Dice', *Englische Studien* 59 (1925), 1–16.

Harmer, F. E. (ed.), *Select English historical documents of the ninth and tenth centuries*, Cambridge University Press, 1914.

Harris, M. D. (ed.), *The Coventry leet book, or mayor's register, containing the records of the city court leet or view of frankpledge, A.D. 1420–1555, with divers other matters*, vol. 1, EETS OS, vol. 134, London, 1907.

Harvey, P. D. A. (ed.), *Manorial records of Cuxham, Oxfordshire, circa 1200–1359*, Oxfordshire Records Series vol. 50, London, 1976.

Hector, Leonard C. and Barbara F. Harvey (ed. and trans.), *The Westminster chronicle 1381–1394*, Oxford: Clarendon Press, 1982.

Hoccleve, Thomas *The Complaint and Dialogue*, ed. J. A. Burrow, EETS OS vol. 313 Oxford, 1999.

   Hoccleve's works: the minor poems, ed. F. J. Furnivall and I. Gollancz, rev. edn ed. J. Mitchell and A. I. Doyle, EETS ES vols. 61 and 73, Oxford, 1970.

   The Regiment of Princes, ed. Charles R. Blyth, Kalamazoo: Medieval Institute Publications, 1999.

Hodgson, Phyllis (ed.), *The cloud of unknowing and the book of privy counselling*, EETS OS vol. 218, Oxford, 1944; repr.1981.

Horstmann, C. (ed.), *Yorkshire writers*, 2 vols., London and New York: Sonnenschein, 1895–6.

Hudson, William and J. C. Tingey (eds.), *The records of the city of Norwich*, 2 vols., London and Norwich: Jarrold, 1908–10.

Hussey, Arthur (ed.), 'Milton wills (next Sittingbourne) – I', *Archaeologia Cantiana* 44, 1932, 79–102.

Idley, Peter, *Peter Idley's instructions to his son*, ed. Charlotte D'Evelyn, Boston: D. C. Heath and Co., 1935.

Isadore of Seville, *Etymologie sive originum libri XX*, ed. W. M. Lindsay, Oxford University Press, 1910.

Jackson, C. (ed.), *The Autobiography of Mrs. Alice Thornton of East Newton, Co. York*, Surtees Society vol. 62, Durham, 1873.

Jacob, E. F. with assistance of H. C. Johnson (eds.), *The register of Henry Chichele, archbishop of Canterbury 1414–1443*, 4 vols., Canterbury and York Society vols. 42, 45–7, Oxford: Clarendon Press, 1938–47.

Jacobus de Voragine, *The Golden Legend: readings on the saints*, 2 vols., trans. William Granger Ryan, Princeton: Princeton University Press, 1993.

Johnson, C. (ed.), *Dialogus de scaccario and Constitutio domus regis*, revised edn by F. E. L. Carter and D. E. Greenway, Oxford University Press, 1983.

Jones, P. E. (ed.), *Calendar of plea and memoranda rolls of the city of London A.D. 1437–1457*, Cambridge University Press, 1954.

Kelly, Susan E. (ed.), *Charters of Abingdon Abbey, part 1*, Oxford University Press, 2000.

Kennedy, P. A. (ed.), *Nottinghamshire household inventories*, Thoroton Society Record Series vol. 22, Nottingham, 1963.

Kingsford, C. L. (ed.), *The Stonor letters and papers, 1290–1483*, Camden Society 3rd series, vols. 29 and 30, London, 1919.

La Viscountess Bindon's Case, 2 Leonard 166, 74 ER 447 (1584); Moore KB 213, 72 ER 538 (1585).

Langland, William, *Piers Plowman: the C-text*, 2nd edn., ed. Derek Pearsall, Exeter University Press, 1994.

The vision of Piers Plowman, 2nd edn, ed. A. V. C. Schmidt, London: Everyman, 1987.

The vision of Piers Plowman: a critical edition of the B-text, ed. A. V. C. Schmidt, London: Dent, 1978.

Will's visions of Piers Plowman, do-well, do-better and do-best, ed. G. H. Russell and G. Kane, London: Athlone Press, 1997.

Lepine, David and Nicholas Orme (eds.), *Death and memory in medieval Exeter*, Devon and Cornwall Record Society n.s. vol. 47, Exeter, 2003.

Lock, Ray (ed.), *The court rolls of Walsham le Willows 1303–1350*, Suffolk Records Society vol. 41, Woodbridge, 1998.

Love, Nicholas, *The Mirror of the Blessed Life of Jesus Christ: a full critical edition*, ed. Michael G. Sargent, Exeter University Press, 2005.

The Mirrour of the Blessed Lyf of Jesu Christ, ed. L. F. Powell, Oxford University Press, 1908.

Lumby, J. Rawson (ed.), *Ratis Raving and other moral and religious pieces in prose and verse*, EETS OS vol. 43, London, 1870.

Luminansky, R. M. and David Mills (eds.), *Chester mystery cycle*, EETS SS vol. 3, Oxford, 1974.

Lyndwood, William, *Provinciale*, Oxford, 1679.

Macaulay, G. C. (ed.), *The complete works of John Gower: the English works*, 2 vols., Oxford: Clarendon Press, 1901.

Macrae-Gibson, O. D. (ed.), *Of Arthour and of Merlin*, EETS OS vol. 268, Oxford, 1973.

Manly, John M. and Edith Rickert, *The text of the Canterbury Tales studied on the basis of all known manuscripts*, 8 vols., Chicago: University of Chicago Press, 1940.

Manzalaoui, M. A. (ed.), *Secretum secretorum: nine English versions*, vol. 1, EETS OS vol. 276, Oxford, 1977.

Marienwerder, Johannes, *The life of Dorothea von Montau, a fourteenth-century recluse*, trans. Ute Stargardt, Studies in Women and Religion vol. 39, Lewiston, NY: Edwin Mellen Press, 1997.

McCarthy, A. J. (ed.), *A Book to a Mother: an edition with a commentary*, Salzburg: Institut für Anglistik und Amerikanistik, Universität Salzburg, 1981.

McGregor, Margaret (ed.), *Bedfordshire wills proved in the prerogative court of Canterbury, 1383–1548*, Bedfordshire Historical Society vol. 58, Bedford, 1979.

Meech, Sanford Brown and Hope Emily Allen (eds.), *The Book of Margery Kempe*, EETS OS vol. 212, Oxford, 1940.

Mézières, Philippe de, *Le livre de la vertu du sacrement de mariage*, ed. Joan B. Williamson, Washington D.C.: Catholic University of America Press, 1993.

Migne, J.-P. (ed.), *Patrologia cursus completus, series Latina*, 221 vols., Paris, 1861–5.

Mitchell, W. T. (ed.), *Registrum cancellarii, 1498–1506*, Oxfordshire Historical Society n.s. vol. 27, Oxford, 1980.

Morris, Bridget (ed.), *The revelations of St Birgitta of Sweden*, vol. I, Liber caelestis, books I–III, trans. Denis Searby, Oxford University Press, 2006.

Morris, Richard ed., *Cursor mundi (The cursur of the world): a Northumbrian poem of the XIVth century in four versions*, EETS OS vols. 57, 59, 99, 101, Oxford, 1874–93.

Mustanoja, Tuano J. (ed.), 'Myne awen dere sone', *Neuphilologische Mitteilungen* 49 (1948), 145–93.

Nicolas, Nicholas Harris (ed.), *Testamenta vetusta*, 2 vols., London: Nichols and Son, 1826.

Northeast, Peter (ed.), *Wills of the archdeaconry of Sudbury 1439–1474: wills from the register 'Baldwyne', Part I: 1439–1474*, Suffolk Records Society vol. 44, Woodbridge, 2001.

Norton-Smith, J. (ed.), *Bodleian Library MS. Fairfax 16*, London: Scolar Press, 1979.

O'Mara, V. M. (ed.), *A study and edition of selected Middle English sermons*, Leeds Texts and Monographs n.s. vol. 13, Leeds, 1994.

Oschinsky, Dorothea (ed.), *Walter of Henley and other treatises*, Oxford University Press, 1971.

Owen, D. M. (ed.), *The making of King's Lynn*, Records of Social and Economic History n.s. vol. 9, Oxford: British Academy, 1984.

Oxford English dictionary, at http://dictionary.oed.com. Oxford: Clarendon Press, 1937–.

Perantoni, Pacifico Maria (ed.), *S. Bernardini Senensis opera omnia*, 9 vols., Florence: Ad Claras Aquas, 1950–65.

Petrarch, Francesco, 'Historia Griseldis. Epistolae seniles xvii.3', in Robert M. Correale and Mary Hamel (eds.), *Sources and analogues of the Canterbury Tales I*, Cambridge: D.S. Brewer, 2002, pp. 655–68.

Letters of old age: Rerum senilium libri I–XVIII, trans. Aldo S. Bernardo, Saul Levin and Reta A. Bernard, Baltimore: Johns Hopkins University Press, 1992.

Phayer, Thomas, *A Foke of Presidents Exactly Written in Maner of a Register*, London: Richard Tottell, 1584.

Pipe Roll Society, *The Great Roll of the Pipe for the twenty-seventh year of the reign of King Henry the Second, A.D. 1180–1181*, Pipe Roll Society vol. 30, London, 1909.

Pizan, Christine de, *The Book of the City of Ladies*, rev. edn, trans. Earl Jeffrey Richards, New York: Persea Books, 1998.

Poos, Lawrence R. (ed.), *Lower ecclesiastical jurisdiction in medieval England: the records of the dean and chapter of Lincoln, 1336–1349 and the deanery of Wisbech 1458–1484*, Records of Social and Economic History n.s. vol. 32, Oxford: British Academy, 2001.

Quintilian, *Institutio oratoria*, 2 vols., trans. H. E. Butler, London: Heinemann, 1920–2.

Ragusa, Isa and Rosalie B. Green (eds.), *Meditations on the life of Christ: an illustrated manuscript of the fourteenth century*, trans. Isa Ragusa, Princeton University Press, 1961.

Raine, James (ed.), *Wills and inventories illustrative of the history, manners, language, statistics etc. of the northern counties of England from the eleventh century downward*, 4 vols., Surtees Society vols. 2, 38, 112, 142, London, 1835–1929.

Raine, James and J. W. Clay (eds.), *Testamenta eboracensia*, 6 vols., Surtees Society vols. 4, 30, 45, 53, 79, 106, London (vol. 1 only) and Durham, 1836–1902.

Redstone, Lillian (ed.), 'Three Carrow account rolls', *Norfolk Archaeology* 29 (1946), 41–88.

Rickert, Edith, 'Some personal letters of 1402', *Review of English Studies* 31 (1932), 257–63.

Riley, H. T. (ed.), *Annales monasterii S. Albani a Johannne Amundesham monacho . . . (A.D. 1421–1440)*, vol. 1, Rolls Series no. 28, London: Longmans, Green, 1870.

   Liber albus: the white book of the city of London, compiled A.D. 1419 by John Carpenter, common clerk. Richard Whittington, mayor, London: R. Griffin, 1861.

Riley, H. T. (ed.), *Memorials of London and London life in the XIIIth, XIVth and XVth centuries*, London: Longman, Green, 1868.

Roberts, E. and K. Parker (eds.), *Southampton probate inventories, 1447–1575* volume 1, Southampton Records Series vol. 24, Southampton, 1992.

Robinson, F. N. (ed.), *The complete works of Geoffrey Chaucer*, 2nd edn, Oxford University Press, 1957.

Robinson, Pamela (ed.), *Manuscript Bodley 638: a facsimile*, Norman, OK: Pilgrim Books, 1982.

Rolle, Henry, *Un abridgment des plusieurs cases et resolutions del common ley*, London, 1668.

Salisbury, Eve (ed.), *The trials and joys of marriage*, Kalamazoo, MI: Medieval Institute Publications, 2002.

Sargent, Michael G. (ed.), *Nicholas Love's Mirror of the Blessed Life of Jesus Christ* New York: Garland, 1992.

Schaff, Philip (ed.), *Anti-Pelagian writings*, Select Library of the Nicene and Post-Nicene Fathers of the Christian Church series I, vol. 5, Edinburgh: T&T Clark, 1887; repr. Grand Rapids, MI: William B. Eerdmans, 1956.

   On the Holy Trinity, doctrinal treatises, moral treatises, Select Library of the Nicene and Post-Nicene Fathers series I, vol. 3, Edinburgh: T&T Clark, 1890; repr. Grand Rapids, MI: William B. Eerdmans, 1956.

Schofield, John and Alan Vince, *Medieval towns: the archaeology of British towns in their European setting*, London: Leicester University Press, 1994.

Sellers, Maud (ed.), *York memorandum book, Part 1*, 2 vols., Surtees Society vols. 120, 125, Durham, 1915.

Sharpe, R. R. (ed.), *Calendar of letter-books preserved among the archives of the corporation of the city of London at the guildhall*, 11 vols., London: J. E. Francis, 1899–1912

Sharpe, Reginald (ed.), *Calendar of wills proved and enrolled in the court of Hustings, London AD 1258–1688: preserved among the archives of the corporation of London, at the guildhall*, 2 vols., London: J. C. Francis, 1889.

Shilton, Dorothy O. and Richard Holworthy (eds.), *Medieval wills from Wells deposited in the diocesan registry, Wells, 1543–1546 and 1554–1556*, Somerset Record Society vol. 40, London, 1925.

Shirley, Walter Waddington (ed.), *Royal and other historical letters illustrative of the reign of Henry III*, 2 vols., Rolls Series, no. 27, London, 1862–66.

Smith, Lucy Toulmin (ed.), *The book of Brome: a common-place book of the fifteenth century*, privately printed, 1886.

Smith, Toulmin and Lucy Toulmin Smith (eds.), *English gilds: the original ordinances of more than one hundred early English gilds*, EETS OS vol. 40, London, 1870; repr. 2002.

Smyly, J. G. (ed.), *Urbanus Magnus Danielis Becclesiensis*, Dublin: Hodges, Figgis, 1939.

Stapleton, Thomas (ed.), *The Plumpton correspondence: a series of letters, chiefly domestick, written in the reigns of Edward IV, Richard III, Henry VII and Henry VIII*, Camden Society vol. 4, London, 1839; repr., Gloucester: Alan Sutton, 1990.

Stell, P. M. (trans.), *Probate inventories of the York diocese, 1350–1500*, York: York Archaeological Trust, 2006.

Stephenson, W. H. (ed.), *Records of the borough of Nottingham*, vol. 1, London: Quaritch, 1882.

Stevens, Martin and A. C. Cawley (eds.), *The Towneley plays*, 2 vols., EETS SS vols. 13, 14, Oxford, 1994.

Stevenson, W. H. and C. T. Flower (eds.), *Calendar of the Liberate Rolls preserved in the Public Record Office*, vol. 1, *1226–40*, London: HMSO, 1917.

Strachey, J. (ed.), *Rotuli parliamentorum*, 6 vols., London, 1767–77.

Stubbs, William (ed.), *Chronica Rogeri de Houedene*, 4 vols., Rolls Series no. 51, London, 1868–71.

T. E., *The lawes resolutions of women's rights*, London, 1632; repr. Norwood, NJ: Walter J. Johnson Inc., 1979.

The Year Books: or reports … with notes to Brooke and Fitzherbert's abridgements, 11 vols., London, 1678–80; repr. with introductory notes and tables by David J. Seipp with Carol F. Lee, Clark, NJ: The Lawbook Exchange, 2007.

Thomas, A. H. [vols. 1–4] and Philip E. Jones [vols. 5–6] (eds.), *Calendar of select plea and memoranda rolls of the City of London*, 6 vols., Cambridge University Press, 1926–61.

Timmins, T. C. B. (ed.), *The register of John Chandler, dean of Salisbury*, Wiltshire Record Society vol. 52, Devizes, 1984.

Tringham, Nigel (ed.), *Charters of the vicars choral of York Minster, city of York and its suburbs to 1546*, Yorkshire Archaeological Society Record Series vol. 148, Leeds: Knight and Forster, 1993.

Twiss Travers (ed.), *Monumenta Juridica: the black book of the Admiralty*, vol. II, Rolls Series no. 55, London, 1873.

Tymms, Samuel (ed.), *Wills and inventories from the registers of the commissary of Bury St Edmunds and the archdeacon of Sudbury*, Camden Society vol. 49, London, 1850.

Walcott, Mackenzie E. C., 'Inventories and valuations of religious houses at the time of the dissolution, from the Public Record Office....', *Archaeologia* 43 (1871), 287–306.

'Inventories of St Mary's Hospital, Dover, St Martin New-Work, Dover, and the Benedictine priory of S.S. Mary and Sexburga in the Island of Sheppey for nuns', *Archaeologia Cantiana* 7 (1868), 272–306.

'Inventory of St Mary's Benedictine nunnery at Langley, co. Leicester, 1485', *Transactions of the Leicestershire Archaeological and Architectural Society* 4 (1872), 117–22.

Warner, G. F. (ed.), *The buke of John Maundeuill*, Roxburghe Club vol. 119, Westminster: Nichols and Sons, 1889.

Weaver, F. W. (ed.), *Somerset medieval wills (1383–1500)*, volume 1, Somerset Record Society vol. 16, London, 1901.

Weaver, J. R. H. and A. Beardwood (eds.), *Some Oxfordshire wills proved in the prerogative court of Canterbury, 1393–1510*, Oxfordshire Record Society vol. 39, Banbury, 1958.

William of Malmesbury, *Willelmi Malmesbiriensis monachi De gestis pontificum Anglorum libri quinque*, ed. N. E. S. A. Hamilton, Rolls Series no. 52, London: Longman, 1870.

Woodbine, George (ed.), *Bracton on the laws and customs of England*, trans. with revisions and notes by Samuel E. Thorne, 4 vols., Cambridge, Mass.: The Belknap Press of Harvard University Press, 1968–77.

Wright, Thomas (ed.), *A volume of vocabularies*, Liverpool, privately printed, 1857.

Zettl, E. (ed.), *An anonymous short English metrical chronicle*, EETS OS vol. 196, Oxford, 1935.

SECONDARY SOURCES

Aers, David, 'Faith, ethics, and community: reflections on reading late medieval English writing', *Journal of Medieval and Early Modern Studies* 28 (1998), 341–69.

'Piers Plowman' and Christian allegory, London: Edward Arnold, 1975.

Faith, ethics, and church: writing in England 1360–1409, Cambridge: D.S. Brewer, 2000.

Alford, John A., 'The idea of reason in *Piers Plowman*', in Edward Donald Kennedy, Ronald Waldron and Joseph S. Wittig (eds.), *Medieval English studies presented to George Kane*, Cambridge: D. S. Brewer, 1988, pp. 199–215.

Allen Brown, R., H. M. Colvin, and A. J. Taylor, *The history of the King's works: II. The Middle Ages*, London: HMSO, 1963.

Anderson, Michael, *Approaches to the history of the western family 1500–1914*, Cambridge University Press, 1995.

Ando, Clifford, 'Signs, idols, and the Incarnation in Augustinian metaphysics', *Representations* 73 (2001), 24–53.

Andrews, Gillian, 'Archaeology in York: an assessment', in P. V. Addyman and V. Black (eds.), *Archaeological papers from York presented to M. W. Barley*, York Archaeological Trust, 1984, pp. 173–208.

Ariès, Philippe, *Centuries of childhood: a social history of private life*, new edn, trans. Robert Baldick, London: Jonathan Cape, 1996.

Arnade, Peter and Howell, Martha C., 'Fertile spaces: the productivity of urban space in northern Europe', *Journal of Interdisciplinary History* 32 (2002), 515–548.

Ashton, Gail, 'Patient mimesis: Griselda and the Clerk's Tale', *The Chaucer Review*, 32 (1998), 232–38.

Astill, Grenville, 'Rural settlement: the toft and croft', in Grenville Astill and Annie Grant (eds.), *The countryside of medieval England*, Oxford: Blackwell, 1988, pp. 36–61.

Aston, Margaret, *Thomas Arundel, a study of church life in the reign of Richard II*, Oxford: Clarendon Press, 1967.

Austin, David and Julian Thomas, 'The "proper study" of medieval archaeology: a case study', in D. Austin and L. Alcock (eds.), *From the Baltic to the Black Sea: studies in medieval archaeology*, London: Unwin Hyman, 1990, pp. 43–78.

Ayers, Brian, 'The urban landscape', in Carole Rawcliffe and Richard Wilson (eds.), *Medieval Norwich*, London: Hambledon, 2004, pp. 1–28.

Ayers, Brian, *Excavations at St. Martin-at-Palace Plain, Norwich, 1981*, East Anglian Archaeology vol. 37, Dereham: Norwich Archaeological Unit, 1987.

Ayoub, L., 'OE *wæta* and the medical theory of the humours', *Journal of English and Germanic Philology* 94 (1995), 332–46.

Baker, Nigel and Richard Holt, *Urban growth and the medieval church: Gloucester and Worcester*, Aldershot: Ashgate, 2004.

Bardsley, Sandy, *Venomous tongues: speech and gender in late medieval England*, Philadelphia: University of Pennsylvania Press, 2006.

Barron, Caroline M, 'The parish fraternities of medieval London', in Caroline M. Barron and Christopher Harper-Bill (eds.), *The church in pre-reformation society: essays in honour of F.R.H. Du Boulay*. Woodbridge: Boydell, 1985, pp. 13–37.

Barron, Caroline, *Pilgrim souls: Margery Kempe and other women pilgrims*, Confraternity of St James Occasional Paper no. 6, London, 2004.

Baschet, Jérôme, 'Medieval Abraham: between fleshly and divine father', *Modern Language Notes* 108 (1993), 738–58.

Batt, Catherine, Denis Renevey and Christiania Whitehead, 'Domesticity and medieval devotional literature', *Leeds Studies in English* new series 36 (2005), 195–250.

Beattie, Cordelia, 'Governing bodies: law courts, male householders and single women in late medieval England', in Cordelia Beattie, Anna Maslakovic and Sarah Rees Jones (eds.), *The medieval household in Christian Europe c. 850–1550: managing power, wealth, and the body*, Turnhout: Brepols, 2003, pp. 199–220.

Beauvoir, Simone de, *The second sex*, trans. and ed. H. M. Parshley, London: Vintage, 1997.

Bell, R. D. and M. W. Beresford, *Wharram, a study of settlement on the Yorkshire Wolds I*, London: Society for Medieval Archaeology, 1987.

Beresford, M. W., 'Documentary evidence for the history of Wharram Percy', in D. D. Andrews and G. Milne (eds.), *Wharram, a study of settlement on the Yorkshire Wolds I: domestic settlement I: Areas 10 and 6*, London: Society for Medieval Archaeology, 1979, pp. 5–25.

Beresford, M. W. and J. G. Hurst, *Wharram Percy: deserted medieval village*, New Haven and London: Yale University Press, 1990.

Biddle, Martin (ed.), *Winchester in the early Middle Ages: an edition and discussion of the Winton Domesday*, Winchester Studies vol. 1, Oxford University Press, 1976.

Blair, John, 'The 12th-century Bishop's Palace at Hereford', *Medieval Archaeology* 31 (1987), 59–72.

'Hall and chamber: English domestic planning 1000–1250', in G. Meirion-Jones and M. Jones (eds.), *Manorial domestic buildings in England and northern France*, London: Society of Antiquaries, 1993, pp. 1–21.

'Palaces or minsters? Northampton and Cheddar reconsidered', *Anglo-Saxon England* 25 (1997), 97–121.

Anglo-Saxon Oxfordshire, Stroud: Sutton, 1994.

The church in Anglo-Saxon Society, Oxford University Press, 2005.

Blamires, Alcuin, *The case for women in medieval culture*, Oxford: Clarendon Press, 1997.

Bloch, R. H., *Medieval misogyny and the invention of western romantic love*, Chicago: University of Chicago Press, 1997.

Bloomfield, Morton W., '*Piers Plowman* and the three grades of chastity', *Anglia* 76 (1958), 227–53.

Boffey, Julia, 'Bodleian library, MS Arch. Selden. B.24 and definitions of the household book', in A. S. G. Edwards, Vincent Gillespie and Ralph Hanna (eds.), *The English medieval book: studies in memory of Jeremy Griffiths*, London: British Library, 2000, pp. 125–34.

Boffey, Julia and John J. Thompson, 'Anthologies and miscellanies: production and choice of texts', in Jeremy Griffiths and Derek Pearsall (eds.), *Book production and publishing in Britain 1375–1475*, Cambridge University Press, 1989.

Boffey, Julia and Carole Meale, 'Gentlewomen's reading', in Lotte Hellinga and J. B. Trapp (eds.), *The Cambridge history of the book in Britain*, vol. 3, *1400–1557*, Cambridge University Press, 1998, pp. 526–40.

Boffey, Julia and A. S. G. Edwards (eds.), *A new index of Middle English verse*, London: British Library, 2005.

Bolton, Jim, '"The world upside down": plague as an agent of economic and social change', in Mark Ormrod and Phillip Lindley (eds.), *The Black Death in England*, Stamford: Paul Watkins, 1996, pp. 17–77.

Bossy, John, 'Blood and baptism: kinship, community and Christianity in western Europe from the fourteenth to the seventeenth centuries', *Studies in Church History* 10 (1973), 129–43.

Bourdieu, Pierre, *Outline of a theory of practice*, Cambridge University Press, 1977.

Bowers, Terence, 'Margery Kempe as traveller', *Studies in Philology* 97 (2000), 1–28.

Brigden, Susan, 'Religion and social obligation in early sixteenth-century London', *Past and Present* 103 (1984), 67–112.

Britnell, R. H., *Growth and decline in Colchester, 1300–1525*, Cambridge University Press, 1986.

'Urban economic regulation and economic morality in medieval England', paper delivered to the 75th Anniversary Conference of the Economic History Society (Glasgow, 2001) at http://www.dur.ac.uk/r.h.britnell/articles/Morality.htm.

Bronfman, Judith, *Chaucer's Clerk's Tale: the Griselda story received, rewritten, illustrated*, New York: Garland, 1994.

Brooks, Nicholas, *The early history of the church in Canterbury*, Leicester University Press, 1984.

Brown, B. D., 'Religious lyrics in MS. Don.c.13', *Bodleian Quarterly Record* 7 (1932), 1–7.

Brown, F. E., 'Analysing small building plans: a morphological approach', in R. Samson (ed.), *The social archaeology of houses*, Edinburgh University Press, 1990, pp. 259–76.

Brown, Pamela Allen, *Better a shrew than a sheep: women, drama, and the culture of jest in early modern England*, Ithaca: Cornell University Press, 2003.

Bryant, J. A., 'The diet of Chaucer's Franklin', *Modern Language Notes* 63 (1948), 318–25.

Bugge, John, *Virginitas: an essay in the history of a medieval idea*, The Hague: Martinus Nijhoff, 1975.

Bullough, Vern, 'On being male in the Middle Ages', in Clare A. Lees (ed.), *Medieval masculinities: regarding men in the Middle Ages*, Minneapolis: University of Minnesota Press, 1994, pp. 31–46.

Burns, E. Jane, 'Saracen silk and the Virgin's chemise: cultural crossings in cloth', *Speculum* 81 (2006), 365–397.

Burrow, J. A., 'The Audience of *Piers Plowman*', *Anglia* 75 (1957), 373–84.

Butcher, Andrew F., 'Rent and the urban economy: Oxford and Canterbury in the later Middle Ages', *Southern History* 1 (1979), 11–43.

Butler, Judith, *Gender trouble: feminism and the subversion of identity*, New York: Routledge, 1990.

Butler, Paul, 'The citole project' at http://www.crab.rutgers.edu/~pbutler/citole.html

Bynum, Caroline Walker, *Holy feast and holy fast: the religious significance of food to medieval women*, Berkeley: University of California Press, 1987.

Caillois, Roger, *Man, play and games*, trans. M. Barash, New York: Free Press of Glencoe, 1961.

Caldicott, Diana, *Hampshire nunneries*, Chichester: Phillimore, 1989.

Cameron, M. L., 'Bald's Leechbook and cultural interactions in Anglo-Saxon England', *Anglo-Saxon England* 19 (1990), 5–12.

Camille, Michael, *Mirror in parchment: the Luttrell Psalter and the making of medieval England*, London: Reaktion Books, 1998.

Capp, Bernard, *When gossips meet: women, family, and neighbourhood in early modern England*, Oxford University Press, 2003.

Carlin, Martha, 'Fast food and urban living standards in medieval England', in Martha Carlin and Joel T. Rosenthal (eds.), *Food and eating in medieval Europe*, London: Hambledon Press, 1998, pp. 27–51

Carroll, Jane L., 'Woven devotions: reform and piety in tapestries by Dominican nuns', in Jane L. Carroll and Alison G. Stewart (eds.), *Saints, sinners, and sisters. Gender and northern art in medieval and early modern Europe*, Burlington, VT: Ashgate, 2003, pp. 182–201.

Carus-Wilson, E., 'The medieval trade of the ports of the Wash', *Medieval Archaeology* 6–7 (1962–3), 182–201.

Chapelot, J. and R. Fossier, *The village and house in the Middle Ages*, Berkeley: University of California Press, 1985.

Chaplais, Pierre, 'The royal Anglo-Saxon chancery of the tenth century revisited', in H. Mayr-Harting and R. I. Moore (eds.), *Studies in medieval history presented to R. H. C. Davis*, London: Hambledon, 1985, pp. 41–51.

Chesterton, G. K., *Chaucer*, London: Faber and Faber, 1932.

Clark, Clifford E., 'Domestic architecture as an index to social history: the romantic revival and the cult of domesticity in America, 1840–1870', *Journal of Interdisciplinary History* 7 (1976), 33–56.

Clark, David, 'The shop within? An analysis of the architectural evidence for medieval shops', *Architectural History* 43 (2000), 58–87.

Clark, James G., 'Thomas Walsingham reconsidered: books and learning at late-medieval St Albans', *Speculum* 77 (2002), 832–60.

A monastic renaissance at St. Albans: Thomas Walsingham and his circle c. 1350–1440, Oxford: Clarendon Press, 2004.

Cole, Andrew, 'Trifunctionality and the tree of charity', *English Literary History* 62 (1995), 1–27.

Coleman, Simon and John Elsner, 'Pilgrimage to Walsingham and the re-invention of the Middle Ages', in J. Stopford (ed.), *Pilgrimage explored*, York Medieval Press, 1999, pp. 189–214.

Coss, Peter, *Lordship, knighthood and locality, a study in English society c. 1180–c. 1280*, Cambridge University Press, 1991.

Craig, L. A., '"Stronger than men and braver than knights": women and the pilgrimage to Jerusalem and Rome in the later Middle Ages', *Journal of Medieval History* 29 (2003), 154–55.

Crane, Susan, *The performance of self: ritual, clothing, and identity during the Hundred Years War*, Philadelphia: University of Pennsylvania Press, 2002.

Crummy, P., 'The system of measurement used in town planning from the ninth to the thirteenth centuries', in S. C. Hawkes, D. Brown and J. Campbell (eds.), *Anglo-Saxon studies in archaeology and history*, British Archaeological Reports, British Series vol. 72 (1979), pp. 149–63.

Cumberpatch, C. G., 'Towards a phenomenological approach to the study of medieval pottery', in C. G. Cumberpatch and P. W. Blinkhorn (eds.), *Not so much a pot, more a way of life*, Oxford: Oxbow, 1997, pp. 125–51.

Cunningham, J., 'Auckland Castle: some recent discoveries', in E. Fernie and P. Crossley (eds.), *Medieval architecture and its intellectual context: studies in honour of Peter Kidson*, London: Hambledon, 1990, pp. 81–90.

Cussans, J. E., *A history of Hertfordshire*, 3 vols. London: Chatto & Windus, 1881, vol. 2, *Hitchin, Hertford, and Broadwater*.

Davidoff, Leonore and Catherine Hall, *Family fortunes: men and women of the English middle class 1780–1850*, Chicago: University of Chicago Press/ London: Hutchison, 1987.

Davis, Dona L. and J. Nadel-Klein, 'Gender, culture and the sea: contemporary theoretical perspectives', *Society and Natural Resources* 5 (1992), 135–47.

Deregnaucourt, J.-S., 'L'inventaire après décès d'Ysabel Malet, bourgeoise douaisianne, en 1369: document pour server à l'histoire de la vie quotidienne de la bourgeoisie médiévale', *Revue du Nord* 64 (1982), 707–29.

Dickinson, J. C., *The shrine of Our Lady of Walsingham*, Cambridge University Press, 1956.

Diekstra, F. N. M., *A dialogue between reason and adversity: A late Middle English version of Petrarch's De Remediis*, Assen: Van Gorcum, 1968.

Dinshaw, Carolyn, *Chaucer's sexual poetics*, Madison: University of Wisconsin Press, 1989.

Dixon, Philip and Beryl Lott, 'The courtyard and the tower: contexts and symbols in the development of late medieval great houses', *Journal of the British Archaeological Association* 146 (1993), 93–101.

Dixon, Philip and Pamela Marshall, 'The great tower at Hedingham castle: a reassessment', *Fortress* 18 (1993), 16–23.

Dobson, R. B., 'Admissions to the freedom of the city of York in the later Middle Ages', *Economic History Review* 2nd series, 26 (1973), 16–22.

'General survey 1300–1540', in David Palliser (ed.), *The Cambridge urban history of Britain*, vol. 1: *600–1540*, Cambridge: Cambridge University Press 2000, pp. 273–90.

Dobson, R. B. and Sara Donaghey, *The history of Clementhorpe nunnery*, London: Published for the York Archaeology Trust by the Council for British Archaeology, 1984.

Dodd, Anne (ed.), *Oxford before the university: the late Saxon and Norman archaeology of the Thames crossing, the defences and the town*, Thames Valley landscapes monograph no. 17, Oxford University Press, 2003.

Dohrn-van Rossum, Gerhard, *History of the hour: clocks and modern temporal orders*, trans. Thomas Dunlap, Chicago: University of Chicago Press, 1996.

Donahue, Charles Jr., 'Lyndwood's gloss *propriarum uxorum*: marital property and the *ius commune* in fifteenth-century England' in Norbert Horn, Klaus Luig and Alfred Söllner (eds.), *Europäisches Rechtsdenken in Geschichte und Gegenwart: Festschrift für Helmut Coing zum 70 Geburtstag*, Munich: C. H. Beck'sche Verlagsbuchhandlung, 1982, pp. 19–37.

Doyle, K. A., 'Thisbe out of context: Chaucer's female readers and the Findern manuscript', *Chaucer Review* 40 (2006), 231–62.

Du Boulay, F. R. H., *The England of 'Piers Plowman': William Langland and his vision of the fourteenth century*, Woodbridge: Boydell and Brewer, 1991.

Duby, Georges (ed.), *A history of private life*, vol. 2, *Revelations of the medieval world*, Cambridge, MA: Belknap Press of Harvard University Press, 1988.

Duffy, Eamon, 'The dynamics of pilgrimage in late medieval England', in Colin Morris and Peter Roberts (eds.), *Pilgrimage: the English experience from Becket to Bunyan*, Cambridge: Cambridge University Press, 2002, pp. 164–77.

Marking the hours: English people and their prayers 1240–1570, New Haven: Yale University Press, 2006.

The stripping of the altars: traditional religion in England c. 1400–c. 1580, 2nd edn, New Haven: Yale University Press, 2005 (first edn 1992).

Dunning, Robert, 'The muniments of Syon Abbey: their administration and migration in the fifteenth and sixteenth centuries', *Bulletin of the Institute of Historical Research* 37 (1964), 103–11.

Dyer, Alan, 'Ranking lists of English medieval towns', in David Palliser (ed.), *The Cambridge urban history of Britain*, vol. 1: *600–1540*, Cambridge University Press 2000, pp. 747–70.

Dyer, Christopher, 'Piers Plowman and plowmen: a historical perspective', *Yearbook of Langland Studies* 9 (1994), 155–76.

'The hidden trade of the Middle Ages: evidence from the West Midlands of England', in his *Everyday life in medieval England*, London: Hambledon, 1994, pp. 283–303.

An age of transition? Economy and society in the later middle ages, Oxford: Clarendon Press, 2005.

Standards of living in the later Middle Ages: social change in England, c. 1200–1520, Cambridge University Press, 1989.

Eames, Penelope, *Furniture in England, France and the Netherlands from the twelfth to the fifteenth century,* London: Furniture History Society, 1977.

Edwards J. F. and B. P. Hindle, 'The transportation system of medieval England and Wales', *Journal of Historical Geography* 17 (1991), 123–34.

Egan, Geoff, 'Urban and rural finds: material culture of country and town', in Kate Giles and Christopher Dyer (eds.), *Town and country in the Middle Ages: contrasts, contacts and interconnections, 1100–1500,* Leeds: Maney 2005, pp. 197–210.

Egan, Geoff, *The medieval household: daily living c. 1150–c.1450,* Medieval Finds from Excavations in London vol. 6, London, 1998.

Elkins, Sharon, 'Gertrude the Great and the Virgin Mary', *Church History* 66 (1997), 720–34.

Elliott, Dyan, *Spiritual marriage: sexual abstinence in medieval wedlock,* Princeton University Press, 1993.

Ellis, R., 'A contribution to the history of the transmission of classical literature in the Middle Ages', *American Journal of Philology* 10 (1889), 159–64.

Emmerson, Richard K. and P. J. P. Goldberg, '"The Lord Geoffrey had me made": lordship and labour in the Luttrell Psalter', in James Bothwell, P. J. P. Goldberg and W. M. Ormrod (eds.), *The problem of labour in fourteenth-century England,* York Medieval Press, 2000, pp. 43–63.

Erickson, Amy Louise, 'Common law versus common practice: the use of marriage settlements in early modern England', *Economic History Review* 2nd series 43 (1990), 21–39.

Women and property in early modern England, London: Routledge, 1993.

Erler, Mary Carpenter, *Women, reading and piety in late medieval England,* Cambridge University Press, 2002.

Fanous, Samuel, 'Measuring the pilgrim's progress: internal emphases in *The Book of Margery Kempe*', in Denis Renevey and Christiania Whitehead (eds.), *Writing religious women: female spiritual and textual practices in late medieval England,* Toronto: University of Toronto Press, 2000, pp. 157–76.

Farrell, Thomas, 'The style of the "Clerk's Tale" and the function of its glosses', *Studies in Philology* 86 (1989), 286–309.

Faulkner, Patrick A., 'Domestic planning from the twelfth to the fourteenth centuries', *Archaeological Journal* 115 (1958), 150–83.

'Medieval undercrofts and town houses', *Archaeological Journal* 123 (1966), 120–35.

'Lincoln Old Bishop's Palace (SK 9777717)', *Archaeological Journal* 131 (1974), 340–4.

Fell, Christine E., 'Some domestic problems', *Leeds Studies in English,* new series 16 (1985), 59–82.

Fenster, Thelma S. and Clare A. Lees (eds.), Introduction to *Gender in debate from the early Middle Ages to the Renaissance,* New York: Palgrave Macmillan, 2002, pp. 1–18.

Fleming, Peter, *Family and household in medieval England*, Basingstoke: Palgrave, 2001.

Fleming, Robin, 'Rural elites and urban communities in late-Saxon England', *Past and Present* 141 (1993), 3–37.

Fowler, R. C., 'Inventories of Essex monasteries in 1536', *Transactions of the Essex Archaeological Society* n.s. 9 (1906), 280–92.

Fox, H. S. A., 'Exploitation of the landless by lords and tenants in early medieval England', in Zvi Razi and Richard Smith (eds.), *Medieval society and the manor court*, Oxford: Clarendon Press, 1996, pp. 518–68.

Franits, Wayne E., *Paragons of virtue: women and domesticity in seventeenth-century Dutch art*, Cambridge University Press, 1993.

French, Katherine L., G. G. Gibbs and B. A. Kümin (eds.), *The parish in English life*, Manchester University Press, 1997.

French, Katherine L., *The people of the parish: community life in a late medieval English parish*, Philadelphia: University of Pennsylvania Press, 2001.

Frese, Dolores, 'Chaucer's Clerk's Tale: the monsters and the critics reconsidered', *Chaucer Review* 8 (1973), 133–46.

Frost, Judith A., 'An edition of the Nostell Priory cartulary: London, British Library, Cotton Vespasian E XIX', unpublished PhD thesis, University of York, 2005.

Gardiner, Mark, 'Vernacular buildings and the development of the later medieval domestic plan in England', *Medieval Archaeology* 44 (2000), 159–79.

'Timber buildings without earth-fast footings in Viking-Age Britain', in J. Hines, A. Lane and M. Redknap (eds.), *Land, sea, and home: proceedings of a conference on Viking Age settlement in the British Isles*, London: Society for Medieval Archaeology, 2004, pp. 345–58.

'Implements and utensils in *Gerefa*, and the organization of seigneurial farmsteads in the High Middle Ages', *Medieval Archaeology* 50 (2006), 260–7.

Garrett, Elisabeth Donaghy, *At home: the American family 1750–1870*, New York: H. N. Abrams, 1990.

Gee, Loveday Lewes, *Women, art and patronage from Henry III to Edward III: 1216–1377*, Woodbridge: Boydell, 2002.

Georgianna, Linda, 'The Clerk's Tale and the grammar of assent', *Speculum* 70 (1993), 793–821.

Gibson, Gail McMurray, *The theater of devotion: East Anglian drama and society in the late Middle Ages*, Chicago University Press, 1989.

Giddens, Anthony, *The constitution of society: outline of the theory of structuration*, Cambridge: Polity Press, 1984.

Gilchrist, Roberta, *Gender and material culture: the archaeology of religious women*, London: Routledge, 1994.

Giles, Judy, *The parlour and the suburb: domestic identities, class, femininity and modernity*, Oxford and New York: Berg, 2004.

Giles, Katherine, *An archaeology of social identity: guildhalls in York, c. 1350–1630*. British Archaeological Reports, British Series vol. 315, Oxford: Archaeopress, 2000.

Girouard, Mark, *Life in the English country house: a social and economic history*, New Haven and London: Yale University Press, 1978.

Given-Wilson, Chris, 'Thomas Mowbray, first duke of Norfolk (1366–1399)', in *Oxford dictionary of national biography*, ed. H. C. G. Matthew and Brian Harrison, Oxford University Press, 2004; online edn, ed. Lawrence Goldman, October 2005, http://www.oxforddnb.com/view/article/12360.

'The problem of labour in the context of English government, *c*. 1350–1450', in James Bothwell, P. J. P. Goldberg and W. M. Ormrod (eds.), *The problem of labour in fourteenth-century England*, York Medieval Press, 2000, pp. 85–100.

Goddard, Richard, *Lordship and medieval urbanisation: Coventry, 1043–1355*, Woodbridge: Boydell and Brewer, 2004.

Goldberg, P. J. P., 'Women in fifteenth-century town life', in J. A. F. Thomson (ed.), *Towns and townspeople in the fifteenth century*, Stroud: Sutton, 1988, pp. 107–28.

'The public and the private: women in the pre-plague economy', in P. R. C. *Thirteenth-century England* 3 (1991), 75–89.

Women, work and life cycle in a medieval economy: women in York and Yorkshire c. 1300–1520, Oxford: Clarendon Press, 1992.

'Masters and men in later medieval England', in Dawn M. Hadley (ed.), *Masculinity in medieval Europe*, London: Longmans, 1999, pp. 56–70.

'Orphans and servants: the socialisation of young people living away from home in the English later Middle Ages', in M. Corbier (ed.), *Adoption et fosterage*, Paris: Editions de Boccard, 1999, pp. 231–46.

'Pigs and prostitutes', in Katherine J. Lewis, Noel James Menuge and Kim M. Phillips (eds.), *Young medieval women*, Stroud: Sutton, 1999, pp. 172–194.

'What was a servant?', in Anne Curry and Elizabeth Matthew (eds.), *Concepts and patterns of service in the later Middle Ages*, Woodbridge: Boydell and Brewer, 2000, pp. 1–20.

'Household and the organisation of labour in late medieval towns: some English evidence', in Myriam Carlier and Tim Soens (eds.), *The household in late medieval cities. Italy and northwestern Europe compared*, Leuven: Garant, 2001, pp. 59–70.

Medieval England: a social history 1250–1550, London: Arnold, 2004.

Goodman, Anthony, *John of Gaunt: the exercise of princely power in fourteenth-century Europe*, New York: St. Martin's Press, 1989.

Graham, Rose, 'Axholme', in *The Victoria history of the county of Lincolnshire*, vol. 2, ed. William Page, London: Constable, 1906, pp. 158–60.

Gray, Arthur, *The priory of St Radegund, Cambridge*, Cambridge Antiquarian Society, 1898.

Green, Judith A., *The government of England under Henry I*, Cambridge University Press, 1986.

Green, Richard Firth, *Poets and princepleasers: literature and the English court in the late middle ages*, Toronto: University of Toronto Press, 1980.

'The *familia regis* and the *familia cupidinis*', in V. J. Scattergood and J. W. Sherborne (eds.), *English court culture in the later Middle Ages*, London: Duckworth, 1983, pp. 87–108.

'*Le roi qui ne ment* and aristocratic courtship', in Keith Busby and Erik Kooper (eds.), *Courtly literature: culture and context*, Amsterdam: John Benjamins, 1990, pp. 211–25.

Grenville, Jane, 'Houses and households in late medieval England: an archaeo-logical perspective', in Jocelyn Wogan-Brown, Rosalynn Voaden, Arlyn Diamond, Ann Hutchinson, Carol Meale and Lesley Johnson (eds.), *Medieval women: texts and contexts in late medieval Britain. Essays for Felicity Riddy*, Turnhout: Brepols 2000, pp. 309–28.

Medieval housing, London: Leicester University Press, 1997.

Haddon-Reece, D., D. H. Miles and J. T. Munby, 'Tree-ring dates from the Ancient Monuments Laboratory, Historic Buildings and Monuments Commission for England', *Vernacular Architecture* 20 (1989), 46–9.

Hall, R. A. and K. Hunter-Mann, *Medieval urbanism in Coppergate: refining a townscape: the archaeology of York* 10/6, London: Council for British Archaeology, 2002.

Hamburger, Jeffrey, *Nuns as artists: the visual culture of a medieval convent*, Berkeley: University of California Press, 1997.

The visual and the visionary: art and female spirituality in late medieval Germany, New York: Zone Books, 1998.

Hanawalt, Barbara, *The ties that bound: peasant families in medieval England*, Oxford University Press, 1988.

Growing up in medieval London: the experience of childhood in history, Oxford University Press, 1993.

'Of good and ill repute'. Gender and social control in medieval England, Oxford University Press, 1998.

Hanawalt, Barbara and Ben R. McRee, 'Guilds of *homo prudens* in late medieval England', *Continuity and Change* 7 (1992), 163–79.

Hanna, Ralph, 'The production of Cambridge University Library MS Ff.1.6', *Studies in Bibliography* 40 (1987), 62–70.

William Langland, Authors of the Middle Ages 3, Aldershot: Variorum, 1993.

Hansen, Elaine Tuttle, *Chaucer and the fictions of gender*, Berkeley: University of California Press, 1992.

Hanson, Julienne, *Decoding homes and houses*, Cambridge University Press, 1998.

Harding, Vanessa, 'Space, property and propriety in urban England', *Journal of Interdisciplinary History* 32 (2002), 549–69.

Harris, Barbara J., *English aristocratic women 1450–1550*, Oxford University Press, 2002.

Harris, Richard, *Discovering timber-framed buildings*, Haverfordwest, Pembrokeshire: Shire Publications, 1993.

Hartshorne, Pamela, 'The street and the perception of public space in York, 1476–1586', unpublished PhD thesis, University of York, 2004.

Harvey, P. D. A., '*Rectitudines singularum personarum* and *Gerefa*', *English Historical Review* 108 (1993), 1–22.

Haslewood, Francis, 'Monastery at Bruisyard', *Proceedings of the Suffolk Institute of Archaeology* 7 (1889/91), 320–3.

'Inventories of monasteries suppressed in 1536', *Proceedings of the Suffolk Institute of Archaeology* 8 (1894), 83–116.

Heal, Felicity, *Hospitality in early modern England*, Oxford University Press, 1990.

Helmholz, R. H., *Marriage litigation in medieval England*, Cambridge University Press, 1974.

Henderson, John, *Piety and charity in late medieval Florence*, Oxford: Clarendon Press, 1994.

Herlihy, David, *The history of feudalism*, Brighton: Harvester Press, 1970.

'The family and religious ideologies in medieval Europe', in *Women, family, and society in medieval Europe: historical essays 1978–1991*, ed. Anthony Molho, Providence, RI: Berghahn Books, 1995.

Hibbert, Francis, *The dissolution of the monasteries as illustrated by the suppression of the religious houses of Staffordshire*, London: Pitman, 1910.

Hillier, Bill, *Space is the machine: a configurational theory of architecture*, Cambridge University Press, 1996.

Hillier, Bill and Julienne Hanson, *The social logic of space*, Cambridge University Press, 1984.

Hilton, R. H., 'Some problems of urban real property in the middle ages', in R. H. Hilton, *Class conflict and the crisis of feudalism*, revised 2nd edn, London: Verso, 1990, pp. 92–101.

The English peasantry in the later Middle Ages, Oxford University Press, 1975.

Hines, John, '*Gerefa* §§ 15 and 17: a grammatical analysis of the lists of nouns', *Medieval Archaeology* 50 (2006), 268–70.

Hogg, James, 'Adam Easton's *Defensorium Sanctae Birgittae*', in Marion Glasscoe (ed.), *The medieval mystical tradition: England, Ireland, and Wales. Exeter symposium VI: papers read at Charney Manor, July 1999*. Cambridge: D. S. Brewer, 1999, pp. 213–240.

Holdsworth, Philip, *Excavations in the medieval burgh of Perth, 1979–1981*, Edinburgh: Society of Antiquaries of Scotland, 1987.

Holmes, Urban T., *Daily living in the twelfth century*, Madison, WI: University of Wisconsin Press, 1953.

Horsman, Valerie, C. Milne and G. Milne, *Building and street development near Billingsgate and Cheapside. Aspects of Saxo-Norman London I*, London and Middlesex Archaeological Society Special Paper no. 11, London, 1988.

Huizinga, Johan, *Homo ludens: a study of the play element in culture*, trans. R. F. C. Hull, London: Routledge & Kegan Paul, 1949.

The autumn of the Middle Ages, trans. Rodney J. Payton and Ulrich Mammitzsch, Chicago: University of Chicago Press, 1996.

Hunt, R. W., *The schools and the cloister: the life and writings of Alexander Nequam*, Oxford University Press, 1984.

Hunt, Tony, *Teaching and learning Latin in thirteenth-century England*, Cambridge: D. S. Brewer, 1991.

Hurst, J. G., 'The Wharram research project: problem orientation and strategy 1950–90', in Della Hooke (ed.), *Medieval villages: a review of current work*, Oxford University Committee for Archaeology 1985, pp. 200–4.

'The Wharram research project: results to 1983', *Medieval Archaeology* 28 (1984), 77–111.

Hyams, Paul, *Kings, lords and peasants in medieval England*, Oxford: Clarendon Press, 1980.

'What did Edwardian villagers understand by law?', in Zvi Razi and Richard M. Smith (eds.), *Medieval society and the manor court*, Oxford: Clarendon Press, 1996, pp. 69–102.

Impey, Edward and Roland Harris, 'Boothby Pagnell revisited', in G. Meirion-Jones, E. Impey and M. Jones (eds.), *The seigneurial residence in Western Europe AD c. 800–1600*, Oxford: Archaeopress, 2002, pp. 245–69.

James, Mervyn, 'Ritual, drama and social body in the late medieval English town', *Past and Present* 98 (1983), 3–29.

James, T. B. and A. M. Robinson, *Clarendon Palace: the history and archaeology of a medieval palace*, London: Society of Antiquaries, 1988.

Jessopp, Augustus, *Studies by a recluse in cloister, town and country*. London: T. F. Unwin, 1893.

Johnson, Lesley, 'Reincarnations of Griselda: contexts for the "Clerk's Tale"', in Ruth Evans and Lesley Johnson (eds.), *Feminist readings in Middle English literature: the Wife of Bath and all her sect*, London and New York: Routledge, 1994, pp. 195–220.

Johnson, Matthew, *Housing culture: traditional architecture in an English landscape*, London: UCL Press, 1993.

Jones, Janet, 'The nunneries of London and its environs, 1100–1400', unpublished MPhil thesis, University of London, 2008.

Justice, Steven, *Writing and rebellion: England in 1381*, Berkeley: University of California Press, 1994.

Justice, Steven and Kathryn Kerby-Fulton, 'Langlandian reading circles and the civil service in London and Dublin, 1380–1427', *New Medieval Literatures* 1 (1997), 59–83.

Karras, Ruth Mazo, '"Because the other is a poor woman she shall be called his wench": gender, sexuality and social status in late medieval England', in Sharon A. Farmer and Carol Braun Pasternack (eds.), *Gender and difference in the Middle Ages*, Minneapolis: University of Minnesota Press, 2003, pp. 10–29.

From boys to men: formations of masculinity in late medieval Europe, Philadelphia: University of Pennsylvania Press, 2003.

Keene, Derek J., *A survey of medieval Winchester*, 2 vols., Winchester Studies vol. 2, Oxford: Clarendon Press, 1985.

'Shops and shopping in medieval London', in Lindy Grant (ed.), *Medieval art, architecture and archaeology in London*, British Archaeological Association Conference Transactions for 1984, Leeds: Maney for British Archaeological Association, 1990, pp. 29–46.

'Tanners' widows, 1300–1350', in Caroline Barron and Anne Sutton (eds.), *Medieval London widows, 1300–1500*, London: Hambledon, 1994, pp. 1–28

'Landlords, the property market and urban development in medieval England', in F. Eliassen and G. A. Ersland (eds.), *Power, profit and urban land: landownership medieval and early modern in European towns*, Aldershot: Scolar Press, 1996, pp. 93–119.

'London from the post-Roman period to 1300', in David Palliser (ed.), *The Cambridge urban history of Britain*, vol. 1, *600–1540* Cambridge University Press, 2000, pp. 187–217.

Kelly, Henry Ansgar, 'Bishop, prioress, and bawd in the stews of Southwark', *Speculum* 75 (2000), 342–88.

Kent, Susan (ed.), *Domestic architecture and the use of space*, Cambridge University Press, 1990.

Kerby-Fulton, Kathryn, 'Langland and the bibliographic ego', in Steven Justice and Kathryn Kerby-Fulton (eds.), *Written work: Langland, labor, and authorship*, Philadelphia: University of Pennsylvania Press, 1997, pp. 67–143.

Kermode, Jennifer I., *Medieval merchants: York, Beverley and Hull in the later Middle Ages*, Cambridge University Press, 1998.

'The greater towns 1300–1540', in David Palliser (ed.), *The Cambridge urban history of Britain*, vol. 1: *600–1540*, Cambridge University Press, 2000, pp. 441–65.

'Northern towns', in David Palliser (ed.), *The Cambridge urban history of Britain*, vol. 1: *600–1540*, Cambridge University Press, 2000, pp. 657–79.

Kerr, Julie, 'The open door: hospitality and honour in twelfth/early thirteenth-century England', *History* 87 (2002), 322–35.

Keynes, Simon, *The diplomas of King Æthelred the Unready, 978–1016*, Cambridge University Press, 1980.

'Regenbald the chancellor (*sic*)', *Anglo-Norman Studies* 10 (1988), 185–222.

King, David J., 'Salle Church – the glazing', *Archaeological Journal* 137 (1980), 332–335.

'The panel paintings and stained glass', in Ian Atherton *et al.* (eds.), *Norwich Cathedral: church, city, and diocese 1096–1996*, London: Hambledon Press, 1996, pp. 410–30.

The medieval stained glass of St Peter Mancroft Norwich, Corpus Vitrearum Medii Aevi. Oxford University Press, 2006.

Knowles, David and R. Neville Hadcock, *Medieval religious houses: England and Wales*, London: Longman, 1971.

Kowaleski, Maryanne, 'The commercial dominance of a medieval provincial oligarchy: Exeter in the late fourteenth century', in Richard Holt and Gervase Rosser (eds.), *The medieval town: a reader in English urban history 1200–1540*. London: Longman, 1990, pp. 184–215.

'The expansion of the south-western fisheries in late medieval England', *Economic History Review*, 2nd series, 53 (2000), 429–54.

Krug, Rebecca, *Reading families: women's literate practice in late medieval England*, Ithaca: Cornell University Press, 2002.

Kuhn, Sherman M. *et al.* (eds.), *Middle English dictionary*, Ann Arbor: University of Michigan Press, 1952–2001; and online version at: http://quod.lib.umich.edu.avoserv.library.fordham.edu/m/med/.

Kümin, Beat, *The shaping of a community: the rise and reformation of the English parish, c. 1400–1560*, Aldershot: Scolar Press, 1996.

Langland, Elizabeth, *Nobody's angels: middle-class women and domestic ideology in Victorian culture*, Ithaca: Cornell University Press, 1995.

Larson, L. M., *The king's household in England before the Norman Conquest*, Madison, WI: University of Wisconsin, 1904.

Laslett, Peter, *The world we have lost: further explored*, 3rd edn, Cambridge University Press, 1983.

Latham, R. E., *et al.* (eds.), *Dictionary of medieval Latin from British sources*, London: British Academy, 1975–.

Lefebvre, Henri, *The production of space*, trans. Donald Nicholson-Smith, Oxford: Blackwell 1991.

Lendinara, Patrizia, 'The *Oratio de utensilibus ad domum regendum pertinentibus* by Adam of Balsham', *Anglo-Norman Studies* 15 (1993), 161–76.

Anglo-Saxon glosses and glossaries, Aldershot: Ashgate, 1999.

Lennard, Reginald, *Rural England 1086–1135: a study of social and agrarian conditions*, Oxford University Press, 1959.

Lerer, Seth, *Chaucer and his readers: imagining the author in late-medieval England*, Princeton University Press, 1993.

Lewis, Katherine, *The cult of St. Katherine of Alexandria in late medieval England*, Woodbridge: Boydell & Brewer, 2000.

Liddy, Christian D., *War, politics and finance in late medieval English towns: Bristol, York and the Crown, 1350–1400*, Woodbridge: Boydell and Brewer, 2005.

Liebermann, F., *Die Gesetze der Angelsachsen*, vol. i, Halle: Niemeyer, 1898.

Locock, Martin (ed.), *Meaningful architecture: social interpretations of buildings*, Aldershot: Avebury, 1994.

Loengard, Janet Senderowitz, '"Plate, good stuff, and household things": husbands, wives, and chattels in England at the end of the Middle Ages', in Livia Visser-Fuchs (ed.), *Tant d'emprises – so many undertakings: essays in honour of Anne F. Sutton*, Bury St Edmunds: The Richard III Society, 2003, pp. 328–40.

Lounsbury, Thomas R., *Studies in Chaucer: his life and writings*, 3 vols., 1892; reprint London: Russell & Russell, 1962.

Luongo, F. Thomas, 'Saintly authorship in the Italian Renaissance: the Quattrocento reception of Catherine of Siena's letters', *Journal of the Early Book Society* 8 (2005), 1–46.

Lutton, Rob, 'Godparenthood, kinship, and piety in Tenterden, England 1449–1537', in Isabel Davis, Miriam Müller and Sarah Rees Jones (eds.), *Love, marriage and family ties in the later Middle Ages*, Turnhout: Brepols, 2001, pp. 217–34.

Luxford, Julian M., *The art and architecture of English Benedictine monasteries 1300–1540: a patronage history*, Woodbridge: Boydell, 2007.

McCann, John, 'An historical enquiry into the design and use of dovecotes', *Transactions of the Ancient Monuments Society* 35 (1991), 89–160.

McClure, Peter, 'Patterns of migration in the late Middle Ages: the evidence of English place-name surnames', *Economic History Review* 2nd series, 32 (1979), 167–82.

McCormick, Betsy, 'Remembering the game: debating the *Legend*'s women', in Carolyn P. Collette (ed.), *The Legend of Good Women: context and reception*, Woodbridge: D. S. Brewer, 2006, pp. 105–3.

MacCulloch, Diarmaid, *Reformation: Europe's house divided, 1490–1700*, London: Allen Lane, 2003.

McDonald, Nicola, 'Chaucer's *Legend of Good Women*, ladies at court and the female reader', *Chaucer Review* 35 (2000), 22–42.

'Games medieval women play', in Carolyn P. Collette (ed.), *The legend of good women: context and reception*, Woodbridge: D. S. Brewer, 2006, pp. 176–97.

McIntosh, Marjorie K., 'Finding a language for misconduct: jurors in fifteenth century local courts', in Barbara A. Hanawalt and David Wallace (eds.), *Bodies and discipline*, Minneapolis: University of Minnesota Press, 1996, pp. 87–122.

Controlling misbehavior in England, 1370–1600, Cambridge University Press, 1998.

Working women in English society, 1300–1620, Cambridge University Press, 2005.

McKinnon, Sarah, 'The peasant house: the evidence of manuscript illumination', in J. A. Raftis (ed.), *Pathways to medieval peasants*, Toronto: Pontifical Institute of Mediaeval Studies, 1981, pp. 301–9.

McRee, Ben R., 'Religious guilds and the regulation of behavior in late medieval towns', in Joel Rosenthal and Colin Richmond (eds.), *People, politics, and community in the later Middle Ages*, New York: St. Martin's Press, 1987, pp. 108–122.

McSheffrey, Shannon (ed. and trans.), *Love and marriage in late medieval London*, TEAMS Documents of the Practice Series, Kalamazoo, MI: Medieval Institute Publications, 1995.

'"I will never have none against my faders will": consent and the making of marriage in the late medieval diocese of London', in Constance M. Rousseau and Joel T. Rosenthal (eds.), *Women, marriage and family in medieval Christendom: essays in memory of Michael M. Sheehan, C.S.B.*, Kalamazoo, MI: Medieval Institute Publications, 1998, pp. 153–74.

'Jurors, respectable masculinity, and Christian morality: a comment on Marjorie McIntosh's *Controlling misbehavior*', *Journal of British Studies* 37 (1998), 269–78.

'Men and masculinity in late medieval London civic culture: governance, patriarchy, and reputation', in Jacqueline Murray (ed.), *Conflicting identities: men in the Middle Ages*, New York: Garland Press, 1999, pp. 243–78.

'Place, space, and situation: public and private in the making of marriage in late medieval London', *Speculum* 79 (2004), 960–90.

Marriage, sex, and civic culture in late medieval London, Philadelphia: University of Pennsylvania Press, 2006.

Malden, A. R. 'The will of Nicholas Longespee, bishop of Salisbury', *English Historical Review* 15 (1900), 523–8.

Malden, H. E. (ed.), *The Victoria history of the county of Surrey*, vol. II, London: Archibald Constable, 1905.

Mander, Gerald, 'The priory of the Black Ladies of Brewood, co. Stafford', in Issac Herbert Jeayes *et al.* (eds.), *Collections for a history of Staffordshire*, 3rd series, Staffordshire Record Society, vol. for 1939, Bishop's Stortford, 1940, pp. 175–220.

Mann, Jill, *Geoffrey Chaucer*, Atlantic Highlands, N.J.: Humanities Press International, 1991.

Margeson, Susan M., *Norwich households: the medieval and post-medieval finds from Norwich survey excavations, 1971–1978*, East Anglian Archaeology Report no. 58, Norwich, 1993.

Marks, Richard and Paul Williamson (eds.), *Gothic: art for England 1400–1547*, London: Victoria and Albert Museum, 2003.

Markus, R. A., *Signs and meanings: world and text in ancient Christianity*, Liverpool: Liverpool University Press, 1996.

Markus, Thomas, *Buildings and power: freedom and control in the origin of modern building types*, London: Routledge, 1993.

Martin, Geoffrey, 'The registration of deeds of title in the medieval borough' in D. A. Bullough and R. L. Storey (eds.), *The study of medieval records: essays in honour of Kathleen Major*, Oxford University Press, 1971, pp. 151–73.

'The governance of Ipswich from its origins to 1550', in David Allen (comp.), *Ipswich borough archives 1255–1835*, Suffolk Records Society vol. 43, Woodbridge: Boydell, 2000, pp. xvii–xxviii.

Mate, Mavis, 'Property investment by Canterbury cathedral priory', *Journal of British Studies* 23 (1984), 1–21.

Mate, Mavis, *Daughters, wives and widows after the Black Death*, Woodbridge: Boydell, 1998.

Mecham, June L., 'A northern Jerusalem: transforming the spatial geography of the convent of Wienhausen', in Andrew Spicer and Sarah Hamilton (eds.), *Defining the holy. Sacred space in medieval and early modern Europe*, Burlington, VT: Ashgate, 2005, pp. 140–60.

Mertes, K. D. M., *The English noble household, 1250–1600: good governance and politic rule*, Oxford: Blackwell, 1988.

Michalove, Sharon D., 'The education of aristocratic women in fifteenth-century England', in Sharon D. Michalove and A. Compton Reeves (eds.), *Estrangement, enterprise and education in fifteenth century England*, Stroud: Sutton, 1998.

Middleton, Anne, 'The Clerk and his tale: some literary contexts', *Studies in the Age of Chaucer* 2 (1980), 121–50.

'Acts of vagrancy: The C version "autobiography" and the statute of 1388', in Steven Justice and Kathryn Kerby-Fulton (eds.), *Written work: Langland, labor, and authorship*, Philadelphia: University of Pennsylvania Press, 1997, pp. 208–317.

Milne, Gustav, *Timber building techniques in London c. 900–1400*, London and Middlesex Archaeological Society Special Paper no. 15, London, 1992.

Minnis, Alastair J., *The shorter poems*, Oxford Guides to Chaucer, Oxford: Clarendon Press, 1995.

Morabito, Raffaele, 'La diffusione della storia di Griselda dal XIV al XX secolo', *Studi sul Boccaccio* 17 (1988), 237–85.

Morris, Colin, and Peter Roberts (eds.), *Pilgrimage: the English experience from Becket to Bunyan*, Cambridge University Press, 2002.

Moser Jr, Thomas C., '"And I mon waxe wod": the Middle English "Foweles in the Frith"', *Proceedings of the Modern Language Association* 102 (1987), 326–37.

Munby, Julian, 'Zacharias's: a 14th-century Oxford New Inn and the origins of the medieval urban inn', *Oxoniensia* 57 (1992), 258–61.

Myers, A. R., 'The wealth of Richard Lyons', in T. A. Sandquist and M. R. Powicke (eds.), *Essays in medieval history presented to Bertie Wilkinson*, Toronto: University of Toronto Press, 1969, pp. 301–29.

Naughton, Joan, 'Books for a Dominican nuns' choir: illustrated liturgical manuscripts at Saint-Louis de Poissy, c. 1330–1350', in Margaret Manion and Bernard Muir (eds.), *The art of the book – its place in medieval worship*, Exeter: University of Exeter Press, 1998, pp. 67–110.

Newman, Christine M., *Late medieval Northallerton*, Stamford: Shaun Tyas, 1999.

Nicholls, J., *The matter of courtesy: medieval courtesy books and the Gawain-Poet*, Woodbridge: Brewer, 1985.

Nichols, Ann Eljenholm, *The early art of Norfolk: a subject list of extant and lost art*, Early Drama, Art and Music Reference Series vol. 7., Kalamazoo: Medieval Institute, 2002.

Nichols, J., *A history and antiquities of the county of Leicester*, 3 vols., London: J. Nichols, 1804; reprinted in 1971 by S.R. Publishers, Ltd, in association with Leicestershire County Council.

Nuechterlein, Jeanne, 'The domesticity of sacred space in the fifteenth-century Netherlands', in Sarah Spicer and Andrew Hamilton (eds.), *Defining the holy: Sacred space in medieval and early modern Europe*, London: Ashgate, 2005, pp. 49–79,

Oliva, Marilyn, *The convent and the community in late medieval England: female convents in the diocese of Norwich, 1350–1540*, Woodbridge: Boydell, 1998.

Orme, Nicholas, *From childhood to chivalry: the education of the English kings and aristocracy, 1066–1530*, London: Methuen, 1984.

Oswald, A., *Wharram Percy deserted medieval village, North Yorkshire: archaeological investigation and survey*, Archaeological Investigation Report Series AI/19/2004, Swindon: English Heritage 2004.

Overton, Mark *et al.*, *Production and consumption in English households, 1600–1750*, London: Routledge, 2004.

Owen, Charles, Jr., *The manuscripts of the Canterbury Tales*, Cambridge: D. S. Brewer, 1991.

Page, William (ed.), *The Victoria history of the county of Hampshire and the Isle of Wight*, vol. 2, London: Institute of Historical Research by Dawson of Pall Mall, 1973.

The Victoria history of the county of Yorkshire, vol. 3, London: Published for the University of London, the Institute of Historical Research, 1974.

Palliser, David M., 'York's earliest administrative record, the Husgabel roll of c. 1284', *Yorkshire Archaeological Journal* 50 (1978), 81–91.

Domesday York, Borthwick Papers no. 78, York: Borthwick Institute, 1990.

'Town and village formation in medieval England', in David Palliser, *Towns and local communities in medieval and early modern England*, vol. 2, Aldershot: Ashgate, 2006, pp. 1–24.

Palliser, David M., T. R. Slater and Elizabeth P. Dennison, 'The topography of towns 600–1300', in David Palliser (ed.), *The Cambridge urban history of Britain*, vol. 1: *600–1540*. Cambridge University Press, 2000, pp. 153–86.

Palmer, W. M., 'The Benedictine nunnery of Swaffham Bulbeck', *Proceedings of the Cambridge Antiquarian Society* 31 (1929), 30–65.

Pantin, W. A., 'The development of domestic architecture in Oxford', *Antiquaries Journal* 27 (1947), 120–50.

'Chantry priests' houses and other medieval lodgings', *Medieval Archaeology* 3 (1959), 216–58.

'Medieval English town-house plans', *Medieval Archaeology* 6–7 (1964 for 1962–3), 202–39.

'The merchants' houses and warehouses of King's Lynn', *Medieval Archaeology* 6–7 (1964 for 1962–3), 173–81.

'Some medieval townhouses: a study in adaptation', in I. Ll. Foster and L. Alcock (eds.), *Culture and environment. Essays in honour of Cyril Fox*, London: Routledge and Kegan Paul, 1963, pp. 445–78.

'The halls and schools of medieval Oxford: an attempt at reconstruction', in *Oxford studies presented to Daniel Callus*, Oxford Historical Society n.s. vol. 16, Oxford, 1964, pp. 31–100.

Parsons, David, 'Transitional architecture in Rutland', *Rutland Record* 6 (1986), 195–201.

Pearsall, Derek, *The Canterbury Tales*, New York: Routledge, 1985.

Pearson, Michael Parker and Colin Richards (eds.), *Architecture and order*, London: Routledge, 1994.

Pearson, Sarah, 'Rural and urban houses 1100–1500: "urban adaptation" reconsidered', in Katherine Giles and Christopher Dyer (eds.), *Town and country in the Middle Ages: contrasts, contacts and interconnections, 1100–1500*, Leeds: Maney, 2005, pp. 43–63.

Pederson, Else Marie Wiberg, 'The monastery as a household within the universal household', in Anneke B. Mulder-Bakker and Jocelyn Wogan-Browne (eds.), *Household, women, and Christianities in late Antiquity and the Middle Ages*, Turnhout: Brepols, 2005, pp. 167–81.

Pennell, Sara, 'Consumption and consumerism in early modern England', *Historical Journal* 42 (1999), 549–64.

Percival, Florence, *Chaucer's legendary good women*, Cambridge University Press, 1998.

Pfaff, R. W., *New liturgical feasts in later medieval England*, Oxford: Clarendon Press, 1970.

Phelps Brown, E. H. and Sheila V. Hopkins, 'Seven centuries of the prices of consumables, compared with builders' wage-rates', *Economica* n.s. 23 (1956), 296–314.

Phillips, Kim M., *Medieval maidens: young women and gender in England, 1270–1540*, Manchester University Press, 2003.

Phythian-Adams, Charles, *Desolation of a city: Coventry and the urban crisis in the late Middle Ages*, Cambridge University Press, 1979.

Pollard, A. W. and Redgrave, G. R., (eds.), *A short title catalogue of books printed in England, Scotland and Ireland and of English books printed abroad*, 3 vols., 2nd rev. edn, London: The Bibliographical Society, 1976–91.

Pollnac, R. B., 'The division of labor by sex in fishing communities', *Anthropology Working Paper* 44, International Center for Marine Resources Development, University of Rhode Island, 1984.

Pollock, Frederick and Frederic William Maitland, *The history of English law before the time of Edward I*, 2nd edn with introduction and bibliography by S. F. C. Milsom, Cambridge University Press, 1968.

Porter, Enid, *The folklore of East Anglia*, London: Roman and Littlefield, 1974.

Pounds, Norman, *Hearth and home: a history of material culture*, Bloomington: Indiana University Press, 1989.

Power, Eileen, *Medieval English nunneries*, Oxford University Press, 1921; reprinted New York: Biblio and Tannen, 1964.

Quennell, Marjorie, *A history of everyday things in England*, 2 vols., London: Batsford, 1918.

Quennell, Marjorie and C. H. B. Quennell, *A history of everyday things in England*, vol. 1, *1066–1499*, 4th edn, London: Batsford, 1969.

Quiney, Anthony, 'Hall or chamber? That is the question. The use of rooms in post-Conquest houses', *Architectural History* 42 (1999), 24–46.

Town houses of medieval Britain, New Haven: Yale University Press, 2003.

Rahtz, Philip *The Saxon and medieval palaces at Cheddar*, British Archaeological Reports, British Series vol. 65, Oxford, 1979.

Rahtz, Philip and Lorna Watts, *Wharram, a study of settlement on the Yorkshire Wolds IX: the north manor area and north-west enclosure*, York University Archaeological Publications no. 11, York, 2004.

Rapaport, Amos, *The meaning of the built environment*, 2nd edn, Tucson: University of Arizona Press, 1990.

Rawcliffe, Carole, 'Curing bodies and healing souls: pilgrimage and the sick in medieval East Anglia', in Colin Morris and Peter Roberts (eds.), *Pilgrimage: the English experience from Becket to Bunyan*, Cambridge University Press, 2002, pp. 108–40.

Razi, Zvi, *Life, marriage and death in a medieval parish: economy, society and demography in Halesowen, 1270–1400*, Cambridge University Press, 1980.

'The myth of the immutable English family', *Past and Present* 140 (1993), 3–44.

Rees Jones, Sarah, 'Property, tenure and rents: some aspects of the topography and economy of medieval York', unpublished Ph.D. thesis, University of York, 1987.

'Historical background', in R. A. Hall, H. MacGregor and M. Stockwell (eds.), *Medieval tenements in Aldwark*, The Archaeology of York 10/2, London: Council for British Archaeology, 1988, pp. 1–8.

'Household, work and the problem of mobile labour: the regulation of labour in medieval English towns', in James Bothwell, P. J. P. Goldberg and W. M. Ormrod (eds.), *The problem of labour in fourteenth-century England*, Woodbridge: Boydell and Brewer, 2000, pp. 133–53.

'The household and English urban government in the later Middle Ages', in Mryiam Carlier and Tim Soens (eds.), *The household in late medieval cities. Italy and northwestern Europe compared*, Leuven: Garant, 2001, pp. 684–98.

'Historical introduction', in R. A. Hall and K. Hunter-Mann, *Medieval urbanism in Coppergate : refining a townscape*, The Archaeology of York 10/6, York: Council for British Archaeology, 2002, pp. 684–98.

'Women's influence on the design of urban homes', in Mary Erler and Maryanne Kowaleski (eds.), *Gendering the master narrative: women and power in the Middle Ages*, Ithaca: Cornell University Press, 2003, pp. 190–211.

'God and Mammon: the York estate of the vicars choral of York', in David Stocker and Richard Hall (eds.), *Cantate Domino: colleges of vicars choral*, Oxford: Oxbow, 2005, pp. 192–9.

Rees Jones, Sarah and Felicity Riddy, 'The Bolton Hours of York: female domestic piety and the public sphere', in Anneke B. Mulder-Bakker and Jocelyn Wogan Browne (eds.), *Household, women and Christianities in late antiquity and the Middle Ages*, Turnhout: Brepols, 2005, pp. 215–60.

Reeves, Marjorie and Beatrice Hirsch-Reich, *The figurae of Joachim of Fiore*, Oxford: Clarendon Press, 1972.

Renevey, Denis, 'Household chores in *The doctrine of the hert*: affective spirituality and subjectivity', in Cordelia Beattie, Anna Maslakovic and Sarah Rees Jones (eds.), *The medieval household in Christian Europe c.850–c.1500*, Turnhout: Brepols, 2003, pp. 167–85.

Revard, Carter, 'Foweles in the frith', *Notes and Queries* n.s. 25 (1978), 200.

Richardson, H. G., Review of *Early charters of the cathedral church of St. Paul, London*, ed. M Gibbs, *English Historical Review* **57** (1942), 124–33.

Riddy, Felicity, '"Women talking about the things of God": a late medieval subculture', in Carole Meale (ed.), *Women and literature in Britain, 1150–1500*, Cambridge University Press, 1993.

'Looking closely: authority and intimacy in the late medieval urban home', in Mary Erler and Maryanne Kowaleski (eds.), *Gendering the master narrative: women and power in the Middle Ages*, Ithaca: Cornell University Press, 2003, pp. 212–28.

'Fathers and daughters: Holbein's portrait of Thomas More's family', in Diane Wolfthal and Rosalynn Voaden (eds.), *Framing the family: narrative and representation in the medieval and early modern periods*, Tempe, AZ: Arizona Center for Medieval and Renaissance Studies, 2005, pp. 19–38.

Riddy, Felicity *et al.*, 'The concept of the household in later medieval England', in Sarah Rees Jones *et al.*, 'The later medieval English urban household', *History Compass* 4 (2006), 5–10.

Rose, Martial and Julia Hedgecoe, *Stories in stone: the medieval roof carvings of Norwich cathedral*, New York: Thames and Hudson, 1997.

Roskell, J. S., Linda S. Clark, and Carole Rawcliffe, *The House of Commons, 1386–1421*, Stroud: Sutton, 1993.

Rosser, Gervase with Patricia E. Dennison, 'Urban culture and the church', in David Palliser (ed.), *The Cambridge urban history of Britain*, vol. 1: *600–1540*, Cambridge University Press, 2000, pp. 335–69.

Round, J. H., *The king's serjeants and officers of state*, London: Nisbet, 1911.

Royal Commission on the Historical Monuments of England, *An inventory of the historical monuments in the city of York*, vol. 3, *South-west of the Ouse*, London: HMSO, 1972.

An inventory of the historical monuments of the city of York, vol. 5, *The central area*, London: HMSO, 1981.

Rubin, Miri, 'Corpus Christi fraternities and late medieval piety', *Studies in Church History* 23 (1986), 97–109.
   Corpus Christi: the Eucharist in late medieval culture, Cambridge University Press, 1991.
Rutledge, Elizabeth, 'Landlords and tenants: housing and the rented property market in early fourteenth century Norwich', *Urban History* 22 (1995), 7–24.
Rybzcynski, Witold, *Home, a short history of an idea*, New York: Penguin Books, 1987.
Rye, Walter and Edward A. Tillett, 'Carrow Abbey', *The Norfolk Antiquarian Miscellany* 2 (1883), 465–508.
Salih, Sarah, 'At home, out of the house', in Carolyn Dinshaw and David Wallace (eds.), *The Cambridge companion to medieval women's writing*, Cambridge University Press, 2003, pp. 124–40.
   'When is a bosom not a bosom? problems with "erotic mysticism"', in Anke Bernau, Ruth Evans and Sarah Salih (eds.), *Medieval virginities*, Cardiff: University of Wales Press, 2003, pp. 14–32.
Salter, Elizabeth, *Chaucer: the Knight's Tale and the Clerk's Tale*, London: Edward Arnold, 1962.
Salzman, L. F., *Building in England down to 1540*, Oxford: Clarendon Press, 1952.
Samson, Ross (ed.), *The social archaeology of houses*, Edinburgh University Press, 1990.
Sandler, Lucy Freeman, *Gothic manuscripts 1285–1385*, 2 vols., Survey of Manuscripts Illuminated in the British Isles vol. 5, London: Harvey Miller, 1986.
Sawyer, P. H., *Anglo-Saxon charters: an annotated list and bibliography*, London: Royal Historical Society, 1968.
Scanlon, Larry, *Narrative, authority, and power: the medieval exemplum and the Chaucerian tradition*, Cambridge University Press, 1994.
Scarry, Elaine, *The body in pain: the making and unmaking of the world*, New York: Oxford University Press, 1985.
Schama, Simon, *The embarrassment of riches: an interpretation of Dutch culture in the golden age*, London: Collins, 1987.
Schofield, John, 'Urban housing in England, 1400–1600,' in David Gaimster and Paul Stamper (eds.), *The age of transition. The archaeology of English culture 1400–1600*, Oxford University Press, 1997, pp. 127–44.
   Medieval London houses, New Haven: Yale University Press, 2003.
Schofield, John and Alan Vince, *Medieval Towns*, London, 1994.
Scott, Kathleen L., *Later Gothic manuscripts 1390–1490*, 2 vols., Survey of Manuscripts Illuminated in the British Isles vol. 6, London: Harvey Miller, 1996.
Scott, R. F., *Notes from the records of St John's College*, Cambridge University Press, 1913.
Scully, Terence, 'Tempering medieval food', in M. W. Adamson (ed.), *Food in the Middle Ages: a book of essays*, New York: Garland, 1995, pp. 3–23.
Segalen, Martine, *Love and power in the peasant family: rural France in the nineteenth century*, trans. S. Matthews, Oxford: Blackwell, 1983.
Severs, J. Burke, Albert E. Hartung, and Peter G. Biedler, P. G. (eds.), *A manual of the writings in Middle English, 1050–1500*, 11 vols., New Haven: The Connecticut Academy of Arts and Sciences, 1967–2005.

Severs, J. Burke, *The literary relationships of Chaucer's Clerk's Tale*, New Haven: Yale University Press, 1942.

Shailor, Barbara A., (ed.), *Catalogue of medieval and Renaissance manuscripts in the Beinecke Rare Book and Manuscript Library, Yale University*, 3 vols., Binghamton, NY: Medieval and Renaissance Texts and Studies, 1984–92.

Shaw, Diane, 'The construction of the private in medieval London', *Journal of Medieval and Early Modern Studies* 26 (1996), 447–77.

Sheehan, Michael M., 'The influence of canon law on the property rights of married women in England', *Mediaeval Studies* 25 (1963), 109–24.

Sheingorn, Pamela, 'Joseph the carpenter's failure at familial discipline', in Colum Hourihane (ed.), *Insights and interpretations: studies in celebration of the eighty-fifth anniversary of the Index of Christian Art*, Princeton University Department of Art and Archeology, 2002, pp. 156–67.

Sheingorn, Pamela, 'The bosom of Abraham Trinity: a late medieval All Saints image', in Daniel Williams (ed.), *England in the fifteenth century: proceedings of the 1986 Harlaxton symposium*, Woodbridge: Boydell, 1987, pp. 273–95.

Short, P., 'The fourteenth century rows of York', *Archaeological Journal* 137 (1980), 86–136.

Silva, Daniel S., 'Some fifteenth-century manuscripts of the Canterbury Tales', in Beryl Rowland (ed). *Chaucer and middle English studies in honour of Russell Hope Robbins*, London: George Allen & Unwin, 1974.

Simpson, J. A. and E. S. C. Weiner (eds.), *The Oxford English dictionary*, 20 vols., Oxford: Clarendon Press, 1989.

Simpson, James, 'The constraints of satire in *Piers Plowman* and *Mum and the Sothsegger*', in Helen Phillips (ed.), *Langland, the mystics and the medieval English religious tradition: essays in honour of S. S. Hussey*, Cambridge: D. S. Brewer, 1990, pp. 11–30.

Slater, T. R., 'Domesday village to medieval town: the topography of medieval Stratford-upon-Avon', in Robert Bearman (ed.), *The history of an English borough: Stratford-Upon-Avon 1196–1996*, Stroud: Sutton, 1997.

Slota, Leon A., 'Law. land transfer and lordship on the estates of St Alban's abbey in the 13th and 14th centuries', *Law and History Review* 6 (1988), 119–38.

Smalley, Beryl, 'Use of the "spiritual" senses of scripture in persuasion and argument by scholars in the Middle Ages', *Recherches de Théologie Ancienne et Médiévale* 52 (1985), 44–63.

Smith, A. A., 'Gender, ownership and domestic space: inventories and family archives in Renaissance Verona', *Renaissance Studies* 12 (1998), 375–91.

Smith, Richard M. (ed.), *Land, kinship and life-cycle*, Cambridge University Press, 1984.

'Families and their land in an area of partible inheritance: Redgrave, Suffolk, 1260–1320', in Richard M. Smith (ed.), *Land, kinship and life-cycle*, Cambridge University Press, 1984, pp. 135–95.

Sommerfeldt, John R., *Aelred of Rievaulx on love and order in the world and the church*, New York: Newman Press, 2006.

Spain, Daphne, *Gendered spaces*, Chapel Hill: University of North Carolina Press, 1992.

Spear, Valerie, *Leadership in medieval nunneries*, Woodbridge: Boydell, 2005.

Speirs, John, *Chaucer the maker*, London: Faber and Faber, 1951.

Sponsler, Claire, 'Eating lessons: Lydgate's "dietary" and consumer conduct', in Kathleen Ashley and Robert L. A. Clark (eds.), *Medieval conduct*, Minneapolis: University of Minnesota Press, 2001, pp. 1–22.

Staley, Lynn, *Powers of the holy: religion, politics and gender in late medieval English culture*, University Park, PA: Penn State University Press, 1996.

Stamper, P. and Croft R., *Wharram, a study of settlement on the Yorkshire Wolds VIII: the south manor area*, York University Archaeological Publications no. 10, 2000.

Stanbury, Sarah, 'Regimes of the visual in premodern England: gaze, body, and Chaucer's "Clerk's Tale"', *New Literary History* 28 (1997), 261–89.

Stenton, F. J., 'The road system of medieval England', *Economic History Review* 1st series 7 (1936–7), 234–52.

Stevens, John, *Music and poetry in the early Tudor court*, London: Methuen, 1961.

Strohm, Paul, *Social Chaucer*, Cambridge, MA: Harvard University Press, 1989.

Hochon's arrow: the social imagination of fourteenth-century texts, Princeton: Princeton University Press, 1992.

Swabey, Ffiona, *A medieval gentlewoman: life in a gentry household in the early Middle Ages*, New York: Routledge, 1999.

Swanson, Heather, *Medieval British towns*, Basingstoke: Palgrave, 1999.

Swanton, Michael, *Anglo-Saxon prose*, London: Dent, 1975.

Tarbin, Stephanie, 'Moral regulation and civic identity in London 1400–1530', in Linda Rasmussen, Valerie Spear and Dianne Tillotson (eds.), *Our medieval heritage: essays in honour of John Tillotson for his 60th birthday*, Cardiff: Merton Priory Press, 2002, pp. 126–36.

Tavormina, M. Teresa, 'Kindly similitude: Langland's matrimonial Trinity', *Modern Philology* 80 (1982), 117–28.

Kindly similitude: marriage and family in Piers Plowman, Cambridge: D. S. Brewer, 1995.

Taylor, Charles, *Sources of the self: the making of modern identity*, Cambridge, MA: Harvard University Press, 1989.

Taylor, John, Wendy R. Childs, and Leslie Watkiss (eds. and trans.), *The St Albans chronicle: the Chronica maiora of Thomas Walsingham*, vol. I: *1376–139*, Oxford: Clarendon Press, 2003.

Thompson, John J., 'Collecting Middle English romances and some related book-production activities in the late Middle Ages', in M. Mills, J. Fellows and Carole Meale (eds.), *Romance in medieval England*, Cambridge: D. S. Brewer, 1991.

Thompson, P., 'Women in the fishing: the roots of power between the sexes', *Comparative Study of Society and History* 27 (1985), 3–32.

Tillot, P. M. (ed.), *Victoria county history of Yorkshire: The city of York*, London: Oxford University Press, 1961.

Tosh, John, *A man's place: masculinity and the middle-class home in Victorian England*, New Haven and London: Yale University Press, 1999.

Trexler, Richard C., *Public life in Renaissance Florence*, New York: Academic Press, 1980.

Tudor-Craig, Pamela, 'Medieval panel paintings from Norwich, St Michael at Plea', *Burlington Magazine* 98:642 (1956), 333–4.

Turner, T. H., 'Original documents: inventory of the effects of Reginald Labbe, d. 1293', *Archaeological Journal* 3 (1846), 65–6.

Turner, Victor, *From ritual to theatre: the human seriousness of play*, New York: Performing Arts Journal Publications, 1982.

Twycross, Meg, 'Kissing cousins: the four daughters of God and the Visitation in the N-Town Mary Play', *Medieval English Theatre* 18 (1996), 99–141.

Tyers, I. and K. Groves, 'Tree-ring dates from the University of Sheffield dendrochronology laboratory: York, 60 Stonegate', *Vernacular Architecture* 31 (2000), 127–8.

Utley, Francis L., *The crooked rib: an analytical index to the argument about women in English and Scots literature to the end of the year 1568*, Columbus, OH: Ohio State University, 1944.

Vasvari, Louise, 'Joseph on the margin: the Merod tryptic and medieval spectacle', *Mediaevalia* 18 (1995), 163–89.

Vauchez, André, *Sainthood in the later middle ages*, trans. Jean Birrell, Cambridge University Press, 1997.

Vickery, Amanda, 'Golden age to separate spheres? A review of the categories and chronology of English women's history', *The Historical Journal* 36 (1993), 383–414.

Virgoe, Roger, 'Some ancient indictments in the King's Bench referring to Kent, 1450–1452', in F. R. H. DuBoulay (ed.), *Documents illustrative of medieval Kentish society*, Kent Records vol. 18, Ashford, 1964, pp. 214–65.

Voadyn, Rosalynn, 'All girls together: community, gender and vision at Helfta', in Diane Watt (ed.), *Medieval women and their communities*, Toronto: University of Toronto Press, 1997, pp. 72–91.

Wallace, David, *Chaucerian polity: absolutist lineages and associational forms in England and Italy*, Stanford: Stanford University Press, 1997.

Webb, Diana, 'Domestic space and devotion in the middle ages,' in Andrew Spicer and Sarah Hamilton (eds.), *Defining the holy: sacred space in medieval and early modern Europe*, Burlington, VT: Ashgate, 2005, pp. 27–47.

Westlake, H. F., *The parish guilds of mediaeval England*, London: Society for Promoting Christian Knowledge, 1919.

Whitehead, Christiana, *Castles of the mind: a study of medieval architectural allegory*, Cardiff: University of Wales Press, 2003.

Whiting, Bartlett Jere, *Proverbs, sentences, and proverbial phrases from English writings mainly before 1500*, Cambridge, MA: Harvard University Press, 1968.

Wilkinson, Louise J., 'The *Rules* of Robert Grosseteste reconsidered', in Cordelia Beattie, Anna Maslakovic and Sarah Rees Jones (eds.), *The medieval household in Christian Europe, c. 850– c. 1550*, Turnhout: Brepols, 2003, pp. 294–306.

Williams, John H., *St Peter's Street, Northampton: excavations, 1973–1976*, Northampton: Northampton Development Corporation, 1979.

Williams, N. J., *The maritime trade of the East Anglian ports 1550–1590*, Oxford: Clarendon Press, 1988.

Wilson, Stephen. *The magical universe: everyday ritual and magic in pre-modern Europe*, London: Hambledon Press, 2000.

Wiltenburg, Joy, *Disorderly women and female power in the street literature of early modern England and Germany*, Charlottesville, VA: University of Virginia Press, 1992.

Windeatt, Barry, '"I use but comownycacyon and good wordys": teaching the *Book of Margery Kempe*', in Dee Dyas, Valerie Edden and Roger Ellis (eds.), *Approaching medieval English anchoritic and mystical texts*, Rochester, NY: D. S. Brewer, 2005, pp. 115–28.

Winkelmes, Mary-Ann, 'Taking part: Benedictine nuns as patrons of art and architecture', in Geraldine Johnson and Sara Mathew Grieco (eds.), *Picturing women in Renaissance and Baroque Italy*, Cambridge University Press, 1997, pp. 91–110.

Wittig, Joseph S., '*Piers Plowman* B, Passus IX–X: elements in the design of the inward journey', *Traditio* 28 (1972), 211–80.

Wogan-Browne, Jocelyn., 'Analytical survey 5: "reading is good prayer": recent research on female reading communities', *New Medieval Literatures* 5 (2002), 229–89.

Wood, Margaret, *Norman domestic architecture*, London: Royal Archaeological Institute, 1974.

The English mediaeval house, London: Phoenix House, 1965.

Thirteenth-century domestic architecture in England, supplement to *Archaeological Journal* 105 (1950) London: Royal Archaeological Institute.

Woolgar, C. M., *The great household in late medieval England*, New Haven: Yale University Press, 1999.

Wormald, C. P., *The making of English law: King Alfred to the twelfth century*, Oxford University Press, 1999.

Wrathmell, Stuart, *Wharram, a study of settlement on the Yorkshire Wolds VI: domestic settlement 2: medieval peasant farmsteads*, York University Archaeological Publications no. 8, 1989.

Wrathmell, Susan, *Wharram Percy deserted medieval village*, London: English Heritage, 1996.

Wright, Thomas, *A history of domestic manners and sentiments in England during the Middle Ages*, London, 1862.

The homes of other days: a history of domestic manners and sentiments in England, London, 1871.

Wyndham, H. P., 'Observations on an ancient building at Warnford, in the county of Southampton', *Archaeologia* 5 (1779), 357–66.

Yates, Frances, *The art of memory*, London: Pimlico, 1992.

Index

Adam of Balsham (Adam of Petit Pont)
41, 42
Aelfric 41
Aelfric Bata 41
affective piety 190–1
apert, fourteenth-century meanings 33–4
aristocratic way of life, comparison with
bourgeoiserie 26–7
artistic depictions of domesticity 14–15, 35–6
aula (hall) 23–4 *see also* hall

beds and bedding
bedding in nuns' households 150–2
fashion for bed curtains and screens 136
goods brought to a marriage by the wife
168–72
relative value compared to kitchen
utensils 127–9, 131–2
Black Death
impact in York 103
impact on urban modes of living 29
Boccaccio, Giovanni, *Decameron* (Griselda
legend) 177, 181–2, 183
boulting-house 23–4
boundaries between plots, significance
of 76
bourgeois (burgeis) domesticity
activities in multi-room houses 21
artistic depictions 35–6
cooking food at home 28–9
establishment as a dominant urban
value 29
impact of the Black Death on 29
link with bourgeois house arrangement 28
privacy for activities within the home 28–9
bourgeoise (burgeis) domesticity in material
culture
bourgeois model of investment 130
cushions 126–7, 131–4
estate associated with 'household' and
'outside' items 129–32
gentry model of investment 131

indicators of peasant and bourgeois
culture 125–32, 135–8
labour of wives 137–8
mercantile model of investment 130–1
peasant model of investment 129–30
relative value of beds and kitchen utensils
127–9, 131–2
silver spoons 126–7, 131–2, 134–5
source inventories 124–5, 139–44
bourgeois (burgeis) houses
adaptable timber-frame construction
29–30
and bourgeois identity 21
as places of work 25–6
comparison with those of the poor 27–8
conventions for organisation of space
23–4
distinctive size and style 21
flexible uses of rooms 24–5
gardens 23–4, 28–9
kitchens 28–9
link with burgeis domestic life 21, 28
places of manufacture and sale 25–7
privies 28–9
surviving inventories of property 23–5
types of rooms 23–4
see also houses, rooms in
bourgeois (burgeis) values 36
bourgeois model of investment 130
discretion 34
domestic values 28
high standards of craftsmanship 31
industriousness 30–1
pursuit of excellence 31
stability 29–30
bourgeoiserie (burgeiserie)
as members of the franchise 18–19
association with the holy family
30–1, 35–6
commercial ethic 20
comparison with aristocrats 26–7
comparison with lives of the poor 27–8

310

definition of the public/private divide
31–2
definitions of 18–19
dominance after the Black Death 29
moral criticisms of outsiders 19–20
neighbour disputes over privacy 31–2,
33–4 *see also* privacy
privacy within the working home 34–5 *see
also* privacy
private activities 33
public and private behaviour 33–4
roles of women 27, 28
status of the householder 29–30
view of themselves as a group 20
way of life 26–7
bread, association with the pantry 59
bread and wine
domestic mealtime ceremonies 53, 59,
60–1
Eucharist ceremony 60–1
brew-house 23–4, 25–6
Brome manuscript (Book of Brome)
anti-feminist cipher puzzles 245–7
'Arise Early' 240, 254–8
contents 235–7, 239–42
culture of gendered play 242–5
desire in the household 240, 254–8
duties of the married householder 240,
254–8
early history 235–7, 239–42
evidence of a household at play 238–9
game texts 240, 241–2
Have Your Desire dice game 239, 240,
241–2, 247–54
household of John Cornwallis 235–7
structure and layout 239–42
use of games to provoke debate about
women 243–7
women readers 237–9
women's assertion of their own desires
239, 242–5
buildings, types of 37–8
boulting-house 23–4
brew-house 23–4, 25–6
cotagium 21–2, 23
cote (hovel) 21–2
cottages 70–1
four-or-more-roomed houses 21
grain-room 23–4
gyle-house 24
hall houses 68–70, 73–4
malthouse 24
one- or two-roomed houses 21, 22–3,
70–1
rental properties ('rents') 119–22

shopa 21–2, 23
shops 70–1
small houses 21, 22–3, 70–1
stone houses 82–4
tenementum 21–2
timber-framed houses 68
see also urban buildings
buildings and contents descriptions
De Nominibus Utensilium (Latin
vocabulary) 41–2, 46
Gerefa lists 45–6
inventories for stock-and-land leases
42–5
inventories of property 23–5
Oratio de Utensilibus (Latin vocabulary)
41, 42
see also nuns' medieval households
burgage plots 73–4
reasons for shape 118–19
stone houses 82–4
burgage tenure, impact of written titles to
urban land 85–7
burgeis *see* bourgeois
burgeiserie *see* bourgeoiserie
burgess status, possession of urban land by
charter 85–7
butler 47–9, 59
buttery
architectural evidence for emergence 38,
49–57
association with the butler 59
distinction from the pantry 38,
39–41
evidence for origins 46
evidence for uses 41–6
location in the late medieval domestic
plan 38, 39–41
reasons for separation of service rooms
62–3
responsibilities of the butler 47–9

camera (room where people slept) 23–4
chambers 23–5, 38, 49–57
chapel, in a burgeis house 23–4
charters *see* property ownership by written
charter
Chaucer, Geoffrey
family situation 29–30, 36
Legend of Good Women 245
Merchant's Tale 229–30
Miller's Tale 22, 24, 30, 34–5
Shipman's Tale 25, 28
Troilus and Criseyde 133
view of the burgeiserie 19–20
Wife of Bath 216–17, 230

Chaucer's Griselda (The 'Clerk's Tale')
    adapting spirituality to lay masculinity
        192–204
    appeal to masculine emotion 185–7
    appeal to middle-rank men 192–204
    domestic politics and wider power
        relationships 204–8
    gender relationships 204–8
    Griselda's character and situation
        194–6
    host and lay male spirituality 187–92
    interrogation of misogyny 204–8
    lay orientation 185–7
    piety 185–7, 204–8
    political statement 204–8
    popularity and interpretations 177–81
    reader's response to Griselda's passivity
        202–4
    Walter's flaws 196–202
Chaunce of Dice game 249–51
children
    of the burgeiserie 28–9
    of the poor 27–9
Church, influence on urban housing
        culture 122
civic leaders, property and status, 79–82
coquina see kitchen
cotagium type of property 21–2, 23
cote (hovel) 21–2
cottages and shops 70–1
counting-house or office 23–4, 25
courtesy books, influence on mealtime
        rituals 61–2
cushions, distinction of peasant and
        bourgeois culture 126–7, 131–4

De Nominibus Utensilium (Latin vocabulary
        for household goods) 41–2, 46
derne, fourteenth-century meanings 33
dispensa (spence), change of name to pantry
        58–9
diversity of medieval society 4
Domesday Book, emergence of the burgeis
        18–19
domestic plan, late medieval 37–8
    architectural evidence 38, 49–57
    arrangement of the chamber block 38,
        49–57
    changes in ideas about domestic space
        57–63
    endurance of the established plan 64
    formal ceremony of mealtimes 53, 59,
        60–1
    household officials 47–9
    influence of courtesy books 61–2

influence of developing domestic
        ceremony 61–2
influence of humoral theory 62–3
persistence of established rules of
        behaviour 64
relationship to domestic organisation
        38–9
serving of bread and wine 53, 59, 60–1
see also buttery; hall; pantry; service rooms
domesticity
    artistic depictions of 14–15, 35–6
    contrast of home and street 15
    contrast of home and work 15–17
    gendered views 14–17
    origins and meanings of the concept 2–3,
        14–17
    privacy and comfort 15–17
    'separate spheres' model 15–17
    source of bourgeois identity 14–17
    see also bourgeois (burgeis) domesticity
domesticity in the late-medieval period
        16–17
    association with the burgeiserie 17
    familiae (households) 17
    multi-roomed timber-frame houses 17
domus (living room) 23–4
dormitory curtains and wall hangings, nuns'
        households 149–50

Etymologie (Isidore of Seville) 41, 42
Eucharist, parallels in domestic mealtime
        ceremony 60–1

familiae (households) 17
family see bourgeoiserie; children; husband;
        holy family; marriage; widows' rights to
        personal goods; wives
franchise, membership of (freemen) 18 see
        also bourgeoiserie
freemen (members of the franchise) 18 see
        also bourgeoiserie
furniture, nuns' households 153–4

games
    anti-feminist cipher puzzles 245–7
    Chaunce of Dice 249–51
    Have Your Desire 239, 240, 241–2,
        247–54
    Ragman Roll 249–51
    see also Brome manuscript (Book of
        Brome)
gardens 23–4, 28–9
gentry model of investment 131
Gerefa 45–6
grain-room 23–4

Griselda legend
  adapting spirituality to lay masculinity
    192–204
  appeal to masculinity, piety and emotion
    181–7
  Boccaccio's *Decameron* 177, 181–2, 183
  conflict between lay male piety and
    models of religiosity 187–92
  Petrarch's redaction 177, 181–5
  see also Chaucer's Griselda (The 'Clerk's
    Tale')
guilds, regulation of crafts 31, 34
gyle-house 24

habitus concept
  open hall in urban buildings 114–15
  rural and urban buildings 103–4
  use of space 95–7
hall (*aula*) 23–4
  familiarity to rural immigrants 114–15
  functions in the late medieval domestic
    plan 37–8
  in urban domestic buildings 69–70
  rural and urban counterparts 117–18
hall houses
  in York 115–17
  'right-angle' and 'parallel' styles 73–4
  timber-framed 68–70
  urban counterpart to the peasant croft
    117–18
Have Your Desire dice game (Brome
    manuscript) 239, 240, 241–2, 247–54
  articulation of desire as an end in itself
    252–4
  comparison with courtly analogues 249–51
  range of fortunes 248–9
  social status and perception of women's
    sexuality 251–2
Holbein, Hans 35–6
holy family
  association with burgeis domestic values
    30–1, 35–6
  embourgeoisement 30–1, 35–6
home
  comparison of burgeis and aristocratic
    conceptions 26–7
  contrast with work 15–17
  distinction from the outside world 15
  domestic values associated with
    30–1
  embodiment of 33
  home visits *see* Visitation
  link with domestic life 2–3
  medieval meanings and associations 1
  place for work and domestic living 26–7

homli, medieval meanings 1
house plan, reflection of household
    structure 103–5
household
  accommodation of the various members
    135–6
  as a social space 232–5
  familiae 17
  orderly domestic regime 28
  origins and meanings 2
  origins of the nuclear family 28
  royal households 47–9
  rural households 111–12
  women at play 232–5
  see also bourgeois; nuns' medieval
    households; peasant household
household goods descriptions
  De Nominibus Utensilium (Latin
    vocabulary) 41–2, 46
  Gerefa lists 45–6
  inventories for stock-and-land leases 42–5
  inventories of property 23–5
  Oratio de Utensilibus (Latin vocabulary)
    41, 42
  see also beds and bedding; cushions;
    nuns' medieval households; silver
    spoons
household officials, organisation of great
    households 47–9
household structure, reflection in house
    plan 103–5
householder
  emergence of 29–30
  duties of ('Arise Early', Brome
    manuscript) 240, 254–8
  hospitality and honour 61–2
  John Cornwallis 235–7
  meanings of 'household' 2, 17
  property and status 82–4
  protection of privacy 31–2, 33–5
  responsibility to supervise the household
    187–92
  ritual of domestic dining 61–2
  social status 29–30, 71–2
  status of different social groups 79–84
houses
  cotagium 21–2, 23
  cote (hovel) 21–2
  cottages 70–1
  distinction by number of rooms 21–3
  four-or-more-roomed houses 21
  hall houses 68–70, 73–4, 115–18
  medieval usage and meanings of 'house' 2
  one- or two-roomed houses 21, 22–3, 70–1
  rental properties ('rents') 119–22

houses (cont.)
  size and style of the burgeis type 21
  small houses 21, 22–3, 70–1
  stone houses 82–4
  tenementum 21–2
  timber-framed houses 17, 29–30, 68–70,
    87–8
  see also bourgeois (burgeis) houses;
    cottages and shops; gyle-house; rural
    houses; urban houses
houses, rooms in and outhouses
  boulting-house 23–4
  brew-house 23–4, 25–6
  camera (room where people slept) 23–4
  chambers 23–5, 38, 49–57
  chapel 23–4
  counting-house 23–4, 25
  domus (living room) 23–4
  grain-room 23–4
  gyle-house 24
  malthouse 24
  office or counting-house 23–4, 25
  parlour 23–5, 35
  servants' room 24
  shop 25–6
  storeroom 23–4
  wine-cellar 23–4
  workshop 25–6
  see also buttery; hall; kitchen; manorial
    hall; pantry; privy; service rooms;
    spence
houses of the poor 22–3
  distinctive urban housing type 119–22
  influence of the Church 122
  purpose-built rental properties 119–22
housewife, medieval meaning 3 *see also*
  wives
humoral theory 62–3
husband
  as bread winner 2–3
  bequeathing goods to his widow 162–4
  gifts to his wife 174–6
  link with the world of work 15–17
  merchant working from home 26–7
  ownership of wife's property on marriage
    162–4, 168–72
  role in the domestic regime 28
  see also Chaucer's Griselda (The 'Clerk's
    Tale')

Kempe, Margery, life of travel and the
  Visitation 259–60, 269–76
kitchen (*coquina*) 23–4
  bourgeois houses 28–9
  cooking food at home 28–9

goods brought to a marriage by the wife
  171–2
relative value of kitchen utensils 127–9,
  131–2

landlords, loss of jurisdiction over free
  tenants 85
landowner, dependency of subtenants
  89–90
Langland, William (*Piers Plowman*) 21–2,
  27–8
  Abraham and marriage metaphors
    211–18
  Abraham as model of pious obedience
    224–31
  Abraham the father 219–24
  contemporary ideas about marriage
    209–10
  the sadness of not being a bird 224–31
linens, nuns' households 155–6
London, patterns of settlement 75
Love, Nicholas 30–1
  meditations on the Visitation 259–60,
    267–9, 273–4

malthouse 24
manor *see* urban manors
manorial hall, layout in Wharram Percy 109,
  110, 111
marriage
  gifts between husbands and wives 174–6
  goods brought by the woman 162–4,
    168–72
  ownership of all property by the husband
    162–4
  see also Chaucer's Griselda (The 'Clerk's
    Tale')
marriage ideologies (Langland's *Piers
  Plowman*)
  Abraham and marriage metaphors
    211–18
  Abraham as model of pious obedience
    224–31
  Abraham the father 219–24
  contemporary ideas about marriage
    209–10
  the sadness of not being a bird
    224–31
married women *see* wives
Marx, Karl 20
mercantile model of investment 130–1

Neckham, Alexander 41–2, 46
nuns, domestic imagery in literature, rituals
  and visions 145–6

nuns' households
  bedding 150–2
  categories of living quarters 148
  comparison with furnishings of the gentry
    152, 154–5, 157–8
  continuity of religious themes and images
    in decoration 157
  decoration of choirs, churches and
    chapels 156–7
  devotional elements in the domestic
    setting 160–1
  domestic details as devotional objects
    160–1
  donations of goods by benefactors
    158–9
  floor coverings 148–9
  furnishings created by the nuns
    themselves 159–60
  furniture 153–4
  household accounts and inventories
    146–8
  linens 155–6
  small household items 154
  utensils for eating and drinking 154–5
  wall hangings and dormitory curtains
    149–50

office or counting-house 23–4, 25
Oratio de Utensilibus (Latin vocabulary for
  buildings and contents) 41, 42

Pantin, W. A. 93, 94
pantler 58, 59
pantry
  architectural evidence for emergence 38,
    49–57
  association with the pantler 59
  connection with bread 59
  distinction from the buttery 38, 39–41
  evidence for origins 46
  evidence for uses 41–6
  implications of name changes 58–9
  location in the late-medieval domestic
    plan 38, 39–41
  reasons for separation of service rooms
    62–3
  responsibilities of the steward 47–9
paraphernalia, widow's right to 164–8
parlour 23–5, 35, 137, 148
Pearson, Sarah 93–5, 117–18
peasant and bourgeois culture
  differences in labour of wives 137–8
  indicators of differences 125–32,
    135–8
  see also servile tenure

peasant croft, as counterpart of the urban
  hall building 117–18
peasant holdings, layout in Wharram Percy
  101, 105–9, 111, 240
peasant household
  conservatism 113–14
  migration of the young to the towns
    112–13, 114–15
  oversight and control by senior members
    111–12, 113–14
  structure and size 111–12
peasant model of investment 129–30
Petrarch, Francesco, translation of the
  Griselda legend 177, 181–5
plot boundaries, significance of 76
poor people *see* children, of the poor; houses
  of the poor
privacy
  Court of Nuisance cases 31–2, 33–4
  definition by burgeiserie 31–2
  definition of private activities 33
  development of 15–17
  indicator of power and possession 34–5
  lack in medieval houses 14
  neighbour disputes over 31–2, 33–4
  public and private behaviour 33–4
  significance of plot boundaries 76
  within the working home 34–5
privé, meanings 33
privy
  in bourgeois houses 28–9
  lack in small houses 22–3
property boundaries, evolution of 72
property ownership
  link between urban and rural
    development 77–8
  link to social status 79–84
property ownership by written charter 84–5
  dependency of subtenants 89–90
  distinction from tenants at will 85–7
  distinction of burgess status 85–7
  emergence of timber-framed construction
    87–8
  rental income from subtenancies 88–9
  types of property conveyed by charter 87

Ragman Roll game 249–51
religious fraternities 189–90
rental properties ('rents') 70–1
  dependency on the landowner 89–90
  distinctive urban housing type 119–22
  income from 88–9
rooms *see* houses, rooms in and outhouses
royal households, organisation and officials
  47–9

rural development, integration with urban
    development 77–9
rural household structure 111–12 *see also*
    peasant household
rural houses, relationship to urban buildings
    117–18
rural society, contrasts and similarities to
    urban society 97–8

'separate spheres' ideology 2–3, 15–17
servants
    accommodation of live-in servants 24,
        135–6
    as part of the household 17
    place in the social hierarchy 71–2
    restrictions on 71–2
    roles in the household 28
    young immigrants to the towns 114–15
service rooms
    architectural evidence for emergence 38,
        49–57
    evidence for origins 46
    evidence for uses 41–6
    location in the late-medieval domestic
        plan 38
    organisation in the late-medieval
        domestic plan 38, 39–41
    wet/dry distinction in service rooms
        62–3
servile tenure 85–7
shop, various meanings of the term 25–6
shop frontage, narrowness 118–19
shopa (workshop or retail space) 21–2, 23–4
shops and cottages 70–1
shops for subletting 87–8
silver spoons 126–7, 131–2, 134–5, 155
small houses (one or two rooms) 21, 22–3,
    70–1
social hierarchy, reflection in urban
    buildings 71–2, 77–8
social status, link to property ownership
    79–84
space
    agent in social relations 95–7
    habitus concept 95–7, 103–4, 114–15
    material culture as engine of social
        practice 95–6, 97
spence
    change of name to pantry 58–9
    evidence for origins 46
St Paul's manorial farm leases, inventories of
    goods 42–5, 46
steward, responsibilities 47–9
stone houses on burgage plots 82–4
storeroom 23–4

subtenants
    dependency on the landowner 89–90
    in urban houses 87–8
    relations with property owners 88–90
tenants at will 85–7
tenementum type of property 21–2
timber-framed houses 17
    adaptable construction 29–30
    emergence of 68
    impact of written charters 87–8
    timber-framed hall houses 68–70
town plans
    burgage plots 73–4
    evolution of property boundaries 72
    evolution of street plans 72
    hierarchy of land ownership 77
    hierarchy of property ownership units
        72–3
    hierarchy of settlement 74
    patterns of occupation 75–6
    primary units of property ownership 72–3
    'right-angle' and 'parallel' hall houses
        73–4
    secondary units of property ownership
        73–4
    significance of plot boundaries 76
    tertiary units of property ownership 74
    urban manors 72–3
urban buildings
    cottages and shops 70–1
    emergence of the urban style 67–8
    emergence of timber-frame construction 68
    fire risk in early timber houses 67–8
    halls in urban domestic buildings 69–70
    reflection of social hierarchies 71–2
    relationship to rural houses 117–18
    rented units 70–1
    rot in early timber houses 67–8
    small houses (one or two rooms) 70–1
    timber-framed hall houses 68–70
urban burgage plot, reasons for shape
    118–19
urban development, integration with rural
    development 77–9
urban hall building *see* hall houses
urban houses
    as adaptation of rural model 93–5
    distinctive urban type 119–22
    relations between owners and subtenants
        88–90
    rooms and shops for subletting 87–8
urban housing culture, influence of the
    Church 122

urban housing style, purpose-built rental properties 119–22
urban identity
    contrasts and similarities to rural society 97–8
    indications in material culture 97–8
    nature of housing 97–8
urban land registries 84–5
urban manors 72–3
    dependence of tenants 78–9
    influence of landlords on tenants 78–9
    links with rural estates 77–9
    owners of the larger primary units 79–82
    status and influence of the owners 79–82
urban open hall see hall
urban property units, reflection of social hierarchy of land ownership 77–8
utensils for eating and drinking, nuns' households 154–5

Van Eyck, Jan 35
Vermeer, Jan 36
Visitation, feast of the
    expressions of devotion to 260–6
    Mary and Elizabeth's meeting 259
    meditations of Nicholas Love 259–60, 267–9, 273–4
    spread of interest in 259–60
    travels of Margery Kempe and Visitation
    unofficial and popular components 266–7
    Visitation offices 260–2
    visual expressions of devotion 262–6

wall hangings and dormitory curtains, nuns' households 149–50
Wharram Percy
    layout of peasant holdings 101, 105–9, 111, 240
    layout of the manorial hall 109, 110, 111
    site location and layout 98–102
widows' rights to personal goods
    clothing 164–7
    gifts and bequests to the woman 172–6
    gifts given by the husband 174–6
    girdles 164–7, 174–6
    goods brought to a marriage by the wife 168–72
    jewellery 167–8
    law regarding personal property of women 162–4
    paraphernalia 164–8
    provisions in the husband's testament 162–4
    wedding ring 168

wills, married women 166–8, 170–1, 172
    see also widows' rights to personal goods
wine see bread and wine
wine-cellar 23–4
wives
    differences in labour contribution 137–8
    duties of the married householder 240, 254–8
    goods brought to the marriage 168–72
    husband's ownership of property 162–4
    law regarding personal property 162–4
    married women's testaments 166–8, 170–1, 172
    medieval meaning of housewife 3
    role in the bourgeois ideal 2–3
    role in the domestic regime 28
    Wife of Bath (Chaucer) 216–17, 230
    women's desires 240, 254–8
    see also Chaucer's Griselda (The 'Clerk's Tale'); widows' rights to personal goods
women
    anti-feminist cipher puzzles 245–7
    articulation of desire through games 252–4
    assertion of their own desires 239, 242–5
    games which provoke debate about 243–7
    gendered views of domesticity 14–17
    Have Your Desire dice game for mixed company 239, 240, 241–2, 247–54
    influence in the design of urban homes 118
    literacy 237–9
    lives of the poor 27–8
    Margery Kempe's life of travel and the Visitation 259–60, 269–76
    participation in domestic play 232–5
    relationship to the household 232–5
    roles in burgeis household 27, 28
    small houses of lone women 22–3
    social status and perception of women's sexuality 251–2
    trading restrictions 18
    travel for visiting or pilgrimage 272–3
    uses of various rooms in the house 24–5
    see also nuns; widows' rights to personal goods; wives
workshop 25–6

York
    Coppergate, pattern of settlement 75–6
    impact of the Black Death 103
    medieval history 102–3
    open hall buildings 115–17